PORT

Henrik Oldenburg

Henrik Oldenburg

PORT

SMAG & BEHAG

Henrik Oldenburg
PORT
Copyright © Henrik Oldenburg
Copenhagen 1999

Printed by:	Nordjyllands Bogtrykkeri
Art Director:	Kirsten Dalgaard
Photographs:	Henrik Oldenburg (HO)
	Birger J. Storm (BJS) and others
Translation:	Linda M. Kronborg
Gastronomy:	Jane Kjølbye
Photo on the cover:	Symington Family

All rights reserved. No part of this book may be reproduced, stored in a retrieval system, or transmitted, in any form or by any means, without the prior permission of the publisher.

In memory of José Estrela Leão (1929-99) who for so many years tried to teach the Danish people to drink better and better Port. And with success.

Printed in Denmark.
First edition.

ISBN 87-90179-16-1

Published by
SMAG & BEHAG
Vimmelskaftet 41-A
DK-1161 Copenhagen K

Phone: + 45 33 97 43 43
Fax: + 45 33 11 17 62

E-mail: admin@smag-behag.dk
http://www.smag-behag.dk

CONTENTS

Chapter 1
The History of Port 13
    The Romans and the Burgundians 14
    The Treaty of Lord Methuen 22
    Pombal and his Company 34
    From Porto Wine to Port 40
    In the shadow of civil war 48
    The years of disaster 54
    Boom 60
    From thistles to carnations 68
    New times - old times 74
    The Revolution in the Valley 79
    The foolhardy purchase of shares 84

Chapter 2
The land of schist 91
    The Valley of the God of Wine 101
    The Valley of the Gods of Weather 103

Chapter 3
Grape varieties 105

Chapter 4
Benefício 111

Chapter 5
From grape to Port 117

Chapter 6
Port types 131
    Vintage Port 138
    Single Quinta Vintage Port 141
    Late Bottled Vintage 144
    Tawny with age 148
    Colheita 149

Chapter 7
Port producers 151

Chapter 8
Port Associations 309

Chapter 9
Vintage years 327

Chapter 10
The pleasure of Port 339

Chapter 11
Tourist in the country of Port 369
    Porto 370
    Douro Valley 376

Index 381

PREFACE

In 1995 I was a guest at a quinta in the Douro Valley. In the small hours of the morning when the old Vintage was served, my host and I were discussing a certain event. He was quite aggravated because he could not find the answer to a question in the quinta's quite spacious library, but that was nothing new, neither to him nor to me.

- No, I'm sorry but there simply isn't any all-round book about Port, I said.

- Well, why don't you write one, then, he replied, and looked as if he actually meant it.

When I returned to Denmark, I spoke of the incident to Portugal's commercial counsellor in Denmark, the legendary José Estrela Leão. I really felt inspired, but wasn't it enough that the Vikings had plundered Lisbon and conquered England. Let the British and the Portuguese keep their Port in peace.

- On the contrary, he said, and waved some documents that he had just received from the Port Institute under my nose. - Do you realize, he said, that in 1994 Denmark imported nearly 400,000 bottles of quality Port, including only Vintage, LBV, old Tawnies and Colheitas - and that the ICEP estimates that Danish wine merchants bought 40-50,000 bottles of quality Port direct from England, mostly Vintage Port.

- Do you know what that means? It means that Denmark imports 450,000 bottles of the best Port for a population of 4.5 million inhabitants. If you look at the pro capita, nobody else in the world drinks as much quality Port as the Danes do!

Well, that was a completely new aspect, and the urge to write a book on Port returned. The English invented Port in Portugal. The French buy the largest number of Port bottles, the Americans buy the most expensive Port, but the Danes buy the best ones!

- You see, José said, it seems only natural that a Dane should write the book on Port. The Danes' have a very high Portculture level, and luckily they have kept out of the historic feud between the Port of the Portuguese and the Port of the British and may therefore enjoy a pleasant glass from both bottles.

That was how it all started. My point of departure was that I loved the beautiful valley of Port, I loved the wonderful wine, I loved the beautiful people who made it.

But that was not enough. Now, all my experience and impressions had to be put into words. Port Wine is actually just a banal table wine, in which fermentation is stopped by adding alcohol, but from a romantic point of view it is the only wine in the world based on hand-picked and foot-crushed grapes, and which therefore goes straight to the heart - if it is a good Port - and otherwise to the head!

I had an idea of the lay out of the book at quite an early stage. It begins with the preconditions of making Port and ends up with what the result can be used for. This is of course all based on my own assumptions. I am a historian. I am no oenologist and no marketing expert, but I have always been fascinated by the world's most clever sailors and adventurers who were pacified and settled down as wine growers in a remote river valley in the north of Portugal and started making the world's best wine.

My background as a historian and a scientist is supplemented by my 22 years as a wine journalist, which gives me a good alibi to ask many questions. Which I did. I was confirmed at a very early stage in my suspicions of the fact that the history of many Port houses has been told and written on a weak background with no sources to confirm the history or distinguish between myth and reality. Tales were told, and even the family-owned Port houses fully accepted the brochures and jubilee publications which had been published throughout the years, which they had even copied from each other, with an uncritical eye.

Also, a lot of Port houses do not have an existing history, so my work in gathering material became much more complicated than I had ever expected. But naturally also much more exciting.

The Port Wine Institute has kindly supported this book financially so that it was possible to publish both a Danish version and an English version. And the financial support also signified that I was able to send all the vital chapters and company profiles to Portugal for comments and criticism, but the evaluations of the wine in the glass are mine only. Most proposals have been followed loyally, but this is my book, my opinions, and my responsibility. A great thanks to all my friends in Portugal for their contributions. And special thanks to Bruce Guimaraens and James Symington for their persistent critique and helpful comments to the technical sections.

My famous fellow-townsman, Hans Christian Andersen, drank Port against sea-sickness, depression, and diarrhoea. I could probably come up with even more failings you could cure by drinking Port, but I have never needed a good reason to drink a good glass of Port.

"Pass the book", I might say. Here it is at last. I have written the book first and foremost for the consumers and for everybody who enjoys a daily glass of Port and want to know a bit more about it.

I can only hope that you get the same feeling in reading the book as I had in writing it!

Copenhagen, October 1999.
HENRIK OLDENBURG

Private lessons in the art of making Port in the beginning of the 1980'ies. The author's skilled tutor is the inventor of the Barca Velha, Fernando Nicolau de Almeida, who was responsible for a lifetime for Ferreira's best Ports.

Demarcated Douro Region

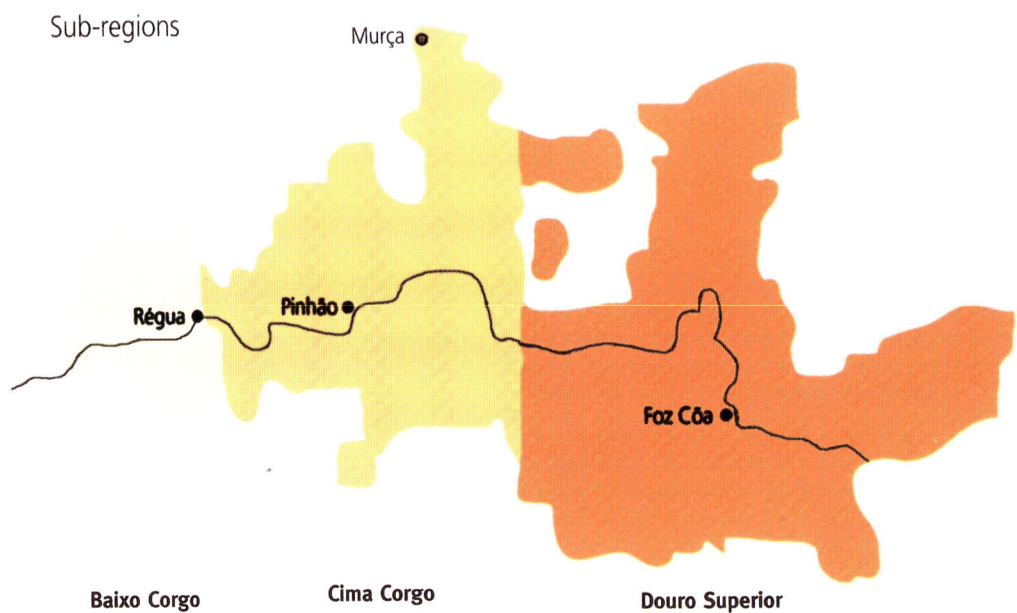

Sub-regions

- Murça
- Régua
- Pinhão
- Foz Côa

Baixo Corgo　　Cima Corgo　　Douro Superior

Chapter 1

THE HISTORY OF PORT

The Romans and the Burgundians

Four years before the young Tribune of the People, Tiberius Gracchus, introduced his historical land reform in Rome in 133 B.C. thereby demanding a temporary stop of the expansion of the frontiers, one of the many expeditionary forces had just taken hitherto unknown territory quite far away from the most attractive goal of pillage, Egypt. This territory lay trans alpina, across the Alps, on the road to the Land of the Gauls.

Decius Junius Brutus was credited as being the first Roman to have crossed the Douro river in 137 B.C. where there must have been a port, for Brutus calls the settlement at the estuary Portuscale - the place today known as Porto - where portus means port and cale signifies the road to Callaecia, the Latin name for Galicia in Northern Spain. The city kept the prefix Portu which gave the name to the later Portugal that was still called Lusitania during the Roman Empire named after a Celtic tribe, who had the audacity to oppose the Romans, rather violently at that, and as late as in 81 B.C. made a desperate attempt to throw the Roman legionaries out of their country. They did not succeed.

The scenario of the Roman colonization included that grapevines had to be planted, for wine was a natural part of the Roman soldier's everyday life. As the wine had to be transported to the different military units, it was only natural to plant the grapevines along the two meander rivers, Tagus in the south and Durius in the north. This was not the first time wine had been drunk by the Douro river, for grape seeds and goblets have been excavated here dating from the early bronze age. But it was the Romans who systematized wine production, and built bridges and dug for gold. Apparently, they were here to stay - which, as you know, they didn't. At the fall of the Roman Empire, Lusitania fell too, but with the visigoths' quick intervention the viticulture was maintained, and the liberal Moors who took the Iberian peninsula in the course of the 8th Century were not allowed to drink wine, as they were Muslims, but they were allowed to invent spirits, and they turned a blind eye to the fact that the underdeveloped local tribes fermented the old grapes and knocked back this golden liquid with unpredictable consequences.

1109: The birth of Portugal

More than 1000 years would pass from the great Roman period till wine was cultivated again along the Douro river. When Northern Portugal had gotten rid of the Moors, it was once again safe to settle as a farmer so why not as a wine grower? This kind of agriculture was by far the most difficult trade to choose, as both the grapes and the

THE HISTORY OF PORT

Yesterday, today, tomorrow. Nothing has changed in the landscape which appeared to the first curious Romans and appears to us today when we visit the Douro Valley. The blue river has cut its way through the steep mountains. The spot in the picture is historical. Here you should pass the dangerous Cachão de Valeira where Baron Forrester drowned in May 1861. (Photo: HO)

wine provided food and sometimes probably also mirth! Some of the so-called Documents of Rights from the 11th Century indicate that it was quite attractive to become a wine grower, and regardless of the quality of the wine, which compared to our standards today was probably quite low, this line of business was quite attractive.

This was especially true after 1109 when King Alfonso VI of Castilla-León governed most of the Iberian peninsula together with his son-in-law Henry, who had been handed over the counties of Minho and Tagus by his father-in-law, and now refused to pass back this territory to the throne and instead proclaimed it as being independent.

This was the birth of Portugal, and that is not all, for with Henry followed the birth of wine too - for the second time. This was due to the fact that Henry came from Bourgogne, France, where he had the title of duke and where a handful of monks from the Cluny cloister had established a convent about 10 years earlier with the purpose of growing wine. The cloister and the vineyard are still there - Clos de Vougeot - close to another ecclesiastical vineyard from the time, Clos de Tart in Morey-Saint-Denis. This was the environment that Henry of Bourgogne came from, and it would be unthinkable that he did not let his Burgundian viniculture influence the wine growing in his new county. We even come quite close to having it in writing, for in Cambridge, England, they keep old manuscripts proving that the wines from the Douro district in the middle of the 11th Century reached prices which were approximately 10 times higher than the prices of other Portugese wines.

Out with the Moors

After the death of Henry, nobility chose Afonso Henriques as Portugal's first king in 1143, and he had barely put the crown on his head, before he was convinced by the surrounding world what Henry of Bourgogne might not even have dreamt about: throwing the Moors out of Portugal for good.

It was, as one says, faith who removed mountains and was now to remove a few thousand infedeles. And this was a sort of religious warm-up for the European princes were on a crusade, the second one actually, and while the South German and French armies were riding directly towards the Holy Land, some of the English and North Germans had chosen the sea route and were going to moor in Lisbon. This was the year 1147. They came, they saw, and they conquered - and pillaged, according to the customs of that time. But they threw out the Moors of Lisbon, which they had promised the King to do, and the soldiers, who had not had enough of adventure, continued towards Jerusalem where they ran into one disaster after another while their more level-headed companions chose to accept an offer from King Afonso. As a reward for their doings, they were given a small piece of land and were asked to settle down in Portugal.

It must have been a motley crew. They came from all over England, and also from Scotland, they came from the Rhine and from the Moselle, from the Flemish fields and from Burgundy, and they were all soldiers of fortune on a crusade, and the odd variety of merchants and a bunch of useful pirates rode with them, and of course an extraordinary number of women, presumably so that the long voyage would not be too boring!

The ones who chose to stay behind were given farm land along the rivers, including the Douro, and here we know from the time of the Romans that the only crop that could be cultivated was wine. So the newcomers began to grow wine, and they must have been good at it, for in the course of the 13th Century viticulture is further expanded. People had developed a good taste of a good glass whether they drank it for religious purposes or because they were thirsty.

THE HISTORY OF PORT

The best proof of the popularity of wine in seen in a royal decree from 1211 issued by Afonso II in which he forbids anybody to cut or even prune the vines, as they are considered royal property all over the country.

After more than a 1000 years, the soldier's, farmer's, crusader's and the ordinary citizens' drink had at last become a royal drink.

The first wine exports

Wine was still cultivated by the rivers. This was for practical reasons, as it had to be transported. Douro must have played a specially important role, for during the reign of Afonso III (1245-79) the town of Vila Nova de Gaia is given the right to charge toll from any boat or ship carrying wine and passing the town. There must have been quite a lot of traffic of this sort over by the Douro river towards the Atlantic sea!

And it was not only due to an increased private consumption. For during the reign of Afonso III, Portugal began to export wine to France, and as Porto with its seaport Vila Nova de Gaia apart from Viana do Castelo a bit further north is the nearest major port of embarkment, it is only natural that all embarkment takes place here.

The trade with the French duchies is extended when Dinis I is to become the first Portuguese king of the Burgundian family (Burgundy again!) in 1279. And there are documents to prove this, dating back from the 14th Century and indicating that Portuguese wine was embarked, specially from Porto and landed in Rouen and Bruges.

But as you know, blood is thicker than water, bullets hit harder than wine, and as the wine exports were weighted against the fortunes of war, war won. Portugal, reigned by a Burgundian family, went to war against England and France and Castile.

These were harsh times, as the name itself indicates: the Hundred Years' War. And it did not only result in blood, injuries and low water in all national purses, it also resulted in Portugal's first commercial treaty, signed on 16 June 1373 allegedly to favour England's sale of wool to Portugal and Portugal's sale of wine to England. This was the first treaty of its kind, but it would not be the last one.

The treaty of Windsor

The war went badly for the Englishmen, and thus also for the Portuguese. When peace finally was agreed upon, the Burgundian male line of descent was extinct with King Ferdinand I in 1383, and the next of kin was his daughter Beatrix who had been married off early to the King of Castile. But the Portuguese had enough of Castile and did not want to risk becoming an appendix to the large Spanish highlands of Castilla-León, so they proclaimed the king's half-brother, João, king in 1385 which gave him the nickname "the illegitimate king".

Naturally it ended in war again between Portugal and Castile, but for once the Portuguese won the great battle of Aljubarrota (1385) when the cloister of Batalha was erected as a triumphal monument. The victory also gave the possibility of strengthening the bonds to England - never knowing when the Castillians would strike again - so João married the English nobleman John of Gaunt's daughter Philippa of Lancaster in the most distinguished royal style.

The wedding was celebrated in a manner consistent with their position, and for the second time England and Portugal signed a commercial agreement giving the British textile manufacturers advantages on the Portuguese market whilst the Portuguese wine growers had direct access to the British market thus pushing out the French. With the signing of the Windsor treaty in 1386 the wine growers of the Douro Valley received the greatest encouragement ever to produce more wine. At this stage, nobody is yet talking about quality.

The good Douro wine

Between the two commercial treaties between England and Portugal, England had lost the command of the sea, and Portugal had won it. With King João aboard, a Portuguese fleet conquered the Moorean town of Ceuta on the coast of North Africa in 1415 where they established a trading post and were rid of the last pirates, and during the reign of João's son, Henry the Seafarer (1349-160), Portugal became the world's leading nation on the great seas.

Henry never found the ocean route to India, even though he was close, but the financially less risky sea route to England was clearly indicated on the Portuguese charts. This was before the time of archives and clerks, but as early as in 1465 there is a document showing that Portuguese wine has been shipped from Porto to Bristol, and it is a reasonable assumption that the wine came from the Douro Valley.

The first written evidence dates 1548 when the geographer, João de Barros, writes in a topographical work of the land between Douro and Minho: "They make a real good wine in these parts, especially in the areas where the ground lies towards Douro and by the Ribas de Pinhão, which is a river converging with the Douro river, and this is where they ship the wine to Porto".

We do not know much about the size of production, but there is a record indicating that Quinta da Eira Vedra (now Eira Velha) produced 70 almudes of wine in 1582, corresponding to approx. 1180 litres of wine). As more and more vineyards in Eira Vedra along the Douro river are mentioned by name in the 16th Century, and even though Portugal's days of glory with the discovery of the ocean route to India in 1498 and the discovery of Brazil in 1502 drags to its close with the Spanish occupation of the country in 1580, this fact does not seem to influence the wine growers in the remote Douro Valley.

They hardly even notice that the king is dead and that Portugal has again become Spanish. But they do, however, notice that England makes peace with Spain in 1604 promising the Spaniards free trade, also of wine. But they probably do not notice that a young German by the name of Cristiano Nicolau Kopke arrives at Porto in 1638 where he establishes himself as a wine merchant.

His aim is to sell Portuguese wine to the North German Hanseatic towns or to anybody who will buy his wine. He purely and simply deals in "wine", especially from the Douro district, and much more than this we do not know. But we do know that his small wine house from 1638 and for many years to come begins to deal in Port and thus becomes a Port house with the oldest roots.

The British in Porto

It was a sign of the times that it was necessary to trade. If you wanted land and influence, you also needed someone to trade with. When Spain refused free trade to the Englishmen in 1655 with the new Spanish states in Latin America, England declared war on Spain. For once England formed an alliance with France, but the English must have had a premonition about the fragility of this new friendship, for at the same time (1654) they also cemented the favourable conditions of trade between Portugal and England in a new treaty, named after the British military dictator Cromwell. This treaty specifically indicates that Portuguese wine is to have a special status upon imPortation to England compared to other wines from other countries. The advantages were of course made reciprocal. It also became easier for the British to sell English wool to Portugal, apart from the fact that the English ships

The archives of Port Wine

Sources are the basis of all historiography and therefore also for the history of Port. Unfortunately, there are only very few written and more or less contemporary narratives from the early times of Port Wine, so one must rely on later documents and oral tradition. Gradually, as trading houses for selling and exporting Port Wine started to appear, so did warehouse books and letters, but all in all reliable source material from before Napoleon is very scarce. There are two reasons for the missing sources – if they ever existed. First of all, many valuable documents and objects were destroyed in fires, most recently at Noval's whose lodges in Gaia burned down in 1981. Secondly, the many ownerships and take-overs have resulted in source material disappearing, typically because a family history follows the family, but the company follows the new buyer. This is seen for example at the sale of Cálem in 1998.

Ferreira is one of the lucky Port producers. They have boxes of source material. They actually have so much material that they had to sort it in 1998 and start a whole new registration. On the basis of the invaluable material two books about the history of this Port house were published in 1988 and 1996: "Um Português" and the wonderful book about "Dona Antónia".

When Cockburn's write their history one day, they have a storehouse of diaries and visitors' books on Quinta do Tua just waiting to tell a story. The diaries and visitors' books have been kept by various members of the family, apparently depending on who was visiting that particular day.

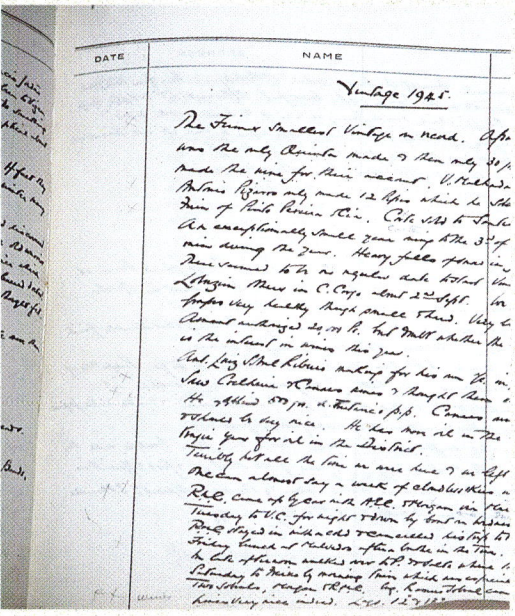

also brought the indispensable dried cod from the North Atlantic to Portugal. The closest fraternization took place in 1660. After some years' of anarchy, Charles II is crowned king and as his wife is Katarina of Bragança, the bonds to Portugal become even closer. This especially affects trade. Commerce is extended, and it is made more attractive to British tradesmen to settle down in Portugal and manage exports to England from Portugal. Especially Porto profits from this. The British tradesmen who until now had usually traded a bit with everybody, are granted a kind of diplomatic status and can only be persecuted if they are arrested while committing a criminal offense. And as they also achieve easy taxation terms and have a full freedom of religion, many of the English are attracted to Porto. In the middle of the 17th Century there are so many Englishmen in Portugal that they feel as settled residents, and the English colony in Porto established its own association called: "The British Factory", an association which will later have great significance for the British Port manufacturers who are mentioned for the first time in 1660 (see page 319f).

The beginning of Warre

A few years later, the misgivings from the union between England and France are confirmed. But it does not last, and in 1660 the French Minister of Finance, Jean Baptiste Colbert, abolishes the internal customs frontier in France and also exersizes customs on certain export goods, e.g. Bordeaux wine to England. The English King Charles II reacts promptly by boycotting all Claret wine from France. Instead they choose to focus even more on wine from Portugal, and the merchants in Plymouth, Bristol and London start to look towards Nantes and Bordeaux and even towards Porto and Viana do Castelo. This tendency is strengthened in 1667 when the English put a direct toll on the importation of French wine. Now only the Francophiles put a bottle of Bordeaux on the table. The year 1670 is a historical year for the English wine adventure in Douro. Two young Englishmen who had grown a taste for Portuguese wine got the wild idea that they wanted to see where the wine grew. When they arrived to the port of embarcment, Viana do Castelo, about 50 kilometres north of Porto, the tale says that they were offered a tasting but were very disappointed at the quality of the wine. They had tasted better, and they wanted to know where the Porto wine came from. The two lads continued their pursuit on mule and by boat up the rough Douro river. By chance they arrived to a peaceful quinta, which some believe is identical to Quinta do Bomfim in the outskirts of Pinhão, where they were treated to dried cod and tomatoes, garlic, bread, sucling pig and to a red wine, which they swore was better than the French wines they were used to drinking in England.

They bought as much wine as they could afford and had it shipped back to Vila Nova de Gaia and back to England. According to the archives and to tradition, a red wine which was added a shot of brandy endured the long voyage better. If this story is true, this was the birth of dessert wine. Well, at least the later so famous Port house, Warre, was borne, for the two young Englishmen settled in Porto and began exporting wine under this name (see page 302ff).

The odd Englishmen

The trade between England and Portugal went better than the countries themselves. These were the weirdest times. Colbert from France presented the first national budget with a surplus in 1669, the same year that the English King Charles II confessed a special love to Catholicism - and to France. The Englishmen were odd in many ways. With one hand they fought wars by tradition, and in lack of a war even civil wars, but with the other hand they started to drink wine, preferably French wine, and preferably French Bordeaux, which for the sake of old relationships and family ties tasted a bit of England.

But the new duties were a menace, Europe was unsettled, so something often happened. Wine imports were coming along fine, as long as the English and the French were fighting on the same team, which they often were when it came to trade, but rarely when it came to politics. There was, however, a comfortable period in the 1670'ies when the two aforementioned daredevils discovered the Douro Valley, for England and France were fighting together against the Netherlands, and it seemed as if they were winning, but then the sly Dutchmen sent a messenger to the Court in London and proposed a marriage between the Netherlander Prince Vilhelm of Orange and the English king's niece Marie, to whom he very practically was cousin. The French Sun King, Louis XIV, could hardly be said to be extraordinarily gifted person, but with the help of advisors he was made to understand that a new alliance was on its way, not only uniting England to the Netherlands, but also reinforcing bonds between England and the Netherlands and Portugal, at least for as long as the British queen was called Katarina of Bragança. Even though London had to fight fires, the plague and civil war, she had enough strength to also fight international plots, and Vilhelm not only got his princess Marie but also via her the English throne when he was persuaded to go to London in 1688 and check out the situation, which signified that the real king, King Jacob, in the meantime was backtracked.

Portugal's reward

Naturally, Jacob fled to France, and England and France were again at war, and again all exports of French wine to England were stopped. The war accelerated as wars usually do, and Spain entered the war traditionally on the side against France whilst Portugal was left again in Europe's furthest corner and was not allowed to join in the game. On the other hand, there was enough peace and quiet to make wine and to protect the interests on the faraway coasts of China. True enough, Portugal was by tradition and morally forced to show sympathy for the block against the Spanish neighbours, which in this case is France, but their hearts were not in it, and the useful footnote in the treaty with France acknowledged that the Portuguese support was only a moral support. They would not participate actively in the war.

This way, they could maintain hostility with Spain and send wine to the theoretical opponent, England. If that is not being sneaky, it is statesmanship. And even better times were approaching for the wine merchants of Porto when the European embers broke out into a big fire in 1702 and when the Wars of the Spanish Succession broke out. It was France, and now also Spain, against the rest of Europe, and it suddenly became dangerous for Portugal to toe the line on the wing, so they quickly changed their political stand, turned 180 degrees and joined the troops against France. And this time they were carrying arms.

The reward made itself felt. The British foresaw a long and tedious war with France, who had become more and more tedious to trade with, so the British Ambassador in Lisbon, Lord Methuen, was ordered to draft a treaty under favourable conditions between England and Portugal concerning the trade between the two countries.

This treaty was thus the fourth of its kind and contained more or less the same objective, but the treaty was to become the most detailed and most extensive one. Some even say that no other treaty of commerce between two European countries has been more efficient and long-lasting.

The Treaty of Lord Methuen

The treaty of Lord Methuen was signed in 1703 and lasted until 1840. The treaty prescribed that the Portuguese bought English wool, and in return the English promised to drink Portuguese wine, which in any case was easier now that the French connection was officially closed. In practice, the Treaty of Lord Methuen dictated Portugal a wine tax of 2/3 of the sum to be paid for the French wines, so even when the war would end eventually, Portuguese wine would have a financial advantage.

Some people at the English Court were not at all pleased at the thought of having to drink Portuguese wine instead of their daily Claret and one can almost understand them. The Douro wine had not yet reached the stage of a port as we know it today. It was a thin, young red wine added a bit of brandy due to the sea voyage it had to endure. Without the brandy it would probably not have been a pleasure to drink it at all.

In spite of the war and of the import prohibition, a census from 1708 indicates that the most wealthy and noblest of all Englishmen were still drinking French wine, the rest drank Portuguese wine, and the Portuguese wine was more or less identical with the wine shipped from Porto and produced in the Douro Valley.

In the second half of the 17th Century, the wine from Douro had developed and became an export product. The Portuguese themselves started to regard it seriously, and later on the English too. Vines were planted generously in Upper Douro, and the wine from the wine town of Porto was a success with the British, for example Vinho de Riba Doyro which later changed names to Vinho de Embarque and again later to the name we know it as today: Vinho do Porto.

The first mention of the name Oporto Wine is seen in an article from 1675, Oporto Wine meaning wine exported from Porto to England. The article mentions that 40 pipes of Oporto Wine has arrived in London, and three years later in 1678, we have the first documented shipload of Vinho do Porto (identical to Oporto Wine) of 408 pipes, which are not necessarily the first pipes to arrive, but the first pipes seen in writing.

The first wave of Port

These are fertile times for the new wine exports from Porto, and whilst Europe is at war, promising young merchants settle down in Porto to be part of the new wine boom. This is the time of the first port houses, even though they are not dealing in Port yet. Following Warre's establishment in 1670, Croft is established in 1678, Quarles Harris in 1680 and Taylor's in 1692 - all with British ancestors and with their objective directed towards London. In 1693 a total of 13,011 pipes of red Vinho do Porto is shipped from Portugal to England, and when Vilhelm III drastically raises taxes on the importation of French Wine, the Oporto wine is on the high road to success. The figures of exports of Douro Wine to England covering the period just before and just after the treaty of Lord Methuen are as follows:

1692-1703: 103,341 pipes
1703-1715: 104,915 pipes

The increase does not seem important at first glance. This is due to the fact that Europe is in the middle of a major war, and that other wine-producing countries as Italy and Greece come on the market as direct opponents to the Douro Wine.

But there is also a third explanation: the vineyards in the Douro Valley, transportation and production - what we today would call infrastructure - could not handle the situation anymore. In the period 1716-1749 new plants are seeded in Baixo Corgo which, according to an eyewitness, is "one big vineyard". The plantation could not have been that massive, but in this period the annual exports do come to a total of about 19,000 pipes at relatively high prices. Furthermore, the first

A pipe of Port

A cask of wine has been called a pipe of Port (pipa in Portuguese) in the Port Wine language for as long as anyone can remember. The origin of the word is uncertain as are the dimensions of the pipe, and there are pipes of many different sizes. The Douro pipe holds 550 litres (145 gallons) whilst the Gaia pipe for export holds 534 litres (141 gallons). Furthermore, at the Port producers' lodges you will see pipes of all sizes from around 500 litres to almost 650 litres, but these pipes are only used for storage purposes. Until the bottling of quality wine outside Gaia was prohibited in 1973, all quantities of Port Wine were measured in pipes. The Douro pipe was a special elongated type, suitable for rolling and stacking aboard the flat-bottomed barcos rabelos, whilst the export pipe of 534 litres (actually 534.24 litres) was very practically divided into 21 small Almudes of 25.44 litres each. The dimensions of the pipe are approximate, as they are hand-made and therefore never completely the same size. Many Port producers still have coopers who make and repair the pipes.

A typical Port Wine cellar in Gaia with rows of the characteristic pipes.

known Portuguese handbook on wine growing is published in 1720 (A Agrigultura das Vinhas) that recommends adding 3 gallons of brandy to each pipe of Vinho do Porto during fermentation to increase the strength and improve quality. The handbook never becomes a bestselling book and is apparently of no great significance. The conservative British shippers are outraged by this recipe, which one of them calls a "devilish" doing, maybe because it was out of their hands and in the hands of the wine producer in the Douro Valley while they were only allowed to add the brandy just before the shipment left the port.

None of their countrymen back in London and Birmingham questioned this doing. But they probably would have been happier with the devilishness. The people, who knew what was what, would have had a bit more fun and become a bit less sour drinking Vinho do Porto - which according to the modern, devilish method was close to what we call Port, even though the addition of brandy is so scarce that the dessert wine is more wine than dessert.

The hierarchy in Porto

But things were shaking up, and the British wine merchants in Porto were beginning to feel the competition. In 1727 they organized themselves in "The British Association" to be able to control the shipments of wine and to be able to keep the prices of wine from the Douro Valley at bay.

But not only the English were attracted to this market. Quinta do Noval is first seen in a document dated 1715, and Burmester was founded in 1730, and many others were founded, grounded and absorbed in the great sea of oblivion. At this stage, England seemed to be the only ones to drink Oporto Wine. Even Heinz "Henry" Burmester with the German name and British nickname was forced to join forces with the Englishman John Nash and established the export company "Burmester & Nash" in 1730, and when they opened their first office abroad in 1768, it was placed in London, not Germany.

Following the motley immigrants, a wine hierarchy was beginning to form in Porto. The German/Dutch families as Kopke, Van Zeller and Burmester lived in and at the outskirts of Rua da Reboleira, just 1 1/2 corks closer to the quay than the British who lived in Rua Nuova, which later became Rua Nuova dos Ingleses and is called Rua Infante dom Henrique today.

But this was the street of the Englishmen. This was where the people who had money lived, and this was where the Factory House lay. This was the heart of the British colony which was so special that it had its own consul and priest. Especially the latter was of great importance with regard to the religious wives. The colony was organized. It was agreed that all goods leaving Porto for England should be imposed a small duty to go to the colony in Porto and to be used for the priest's salary, among other things.

As you can imagine, not all exporters remembered to pay these duties on time, and petitions are recorded from the treasurer to the English foreign minister, in which he regrets the empty till and regrets even more that the priest might have to be laid off. Hopefully these prayers were heard.

Port with problems

It soon became everyday with regular working hours in the street of the English and also in the rest of Europe. After more than half a century of endless wasting wars peace was finally agreed upon in 1720, and the following 20-30 years saw alliances and agreements to avoid major wars and to keep the inevitable local wars local.

Peace also meant peace to be able to produce wine, peace to trade wine and peace to drink the one or two daily glasses of wine. The English liked the fortified red wine. In 1728, the English imports of the new dessert wine increased to 18,208 pipes, and neither the wine merchants nor the wine growers were able to follow demands. More plantations were urgently required. The vineyards expanded and new plants were planted, not only on the mountains sides but also in the lowlands. The quality of the wine decreased and demands increased, and when quality decreases so do demands in its tidings. The result was that exports, which at the time were about 16,000 pipes a year around 1750, fell to 13,000 pipes in the years 1754-56. And the fall in price was even more drastic, from 60,000 Reis a pipe to 8-12,000 Reis a pipe when times were none too good. And the name devaluated as well, just as we have seen in our days with the Chablis wine.

If we were to write a scenario in the art of ruining the reputation of wine, the Oporto Wine from these years would be the background material starting with the lack of grapes, which were compensated for by new plantations, and continuing with haste instead of patience. There is not time to wait when a market is in urgent need of wine. Quality decreased. And to stretch the harvest, water and cheap Spanish wine are poured into the casks. And to take off the sharp taste, sugar is added. And a little more brandy is added to be able to wash it down. And prices are dumped to be able to sell it.

For the first time market mechanisms are no doubt ruling the decay. This is also the time (1727) when the young Peter Bearsley, the head of the later so famous Port house, Taylor's, makes his daredevil voyage into the Douro Valley and notes that with some luck the thin wine can be improved by adding elderberry syrup (baga).

The big bang in Lisbon

During his Odyssey to the wine land between Régua and Pinhão, Peter Bearsley must have realized that it would be somewhat practical to tie closer relations between the wine growing by the Douro river and exports from Porto. In 1744, he buys the property Quinta dos Alambiques in Lugar das Lages with his brother Bartholomew. This is the first time a British shipper buys a quinta in the Douro Valley and thus becomes partly self-sufficient in grapes. Taylor's do however still own the quinta.

A year later, in 1745, when England was again at war with France, the Exchequer was again in need of money. But so as not to break the treaty of Lord Methuen, no extra duties were laid on wine, but instead on the casks that the wine was transported in. From now on, a duty of £4 had to be paid for every pipe touching a British port. This resulted in an expected fall in exports, falling prices due to the sudden surplus, and in 1775 the first violent quarrels between the wine growers in the Douro Valley and the wine exporters in Porto arose.

The wine growers wanted prices that the wine exporters did not want to pay. Production increased, exports decreased. A pipe of good wine was sold at £2-3 which is below the price of production, and on top of that the 1755 vintage was of such a questionable character that the wine merchants cancelled their buying trips to the Douro Valley. To emphasize their disapproval they sent a harsh message to the wine growers telling them in short pithy words that if the quality of wine did not improve, they would not sell it - they would not even taste it! The wine growers were furious. This could only end with a bang.

And the bang does not fail to come. On the 1st November Lisbon is destructed by the largest earthquake in the history of Europe. More than 3,000 people die, and the capital is levelled with the ground.

A Quinta in the Douro Valley

Just as Bourgogne has its domaines and Bordeaux its châteaux, the Douro Valley has its quintas. They all mean the same: a combination of buildings and land, but the quinta's name has no commitment involved like a domaine or a château. Only the land is classified, not the quinta nor its name.

Originally, the quinta was a country house for habitation, but gradually it included a winery, and it was therefore quite practicably divided into three parts: one part with a kitchen, dining room and sleeping quarters, one part for the crushing of grapes and vinification (adega) and one part where the wine could lie in pipes before the transportation to Gaia (armazém).

There are still quintas with all three functions, some of them even offer facilities for tourists and guest rooms, and in many cases the original quinta is used for living quarters whilst a new building now holds the vinification plant and storage facilities. Here are four types:

Top left:
Production quinta: *Sandeman's Quinta do Vau is only used as a winery. No living quarters and no storage. When the wine has been produced, it is transported to a vinification centre.*

Top right:
Guest quinta: *Ferreira's Quinta do Porto is only used for living quarters with beautiful guest rooms, a swimming pool, table tennis, darts and other leisure activities for the invited guests. Wine is no longer produced on this quinta.*

Bottom left:
Tourist quinta: *Fonseca's Quinta do Panascal is well-equipped for a pedagogical tour. Visitors can come unannounced, rent a tape recorder and walk around the quinta and learn something about the everyday life on a quinta. They might even be offered a small tasting. The quinta is part of the tourist project: "Rota do Vinho do Porto" (see also from page 376) but is also used for producing wine.*

Bottom right:
Omnibus quinta: *The Barros family's Quinta de São Luiz is big and spacious. Here you will find all the functions of a quinta: living quarters and guest rooms, a large, modern vinification plant and an armazém for storage purposes.*

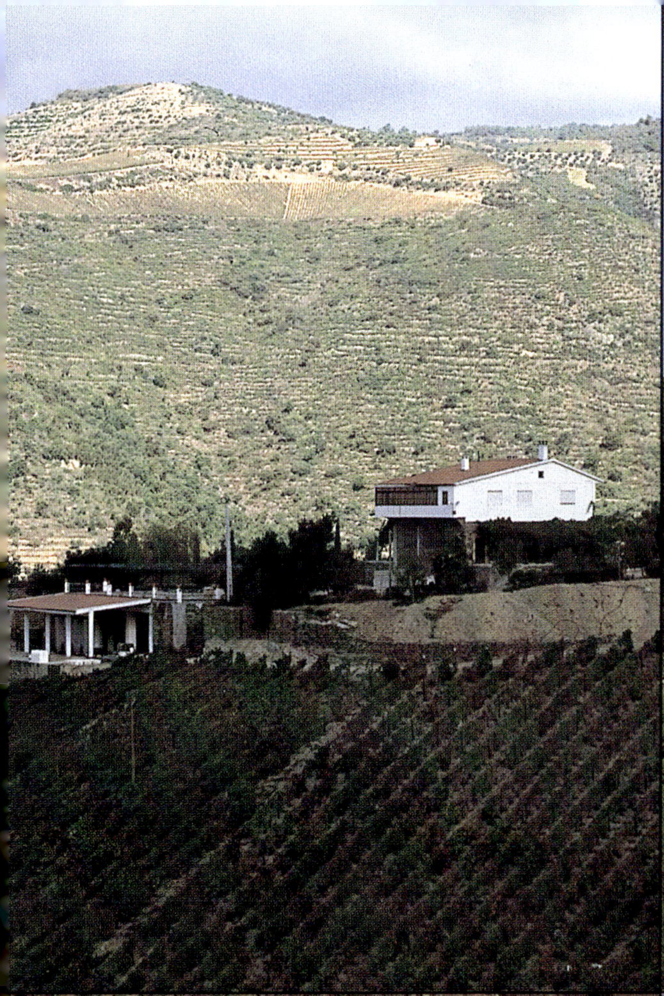

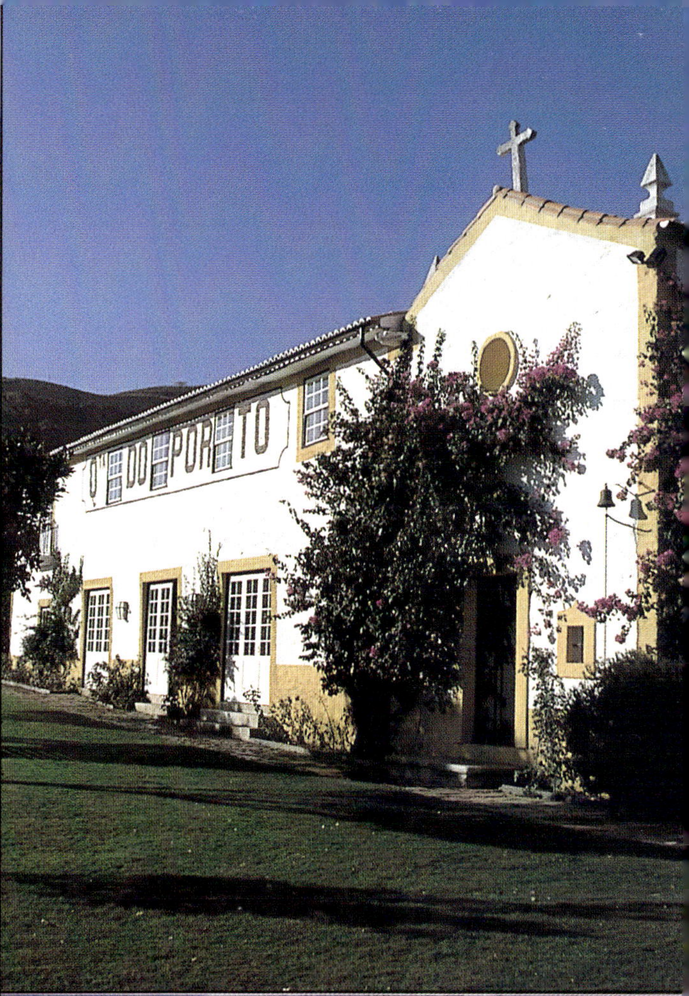
Q.TA DO PORTO

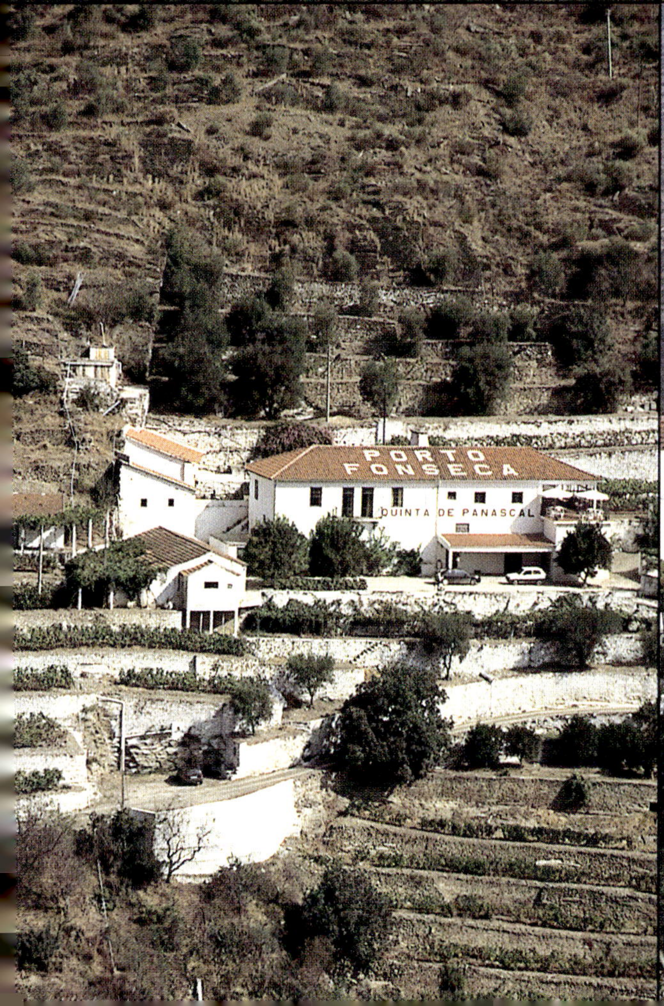
PORTO
FONSECA
QUINTA DE PANASCAL

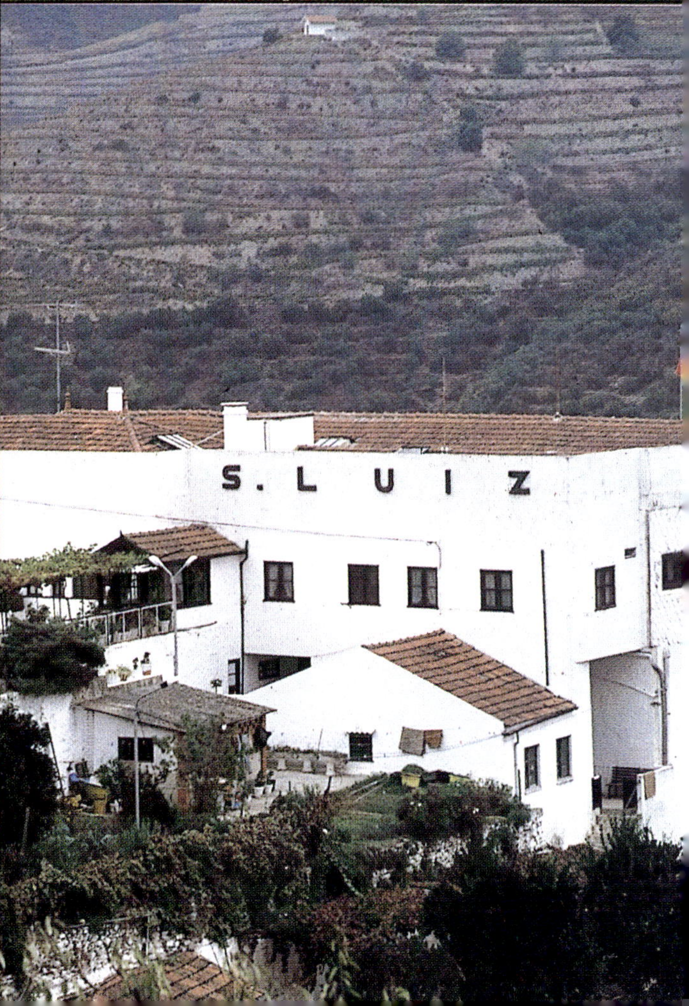
S.LUIZ

The meeting in the Douro Valley

Fortunately for Lisbon, and thus Portugal, and thus wine exports, the new king, King José I, had employed a new, strong man, Sebastião José de Carvalho e Melo, in 1750, to shape up finances. Both the king and Carvalho, also known as the Marquis of Pombal, which was to become his future title, had to flee Lisbon during the earthquake, but the last tremors had barely died down when Carvalho could present a plan for the reconstruction of the city and for the bailout of city finances.

The bailout also included an evaluation of the falling exports of Vinho do Porto, which was still a considerable part of national exports. It is said that the blood was boiling so fiercely in the Douro Valley that the farmers were seriously considering uprooting the vines and planting other crops so as to avoid the battle with the wine merchants of Porto every single year. But if this threat was ever realistic in order to discontinue wine production, they were drowned by the plain fact that the farmers very well knew that the steep mountain sides could not be used for anything else than vines and hens. And the hens were not worth much effort.

In December 1755, an interesting meeting took place here when three of the Douro Valley's most outstanding figures sat down to discuss the unbearable situation:

Dr. Luis de Beleza Andrade,
an important wine grower with lodges in Gaia

Dr. Frei João de Mansilha,
a locally-known Dominician

Dr. Bartholomeu Pancorbo,
a Spanish nobleman, who made a living as a wine exporter in Porto

The latter had good contacts on the Continent and wanted a broader export to the European Continent; friar Frei João was not into wine growing but represented common sense, which they must have had a feeling would be necessary. And according to history, he was the one to come up with the final proposal, namely first of all to re-introduce dignity to the Douro Valley (and on the export market), to limit the too many vineyards covering to wide an area, so both producers, wine growers and buyers could have a knowledge of where the best and the poorest wine came from. The Portuguese historian, Moreira da Fonseca, has looked into the content of the epoch-making meeting and says that a proposal for the control and the improvement of cultivation and exportswas prepared on the basis of this meeting, and as the three mentioned kingpins all agreed quite nicely to the terms, and as Pancorbo was on good terms with the Prime Minister's brother, Paulo de Carvalho, the dispatch went directly through him to the supreme authority of the country. The considerations were presented by the end of 1775, and after several amendments Minister Sebastião José de Carvalho e Melo signed this document on 10th September 1756.

The state monopoly

The radically new issue in Carvalho's law was the establishment of a state organ to control the wine process from the cultivation of grapes to exportation. It was called the *Companhia Geral da Agricultura das Vinhas do Alto Douro* (which actually means "the company for the cultivation of vineyards in upper Douro", later known as Real Companhia Velha, among the people just known as "The Company". In July 1757, the Company was fully operational. It was headed by a president, 12 deputies and 6 councillors and also included the "infantry", a bunch of clerks, tasters, commission agents, errand boys and all relevant what-nots in the manning of a state monopoly. And it was a real state monopoly. Carvalho must has given up the

1756 it says to the left in the register with the instrument of foundation of the Company, created by Marques de Pombal. It lies in the archives of Real Companhia Velha.

attempt to settle the squabble between the uncompromising local farmers and the belligerent English shippers and chose in-stead to take a strong line. Therefore the Company in practice took care of all the things that the farmers and the shippers disagreed upon: the control of the cultivated areas, the regulation of the prices of grapes and wine and the assurance of the repution of Douro wine. The Company, as well as Pancorbo, also wanted exportstargeted at other countries than England. Therefore the Company needed a monopoly on the entire process from the first picked grape to the last pipe on its way out of the seaport of Porto.

As so very often, this took place before by a heavy-handed state intervention: both parties, both the farmers as well as the shippers, believed that they had been treated unfairly. However, there was no room for discussion, as the intervention had been dictated by the King's right hand, and the involved parties were discretely told that if they were not satisfied, the farmers could cultivate whatever they wanted, and the English could go back to England.

The law included 53 articles, of which the most important ones were the following:

§ 10: The Company must ensure the good name of the Douro wines and a decent price for the parties trading wine. High prices entailing that nobody can afford to drink wine should be avoided as should low prices resulting in financial disaster to the wine growers. The capital of the Company is set at 1,200,000 Cruzados, half of which comes from good and merchantable wines, the other half in currency so that the company may carry out its obligations to both the wine growers and to trade.

§ 14: The Company must settle Douro wines of the finest quality, in good state and unadulterated, at a price of 25,000 Reis a pipe of a regular size. A wine of a cheaper quality, but which is still drinkable and acceptable for shipment, is paid for at 20,000 Reis a pipe. The Company will continue to buy such wines at these terms in the years to come, if there is an overproduction or a lack of wine so that the wine growers are secured financially in years of overproduction and must in return keep prices down in years with low production.

§ 29: It is vital for the export of Douro wine that it is divided into wine from Upper Douro and its nearest surroundings and wine from the rest of this area, which is only produced for local consumption so that the latter does not damage the reputation of Douro wine. A map of all vineyards on the northern and southern banks of the Douro river is to be drawn up indicating all farmers producing wine for export and indicating the size of production for the past five years so that no vineyard proprietor may sell wine without notifying the Company or sell pipes of Douro wine to the Company or for export exceeding the quantity that is defined in the above-mentioned registration. Any violation will be fined nine times the value of the wine which is sold illegally and entail that the proprietor loses his right to sell wine.

§ 30: It is prohibited to introduce wine from other regions or countries to the demarcated area for Douro wine.

§ 33: To be able to ensure a sound and fair trade between wine growers, buyers and sellers of Douro wine, the Company maintains its right and duty to buy wine for export to the aforementioned prices of 25,000 Reis and 20,000 Reis, respectively, according to the quality of the wine. For wines of an inferior quality for local consumption only, another tariff will be applied, depending on the destination of the wine.

Douro wines and other wines

With the well-defined distinction between Douro wines and "other wines" mandated by the articles, it was obvious that some kind of clear-cut delineation had to be decided upon for a precise description of what was within the Douro area and what was not.

Therefore, a committee was appointed to draw up a register, a *Tombo General das Duas Coastas,* in which it should be indicated who made the best wine for export (Vinhos de Carregação) on both the northern and the southern bank of the Douro river to be measured according to the prices at which the wine was sold. As stated in § 29 there was to be a sharp distinction between wines which were suitable for export and wines for local consumption. And this was where the delineation was to be drawn. The elastic word feitoria (a place where something is made=feito) was included and marched right into the Port parlance. Feitoria is seen in the English translation Factory. It was decided to delineate a feitoria zone around the best vineyards, and the Douro Valley was thus the world's first demarcated wine region according to the law of 10th September 1756.

When the Company started in office in July 1757, the last formalities were put into place, and then it was time for the hard work. In the period between 4th October and 9th November 1758 a total of 201 brands were laid down, most of them as granite slabs, with the inscription Feitoria and the year of 1758, and in some cases also a serial number chiseled in the slates, and in the period between 17th April and 4th May 1761 a further 134 granite slabs were laid down. Of these 335 slates, 103 have been found. The rest are lost, some have been dug up and used for other purposes, for example as foundation stones in houses (!), some of which are built into the walls; others are still being excavated at random, plus the 103 slates which can still be seen. It goes without saying that the work in this trackless terrain was very strenuous, but the demarcation had a very high priority, and even though there were some discussions with dissatisfied site owners, who believed that their land had been underestimated, the government cut through severely and settled the disputes before the corrected demarcation in 1761. The topographical map, which was used for this historic demarcation, was finalized on the 17th November 1761 and sent to the archives in Lisbon, but unfortunately it has since disappeared.

The modern aspect of demarcation is emphasized in the Port Institute's interpretation of this first demarcation both for today and for the future, i.e. not only acknowledging or refusing the existing vineyards but also envisaging which areas and which fields had potential possibilities. Still, the main idea of the demarcation is to maintain production very close to status quo, and both production and exportsshould be controlled solidly by the Company. This is also seen in a special clause monopolizing the trade of wine and the sale of wine, brandy and vinegar to the four Brazilian colonies, Rio de Janeiro, São Paolo, Bahia and Pernambuco.

In one breathless month, from 4 October to 9 November, 1758, 201 brands were laid down into the schist, bearing the name "Feitoria" and the year "1758", the proof of the first demarcated wine district in the world. Burmeister's Arnold Gilbert has found one of the family's Quinta Nova de Nossa Senhora do Carmo.
(Photo: Porto Burmester)

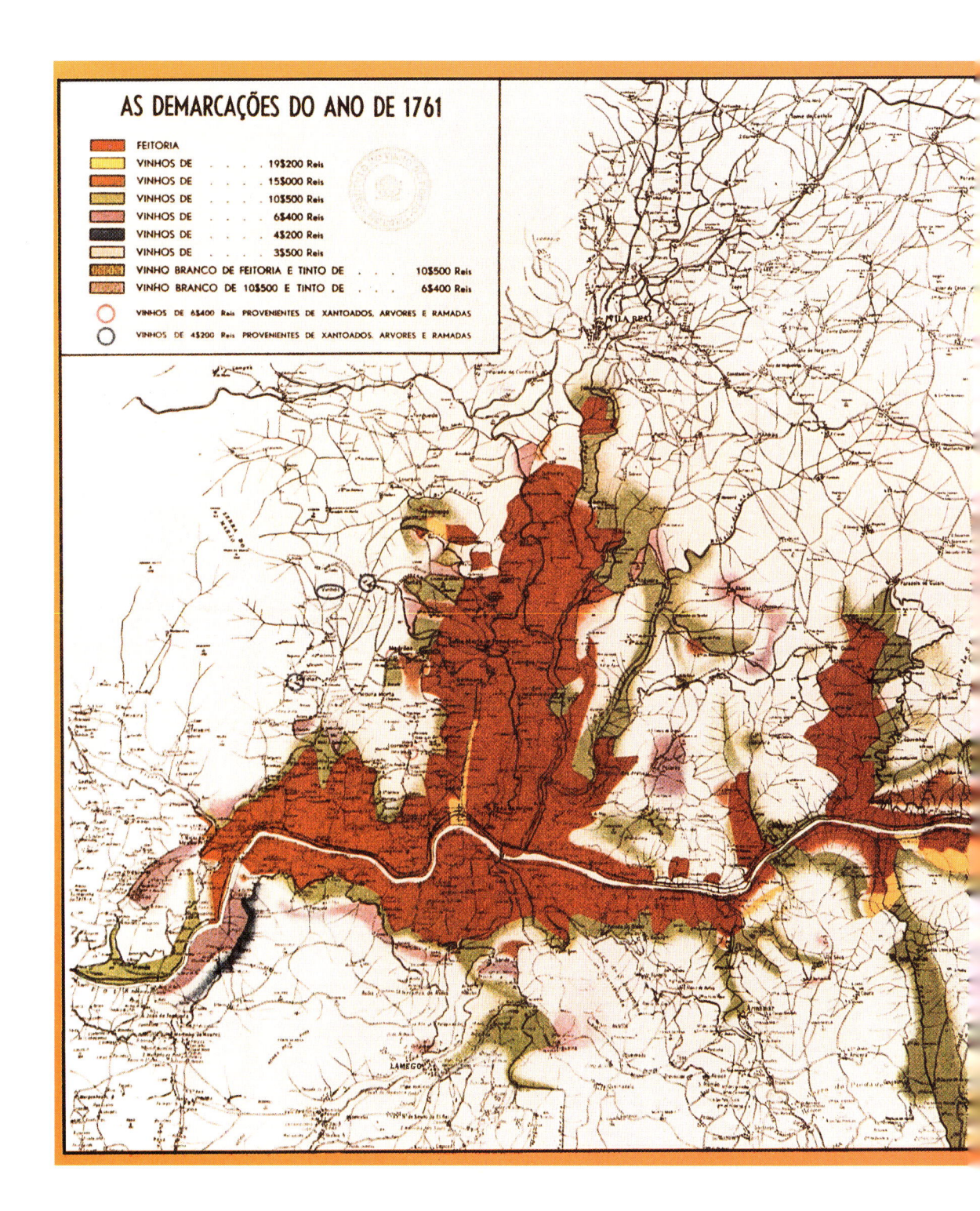

The map of the demarcated area from 1761 is just as faded as it is historical. It shows the worlds's first, clearly demarcated wine district structured according to the value of the wine sold.

ESCALA 1/80.000

Pombal and his Company

The Company was Pombal's creation and therefore it had his whole-hearted support, regardless of the opinion of others, and Pombal was invaluable for the Company in its first years, for he stood unfailing and strongly by King José's side. However, when the king died in 1777 - the same year as Port exports had reached a 20,000 pipes of wine a year, Pombal suffered a series of political defeats and had to retire.

But there was so many other things going on in the world. The American Civil War had started, and after the king's death, Portuguese nobility saw a possibility of getting rid of the unpopular marquis. And so they did. King José's daughter, Maria, became Queen Maria I, and the second crown befell the family when she was bequeathed to her uncle, Pedro III. None of them were in favour of Pombal who is sent into exile, and nobody reaches out to help the preserver of Portugal.

Pombal was strongly criticized, especially of being too autocratic and too punctilious, but his ability to stimulate the wine growers and the exporters is said to have been genuine - and showed results. Prices were stabilized, and the falling export that had led to the foundation of the Company, rose again from the fatal 13,000 pipes in the years 1754-56 to approx. 20,000 pipes a year after the foundation of the Company. And furthermore, it is important to note that the name of Vinho do Porto was now definitely established and was given all the support possible by a minister. On the other hand, the Company soon suffered the fate of so many state monopolies with the urge to control everything - including the state monopoly: power leads to abuse. This is seen in all British records, even though they are written by subjective parties in the matter: increasing amounts are ear-marked on the budget for bribing the Company's officers. A silver coin once in a while would make them read the wrong result of a test so that the shippers had a poorer wine approved than the one holding a control brand, and at the right price you could even purchase an approval to be dedicated to any one wine. Some even say that Pombal himself had bartered some of the bilhetes, which accompanied every export of Oporto Wine, and that he used them to export wine from his own vineyard by Carcavelos under the good name of Oporto Wine.

The first scandal

It soon became everyday life within the Company. At the same time of the fall of the Marquis de Pombal, the agent of the Company, the aforementioned Dominician, Padre Frei João de Mansilha, is brought down, allegedly because he showed "extreme zealousness" in his efforts to promote the Company. He is held in solitary confinement for some time in the Cloister of São Domingo in Lisbon, is convicted soon after and forever banished to the Cloister of Pedrógão Grande.

This was a sign of new times. Queen Maria limited the Company's rights the same year, first by decree of 9th August, followed by a quick intervention of 22nd September the same year, entailing that the Company lost its monopoly on the exportation of wine to Brazil and a similar monopoly on the sale of everyday wine to the small bars and taverns in the Douro Valley.

This quick intervention saved the Company from being uprooted, for the whole thing was a mess. In the meanwhile, the resentment against the monopoly was growing rapidly and not only among the British wine merchants. The iron discipline was rusting. This was not only felt by the Marquis and the Dominician, but also rubbed off on the quality of the wine. Around the time of the dismissal of Pombal, approx. 20,000 pipes of wine a year were being exported, and now exports soared - in spite of the rigid demands on production - to more than 27,000 pipes in 1777 and in the following years. The reason is simple enough: foreign table wine was trickling into Portugal and into the demarcated district. And things became even worse, for in 1787 exports reached a high 34,000 pipes, and in the years 1788-90 an average of 41,000 pipes a year were exported! The

From the beginning the Company scrupulously controlled all properties and lots along the Douro river. This original map is from 1756 and indicates ownership and location, production and prices.

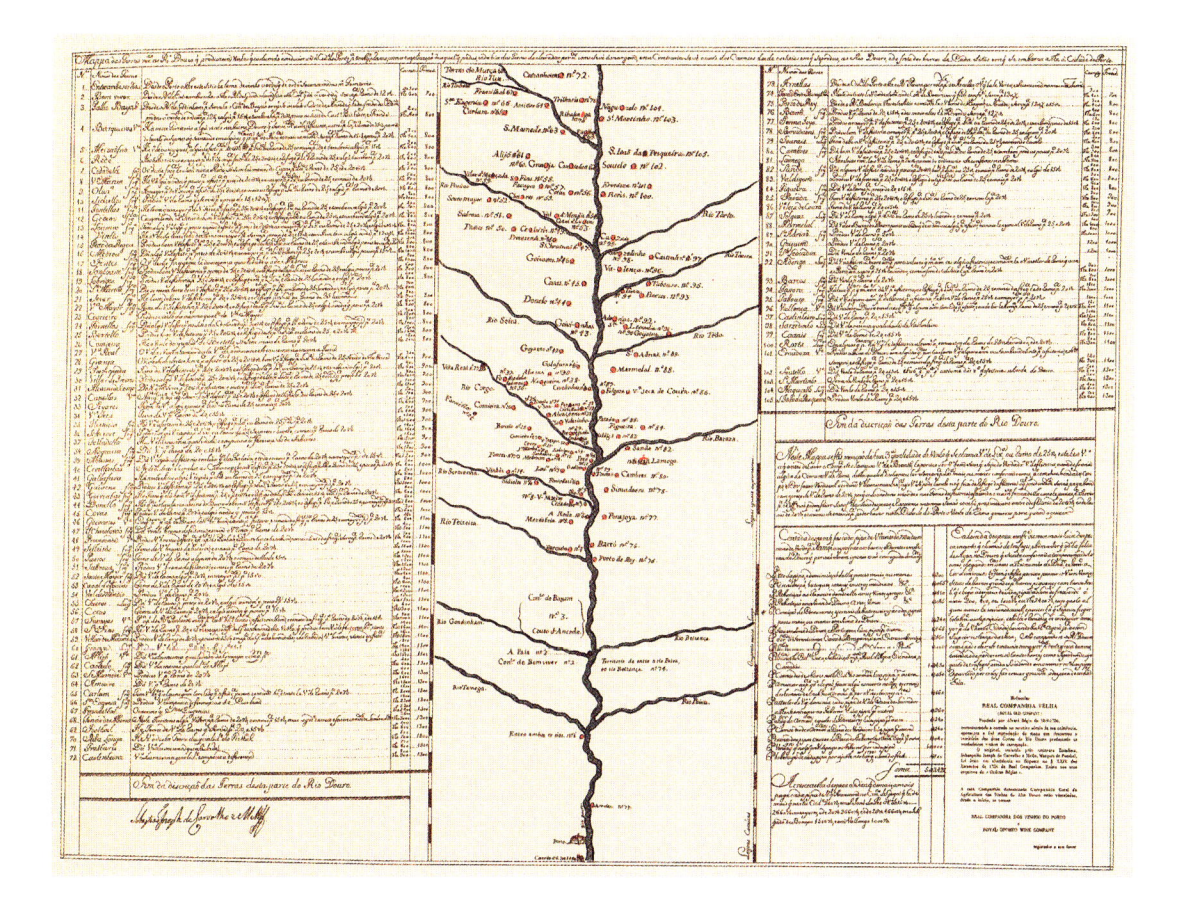

harsh figures for the export of Oporto Wine illustrate the much too rapid growth:

1756: 12,211 pipes
1757: 12,488 pipes
1758: 17,327 pipes
1759: 19,425 pipes
1760: 21,290 pipes
1761: 18,281 pipes
1762: 27,085 pipes
1763: 12,242 pipes
1764: 17,186 pipes
1765: 19,534 pipes
1766: 21,272 pipes
1767: 20,242 pipes
1768: 22,471 pipes
1769: 22,922 pipes
1770: 16,469 pipes
1771: 22,363 pipes
1772: 20,358 pipes
1773: 20,129 pipes
1774: 23,214 pipes
1775: 24,013 pipes
1776: 22,620 pipes
1777: 26,833 pipes
1778: 22,890 pipes
1779: 29,575 pipes
1780: 27,716 pipes
1781: 21,059 pipes
1782: 25,923 pipes
1783: 19,741 pipes
1784: 21,795 pipes
1785: 24,567 pipes
1786: 23,555 pipes
1787: 34,017 pipes
1788: 36,608 pipes
1789: 39,645 pipes
1790: 46,808 pipes
1791: 45,390 pipes
1792: 55,123 pipes
1793: 31,113 pipes
1794: 52,654 pipes
1795: 53,392 pipes
1796: 38,584 pipes
1797: 28,757 pipes
1798: 64,402 pipes
1799: 56,699 pipes
1800: 55,896 pipes
1801: 21,208 pipes
1802: 23,801 pipes

SOURCE: *Instituto do Vinho do Porto*

The easy solution

In 1781, the Real Companhia Velha noted that a shipment of Port was sent off to Katarina II of Russia. Unfortunately this was an isolated occurrence. Otherwise, there was a growing concern with regard to the galloping export figures in the late 1780'ies, especially because everyone in the business knew that these figures had not been obtained honestly.

Something had to be done, and only the Queen could do it. The first problem was the surplus production; the other problem was that this surplus production was especially due to wine brought illegally into the demarcated area. The matter could therefore be approached from several angles. One could either tighten the control of wine from abroad, punish the responsible parties according to the Demarcation Act, or, extend the demarcated area so that the wine which was necessary for the increasing exportation could be legalized.

The Border Commission appointed by the Queen chose the last and obviously easiest solution. The Commission visited Douro several times with the mandate "to extend the demarcated district temporarily and for as long as experience proves it to be favorable and in common interest. The extension will be considered as being outside of the demarcated district, as soon as it is estimated to have a detrimental effect on trade and the export of legal wine". And so on

THE HISTORY OF PORT

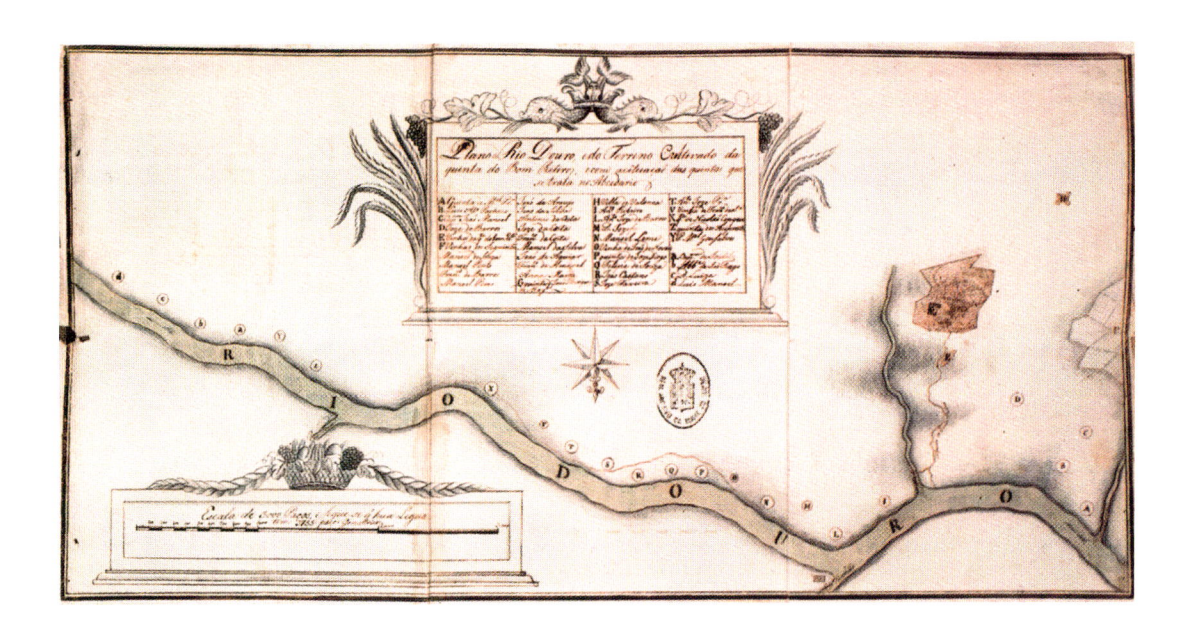

After rigorous demacation of the Port Wine district under Pombal, Queen Maria allowed several extensions in the late 18th Century. The illustration shows a map with a petition from a small farmer explaining why his land should be included in the demarcated area. It is dated 1789.

and so forth. The Queen recognized the shortage of "legalized" wine in the increasing export as being a vital national cause. And in May 1788 she intervened directly in the work performed by the Commission and the Company and commanded an immediate intervention, upgrading a number of properties which were "known to have a good reputation and able to produce wines for exportation of a quality, which were as adequate as the ones included in the new demarcation", to be included in the Factory Zone.

In September 1788, the Commission was able to present its first results, and on 6th September 1788 the Company's management was informed of the new extensions, and of which properties and vineyards had been promoted to Feitoria status, and of the fact that the rules for cheap table wine had also been adjusted. Peace was finally restored. A royal decree of 17th November 1788 even gave permission to plant and produce red wine outside of the demarcated area against a guarantee of 15,000 Reis a pipe to be paid by the Company. The moral must have been that if it is legal to produce wine, there is no reason to cheat. But on 13th January 1789, the Queen had to give a temporary permission again, which "as an exception and solely for this year" made it legal to purchase wine cultivated outside of the new demarcated area.

But this was not enough. In May 1790, the Company's management had to request the Queen's permission to include "certain small vineyards" in the demarcation area, even though they did not - according to law - produce wine which was adequate for exportation. The Queen was urgently requested to include these vineyards in the demarcation area, and the matter must have been quite urgent, for one week later on 19th May 1790, her Majesty gave her approval. Not only "certain small vineyards" were included - the extension was so massive that from a historic point of view it is considered an important revision of the 2nd demarcation.

The long way from the grapes to the exportation of Port Wine was for many years split between two worlds: the wine growers and the wine producers in the Douro Valley and the wine merchants and the exporters in Gaia. The hardest work was transporting the finished wine to Gaia. It was hard work for the oxen, but also hard for the farmer who had to walk alongside the cart carrying the Port Wine.

Douro becomes navigable

However, things were soon in pretty bad shape again. In May 1791, the Company was forced to request another extension of the demarcation area. The Queen sees it fit to approve this extension later on in the year, and the Company's arguments for the application are historical: the production of Vinho do Porto has now increased so much that there is not produced enough table wine.

Exports go galloping. But the oxen carrying the pipes from the Douro Valley are galloping no more, for there are two reasons for the soaring success of Port in these years: the English have transformed Douro Wine to Oporto Wine and Oporto Wine to Port - and the Douro has become navigable so that the wine is now carried by boat from Upper Douro to Porto.

In 1780, the Company had begun to improve the possibilities of sailing on the Douro river by cutting a channel through the cliffs. This resulted in a small waterfall by San Salvador da Pesqueira, and the boats could now sail right up to Barca d'Alva.

At the extension of the demarcated area in 1788, the Queen had chosen to include some vineyards close to Cachão, but not only were they East of the previous demarcation, they were also miles from anywhere, for there were no passable roads, and the "Cachão da Valeira" hindered any navigation on the Douro river. Some infamous

It helped both the oxen and the farmers when the Douro became navigable towards the end of the 18 th Century. Now the pipes of Port Wine were rolled aboard the sharp-nosed barcos rabelos, and there was room for quite a few pipes aboard when they were properly stacked. It now became attractive to the shippers to buy land and property in the Douro Valley.

groups of rocks in the middle of the river acted as damns thus producing waterfalls and undercurrents which could even subside the sturdiest boat.

But now the Portuguese got cracking, and in the course of 1792-93 the Douro river was made navigable right from Barca d'Alva by the Spanish border, enabling the sharp-nosed Port boats, barcos rabelos, to carry pipes all the way to Porto and Vila Nova de Gaia. At the same time, roads between Porto and Foz do Douro were made passable, but yet another 100 years would pass before the railroad was introduced in 1887.

At least the wine could now be produced, transported and exported all in one go. And there was a great demand for Douro wine which in the course of a few years had changed from being a practical and drinkable everyday wine to becoming a British prestige aperitif. This resulted in the "second wave" of new British Port houses, of which the following still exist:

1784: Smith Woodhouse
1790: Sandeman
1790: Martínez
1797: Gould Campbell
1798: Dow's

From Porto Wine to Port

What attracted the hopeful, young Englishmen to settle as Port exporters in the late 19th Century was the fact that the Oporto Wine had become Port. The dessert wine had replaced the fragile table wine which was somewhat difficult to transport across the sea to England. When adding brandy, transportation no longer posed a problem. Port became increasingly popular in England, and from now on the French Claret was no longer considered real competition.

The transformation from table wine to dessert wine did not take place from one day to another, and it was one of the few things that Pombal had not legislated, but which was a matter between the farmers and the shippers. Eventually there was no doubt that brandy had to be added for the keeping qualities, so the question was only at which stage.

The shippers maintained for a long time that they were the ones who should give the wine a shot of brandy before commencing the voyage to England, and at this point the wine had ceased fermenting and was quite dry. But the farmers maintained that the wine was easier to handle if they were the ones to add the brandy, because it meant that the wine was less perishable on its way from Douro to Porto.

The most important issue was, however, that port had put a distance to red wine. This is emphatically put by Samuel Johnson (1709-84) who in his mature manhood years determined that "Claret is for boys, port is for men". In Sandeman's archives there is an interesting description of how the shippers travelled every Spring all the way from Porto to the annual wine festival in Régua to talk to the small wine growers and farmers and to taste the wine which had been harvested the year before. Deals were made according to how much the Company had allowed - and these rules had to be followed. First, the Company bought all the wine for the home market. The best qualities were kept for exportation, and each Port house had to let all purchase and all shipments go through the Company.

This account is dated 1814, but the shippers had begun to visit the Douro Valley regularly long before, and eventually it became common to buy land and property there so that they were closer to the grapes and could control the addition of brandy.

The transformation of Oporto Wine to Port took place in the second half of the 18th Century. In Pombal's detailed demarcation and directions from 1755, the wine is consistently mentioned as Vinho do Douro, i.e. Douro wine. But on 8th February 1767, Port is seen for the first time in print, and this the earliest existing example - found in a catalogue from Christie's Auctions in London where a lot of red Port is put up for auction.

The development hereafter is next to explosive. The simple table wine which has been added a shot of brandy, so it could be enjoyed with some relish, has not only become a decent dessert wine but has become so sophisticated that another catalogue from Christie's archives from April 1773 indicates a lot of "Port Wine 1765", which is the earliest mention of a Vintage Port.

Port in print

Things developed rapidly now. In 1788, John Croft writes that Port should be matured for approx. four years in pipes before it is shipped, i.e. more or less as a modern Late Bottled Vintage. The four years of maturation also entail that the brandy is added during or immediately after fermentation - otherwise the wine would no doubt have been perishable.

The oldest British Port house, Warre, is one of the first Port houses to lend its name to this new turn. The oldest example is, however, a lot of "Barnes Port", which is sold at Christie's in 1800, followed by "Plaskett's Port" (vintage year 1799) in 1804, and in another catalogue from Christie's, Croft's is indicated at 67-69 Shillings for 12 bottles in February 1810, and a lot of "Warre's Port" is put up for auction on 18th November 1812 at 56 Shillings a crate (it is underlined that the crate contains 12 bottles). There is also a note about the first matured Vintage Ports on an auction held in July 1813 where one can purchase "Warre's Port 1805. Laid in 1808".

Not only was the dessert wine revolutionized, the bottle was too. Around 1760 the first bottles with almost vertical sides are produced; and the bottles can now be packed in cases, signifying that the common man does not have to buy only one pipe at a time.

This stirs the imagination, and from 1775 Vintage Ports are produced and bottled rather systematically. Christie's has several examples from the 1770'ies and the 1780'ies, and even "The Times" announces "Red Vintage 1788" for auction in April 1793. And while Christie's can present a 1765 Vintage as the first Vintage Port, the English writer, Warner Allen, says in his book: "A History of Wine" (1952) that the year 1775 is "the first vintage worthy of being called a Vintage Port", and this seems to be the common opinion of British Port houses. Furthermore, the 1779 Vintage is the oldest, recorded Vintage being sold as Vintage Port by several shippers.

In all circumstances, this all takes place a few years before the first French red wine is vintaged: Château Lafite, 1787.

Record and revolution

In 1792, when the French guillotine began reducing the number of the French population, the shipments of Port reach a sky-high record: 55,123 pipes. Regardless the instant enthusiasm, this situation cannot go on. And it does not. A year later, King Louis XVI is beheaded on the scaffold, and France goes to war against most of Europe, including England and Portugal. Apart from the practical problems of exporting wine in war times, a difference of opinion is noted for the first time between the English in Lisbon and the English in Porto.

More and more Englishmen, especially among the young generation in the British Port colony, sympathize with the French revolution and feel somewhat split when their country of birth, England, and their native country, Portugal, try to put a stop to the revolutionary ideas.

One of them is a young Scotsman, George Sandeman, who had settled as a wine merchant in London in 1790, and who sometime in the 1790'ies (Sandeman's own archives claims it to be 1796) made a bold voyage to the Iberian peninsula to find out if he wanted to trade in Sherry or Port. As we all know, he ended up doing both.

Sandeman was in his twenties and did not see eye to eye with the intransigent British politics with regard to revolutionary France. On the other hand, the British embargo of French wine was his great chance, and even though his heart went out to the unhappy French revolutionaries, his purse most certainly approved of the poet, Jonathan Swift's national epic from the time of the Declaration of War in 1793:

Be sometimes to your country true,
Have once the public good in view.
Bravely despise Champagne at Court
And choose to dine at home with Port.

This was a common, British point of view attracting more and more devotees. In 1798, the shipments of Port from Porto to London reached a sky-high 64,402 pipes. This record was not beaten until more than 90 years later, and in 1799 the shippers of Port noted that Port now made up more than half of Portugal's total export.

Considering that Spain and England were constantly at war with each other at sea, this was an incredible number of pipes of Port going off to London, and it was astonishing that Portugal succeeded in taking sides with the English without their large neighbour Spain interfering.

But, in 1801, they eventually did. Whilst Great Britain was trying to pull herself together in the League of Armed Neutrality, and Nelson made a small trip to Copenhagen to wreck the Danish fleet, Spanish troops occupied Portugal and closed down the major seaports of Lisbon and Porto. The overseas export of Port falls drastically from nearly 56,000 pipes in 1800 to slightly more than 21,000 pipes in 1801.

The peace treaty between France and England, signed in Amiens in 1802, did not bring back "the good old days" immediately. Even though both the English and the French were fed up with wars and the costs of having them, peace did not last. Napoleon protected French industry and introduced tariff barriers against England, and the English retaliated by boycotting French wine. In May 1803 war broke out again.

When Spain joined sides with the French a year later, the export of Port was threatened by black clouds. Napoleon proclaimed himself Emperor, his brother became King of Spain, and Nelson brought Port into the history of war by dipping his finger in a glass of Ruby Port and tracing his strategy on a map with his finger before the sea battle at Cape Trafalgar in 1805.

Nelson's touch

Nelson's "touch" was the best thing that happened to Port in these years. Sandeman's archives contain a document indicating the Port exporters' hardships. George Sandeman sent this document to the house's customers in August 1805, a few months before Nelson was victorious at Trafalgar making sailing to England possible again. The letter informs the customers that a convoy is on its way from London to Porto and kindly request orders for Port and Sherry.

Another document in the Sandeman archives dates April 1809 and ensures Sandeman's customers that the utmost will be done to procure Port and Sherry, apparently at the same prices as in 1805, but with an important note: that a sup-

Port Wine entered world history via Lord Nelson's left indexfinger. Shortly before the battle of Trafalgar in 1805 the English Sea lord visited Lord Sidmouth and on A.D. McCormick's painting he explains histatic by dipping his finger in his Port Wine glass and drawing a map on the table top. Nelson's touch was his last encounter with Port. He did win the battle, but died.

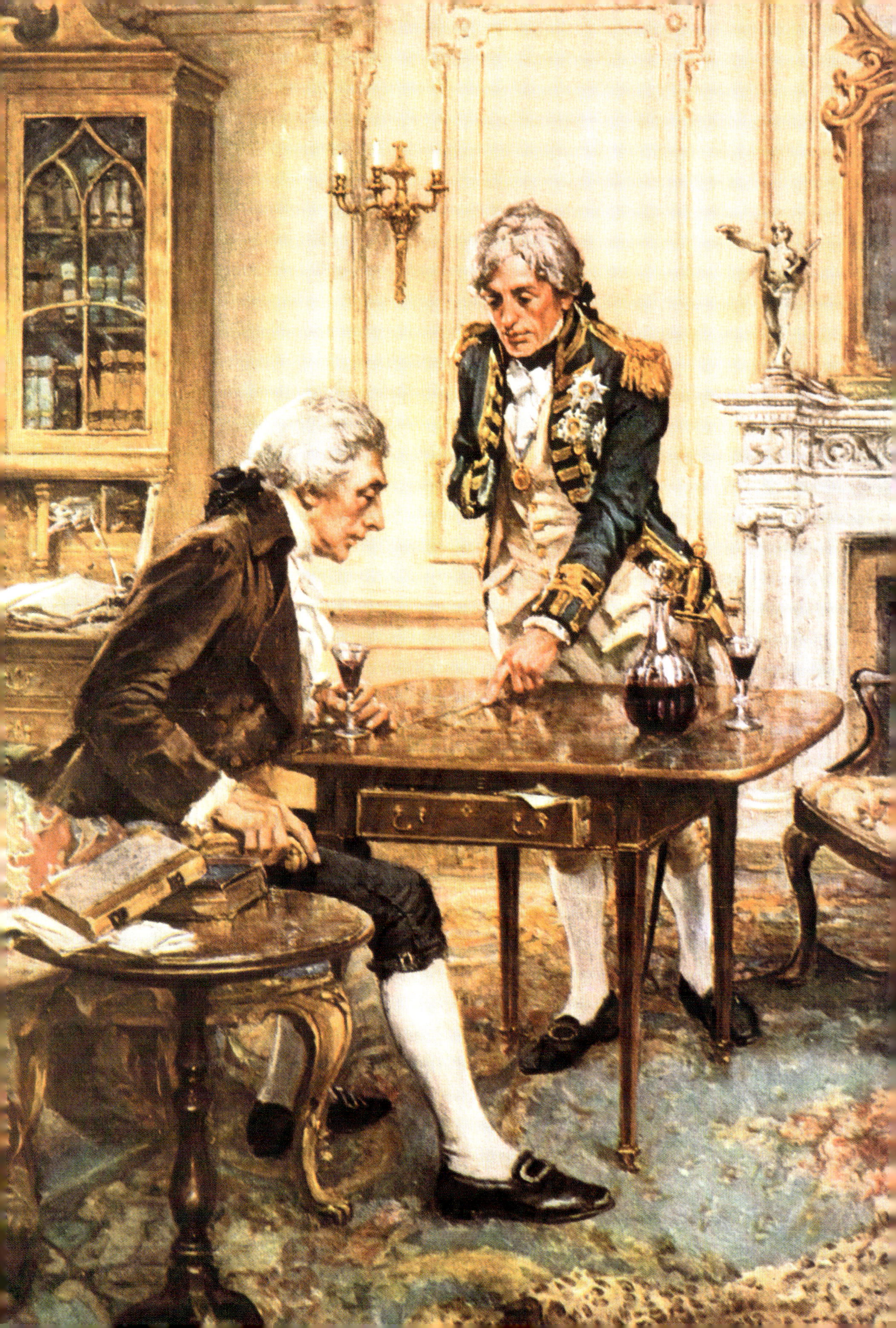

plementary duty will be accrued; one could almost call it danger money, "if the French are at Oporto".

Which they were. In 1806, Napoleon had ordered a blocking of England which naturally also included the British importation of Port, and as Portugal refused to join the embargo against England a year later, French troops occupied Portugal by land while an English frigate brought the Portuguese king safely to Brazil by sea.

It could have been the love of a daily glass of Port that led to the illogical British reaction towards the countries that were forced by Napoleon to join the blocking of the mainland. The pro-English Denmark was attacked without notice by the English navy in September 1807, while the just as pro-English Portugal was patted gently and promised military assistance against both the Spaniards and the Frenchmen.

Portugal needed the encouragement. This financial situation was in a terrible state, because export was not as it used to be, and Portugal was being flooded with English goods at high prices, whereas they were not allowed to sell anything themselves. The merchant navy was as good as useless, and the only regular trade going on was with the Azores and Madeira - apart from the quantities of Port still being shipped to England. If one imagines how bad infrastructure in Portugal was at the time, and how difficult times were, one acknowledges that it was much more difficult to advance by road from Lisbon to Porto than by sea from Lisbon to Rio de Janeiro.

Portugal abided by - and survived - the British conditions. Therefore the English-Portuguese ties were strengthened during the Napoleon wars. This was also because many of the young sons of Port merchants participated actively in the British army, and a certain William Warre wrote an enthusiastic letter to his father on 15th May 1810 stating: "Lord Wellington has asked me to procure a hogshead of very fine, old Port regardless of the price and has asked me to convince you to take good care of the wine in London." Lord Wellington, and especially his Quarter Master, General Calvert, were taken in by Sandeman's 1797 and was according to this statement: "the finest ever known" - and after tasting it - Calvert ordered two pipes to be forwarded to his address in London.

Critical years in Portugal

Even though wars were going on everywhere, there was still a time and place for the daily glass of Port. In 1808, Portugal was being occupied by a French support army, which, however, was detained by small battles on their way through allied Spain (!), but the English set their own speed at sea, and at the announcement of the French attack on Portugal, a British corps under Sir Arthur Wellesley, the later Port-loving Lord Wellington, was sent to Portugal in haste where he won his first battle against the French at Vimeiro in August 1808.

Luckily for Portugal and for Port, Napoleon needed his soldiers to fight the uprise in Spain, so they retreated, and when they tried to charge Portugal again in the spring of 1809, and even reached the occupied principal seaport of Porto, Wellesley returned in haste and not only threw the French out of Portugal but well into Spain.

But a year later there was trouble again. The French returned to Portugal with fresh troops, and the English had to fight hard before ending the battle. When Spring came, the French troops lacked supplies and were thrown out of Portugal once again and far into Spain - and this time, they did not return.

Neither did the Portuguese king, at least not in the beginning, even though the kingdom was formally re-instated on the Conference of Vienna. The political unrest was smouldering beneath the surface in Portugal, and in 1815 the colony

Export in 1811

In the spring of 1811 the French have to evacuate Portugal because they were short of supplies. Wellesley pursues them far into Spain, for on the high seas the British are in command. And that is also why the shippers in Gaia manage to send a total of 18,536 and a half pipes of Port to England in spite of war and the Continental System. In Ferreira's archives there is a detailed list of whom the shippers were:

Real Companhia Velha	7438	pipes
Bernardo de Clamouse Browne et Comp.	1238	pipes
António Joaquim de Carvalho	1054 1/2	pipes
Vanzellers & Comp.	1053	pipes
Joaquim José de Figueiredo	988 1/2	pipes
Tomás da Rocha Pinto	732	pipes
Nicolau Kopke & Comp.	620	pipes
Butler Tyndale & Comp.	605	pipes
Joaquim da Costa Lima e Cunha	543 1/2	pipes
Geraldo Galway	531	pipes
Nogueira & Frutuoso	510 1/2	pipes
Daniel Bull & Sylvius	532	pipes
Patrício Hely	330	pipes
Luís Caetano de Sousa	282 1/2	pipes
João Henriques de Magalhães & Comp.	276	pipes
Ana Perpétua de Barros e Mello	262	pipes
José Gonçalves Ferreira	260	pipes
Quarles Harris & Filhos	257	pipes
Machados & Comp.	257	pipes
Domingos Ferreira Pinto & Teixeira	171 1/2	pipes
Manuel José de Amorim	162	pipes
João José da Costa e Silva	150	pipes
José Bernardo Ferreira	101	pipes
T.M. Correia de Aguiar	77	pipes
António Pearce Tremlett	68	pipes
Manuel Perreira Viana de Lima	56	pipes
João Manuel Martins	55 1/2	pipes
António de Sousa Lobo	39	pipes
João Leite de Magalhães	32 1/2	pipes
Burmeister & Comp.	10	pipes
Joaquim José Fernandes da Silva	7	pipes
José Guedes Amorim	5	pipes
Martins Lopes & Comp.	5	pipes
Schindler & Rahm	4	pipes
Viúva Souto e Freitas	2	pipes
I alt:	18536 1/2	pipes

of Brazil declared herself as an independent kingdom - certainly in a personal union with Portugal - while Napoleon was arrested and locked up on the island of Saint Helena where he immortalized - not Port but Constantia wine. The French Revolution had started a wave, which now nearly 20 years later, reached the faraway coasts, especially Spain's former colonies in South America, but which also broke on the European Continent. The historian, A.H. de Oliveira Marques, who wrote the History of Portugal, calls the period just before and just after the fall of Napoleon the most critical times in the history of Portugal. First there was the earthquake in Lisbon, then wars and sieges which took place year after year, and then the Frenchmen's recurrent predatory expeditions - there is a tale about a certain episode on 25th May 1808 when 90 wagons loaded with gold and silver from the Portuguese churches, followed by 33 wagons loaded with money left for France - which are all to blame for the lack of art and architecture in Portugal. And when the king fled, the ruling of Portugal was practically left to the British General, William Beresford.

"From 1808 to 1821 the country could either become a British protectorate or a Brazilian colony", Marques states. Beresford was disliked, and whenever he was confronted with any kind of reluctancy, he rushed off to Brazil to complain resulting in the weak king giving him even wider powers.

The Spanish threat

King João knew that there was some unrest back home in Portugal, but he did not even make a move to go back. The air in Lisbon was certainly full of sultry revolutionary ideas which spread because the king was as weak as he was. When the Conference of Vienna had ended, and the British troops had left Portugal, there was no royal house, no life guards, and no English soldiers to stop an uprise. Especially the British Port producers must have had many a sleepless night at the thought of revolution - or a new Spanish intervention, now that Spain was about to lose her precious South American colonies.

A letter from the Port house Ferreira's archives shows that this was their worst fear. The letter is written by one of Ferreira's agents in London, Joaquim Máximo on 30th May 1817 giving a situation report to his principals, Luís and António Bernardo Ferreira, partly in Spanish: "Do not be surprised at the fact that I am writing to you in Spanish. I have a nasty suspicion that our dear Portugal will soon be praising [the Spanish king] Ferdinand, and thus our language will be bristling with Spanish words. Oh, these are terrible times ...".

It did not, however, end that badly. The Spaniards probably wanted to invade Portugal, but they were weak, and the reinforced European balance of power would not have accepted this. Talleyrand had at the Conference of Vienna proposed that one of the Portuguese princes become King of Portugal and the other King of Brazil - or vice versa - the important issue being that a quick decision was made, before the English - out of fear of a revolution in Portugal - lost their patience, meddled and abolished - as they had threatened to - the Companhia das Vinhas do Alto Douro.

When the mentally unstable Queen Maria died in 1816, and a military uprise in Lisbon was suppressed ruthlessly a year later, it was obvious that something had to be done. This was made even clearer when a liberal, secret society was formed in 1818 with members from both the outer circle of the royal house and from the Port house of Ferreira, with the objective of bringing a dynamic, liberal government to Portugal, thus dethroning the king. The secret society was no more a secret than rumors reached Rio, and after a minor liberal uprise in Portugal in August 1820, João had to admit that it was more important to be King of Portugal and maybe lose Brazil than be King of Brazil and lose Portugal for sure. He was acclaimed upon his return in 1821 - also by the liberals. But as he had feared, he did lose Brazil, who chose his son Pedro as the first Emperor of the now independent kingdom.

Coup d'état and black clouds

The British Port shippers had one comfort in their continuous state of uncertainty in Porto - all was well with the Port exports to England. The 1811 vintage was called a "Comet Vintage" and was even outdone by "The Waterloo Vintage" in 1815, which has gone down to history as one of the most exquisite vintages - presumably because more people have heard about it than tasted it.

The following four vintages were mediocre; exports fell as did prices. The 1820 vintage was shipped by most of the shippers as a Vintage Port, perhaps due to the previous weak years, but several doubtful vintages followed and more riots. The Vintages of 1820 and 1821 were almost impossible to sell, and according to the archives of Ferreira this was due to the fact that they were too sweet.

When João VI died in 1826, Pedro was called home to Lisbon to become king, but he declined, and offered the throne to his 7-year-old daughter Maria II (the then Gloria) and instated his ultra-Conservative brother, Dom Miguel, to be her guardian. This could only result in a violent confrontation between the military extremists and the Church and the new liberal ideas. And this is exactly how things went.

The year after the Spaniards offer to help the right-wing supporters, whilst the English support the liberals, and as the English are by far the strongest, Dom Miguel is forced to promise to abide by the Constitution. But this promise does not last for long. As soon as the last Englishman is well out to sea, he heads a Coup d'État, sets the Constitution aside, dismisses all the liberals in Government and proclaims himself king. Suddenly the outlook for Port and for the British colony in Porto is black. But help is near. Pedro abdicates as Emperor of Brazil and sails to England to obtain support for a final confrontation with his treacherous brother, Dom Miguel. And he succeeds. In 1832, he goes ashore and conquers Porto. In July 1833, he is received with open arms in Lisbon, and a year later Dom Miguel is forced to surrender for good and goes into exile. The now 15-year-old Queen Maria returns and marries wisely to Ferdinand of Sachsen-Koburg, but it is still smouldering beneath the surface in Portugal - as in the rest of Europe. This is the time of revolutions, and a civil war is not easily forgotten.

Pedro I, Emperor of Brazil won the exhausting brothers' war against Miguel in 1832-1833.

In the shadow of civil war

All was not well in Portugal - and neither in England for that matter. In 1810, Portugal signed a new commercial treaty with England to boost Portuguese wine, especially Port, in times of war and crises, but nevertheless Port exports fell from a little more than 40,000 pipes a year between 1777-1810 to 28,000 pipes between 1812-1834. And it seemed quite insignificant that the citizens of London had started to import crystallized plums and pears from Portugal.

First there was the war, then the crisis, then came internal political unrest and finally financial problems in England, for even though the British had won the Napoleon wars, they had paid a high price.

In 1817, the riots between workers and the police in London were so serious that the British constitution, The Habeas Corpus Act, was set aside for the first time in the long history of England. In 1819, a peaceful workers' meeting in Manchester developed into a small civil war with many casualties, and in December of that year Government approved the much hated Six Acts which in practice abolished the freedom of the Press and of Assembly.

More and more people were suffering from poverty. On the faraway Continent one revolution was followed by the next, and in 1824 the British Minister of the Interior, Robert Peel, abolished The Combination Act which since 1799 had prohibited workers to go on strike or to organize in trade unions. In 1826, a new financial crisis breaks out in London, and several Port importers have to shut down.

In 1828, amendments are made to the corn law to stabilize corn prices. The Duke of Wellington tries his hand at politics without success. Ireland threatens to tear herself loose, and England is in financial difficulties. This effects the importation of luxury goods such as Port. In 1832, the Parliamentary reform is finally introduced in Great Britain, giving more influence to the Middle Class - but none to the working class.

The upper class is still moaning about England being in need of a strong leader. Well, they find - not him, but her in the form of 18-year-old Victoria of Sachsen-Koburg who becomes Queen in 1837. This is also the year when the fantastic Vintage Port of 1834 is released for export from Porto. Peace is restored at the British dinner tables, and the decanter of Port is once again served with honour and dignity.

Cockburn, Graham, Fonesca

In the years of unrest, an increasing number of young British men wanted to try their luck abroad. Three of the old Port houses were founded in these years: Cockburn's (1815), Graham's (1820) and Fonesca (1822), and if the young people listened closely enough, they could hear their older countrymen sitting in the Factory House reminiscing of old times during the war when there were so many British ships in the seaports that it had been safe to ship Port to England. When the war was over, the marine had disappeared, and the infamous Algerian pirates were replaced by new colleagues from other countries lurking outside the major seaports, and it was no secret that some of them had specialized in attacking ships carrying Port bound for England. This situation was quite unbearable - one could almost wish for the return of the times of the war.

Ferreira's English agent, J.M. Virgiano warned his superiors in a letter from London dated 18th November 1815: "Do not send shipments at this time of the year, for the weather is very unstable at sea, and there is also quite a lot of piracy from the Algerian privateers". This was just after the war, and the Mediterranean and the Atlantic Sea were calm and smooth for pirates and other hoodlums to ravage.

Pirates or not, there were also those riding on the crest of a wave, among others Manoel Pedro Guimaraens, who had taken over the merchant house Fonseca & Monteiro in 1822, and who in 1840 had distinguished himself as the second largest shipper of Port. There was also young Robert Cockburn who in the middle of the Congress of Vienna in 1815 decided to live on selling and shipping Port. Or there were William and John Graham, Scotsmen like young Cockburn, who in 1820 were paid 27 pipes of Port for a bill of exchange, which had fallen due, and were reprimanded by their father in Glasgow. He did, however, forgive them later on when he could see that there was money to be made in sending Port from Porto to Scotland.

But apart from the piracy, the problems that arose did not so much arise in Porto as they did in the Douro Valley. Here the meagre years had been exploited to scrutinize the efforts and contribution of the Company. There were more Port producers now, and they stood stronger than ever before, especially because the Company's political backing was too busy with more urgent matters.

Especially the British shippers were sick and tired of the Company's magisterial attitude. They also believed that the brandy which the Company allotted them was of a very poor quality. The attitude among the producers was clear enough: if the Port was to surpass this period of stagnation, the monopoly of the Company had to be broken. The new keyword was free trade - both in Régua and in Pinhão as well as in London and Paris.

Dissolution of the Company

The civil war did not improve matters between the British Port shippers and the Company. To put it bluntly, they had each backed their own horse and the shippers won. The Port producers had also been forced into the civil war against their will.

When Emperor Pedro took the city of Porto in 1832, the Company was occupied by the Miguelist followers and opportunists, and in August 1833 the Company's lodges came under fire, under the command of one of Miguel's generals, and many thousands of litres of good Port spilled into the Douro river so that they would not fall into the hands of Pedro's men, i.e. into the hands of the British. According to Sandeman's archives, more than 27,000 litres of Port were wasted. Ferreira's archives indicate an astronomous 10,000 pipes of Port and aguardente.

The fire that followed was only put out after many complications, for example the lack of something quite so banal as water. The Company was accused, and rightly so it seems, of having been the base of the Miguelists, thus causing Portugal to lose the civil war. The British reminded the Portuguese that Charles Noble from Warre and other highly esteemed Port merchants had been imprisoned for their liberal point of view and that the entire British colony had been under siege, because nobody could foresee the outcome of this fratricidal war.

At this stage, the British Port producers felt badly treated by the Government. They had supported the legitimate regent, and incidentally they had also - in spite of the Company's querulousness - expanded the export markets to include Germany, France, Brazil - and even Russia. That was a good point. And maybe this was why the returned Queen Maria dissolved the Company after peace was restored in Évora-Monte in December 1834. Port had gained its free trade status.

And one must say that the rumour spread. New Port houses shot up along the quays in Gaia in a dense fourth wave, of which some naturally did not even survive the ripple, but many did and did not let go - and they were not all British: Niepoort (1842), Romariz (1850), Rozès (1855), Cálem (1859), Krohn (1865) and Delaforce (1868).

The pitfalls of free trade

The free trade had the wind behind it from the beginning. Stocks were depleted in all the countries who drank Port by tradition, following several years of unsuccessful exports so that all the producers had to do was to fill them. And now the Port shippers could set their prices.

But it was soon to be seen that free trade also has its disadvantages. With the dissolution of the Company there was no authority to control the planted area which suddenly increased drastically - and not only within the demarcated area. Vines were planted in any spot where one could dig a hole. Production soared, the importing countries quenched their thirst, and after three years of free trade the Port producers did not feel anything had improved. They had gotten rid of the Company, but they had also gotten a new problem on their hands which was just as serious: Surplus. And an overproduction, at that, which could not be controlled or not even localized, for competition had revived the temptation to smuggle cheap grapes into the demarcation area and cheap wine out of the demarcated area and further on to Vila Nova de Gaia where it emerged as fake Port.

The sour fruit was again to be found on the dinner table, and the Port shippers had to swallow the bitter pill. Times had been bad with the Company, but times were even worse without. So in 1838, the Company was revived - although it never regained its full strength. Actually its strength was reduced to such an extent that it became a state-guaranteed puppet on a string in the game of the annual overproduction. Some did suggest to scrutinize the Commission's recommendation of 1788 concerning the expansion of the demarcated area, and especially the lines regarding the expansion only being temporary, and simply reintroducing the demarcation indicated by Pombal in 1756, but there were too many interests at stake in the new demarcation and the suggestion therefore fell on deaf ears.

To pass the time during which no Port could be exported, the farmers planted more vines. This was a self-increasing folly and the sole comfort was, if any, that the surplus product at least was non-perishable.

Joseph James Forrester, hothead and baron, came to the Douro in 1831 to deal in wine but instead, he spent his time mapping the Douro river and thus earned the title of baron. He died in 1861 when his boat capsized on his beloved Douro river. At that time he was a little more matured than in Roquemont's painting from the 1840'ies.

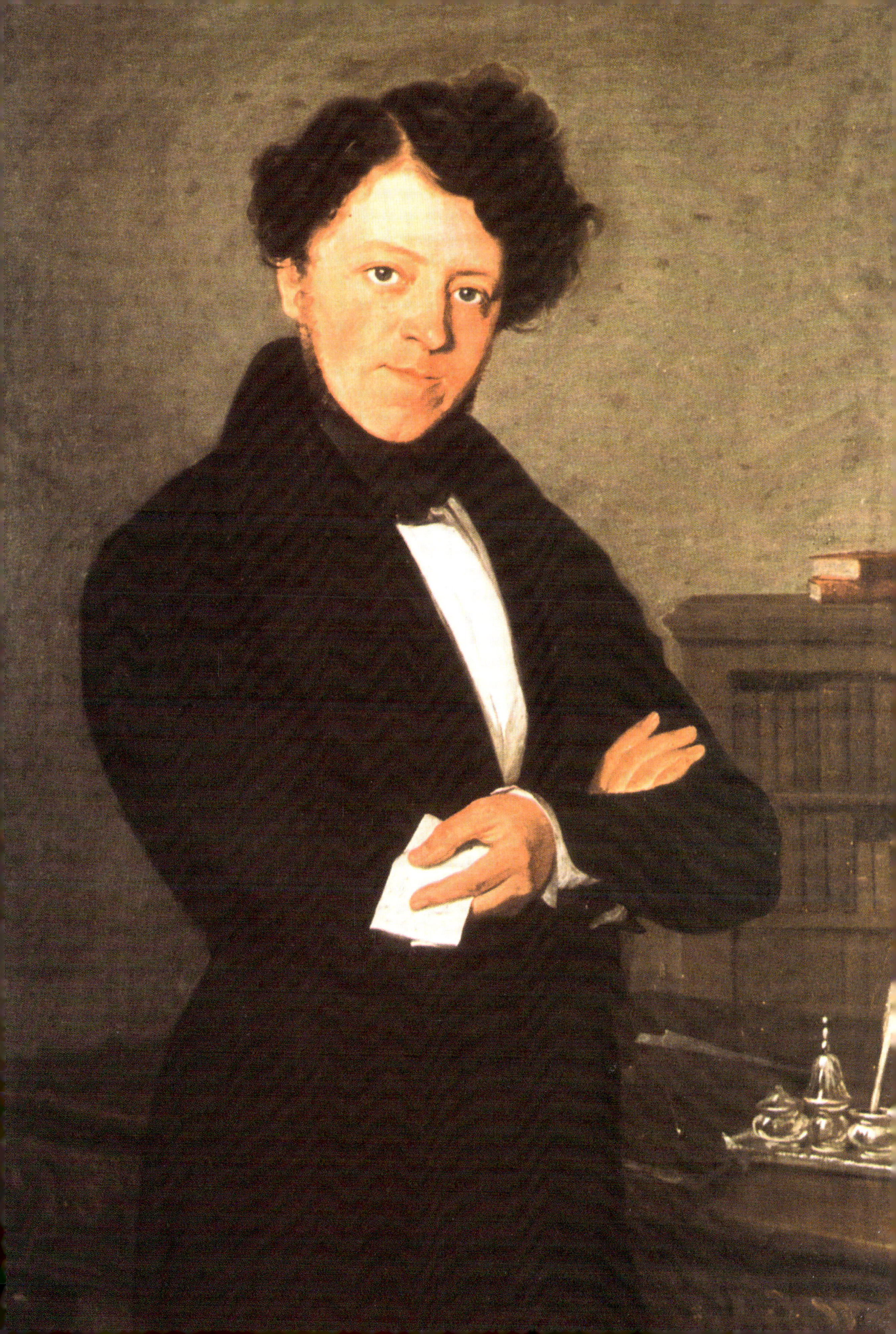

Fermentation and fraud

The years up until and after 1840 were no fun. Between 1837 (an excellent vintage!) and 1844 (a reasonable vintage) harvest was rather mediocre. This resulted in a lack of interest on the part of the British. Furthermore, the Methuen Treaty expired in 1840. A new commercial treaty was signed in 1842 but never obtained the same importance as the old one. Ferreira's archives indicate that the years 1841-43 were decidedly years of crisis. And there was good reason for Joseph James Forrester to publish the small controversial pamphlet in 1841: "Uma palavra ou duas sobre o Vinho do Porto" - a word or two about Port, in which he rather openly accuses the wine business to deliberately swindle with Port.

According to Forrester this swindle especially referred to the illegal addition of elderberry syrup, sugar and very sweet dessert wine. In his opinion, Port should be a "natural wine" of which the fermentation should not be stopped by adding alcohol but is allowed to cease fermentation naturally. He also attacked the Company tasters whom he believed to be corrupt and incompetent, as they much preferred the dark wines to the light wines uncritically, without even tasting them.

The critics maintained that Forrester's criticism was "putting old wine into old bottles" and to some extent they were right in their assumption. There was nothing new in his points of criticism, but this does not signify that they were not reasonable. His countrymen in London and in Porto were not too fond of him, but they all knew that he was right when he said that it was the taste of the British that dictated the vinification in Pinhão. The discussion of whether or not to add brandy was not new either, even though it might be benificial. However, there were good arguments against Forrester, for example in George Sandeman's account of how he handled the historical Waterloo Vintage 1815:

"I selected three pipes drawn from the same tonnel, to one of which I put one-third of the usual quantity of brandy, to the second two-thirds, and to the last a full dose of brandy. Recollect that this was one of the finest vintages I ever had to deal with, and the tonnel was one of the best of the year. I bottled all three pipes at the same time, and between one and two years afterwards I found the first pipe becoming sour, and was obliged to start it again into cask and dose it with brandy. In three or four years I was obliged to do the same with the second, but the third was so much liked that I was offered a guinea a bottle for it." The addition of brandy to cease fermentation proved useful, both with regard to its-keeping qualities and with regard to taste. But what could one do with the surplus production and the swindle with alien wine. Even Forrester had no good ideas for that.

The Company's second failure

But what lacked in common sense and what the politicians and the Company had given up on, nature handled. In 1851, the first attacks of white mould fungus (Oidium) were observed on the vines in the Douro Valley, and in the following years the fungus devoured so much that production fell drastically.

In the course of the 1850'ies Oidium was controlled - according to several hoax stories because Forrester found out that one could treat the vines with sulphur. At this point even the stocks in Gaia, exportation and quality had fallen drastically so that exports only reached around 30,000 pipes in 1859, which was more or less the same as 80 years earlier in spite of the many new plantations in the Douro Valley. A census carried out by Ferreira's Dona Antónia, or at least upon her request, indicates the production of some of the quintas in the critical years of the 1850'ies as follows (the numbers are in pipes of Port):

Quinta	1853	1854	1855	1856
Vesúvio	313.5	278	169	69
Vargelas	76	69	35	13
Granja	43	9.5	5	4.5
Nogueiras	12	1	0.5	0

This drastic decline is confirmed in Sandeman's archives. In 1855 8,000 pipes of Port were produced compared to 80,000 pipes in a normal year. And it did not help exports that a permanent stage coach was introduced between Lisbon and Porto this same year, or that gas lighting was introduced in Porto, or that an uninvited guest, called the cholera, arrived in this country, supposedly spread by two sailors from Barca d'Alva. Production fell, as did the quality of Port. The situation became so critical that an impartial appraisal by Government in 1859 maintained that the reputation of Port had suffered to such a degree that "the Port approved for exportation is of such a quality that it should be destillated".

That was plain speaking without beating around the bush, and the Company came to a sad end even though it was not completely or even half to blame for the mess. By royal decree of 7th December 1865 the Company was finally dissolved for the second and last time, at least for the time being. The exports of all Portuguese wines from any Portuguese sea port and from any producer were declared free. The Company had lost its privileges, and from now on it was an ordinary Port producer.

The years of disaster

The so-called "Second period of free trade" (1865-1907) had a tragic start. In 1861, one of the most colourful personalities of the Douro Valley, the afore-mentioned Joseph James Forrester, a bad-tempered Englishman with bad-tempered Scottish blood, died in a tragic accident on the Douro river.

Forrester had arrived to the Douro Valley in 1831 to work for his uncle's firm "Forrester Port", but he soon proved to have many other talents than selling and exporting wine. He fell passionately in love with Port and its country, but his love was for the Douro Valley and not for Vila Nova de Gaia. He fought for a pure and genuine wine, no matter what it must have tasted like, for he was, as mentioned, opposed to ceasing fermentation with alcohol and became spokesman for the puritan Douro wine. Fortunately, he also had other, more positive points of view. He had a burning enthusiasm towards the topography of the Douro Valley, and showed a talent as a cartographer. He elaborately drew detailed indications of the wine districts in the Douro Valley on parchment paper. These maps are a piece of history and were not surpassed until the camera was brought into the Douro Valley many years later. And at the same time, the maps had many practical functions. First of all, it became easier to have an accurate layout of the demarcations and the ownership of the different plots, and second of all, they made it possible to analyse the Douro river's course which contributed towards making transportation easier. Forrester's efforts were so significant that he was appointed baron in 1855, and when he sailed out on his last voyage on his beloved Douro river on that fatal day in May 1861, he had become one of the most esteemed personalities of the Port province. On this day, he was with Dona Antónia Adelaide Ferreira (also known as Ferreirinha) and her husband, Francisco Torres. They had set sail from Vesúvio with the purpose of having dinner at Régua, but after two days of heavy rain, the river waters were overflowing, and the boat capsized at Cachão da Valeira.

Everyone on board fell into the river, but according to a persistent hoax water story, Forrester drowned due to his integrity whilst the two ladies survived due to their vanity. Forrester was pulled down because he had a belt with silver coins for paying the farm workers tied around his waist, whilst the bulky crinolines of the ladies saved them from drowning.

When the railway was built in 1887, it not only signified a smoother traffic for the pipes of Port. The railway was built very close to the quintas so that the Port Wine people could go out their back door and step onto the train – like here at Cálem's Quinta da Foz. The small Douro train still runs today, not according to a schedule but rather upon the request of the quintas.

QUINTA
DA FOZ

The cure that did not cure

If the final dissolution of the Company was to be a cure, and one might suppose that this was the point, it was very quickly easy to see that the cure did not help. From the low exports in 1860 of 33,224 pipes due to the impact of Oidium, exports rose to around 52,000 pipes in the 1870'ies and to around 60,000 pipes in the 1880'ies and fell again drastically to nearly 55,000 pipes in the 1890'ies and even lower around the turn of the century. Overproduction was no more to blame for these results, which were due to a poor economy.

The increasing figures in the 1870'ies, 1880'ies actually cover the fact that in 1863, the first attack of the wine louse, Phylloxera, was noted on Quinta do Montes by Gouvinhas. This is colourfully depicted in the history books as how even the wealthy families of the Douro Valley went bankrupt and had to see their former so prosperous children walk around barefooted and in rags on the country roads, and naturally there must have been some sad destinies following the wake of the lice, but lice or no lice, exports rose increasingly and reached an incredible record of 75,000 pipes in 1886 - the same year that Porto got electricity, but the top had been reached and now there was only one way to go: downwards. And so it did.

In 1871, the "Anti Phylloxera Committee" was formed under the leadership of Batalha Reis, in the following years the vines were grafted vigorously on American roots. But these things take time, and the new vines also needed time before they could produce grapes, and as time requires patience and the market did not have any time for patience, the Port shippers faced new problems. 1878 should have been a festive year, as this was the year the population of the Douro district topped the 296,000 mark, and the railroad from Porto had been extended to Régua (and the year after to Pinhão), but there was not really anything to celebrate apart from the fact that this vintage was the last of the pre-phylloxera vintages for Port.

But happy days were short-lived. Just as short-lived as was the taste of the "replacement wine" which since the invasion of phylloxera had been shipped to England. The British consumers could easily taste that the new shipments of Port did not taste as good as they used to - simply because due to phylloxera, most of the grapes had to be purchased outside the demarcated area and were exported under false names. The English still chose to be blind to the fact because the global market was short of wine due to phylloxera which had also ravished France and Italy, but it was also due to the fact that the British import duties has been lowered so that it had become a bit cheaper to drink Port. And that seemed to be some sort of compensation.

But then Portugal suffered financial problems and in 1889, 100 years after the French revolution, the first of many financial "balloons" burst in Portugal. At the same time the Brazilian Empire was overthrown by the army, and the royal family and all their faithful subjects fled to the depressed Portugal. On top of all the other incidents, a new uninvited guest arrived at the vineyards of Douro: mildew. Mildew was detected for the first time in 1893 and resulted in the reduction of the wine district so that 25 years would pass before the same number of vines would be reached again.

As in 1834, the British Port producers were furious with their Government. This situation culminated in 1889 when the skippers closed their armazéns in protest against the Government - a somewhat passive protest resulting in more anti-British demonstrations. And none of it helped anyway. Amidst all the misery, a lot of effort had to be put - for the umptieth time - into recreating the good name and reputation of Port. At the same time the struggle went on with other potential abusers of a product, which was well-established on the global market, but which was unprotected by name. Especially France was confronting similar problems with her wines, and at conferences held in Paris in 1883, in Madrid in 1891 and in Brusselles in 1900 the Portuguese delegates fought vividly to establish a monopoly of the term Vinho do Porto - or Port as the drink was called at international level and which was a temptation to parasites.

The new boundaries

Not many celebrated New Year's Eve as 1899 turned into the year 1900, neither in the Douro Valley nor in Vila Nova de Gaia. The atmosphere was dull, the trade outlook just as dull and enthusiasm half-hearted. The air was just about as cold as the blue Douro river in the night.

The grape growers, the producers, the shippers and the politicians could only agree on one thing. Something had to be done about the situation. Free trade or no free trade - discipline and control had to be restored, and if all the countries in the world were to respect the Porto name for its history and reputation, it was important to shine up the reputation first.

The matter was of great significance to the nation and ended up on Minister president João Franco's table who in 1907 had arrogated dictatorial power on himself without King Carlos I intervening. The same year he had signed a new Act on Port, in which it is established that Port is a Portuguese product, which may only be produced in the Douro Valley, and which may only be exported from Porto's estuary (by Vila Nova de Gaia) or from the seaport of Leixoes.

João Franco could easily contain himself from reopening the Company, but he did introduce two new institutions which together had the same functions, but which were not as powerful as the Company had been in its days of glory. The first institution was called *Comissão de Viticultura da Região Duriense*, the other *Oporto Customs House* which was given an English name because Great Britain was still the most important importing country of Port. The new Act was only in effect for about one year before João Franco chose to revise it, especially as too extensive permissions had been handed out for the planting of new plants. The permissions were now reduced, but instead an area at the furthest end of the river would be included in the demarcation area. This time results were, however, more fortunate, and apart from a few minor adjustments in 1921, the boundaries of the demarcated Port district are unchanged from that time and until today.

The world at war

The years 1908 and 1909 were disastrous for Portugal. On 1st February 1908, King Carlos and Crown Prince Luis were assassinated by anarchists during a ride in Lisbon, and in three hours of the morning of the 23rd December 1909 Porto endured the worst flooding it had ever experienced. The Douro river rose by 27 meters, and Sandeman alone lost fortunes for £ 35,000.

These disasters were followed by new political crises. First of all, King Carlos' second oldest son, Manuel, who had been proclaimed King after the assassination of his father and brother, was forced to abdicate in October 1910 after violent street fights in Lisbon, and Portugal was proclaimed republic. The properties of the Church were confiscated, prominent Catholics were ordered to leave the country, and the teaching of religion was abolished in the schools.

Whilst the fighting between anarchists and royalists in Lisbon was fierce, not one shot was fired in Porto. And even though the riots continued in Lisbon and led to the first general strike in the capital in 1912, followed by the republican government having to declare the city in a state of emergency, the troubles never reached the everyday life in Porto. The reason for this was that there were not many royalists in Porto - not even among the royal British Port shippers. They did not have much respect towards the corrupt and incompetent monarchy, and the country did not need another unrest. However, the promised improvements failed to materialize, and this worried the Port merchants, for exports were very sensitive to the political situation. When things at last seemed to have settled down in Lisbon in the spring of 1914, and it was time to let differences be differences, the first World War broke out on 28th June 1914 following the assassination in Sarajevo. At first, Portugal tried to take advantage of her geographical position and stay out of the political arena, but that did not last for long. The neutral seaport of Porto became a cloak for the German ships (when the war broke out 80% of the German merchant navy lay in foreign seaports), and when

The price for having the lodges so close to the river in Gaia has for generations been paid by floods. The woman on the photo is standing in front of the tide gauges from Cálem's cellars. The worst flooding began the day before Christmas in 1909. As you can see the period from December to February is the worst.

THE HISTORY OF PORT

the British demanded that Portugal, who had signed a non-attack pact with England, show her hand, the National Assembly voted to go to war with the Allies in November 1914.

Even though some time passed before this decision was made practice - there was some local unrest and a couple of government crises to be settled - both England and Germany acknowledged Portugal as a party in the war, and internally the drastic step was taken to expel all citizens of German heritage - also those families who had been Portuguese for several generations. This hit, among others, the German Port family, Burmester (see page 161f).

Gaia gets her free port

Nobody can maintain that Portugal had an impact on the Allies' victory, but they had bet on the right horse, and when the Treaty of Versailles was drawn up in 1919, Portugal was also rewarded a special prize. It was incorporated in the treaty that it was forbidden to mix any other wine in Port. The name Port was monopolized as a dessert wine to be shipped from Porto and to be produced from grapes from the Douro Valley. Also France got their monopoly on Champagne and Cognac.

Portugal's lack of commitment in the War might have been the reason that the pot kept on boiling in Lisbon. The steam had not been let off on the battlefield, but in 1921 it was. The military in Lisbon overthrew the three-month-old Government in May, and a new revolution in October overthrew the reigning Government that had been formed in May, and two more Government were formed and overthrown before the end of that year. But still nobody in Porto heard the din in Lisbon. In 1921, the Port producers and miraculously also the necessary number of politicians agreed to give Port its definition as a result of the Treaty of Versailles, and it was now established by law that Port should go through a certain maturation process before shipment could take place. This process was to take place at an indicated areas in the seaport of Vila Nova de Gaia, and for this purpose the concept "Gaia Entrepôt" was founded; a duty-free area like any other freeport and a legal clause which included a significant extension of the demarcated area, because the new free port had been defined as the place where the firms of Port merchants already had their lodges.

In 1926, Gaia was given its "entreposta" or its status as free port, which made the Act on the bottling of Port Wine more logical. 70 years later, the signs are fluorescent, but otherwise not much has changed. The many lodges are still lying shoulder to shoulder so that the slim barcos rabelos can come alongside with their heavy cargo of pipes of Port.

Boom

The boom from the First World War had nothing to do with the boom of the 1920'ies. But just as any other boom, the Port Wine boom was quite hollow, and the large export figures were hard-earned. Prices for grapes dropped again, signifying that many small farmers had to forfeit, and still production was soaring as if a new record just had to be set every year. But this was just not so, for the world market was satiated. The war had reduced the world population, especially the male population, and following the war, the Spanish flu raged and reduced it even more. As if this was not enough, the happy charleston of the 1920'ies danced right into a gigantic financial crisis starting with Black Friday in New York on 24th October 1929 and spreading in the most gruesome way just as the Spanish flu had done.

In Portugal, the crisis hit a nation already in deep crisis. In 1926, General da Costa had overthrown President Machado with a coup d'état, and now the Portuguese who had the strength and urge could celebrate the 40th government since the introduction of the Republic in 1910! If they wanted to waste Port Wine on this occasion they could also have celebrated the fact that Portugal had lived through 18 revolutions and coup d'états in the same period. Well, 19, as general da Costa was overthrown himsef the same year and deported to the Azores. Peace and order was not preserved with the assistance of the military and the police. It came quite unexpectedly from a doctor of economics who in 1928 became Minister of Finance, and surprisingly quickly had the poor Government finances under control. He also presented a proposal for the integration of Port Wine interests - but then he had more important things to do and took control as dictator in 1932, still under the title of prime minister, but António de Salazar soon sat well in his chair and did not have to ask anybody's opinion.

So it was very easy for him to implement a radical division of the Port Wine industry later in 1932. A Port Wine producer, who lived through this period, once told me that it was a unanimous decision - unanimously approved by Salazar's one vote - but no more was required at the time. And just as in the time of the Company, there was a need for somebody to take a strong hand with logical ideas, and whether or not you liked Salazar's way of doing things: nobody felt like disagreeing with him.

In the roaring 1920'ies the women were given access indirectly to the pleasure of Port Wine. They were used as eye-catchers on the colourful posters promoting this art. But they were not yet allowed to join in the after-dinner drink of Port!

EXPORTA
VINHOS
PORTUGUEZES
BORGES &

OS VINHOS DO PORTO
DE
A. RAMOS PINTO
SÃO UMA TENTAÇÃO

KOPKE'S
House Founded
1638
PORTS

SANDEMAN'S
PORT

The transportation of Port Wine has always been hard labour. Here the poor oxen carry their heavy loads - pulling the pipes up and over the cobble stones in Gaia. The photo is from Ferreira's archives.

State monopoly on brandy

The main idea of the new Act was that the production and trade of Port Wine were to be separated. To control production and maintain the interests of the wine growers the *Federacão dos Viticultores da Região do Douro* was established, better known as Casa do Douro - and to watch over the interests of trade and exports the *Grémio dos Exportadores de Vinho do Porto* (The Association of Shippers) was established by Act of 18 November 1932. *The Instituto do Vinho do Porto* (the Port Institute) was also established in 1933 with the task of coordinating interests and activities (these three important organizations are defined on page 309ff).

At the same time, the sale of brandy was nationalized in 1933 under the Juncta Nacional do Vinho, which from then on would have the monopoly on the sale of brandy to the Port Wine producers. This way, everything was organized, but it hit the people who had combined the sale of Brandy with the sale of Port hard, especially Manoel Poças (See page 246f).

In relation to the new law, the demarcated area was adjusted again (1932), and this and other things signified a new organisation of production and exports. But the wine producers had experienced the bad years bodily. After the fine vintage year of 1927 Vintage was declared by 30 shippers, which was a record, only Boa Vista declared Vintage in the year of the market crash in 1929, nobody declared in 1930, and in 1931, which would prove to be a vintage year of an exceptional quality, only three shippers had the courage - and the money - to declare Vintage. Noval has since become famous for its 1931' as for Nacional 1931, the two most expensive Ports

A dozen farm workers have to go onto the bank and pull the heavy barco rabelo against the stream. The bridge in the background shows that Alvãos' photo must date from around 1940.

ever to be sold on auction. After the intervention, the financial situation improved in the beginning of the 1930'ies, in spite of unemployment and times of crisis in many other countries. Both 1934 and 1935 were good vintage years, 1935 maybe sligthly better, and exports rose again. Between 1933 and 1939 exports and consumption on the home market were at about 75,000 pipes a year, but then the Second World War started and sealed off Europe. It became dangerous and difficult to sail the seas, and many of the traditional Port Wine drinkers participated in the war, so in the five years of war exports fell to around 30,000 pipes a year.

But as Portugal had kept out of the war and grew stronger while the rest of Europe was bleeding to death, there was more and more Port Wine to sell - and less and less people to buy it.

Fantastic year of peace

If you want an idea of how well Portugal was doing in the Second World War, you should read the German author Erich Maria Remarque's sad novel: "Night in Lisbon" from 1962. Here you see Lisbon as a bright spot on the map of a blacked-out Europe, the only city on the Continent with passage to the free world and where all the treasures of Europe were gathered, especially those of the Jews.

But during the Second World War the Port Wine producers were a disunited people. More and more of the British were volunteering or were drafted, and the first only returned in 1945 for the grape picking season. Some of them returned much later, as for example John H. Smithes from Cockburn's who had participated in the war as a rear gunner on a mosquito. When he had left

The War Vintage - or the Peace Vintage, if you like, of 1945 was of an excellent quality, but the production was limited and it was hard to sell.

Quinta do Tua, he knew that 8 of 10 rear gunners died on the job, but he managed to survive and returned to the Douro Valley in winter and wrote in the quinta's diary on 8 January 1946: "We are back at last. I don't know quite what I feel - I only know that I feel and that I love Douro and its People. I am content".

And he had reason to be, for when he approached the young wine in the quinta's armazém, he must have sensed that something great was on its way with his fine legendary Port Wine nose, and Vintage 1945 proved indeed to be very small in yield but very big in quality - so big that it was the only Vintage that could be compared to Vintage 1912.

8 shippers declared this Vintage a couple of years later, but it was still difficult to sell it. The situation was grotesque. After no 1939's and five small vintage years during the war, finally a sensational vintage year, but the potential customers had no money to buy it. Europe was living off ration cards and quotas, and the home market did not have a tradition of drinking such sublime vintages as Vintage 1945.

Portugal was actually doing quite well. After Salazar had forbidden the Portuguese to vote for other parties than his own fascist party "União Nacional" before the war, he allowed other parties to run for election in 1945, but nobody felt like it. And things were going well. Portugal had no war wounds and no disabled persons, except from a few of the volunteers. There was no shortage of goods. Only a shortage of the markets to deal with.

The dark times continue

Belgium and Luxemburg were the first to open the doors to Port Wine in autumn 1945. But they were small export markets, and the big export markets, England and France, who had bought more than 50% of all exported Port Wine before the war, were still to come. England, who in the late 1930'ies had taken 48% of the Port Wine exports, had shortly after the end of the war entered the scene with a Labour Government who promised the English that the old benefits would soon return, but this was easier to say than to keep, and instead of free access to all goods, the government introduced a ration scheme for imports, and apart from that the shippers had to obtain export licenses from the British embassy in Lisbon. These licenses were equally distributed between the importers and the shippers and were handed out according to the exports to England and France upon the outburst of the war. But there was no exports to Germany, so a Port Wine house such as Burmester, who by tradition sold quite a lot of Port Wine to Germany, was put in a nasty spot.

It was not until the monetary reform in 1949 that Germany could import freely again, and the same year the import restrictions on wine to Great Britain were abolished and the free trade reinstated. As a "cadeau" to the new Age of Enlightment, the electric signs were lit again, and it was a very special day when Sandeman's Don lit up once again.

Otherwise the years for the Port Wine business were glum, and even though the shippers were favoured by the splendid vintages 1947 and 1948, things were slow. Those who remembered the boom after the First World War were probably expecting the same situation, but there was no boom. Cockburn's remembers that there were months after the war when only 1/2 pipe of Port Wine was shipped - a month!

Some had to close down, others were taken over. A new generation entered the scene with new ideas and new energy, some even had money to invest in modern techniques, and many began to take an interest in planting and vinification. But exports were still slow.

Regardless of the good vintage years, the years around 1950 to 1955 were considered years of crisis. In a year like 1952 the exportation of Port Wine to England fell by more than 1/3 in the course of six months, and the crisis could no longer be explained by times when money is short or restrictions. Now the women and the young generation were to blame.

Very à propos, a woman ascended the throne in 1952, and very symbolically Queen Elizabeth has never supported the consumption of Port Wine in England. Habits were changing too. After the First World War women had started to sit at the table, after the Second World War, men had started to help in the kitchen. In an interview in "The Daily Mail" in 1952, the young, newly-appointed director, Patrick Sandeman, from the house of Sandeman, incautiously published his indignation about the fact that English men had begun to do the dishes instead of enjoying a glass of Port after dinner. He did, however, pour oil on the troubled water straight away: " I don't. I do the dishes - and then I enjoy a glass of Port"!

Just after the war the English had no money to spend on Port Wine. Then followed import restrictions and shortage in goods, and now a new generation was growing up who had not been used to drinking Port Wine and who therefore did not miss it. Other countries were beginning to show an interest in Port Wine, however, but not to the degree that it would replace the British market. Not until the beginning of the 1970'ies did exports reach the same figures as in 1920'ies and the 1930'ies.

A milestone was reached in 1963 when France became the first country in the long history of Port to catch up with England as the largest importer of Port Wine.

Emergency: Barca Velha

As the English would no longer drink Port Wine - especially the expensive Vintage Ports, because they simply did not have the money for them -

Fernando Nicolau de Almeida, who invented the red wine "Barca Velha" because the foreign markets did not want or could not afford to buy Port Wine. Today, "Barca Velha" is the most expensive table wine in Portugal. (Photo: HO)

then the Port Wine producers had to think of something else. Ferreira's technical director and wizard, Fernando Nicolau de Almeida, had an idea. Whilst the world would not buy Vintage Port, but they had no objections to drinking red wine. So why not produce more red wine and less Port Wine, or even better: make a red wine which was the equivalent of a Vintage Port. He told me that he had been so enthusiastic about the idea that he had not listened to the worried objections around him, of which the most common objection was that "when the grapes are perfect for Port Wine, they cannot be perfect for red wine". But as Max Schubert with his Australian "Grange Hermitage", Almeida knew with his fine Port Wine nose that he was on to something special. Some of Ferreira's best grapes for Port Wine came from Quinta do Vale do Meão close to the Spanish border. Here, he chose Tinta Roriz, Touriga Francesa and Tinta Barroca from a height of 100-600 metres and mixed with grapes bought from small farmers. This would result in a wine characterized by Tinta Roriz. He did not use Touriga Nacional which was the most popular Port Wine grape.

The first vintage appeared in 1953. The grapes were nursed from the first grape that was picked - all by hand naturally - and after several attempts Almeida was finally satisfied. The wine was laid in casks in the remote quinta for the winter and was then transported into Gaia for mixing and maturation. Whilst Almeida was waiting for the wine to mature and be bottled, it was named after one of the old, traditional Port Wine boats and was called *Barca Velha*, the old boat.

When Almeida finally launched it, it was gone in two minutes. The rumour had enticed the market, and suddenly there was a certain prestige in owning and tasting Portugal's new red wine, which soon became the most expensive and the most in demand. It still is, especially because Almeida was very critical and only wanted to produce Barca Velha in the very good years - or whenever it suited him. He made a '54, because there was a demand, then he made a '57, a '64, a '65, and a '66, after which the mythe needed a rest, and he did not make the wine again until 1978. When it was released sometime in the 1980'ies, the reputation of Port Wine had long been restored.

Vintage Capers

Other Port Wine houses went their own way. They needed a new type to replace the expensive Vintage Port, preferably a type with a resemblance to Vintage, but which was cheaper and had a faster maturation.

Taylor's had a brilliant idea, one of those ideas that fortunately come as a revelation just at the right time. Quinta de Vargellas had for some years yielded a lot of grapes of prime quality but had not used them for Vintage Port, either because the vintage year was not interesting enough, or because the market simply did not want to buy Vintage Port.

Under the management of "Dick" Stanley Yeatman they decided to revive a Vargellas Vintage, i.e. a Vintage solely made from grapes from this quinta. This had been done before in 1910, but the idea had been abandoned again, because Taylor's and the other major Port Wine houses had chosen to sell the company name instead.

Now they wanted to try again and openly market Vargellas wine as an excellent Reserve instead of Taylor's expensive Vintage Port. For various reasons they had to wait until 1958 before the first "modern" Single Quinta Vintage Port from Vargellas was born, but according to the idea it was cheaper and drinkable at an earlier stage than the classic Vintage Port from Taylor's.

Quinta do Noval chose another solution. According to the van Zeller family, Noval's English importer, Jack Rutherford, had experimented in the 1940'ies with a Vintage Port, which was allowed to lie in casks a bit longer than usual, but which was drinkable at an earlier stage without losing its character of a Vintage Port (see page 145).

The hard-pressed situation on the English market made Noval's owner, Luis Vasconcelos, meet the challenge, and soon the first Late Bottled Vintage was born: Noval LBV 1954.

Like Ferreira's red wine from Port Wine grapes and Taylor's Single Quinta Vintage Port this wine was considered a "bastard" by Port Wine connaisseurs, and the other Port Wine houses were reluctant to accept it in the beginning. Later, however, they copied the idea. But more than 10 years would pass before the Port Institute approved the LBV type, especially influenced by Taylor's ability to make an LBV 1965, bottled in 1969, and which looked as if it would found a school.

But by then the Port Wine fog was clearing, and Noval's LBV was altered.

From thistles to carnations

Apart from captain Henrique Galvão's one-man protest in 1961 when he took 620 hostages aboard the cruiser "Santa Maria" and sailed them to liberty in Brazil, followed by a tail of warships, life in Portugal went on as usual, carefully monitored by Salazar and his party members in União Nacional which since 1953 had been the absolute ruling party in Portugal.

But Galvão's lonely protest was soon followed by other protests. In 1962, a handful of officers rebelled against the regime but were immediately suppressed, and then followed the riots in the African colonies of Angola, Mozambique and Guinea-Bissau. It started as something Salazar called "boyish pranks" but in the course of 1962, more than 62,000 Portuguese soldiers were sent to Africa to deal with the boyish pranks, but they did not succeed.

The riots escalated, as troubles spread all over the African continent, and Portugal spent a fortune in keeping the riots down, even though Salazar should have learned a lesson from France's dearly bought experience in Algiers. In only a few years, the surplus from the fat years of war was exhausted without a solution to the African situation. At the new year of 1967, the expenses for Portugal's inconclusive colonial wars in Africa were more than 40% of the income.

In 1968 things went completely wrong. Young officers, who had been sent to Africa because they were troublesome to have running around the streets of Lisbon and Porto, formed a protest organisation against the war in Africa, Movimento das Forcas Armadas, and well-known concepts, such as civil war and mutiny, started to lurk. At the same time, the once so abundant national purse was empty, Salazar had a stroke and had to give up after 36 years of a heavy-handed treatment of Portugal. He was hospitalized and disarmed. He hardly noticed at all. He had isolated himself for years and had no more energy.

Neither had the rest of Portugal who lacked coal. Portugal had one of the world's largest deposits of tungsten, but there was no money to light the bulb, and no money to buy electricity from abroad. The solution seemed simple: the Douro river had to be dammed up even more than it already was. There was no room for romantic notions. When the work was implemented, history's last barco rabelo had sailed Port Wine down the Douro. A few years later the dams were made passable thanks to subsidies from the World Bank, so the Douro became navigable from Porto to the Spanish border - and vice versa. But by then it was too late for Port Wine to benefit from this initiative - only tourism would benefit at all.

The golden 1970'ies

It was no thanks to Portugal that increasing prosperity in the late 1950'ies resulted in a boom in

THE HISTORY OF PORT

the exportation of Port Wine. There was a good reason for Harold Macmillan in 1959 to be able to run for election in England - and win - on the slogan: "You have never had it so good!" The English had never had it so good - for as long as they could remember.

People simply had more money to spend - even in Germany with the Marshall aid and Wirtschaftswunder resulting in export figures reaching sky-high limits from the lean years before the war without, however, ever reaching the magic figures of the 1930'ies:

1933 - 1939	75,633 pipes
1940 - 1945	30,954 pipes
1946 - 1960	46,634 pipes
1961 - 1965	56,549 pipes
1966 - 1970	68,142 pipes

The good Lord favoured the Port Wine producers in the 1960'ies. 1960 itself was a great Vintage year, which unfortunately has always been overshadowed by the excellent Vintage 1963, one of the best of this century. Then came Vintage 1966, yet another classic vintage year, and Vintage 1967, a reasonable vintage year, and the decade saw another success: 1970 which from the first tests taken from the cask were compared to Vintage 1963, even though the style was different from one house to another.

Note the export figures above, and then see how they seem to explode after 1970:

1971 - 1976	88,361 pipes
1977 - 1981	118,000 pipes

(Source: IVP)

First they built dams so that the Port Wine boats could no longer sail the Douro, then they made floodgates so that the tourists could sail the Douro again. But by then the pointed barcos rabelos had sailed the Douro past Cachão de Valeira for the last time. (Photo: HO)

In the course of the 1970'ies exports reached quantities which were more than double the quantities in the difficult years after the war. There were many reasons for this, also political reasons, but if you only take Port Wine into consideration, there were a few events around 1970 which made a difference.

First of all, there were problems with the Americans, for as a side effect of the Californian wine revolution, the production of the Californian "Port Wine" in the late 1960'ies was 10 times that of the "real thing" from Portugal. The same problems were encountered with wine producers from Australia, so in 1968 a resolution was passed that the wording Vinho do Porto was to be printed on every single bottle of Port exported to the United States, Australia or other dubious countries. A large percentage of exports was still carried out on pipes to the traditional markets, and the bottling took place in London, Brussels, Paris or Copenhagen, as it always had, but some felt that it did not have to be so forever.

There were also problems with the countries who had never ratified the Versaille treaty and its protection of Port Wine, especially the USA and Spain. In 1904, a large lot of Tarragona Port Wine had appeared on the British market, and now the Californians had also started to export their own Port Wine, and nobody seemed to dare limit the wine producers liberty in this great land of freedom.

Things went completely wrong when Californian and Australian bottles appeared with the wording "Vintage Port". The producers claimed that it was a matter of style, which they believed could be compared to Danish pastry and German sausages. It seemed less important to the inhabitants of Porto that the contents tasted more like Tawny.

Something had to be done to protect Vintage Port, which was the precious and prestigious type, and the only way to ensure that every single bottle of Vintage Port was bottled under Portuguese control and equipped with clear text so that nobody could be mistaken of its content. This way the Portuguese would also be able to neutralize the shady wine merchants in Europe who were adding anything cheaper in their Port Wine.

For once, the idea was quickly brought to action. After 1973, it was forbidden to bottle Vintage Port in any other place than in Gaia Entrepôt. With a quick edge-of-hand blow the right owners had obtained a monopoly on Vintage Port. They had never imagined that it would be this easy or that it would found a new school. But it did. In the course of a few years, 75-80% of all Port Wine was bottled in Gaia.

As a consequence of the new Act the Port Wine houses were allowed to keep their own "surplus". Previously, nearly all Vintage Port had been shipped to England, France, and the other big markets for bottling; now only pre-ordered quantities were shipped. The rest was stored for better times - at higher prices.

The German Nemesis

When the excellent 1970'ies were introduced in the market, and bottling was monopolized to avoid fraud and misunderstandings, Nemesis hit the Port Wine business.

In 1973, a routine check of some bottles of Port Wine was carried out in Germany, and somebody suspected that the wine was synthetic. It proved to be the brandy. Measurements were carried out, and if the brandy really was vegetable-based, the wine in the bottles would have to be at least 300 years old. It was not, and the brandy was not vegetable-based but produced on the basis of petrol and bought at a cheap price in France by Casa do Douro. It was traced to somewhere in Yugoslavia, but seemed to be produced in North Africa. It was not poisonous, but the mere idea - presumably brought about by the monopolization and the following grief of the wine merchants all over Europe, led to the importation of Port Wine being forbidden in Germany, France and England, until things had been sorted out.

"That issue damaged the Port Wine business far more than the revolution a year later", James Symington once said. For the famous Carnation Coup on 25th April 1974 was very much a phenomenon in Lisbon, and the only vineyards and properties, which were affected by the revolution and the glittering promises of "free land for everyone", were the isolated farms in Alentejo. In Porto and Gaia it was noted that the country had a new rule, but not many Port Wine people noticed any revolts or a re-distribution of values apart from the Real Companhia Velha owner Manuel da Silva Reis who had to leave for Brazil in a hurry.

The traditional bottling of Vintage Port on the best export markets could have major consequences: to the left Cockburn's Vintage 1963 in an original bottling from Gaia in the regular bottle; to the right the same wine, bottled in Copenhagen by a Danish wine merchant – in a Champagne bottle – as he probably had nothing else at hand! The wine has a perfect taste, but the packaging is somewhat special!

The calm after the storm

The revolution did not cause any damage to the Port Wine business, but the fear thereof did make many people nervous. Many people wanted a revolution, probably even among the Port Wine producers, but nobody wanted to be overrun, and nobody wanted this situation to last. But when the upheaval finally started it lasted for two years before the consequences could be foreseen. Two years in which nobody knew if they would be overtaken, sold or nationalized.

The carnation also bloomed in the colonies in Africa. Many of the young officers, who had been drafted to these distant armies, were active students from the uprise at the universities in 1968 - 1970 and they had not forgotten Mao's little red book. They would not put up with bad management in a meaningless war, and as they had no military background and did not know the line of command they went straight to general António Spinola for support for their uprise.

General Spinola was a figurehead of no importance at all, but with him at the lead the officers who were faithful to the government, were paralysed, even though the coup d'état actually only was a coup d'état of majors, and there was a large gap from the ideology between the relatively loyal general and the young majors and captains who were left-wing - absurdly also influenced by the new Marxist movement whom they had been sent to Africa to fight against.

They mobilized and from a military point of view they raised a mutiny against their peers and moved the battlefield from Angola to Lisbon.

The revolution started on 25th April 1974 and it ended on practically the same day with hardly any victims and without the soldiers using their weapons. This was the point of the so-called peaceful revolution: the population put carnations in their rifle barrels to celebrate the expected freedom and have their men and sons home sent home from Africa.

Marxist hangover

The revolution was successful - but what was next? Especially the British Port Wine shippers slept lightly in the nights to come, for it was soon evident that the conquerors did not know what to do with their victory. The liberals wanted freedom. The communists wanted power.

The oil crisis was smouldering as was the civil war in Angola which did not make things easier. But it did help on the public feeling that the communist leader, Alvaro Cunhal, was a Stalin-loyal orthodox. It actually saved Portugal from communism, and at the spring elections of 1975, the communist party only got 12.5 % of the votes against socialist Mário Soares' 37.8%, but with support from both left-wing and right-wing parties the provisional head of government and the party communist, Vasco Gonçalves, managed to stay in power and promised his people a fair share of the means of production and property. If the Port Wine producers had slept lightly before, they dared not sleep a wink now.

It was their good fortune, and probably also the good fortune of Portugal that the notions of the communists and their allies among the young officers were more based on romantic theories and manifests than on reality. The rural population whom they wanted to save according to their theories did not want to be saved at all. The farm workers were, what the theorists sitting behind their desks never understood, not just farm workers but also small proprietors, and quite satisfied with their life and situation so that several of the stationed communist commissioners were physically thrown out of their offices and had to go back to Lisbon with a message they did not understand and which Marx and Mao had never anticipated. The communists hang on to their delicate power as long as they had the support of the young officers, but for them the happy days of revolution soon came to an end. In November 1975, they were disarmed by elite troops under general Ramalho Eanes, who had not been active himself in the Carnation Coup and who therefore had clean hands so that at the first free election in spring 1976 he was elected President.

But the strong man was the socialist, Mário Soares, who obtained 36% of the votes for his programme of human socialism in a new society with room for private property rights.

The Port Wine people could sleep safely once more.

The hot summer of 1975

One of the consequences of the Carnation Coup was that Salazar's corporate system was abolished in September 1974. Another consequence was that the Port Wine shippers' association, the Port Wine Institute and the Casa do Douro had to be re-organized under another form, but as long as the communist party has any influence, the threat of nationalization overshadowed any ideas of re-organization of the associations which could be closed down. So nothing happened except that the shippers' association was placed under the IVP.

In the hot summer of 1975 (verão quente) the risk of nationalization was close. Parts of Portugal's industries were nationalized in March 1975, and the Port Wine producers had no idea what this would entail. They belonged to Portugal's recognized "capitalists", and the outcome of the exportation of Port Wine was very important to the Treasury. If the communists won the election or stayed in power, they would lose their properties. Some of the British shippersstarted to make travelling plans to return to their motherland and had meetings with their employees to discuss the situation. The communists asked them to overtake the means of production, but the employees were reluctant to. On the contrary, they picketed to stop the communists and opportunists of penetrating the valuable lodges in

THE HISTORY OF PORT

Gaia and the distant quintas in the Douro Valley, and as the Marxists had no support from the farm workers, the theory fell through. This is how things went on one hot summer. It was hot - boiling, but things did not boil over. And the heatwave September brought cool rain and cooled down the Marxist passions and everything went more or less back to normal.

In the hot summer of 1975, Real Companhia's owner, Manuel da Silva Reis, bought the firm Sousa Guedes and its Quinta das Carvalhas with the round Casa Redonda (on the peak of the mountain in the background). Today, it is a useful direction finder in the Douro Valley. But Silva Reis had no time to enjoy the view or the small town of Pinhão, as he had to escape to Brazil and did not return until the overpressure of that hot summer had passed. (Photo: HO)

New times - old times

The older generation in the Port Wine business remembered a lot of talk about the weird summer of 1899 when a plague raged in the Douro Valley so that the shippers could not visit their quintas before harvest. Now they would be able to tell their grandchildren of a new weird chapter in the history of Port and tell them of the time in 1975 when the Port Wine had to be transported in convoys to avoid it being stolen on the long way to its destination.

In the eyes of the shippers the Casa do Douro legally robbed them when the price of brandy escalated in autumn 1975 and was raised without warning from Esc 11,000$00 to Esc 22,000$00 a pipe. Casa do Douro had very quickly adapted to the new rulers, or was it vice versa, whilst both the shippers and the small farmers had great difficulties.

To avoid losses during transportation, many had chosen to leave as much Port Wine as possible in the Douro Valley where things were calmer than in Porto. But this signified that they had no room for a new vintage, for the small farmers had rashly gotten rid of their casks and vats which they rarely needed. But they did now.

On the other hand, the shippers had plenty of room. Many of them had kept their Port Wine in the Douro Valley, some of them had small harvests, then there was the revolution, and unrest had also drained their stocks so that they really needed an abundant vintage, preferably a good one. But quantities were more important than quality.

But both in 1973 and the revolutionary year of 1974 the harvest was bigger, and 34 shippers declared Vintage in 1975 - and they needed every single bottle.

They also needed bottles, for after the political unrest it was approved at a meeting held at the Port Institute on 27th November 1973 that all Vintage Port from 1st January 1974 had to be bottled in Gaia. As no Vintage was declared in 1973 due to the hot summer of 1975, and as 1974 was only declared by 11 shippers, the Vintage 1975 was the start of new times for the Port Wine business.

The new times, however, were remarkably the same as the old times.

Into the hands of strangers

Some did, however, wake up to a hangover in the 1970'ies. This was not so much due to the revolution as to economy. Heavy succession duties and disagreements within the various families and whether or not to keep the Port in the hands of the family coincided with the desire of the multinational companies to distribute the financial risk and rely on as many products and markets as possible. So the Port Wine houses wanted to sell, and there were a lot of buyers around. It had been a long tradition for a Port Wine house to be taken over by another Port Wine house when there were problems of succession or financial problems, and even though families as the Symingtons and Barros-Almeidas bought houses and grew - it was still all within the business. The new line started when Harveys of Bristol bought Cockburn's in 1962 and put the Port Wine business into the hands of strangers.

This development accelerated and reached a peak when the whisky magnate, Seagram, purchased Sandeman in 1979.

The ownership in the 1950'ies had been concentrated within the families, but this course of action changed, expecially in the course of the 1970'ies, to become company-owned. The list below speaks for itself:

Cockburn's is owned by Allied Domecq
Croft is owned by UDV
Delaforce is owned by UDV
Ferreira is owned by SOGRAPE
Martínez is owned by Allied Domecq
Noval is owned by AXA
Offley Forrester is owned by SOGRAPE
Porto Cruz is owned by La Martiniquaise
Ramos-Pinto is owned by Louis Roederer
Robertson is owned by Seagram
Rozès is owned by Vranken-Lafitte
Sandeman is owned by Seagram

In most cases, they were prosperous, which resulted in stability and fresh capital - and better Port Wine. Some even rode out the storm, for example the Symingtons who had been very close to selling Quinta do Bomfim in the 1950'ies, but whose financial situation improved and who bought Graham's and Smith Woodhouse in 1970 and Quinta do Vesúvio in 1989.

Sometimes things went well, sometimes they went badly. Some grew, some closed down, and some even appeared on the market, such as Churchill Graham who was founded in 1981 as the first new, British-owned Port Wine house in more than 50 years.

Unity and prosperity

Some of the family houses were sceptical towards the new "multinational" colleagues. They doubted that their colleagues had the best intentions and if they would co-operate with regard to mutual problems or whether they would feather their own nests. Nobody knew.

But at this point, everyone rejoiced in the promising Vintage 1977, which was "only" declared by 33 shippers against 34 shippers in 1975, but which still outshined the quality and expectations of this hot summer.

The parties also agreed when the "Luso-Magyar" deal was negotiated in 1977 ensured global protection against copies. The wording of the agreement was frail it was not signed until 1981, but it proved that the Port Wine people stood together.

When the former so renowned Vintage 1977 was bottled in 1979, its success was measurable. For the first time since 1925, the Vintage 1979 gave an export of more than 110,000 pipes of Port Wine. It was the start of the best decade within the history of Port - later surpassed in the 1990'ies!

Let us look at the figures for the sale, exports and the stock of Port Wine in the 1980'ies and 1990'ies, measured in pipes (of 550 litres):

Year	Home market	Exports	Total sales	Production	Acc. stock
1980	16.733	111.728	128.461	127.972	-489
1981	14.562	99.360	113.922	100.536	-13.865
1982	14.103	104.158	118.261	109.079	-23.046
1983	13.732	105.899	119.631	102.395	-40.285
1984	13.110	107.726	120.836	108.861	-52.261
1985	13.593	115.381	128.974	120.851	-60.385
1986	16.505	124.168	140.673	148.329	-52.729
1987	18.298	124.407	142.705	169.177	-26.257
1988	20.447	130.575	151.022	153.696	-23.639
1989	19.596	127.755	147.351	216.825	45.798
1990	22.197	124.746	146.943	193.194	92.022
1991	21.408	120.292	141.700	147.456	97.735
1992	21.260	120.059	141.319	101.333	57.722
1993	25.916	129.381	155.297	108.184	10.610
1994	14.661	140.182	154.843	136.818	-7.415
1995	21.090	146.879	167.969	163.528	-11.856
1996	21.324	146.491	167.815	164.651	-15.020
1997	22.349	141.973	164.322	166.500	-12.842

Source: IVP

The right column, accumulated stock, means that one year of deficit or surplus is transferred to the next year.

But these figures are total figures for the entire industry. The subtle *Lei do terço* (defined on page 310) does not permit extra sales in relation to the stock nor that less sales are transferred to the next year. This is why the sale of Port Wine practically exploded in December 1990, as the shippers' unused quotas would be lost by the end of the year.

As you can see by the figures, there was a deficit throughout the 1980'ies in the relation between production and sales. This continued until the record-breaking year of 1989 when production followed sales, especially because the autumn of 1988 had forewarned a large price increase on quality Ports.

Things were going so well that the Port Wine shippers nearly forgot that Casa do Douro had nearly doubled the price of aguardente in 1980.

The palmy year of 1985

In the fantastic 1980'ies, the vintage year of 1985 was the most palmy year ever. The national euphoria was already great, for Portugal was, along with Spain, joining the EEC and had to get rid of the remaining Marxist ties and profess to western democracy. This gave stability within the industry and a great faith in the future.

When the Port Wine houses began bottling the Vintage 1983 in the summer of 1985, they could rejoice in the fact that they had been blessed with three excellent Vintage years in only four years: 1980, 1982, and 1983. During the bottling process they could enjoy yet another great summer, which was just as hot at the revolutionary summer 10 years before - but more calm!

"Never can the grapes have been gathered under better weather conditions than this 1985 vintage", Michael Symington wrote in his journal at Quinta do Bomfim in October, and a couple of months' later the shippers rejoiced and noted the largest exportation of Port Wine ever: 115,381 pipes in the calendar year of 1985.

Exports rose by 7.1% in quantities and around 27% in value. The warehouses had practically no stocks taking into consideration the production lacked 60,385 pipes.

The shippers could thus set their price as they wanted - and they set it high. When the successful Vintage 1985 was offered "en primeur", the opening prices were 30-40% higher than for 1983, especially because the Americans had acquired a taste for Vintage Port. The British were for once more reserved, but who cared, there were dollars ahead.

The record-breaking vintage also included some bottles with inexplicable acid flaws, but this had now become a consumer problem. The impatient consumers could just have waited a bit longer, and the patient consumers have not found out yet.

The last hopeless Vintage

1985 was also the year when James Symington with justified pride told us about the new technique and its bliss. "You cannot compare the Port Wine from old times to the Port Wine of today. We make a far better Port Wine today than in the so-called "good old days". The control of vinification and preparation has improved, and work in the field is carried out much more professionally. In earlier days, Port Wine was not a question of techniques but more a craftsmanship, which sometimes succeeded, and sometimes didn't. Today not much can completely fail".

He was right. Since 1973, Vintage has been declared every single year, and when 1973 was declared in the hot summer of 1975, we can easily say that 1971 was the last Vintage when there was not an applicable technique to make a good Port Wine from bad grapes, and is thus the last year without Vintage - just as we say that the 1977 is the last completely unsuccessful vintage year in Bordeaux.

The Port Wine was entering the IT age, and not only the stocks in Gaia profited from this new magic. Also the remote quintas were beginning to dream about new techniques but first the wiring had to be laid out so one could begin to speculate in the electric pumps and later in computerized vinification plants.

But also the Port Wine people were undergoing a development. The first pioneers after the war had been replaced in the mid 1960'ies by a new generation, who were educated at posh universities and who knew everything about acids and bases. They had no longer only trained their noses in the cold cellars and sterile labs in Gaia.

Autovinification was introduced when there was a shortage of manpower and died when electricity was introduced. This process is detailed on page 126. This was the beginning of the electric adventure. The pumps were pumping, and even though half of the best Port Wine was still treated manually around 1970, the process was under far better control, because you could press a button to regulate the temperature control accordingly. The experts discussed the pros and cons of foot-crushing methods, but they did agree upon the

An Act was almost passed approving the Douro Valley's qualities of terrace land, like the Rhine and the Moselle, but then the first winding patamares were introduced in the 1960'ies and since then the hazardous ao alto planting in the 1970'ies. Ao alto is like being in the first carriage of the roller coaster. It could only go wrong. But it didn't. (Photo: HO)

fact that the significance of cooling down and macerating, another modern expression, was becoming more and more important.

Also the rugged landscape of the Douro Valley was changing. The risk of a shortage of labour from the distant villages was compensated for by modern tractors. But if they were to use petrol for fuel instead of Caldo Verde, the traditional terraces had to be replaced without the steep stone walls.

The solution was introduced in the late 1960'ies. They were called patamares and are described on page 96. The revolutionary aspect of the patamares was, as you can see on the photo on page 96, that they were divided into different levels as the traditional terraces, but had winding paths between the levels instead of stone walls so that small tractors could work their way through.

And when João Nicolau de Almeida and his uncle, José Ramos-Pinto Rosas, in the late 1970'ies presented the bold ao alto method (see page 97), you could easily get the impression that the vineyards were turned upside down. Things had changed in the Douro Valley.

The Revolution in the Valley

Whilst the first vertical rows of vines were being planted on Ramos-Pinto's Quinta do Bom Retiro, and the rest of Europe was collecting itself in the wake of the oil crisis with increasing unemployment figures, the small wine growers and farmers in the Douro Valley started to get an opinion of their own with regard to the Port Wine industry.

The grape growers supported themselves by cultivating grapes which they sold to the large Port Wine houses. This was a tradition, which had not changed much throughout the years except that the oxen carts had now been replaced by lorries. But now the farmers began to note that more and more of the shippers' old quintas were being modernized with visible signs of prosperity, for example swimming pools with cool, clear water, refrigerators, freezers, televisions, bathrooms and electric stoves, and the old coaches and pick-up trucks had been replaced with Mercedes' and BMW's in the garages. The grape growers wanted part of the prosperity, and they were not of the opinion that this could be achieved only via the prices of grapes. In the beginning of the 1980'ies they were backed by some of the private quintas whose owners were dissatisfied with the state of things. So far, they had supported themselves by selling Port Wine to the large producers, as legislation only permitted sales and exports from Gaia's Entreposta, and that was the only place they did not feel like setting their feet.

In the aforementioned golden year of 1985, the state of affairs had become so unequal in the sense that the small farmers and the small quintas in the Douro Valley were delivering grapes or wine towards around 90% of the total Port Wine production - but their sale of Port Wine was a mere 1.6%. And what was even more grotesque: the well-established shippers in Gaia only owned 6% of the cultivated area in Douro, but had 98.4% of the total sales of Port Wine and 100% of the total exports.

They did not need a revolution to change things. This was thanks to an odd distribution of seats on the board of the Port Institute, which did not match reality. The 12 seats on the board were occupied by 6 small farmers, 3 shippers, 1 Quinta owner, 1 co-operative, and 1 "outsider", namely the Real Companhia Velha, who was not a member of the Shippers' Association, but who by tradition was granted a positive treatment. It was not even necessary to vote on the issue. When the proposal was presented, it was approved immediately. The Act of 7 May 1986, brought into effect in June of the same year, approved selling and exporting Port Wine direct from the Douro Valley without the wine having to go via Gaia. But naturally the small producers and quintas had to abide by the same rules and regulations as the large Port houses.

This was very positive for the small quintas such as Infantado, Romaneira and Côtto, who had complained for a long time because they had not been allowed to export their Port Wine. And even the

THE HISTORY OF PORT

If you travel a bit away from the Douro river and the large quintas, the Port Wine country consists of many small holdings and cottages with a few rows of vines. This patchwork had a whole new value when the new Act on direct sales and export from the Douro was introduced in 1996. (Photo: HO)

large Quinta do Noval was looking at better times. In 1982, the van Zeller's began building a large lodge by Pinhão with room for the maturation of 7,500 pipes of Port Wine, which was five times their annual production.

In 1985, the van Zeller's inauguarated the "Cathedral" in Douro. A year later, the Act on direct exports from the Douro Valley was passed, and in 1991 Noval moved their address permanently from Gaia to Pinhão.

New money in the till

The shippers shrugged - and there was not much else they could do. The private quintas were no threat to the export market, but several of the major producers experienced a shortage of the normal quantities of grapes and wine, because more and more of the small wine growers and farmers were now trying to be exporters.

In the meantime, while the new Act on direct exports from the Douro Valley was being prepared, the shippers had something else to think about. Portugal had become presentable, the communists had been pacified, and from the New Year of 1986 Portugal would enter into the EC. The World Bank marked this event by welcoming the Port Wine producers into the fine credit-worthy company.

But back to the golden year of 1985: more Port Wine was being sold than produced and the-

THE HISTORY OF PORT

re was no indication of this situation changing. As from 1986, a considerable new planting and re-planting of vineyards in the demarcated area was permitted - with very generous financial support from the World Bank, granted as a loan, which was interest-free for the first seven years. This implied that a total of 1,200 ha could be planted or re-planted, corresponding to a quantity of grapes for 6,000 pipes of Port Wine. The loans were granted in portions for the planting of 9.7 ha per property in the A and B categories on the condition that only the 5 "noble grape varieties" were used. The plan was to replant a total of 2,500 ha of vineyards, which had lied fallow or had been used for other crops, in the course of a few years. Only fields in categories A and B were included (Please see explanation on page 116) which would give a logical qualitative improvement, as less than 50% of all Port Wine in 1985 came from A and B fields.

The planned systematic planting and replanting would also give the possibility of cultivating only the best grape varieties, which had certainly not been the case before when planting was carried out at random and rejects, if any, took place in the adega. So this was yet another improvement.

Naturally, there was always the hope of a surplus production which would not be available until five years later when the grapes from the new planted vines, approved for the production of Port Wine, would be absorbed by the demand for Vintage, LBV, and other fine types. There was a risk of an overproduction (or a fall in the sales and/or exports), which would then especially affect the small farmers in Lower Douro. But that was consi-

The local newspapers were understandably very honoured when the many foreign heads of state accepted the invitation to join the Confraria fraternity. Especially ascetic Fidel Castro was seen with a glass of Port Wine in his hand.

O Comércio do Porto

Diário - Ano CXLIV - N.º 139 - 130$00 (IVA Incluído)   Director: Luis de Carvalho – Director-adjunto: A. Santos Martins   Domingo, 18 de Outubro de 1998

CASA DAS LÂMAPADAS, LDA.
MATERIAL ELECTRICO
ILUMINAÇÃO
PORTO · LISBOA

Cimeira do Porto generoso

Juan Carlos de Espanha, Fernando Henrique do Brasil, Fidel de Cuba, Fujimore do Peru e demais chefes de Estado e de Governo, participantes na VIII Cimeira Ibero-americana, viveram ontem um dia muito especial na Invicta. E não só porque «vestiram» de Infante D. Henrique e foram entronizados como membros da Confraria do Vinho do Porto: também porque, mesmo debaixo de chuva, o povo da cidade – tão generoso como aquele néctar de deuses que se produz nas margens do Douro português – desceu à rua para viver o grande acontecimento.

dered to be speculation. And that is why it was quite unexpected when the stocks in Gaia started to abound in the beginning of the 1990'ies.

The good times for Port

Shortly after the fantastic harvest in 1982, times were a bit more fun. These were the good times for the Port Wine producers. The Brotherhood had been introduced with its scarlet red capes and ceremonious forms which were however interpreted with a gleam of enthusiasm.

The idea of establishing a Port Wine Brotherhood (Confraria do Vinho do Porto) was far from new. It had already been discussed back in 1964, but Salazar had not allowed such private associations, so the dream had to wait until the fall of Salazar. Then the revolution followed when it was forbidden to establish private associations for other reasons, so it was not until November 1982 that Chanceler *Fernando Nicolau de Almeida*, Almoxarife *Robin Reid*, Copeiro-Mor *José António Ramos-Pinto Rosas*, Almotacé *Michael Symington* and Fiel das Unsanças *Manuel Pintão Poças* could put on their red capes and put Henry the Sailor's hat on their heads.

The main purpose of the fraternity was to spread the knowledge and love of Port Wine, and brothers and sisters from the various Port Wine houses took the task upon themselves with enthusiasm and catching gaiety. They had a lot of fun and enjoyed each other's company, and this was a good thing in a business with tough competition between the houses.

The first, major international assignment of the fraternity was to participate in the Port Wine festival in Copenhagen in November 1988 when they contributed with pomp and circumstance towards promoting Port Wine as a happy and festive drink.

But the fraternity had already made their mark when they celebrated their one-year anniversary and admitted Queen Elizabeth and Prince Philip as sister and brother in 1983. In 1986, the Swedish King and Queen were "enthroned", and in May 1988, the same year as the brothers and sisters went to Copenhagen (Please see page 314-315), Portugal's socialist President, Mário Soares, became a fraternity brother. To the great vexation of the inefficient Sherry people, the Confraria also invited the Spanish King Juan Carlos to become a Port Wine brother, and to their even greater vexation he accepted and was admitted to the fraternity in May 1989.

The Confraria's best scoop was in October 1998 when 23 celebrities from the Iberian/American conference in Porto were made members with Cuba's Fidel Castro, Argentine's Carlos Menem and Chile's Eduardo Frei as prominent members. This effort surpassed normal diplomacy. What all the foreign ministers had not been able to do, Port Wine accomplished.

The battle against Casa

But behind the flowering robes there were problems. When the fraternity brothers came to Copenhagen in November 1988, they brought the latest figures with them: it looked as if Port Wine would set a new record for 1988, and these figures proved to be correct. When 1988 turned into 1989, 151,022 pipes of Port Wine had been sold in one year only, corresponding to 9,200,000 cases of Port Wine. The remarkable thing was that England was now only the fourth largest buyer after France, Belgium and Portugal, whilst Denmark was in a sixth place.

The joy of these exports was followed by some disappointment as the annual harvest was small, so small that the allowed amount of wine could not even be fulfilled. This year's beneficio was set at a total of 140,000 pipes of basic wine plus the 35,000 pipes of aguardente giving a total of 175,000 pipes of Port Wine, but the efforts only resulted in 153,696 pipes of Port Wine, which was unfortunate, because normally the remaining beneficio may not be transferred to the following year. Nevertheless, the Casa do Douro gave its permission, and when the harvest of 1989 exploded and set a new record, and sales could not follow, it resulted in a surplus production.

And this was not all. In 1989, Casa do Douro raised the price of aguardente by 20%, and in 1990 a dispute between the shippers and Casa do Douro burst into flames. A permission for the production of 115,000 pipes had been given, but via the Casa do Douro this figure was drastically increased to around 157,000 pipes.

Also, nearly 40,000 pipes of aguardente were necessary for this quantity of Port Wine - and the Casa do Douro simply could not provide these quantities. So on the one hand Casa do Douro had approved an overproduction but on the other hand they had not bought enough aguardente.

The shippers were discontent. Cristiano van Zeller claimed that the Casa do Douro had abused its position and treated the shippers unfairly and documented the following: on the family's Quinta do Noval a production of 170 pipes of Port Wine was approved from their A fields of a total beneficio of approx. 85,000 pipes in 1982. In 1991, Noval could only produce 133 pipes of the total beneficio of 110,000 pipes.

At the same time, Casa do Douro approved a new basis of calculation for the allocation of beneficio in 1991 (See page 114f) without any reason and without informing the shippers. When the small farmers demonstrated, the Casa do Douro complied immediately.

Things did not improve when the Escudo was devaluated resulting in a fall in income, the stocks in Gaia growing - and the consumption on the world market was slow. For the sixth year in a row the production of Port Wine was larger than its sales. The farmers who had planted new vines in the 1980'ies in good faith and with the support from the World Bank, now had to pay back their loans - but without sales, no income!

Mesquita Montes - for many years the Casa do Douro's powerful director and the evil spirit of the Port Wine shippers. (Photo: BJS)

When some of the co-operatives asked for money owned to them by Casa do Douro, they received nothing. The state-controlling body had spent its savings on shares in private real estate.

The foolhardy purchase of shares

It was a regular bombshell, the greatest in Gaia since the Miguelists in 1833 fired at the Company's lodges, when Casa do Douro's Mesquita Montes announced in July 1990 that Casa do Douro would purchase 40% of the shares in Real Companhia Velha and had actually already bought them. The price was £ 37,500,000 or US$ 72,000,000.

The announcement was made inconveniently and quite on purpose a few days before the Port Wine industry's annual holiday period. It was a surprise because rumors the year before had talked about Italian investors who wanted to buy shares in Real Companhia Velha, but those rumors had been denied.

Now the rumors proved to be true. Portugal's impartial arbitrator, the Procurator General, called the deal "incompatible" with Casa do Douro's position as state-controlling body. But the evaluation of the arbitration was incontrovertible. This meant that the state-controlling body would become co-owner of the former state monopoly and thereby should control itself.

The shippers were furious. They had already often criticised the small committee of four men who decided the size of the annual harvest. The committee consisted of 1 representative from Casa do Douro, 1 representative from the Port Institute, 1 representative for all the shippers and the owner of Real Companhia Velha, Silva Reis. The news of Casa do Douro's purchase of shares was announced by the exporters' association's president Manuel Pintão Poças as follows: "It is a insult to the Port Wine industry, and Casa do Douro's action clearly shows that it should be placed under the Port Institute. Casa's policy in the 1980'ies has been strongly criticised and is very political. Casa is to blame for the panic on the Port Wine market in the late 1980'ies, for it dictated a limited production in the good years in the early 1980'ies (1982, 1983, 1985) to get rid of their own stocks, so when the vintages of lower quality appeared in 1988 and 1989, there was a sudden shortage of quality Port Wine on the market. Then followed an excessive production, and that was Casa's fault too. Now they need the money, so what will they do? Maybe they will dump prices, maybe they will use the surplus production in Real Companhia Velha when the others have no more, maybe they will see to an overproduction and then afterwards when the wine cannot be sold they will repurchase it. Well, it's possible! Everything is possible when it comes to Casa do Douro!"

The business is shocked at what the Casa do Douro has done, the sober-minded Michael Symington wrote in a news letter. The most shocking thing is perhaps the fact that Casa do Douro can conceive doing such a thing, Peter M. Cobb wrote in his harvest report. With their blundering purchase of shares, Portugal has established itself as a regular banana republic was Manuel

Pintão Poças' evaluation of the situation. The much scolded Mesquita Montes also had a comment to make. When he visited Copenhagen in 1990 to profile Douro wines he explained that the balance between exports from Gaia and the Douro Valley was unfortunate, and by buying the shares he had seen to it that the money stayed in the valley. "The co-operatives cannot export with no markets to export to, and nobody is there to help them", he said. And anyway he saw nothing offensive or illegal about Casa do Douro's purchase of shares, for the Casa was state-controlled, but only with regard to quantities, not with regard to quality.

And with regard to the future, he could easily imagine that Casa would waive their state-controlling rights which had been dictated by Salazar and that the controlling function would be passed on to the IVP.

Power to the Institute

If the shippers had heard this it would have been grist to their mill. But they did not, and the disguised offer was not followed up. Instead, they worried about the export market and feared that the trouble between Gaia and Régua would influence the foreign markets which had become so important to the shippers, as exports in 1989 were early 87% of the total sales, and in 1990-1991 only fell to approx. 86%. It was a very sensitive issue.

In the spring of 1991, Cristiano van Zeller was elected chairman of the board in the exporters' association after Pintão Poças. He was just as sharp as his predecessor: "It is an absurd situation and the Casa should immediately be deprived of its political influence. It is an unbearable situation that the producers have now got a competitor who has been appointed by the state to control the harvest quantities and the classification of vineyards, to control the stocks of all the producers, to decide who may produce Port Wine, and how much may be produced, and who has the political power to intervene in the market and purchase unsold wine. We even pay for the grapes and the alcohol via the Casa.

The Casa's functions should be transferred to the Port Institute who is an impartial body so that the Casa may carry on their private activities. The IVP would be far better at handling matters, which the Casa has never been capable of. The Casa has never had a proper view of production, and far more Port Wine was produced than necessary. And while figures and information from the Casa is always late and incorrect, the IVP is always prompt and their figures are credible".

However, the Port Institute did not have the necessary power. Manager Leopoldo Mourão was forced to retire because he had been too weak in the confrontation with Casa do Douro. Mesquita Montes seldomly reacted to criticism, but on 17 May 1993, the newspaper "O Publico" finally announced that he had decided that the Casa do Douro had to annul the deal.

This tormenting situation also had an impact on Casa do Douro and Mesquita Montes. In 1991, the sale of aguardente was liberalized, and in 1995 the CIRDD was founded (See page 311) and took over some of Casa do Douro's most important functions. And Mesquita Montes retired.

Prosperity in the 1990'ies

The new Act on direct exportation from the Douro Valley stopped all extravagant purchases of real estate. All the small wine growers now dreamed of owning their own property, and the patchwork in the Port Wine valley remained. A statement from 1990 indicates that approx. 28,000 wine growers and farmers owned on an average 1.07 ha each, and 2/3 of them made 25-26 hl at the most a year, corresponding to less than 300 crates of wine. The permission to export was to most of them just a theory - but it was favourable with regard to the prices for grapes.

Another statement from 1990 indicates, however, that the world consumption of Port Wine had doubled compared to 1970, and as the figures on page 76 show, sales and exports soared after 1993. With these figures in mind, the producers made a move to touch one of the last holy cows in the business: bulk sales.

Even though the bulk sales of Vintage and LBV had been prohibited since 1973, and the finest Tawnies could not be shipped in bulk either, the total bulk sales were uncomfortably large and not at all favorable to the reputation of Port Wine. In 1980, bulk sales were around 45% of total exports against 55% bottled Port Wine.

From April 1992, all old 70 cl bottles were forbidden, and by decree of 12 October 1995 a temporay prohibition against the exportation of Port Wine in bulk was introduced. The decree entered into force five days later and would soon indicate how much exports would decrease when the price of Port Wine increased.

But the producers were in for a good surprise. Bulk sales were reduced by 25% when the decree entered into force, then completely disappeared and were not reflected on the total export figures at all. Boldness was thus rewarded. And now, every bottle of Port Wine could be controlled during the whole process before it was set on the dinner table in London, Copenhagen, Stockholm, New York, or Hong Kong.

The new Act was valid from 1 July 1996. This was the last time a bottle of Port Wine made from grapes from the south of France or Spain was ever opened.

1996: a new golden year

1996 was similar to 1985 in many other ways. Apart from the prohibition against the exportation of bulk wines, the new wine route "Rota do Vinho do Porto" was inaugurated in September 1996, and Vintage 1994 was bottled.

Before the wine route along the Douro river becomes the new tourist attraction, many are hoping for, reparations are required, otherwise the tourists will never go there! (Photo: HO)

The wine route had the same good purpose as the establishment of the Confraria: to increase the interest of Port Wine, but it also had the purpose of bringing tourism to the isolate Douro Valley. This would be a benefit to the producers and wine growers who lived there; it would create an interest for Port Wine and hopefully maintain the local people who were a bit too much in a hurry to move to the cities.

Rota do Vinho do Douro was inaugurated with a voyage from Porto to Régua. This was one of the benefits of the new political season, namely that locks and dams were to be made navigable so that one could travel on the Douro river by boat.

At the same time, tourist facilities were built or renovated. There were for example no hotels, except for a couple of run-down hotels in Régua, a minute hotel in Pinhão and a slightly better hotel in Lamego, so tourism requested that the large and small quinta owners to open their doors to the expected flow of curious visitors.

It was surely the dream of any Port Wine-loving tourist to be able to wake up in the morning on "your own Port Wine Quinta", open the shutters, look at the vines, hear the chicken cackle a "good Morning to you" and to begin a new day in the Port Wine country.

However, not all the Port Wine people were happy. Some saw a horrifying image of the Douro Valley as Portugal's Napa Valley - others believed that it was a great idea. Tourism, visits, interest, sales, turnover, more interest, more sales, more turnover. As mentioned in the chapter about tourism (see page 376ff), the dream has slowly developed since 1996. And whether it is the merit of the prophecy of tourism or not, it is simply impossible to find a quinta "for sale" today. The Symington family were fortunate to be able to re-purchase the Quinta da Senhora da Ribeira in 1999, but Taylor's had to pay more than they wanted to in 1998 when they had to outbid a well-known Danish wine importer for Quinta do Junco.

It was a sensation when the somewhat obscure Quinta Ventozelo was bought by Spanish investors in the spring of 1999, as it was common knowledge that not much was for sale in the valley, and nothing at all by the river. Real property in the Douro Valley had become a seller's market!

American hysteria

Vintage 1994 also became an item on the seller's market! In the months prior to declaring Vintage 1994 I visited the Douro Valley three times and know for a fact that there was more talk about the new wine route and the decline of bulk sales than there was talk about Vintage 1994.

It was a promising vintage, no doubt about that. Gordon Guimaraens explained to me that it had the same fruit and structure that he remembered from 1970, and Michael Symington wrote in a news letter: "1994 has this wonderful flowery freshness of violets mixed with fresh hay, which I have only noted a few times over the years. Vintage 1995 had the same qualities as did Vintages 1966 and 1970. And I believe that Vintage 1994 has those same qualities. It will become an excellent wine, so my only problem is whether or not I will live to taste it"!

A total of 46 shippers declared Vintage, which was the greatest number ever, but this could also be due to the fact that no really good vintages had been declared since 1985, and that 1993 was a failure with only one shipper declaring Vintage, namely Quinta da Romaneira who declared it with a grin and a shrug. The euphoria of this vintage is more due to the reception of the wines than to the wines themselves. The part of the American media who moves lightly between success and failure was very quick in proclaiming that Vintage 1994 was phenomenal, and when Robert M. Parker and "The Wine Spectator" - in their mutual urge to outbid - plastered Taylor's, Fonseca, and Noval with 100 points, all hell broke loose in Oklahoma.

Quinta Ventozelo was bought in the spring of 1999 for Spanish Pesetas and is the latest quinta to be sold. There are many buyers but not many quintas for sale - and none near the river. (Photo: HO)

The American public who never touches wines under 90 points ran amok - and the Port Wine producers followed.

We were not talking about months, but weeks, after which there was not a drop or a bottle left of Taylor's, Fonseca's or Noval's, and when they were gone, the euphoria passed on to the other brands. The most embarassing thing was that some of the producers in Gaia, whom one might expect to show some moderation in the euphoria were just as high as prices were. A respectable house as Cockburn's practically boasted about selling 99% of their Vintage 1994 to the United States - and were sorry that they did not have another 99% to sell!

Pure madness

There were several aspects to the American hysteria wrecking the Port Wine market. Now retired Bruce Guimaraens had the following to say about the 100 points even though he was quite happy for his son David's success with the Taylor's and Fonseca wines: "As far as I can see it is pure madness to give a wine 100 points, which is only two years old and which most probably will not top for the next 50-60 years. How can anyone evaluate it at this stage? How can you look at a two-year old girl and say that she will grow into a beauty at the age of 20? And even if she does, she will probably have a zit or something else reducing her to a 99-point girl"!

In London, the prices of a case of Vintage Port 1994 rose and cost 40-50% more than the acceptable Vintages 1991 and 1992. And the same thing happened in Copenhagen. A Vintage 1994 cost more than a young Vintage had ever done before. A wise man said to keep cool: "One hundred years ago the nouveau-riche Americans bought art they did not understand. Now they are buying Port". Wise words, for the euphoria lasted as long as it had with Vintage 1977 which was also outbid by the American market. "The way the Vintage 1994's were snapped up, you would have expected an increased American interest in old Vintage Ports. But nothing happened", James Symington noted. Huyshe Bower, co-owner of the two 100-point wines from Taylor's and Fonseca had the same experience.

But there was another negative aspect. You may well be of the same opinion as a practical salesman that it does not matter who buys the goods as long as they are sold: but Vintage Port is not Coca Cola or chewing gum that never changes and can be produced infinitely.

A famous producer once said: "Don't quote me on this, but I suspect that most of Vintage 1994 will be drunk before the year 2000, for when these wines have obtained 100 points, they will be served on the American dinner tables as from tomorrow. You see, it is prestigious to be able to serve top quality products. And patience is not an American virtue ..."

Not many want to be quoted by name. But Bruce Guimaraens said in his book "Vintage Port" which was published in June 1999: "It is a sad fact of life that most Vintage Ports, particularly in the United States and Holland, are consumed within a few months after being declared".

Never-ending hysteria

Vintage 1995, which is expected by some producers to be just as excellent as Vintage 1994, maybe even better, was introduced on the market at the expected high prices. But the Americans had lost their urge. Now other bottles were popular, and Port Wine lost their interest.

On the traditional European markets, the importers and wine merchants had been disappointed when the Americans had been allocated nearly all of Vintage 1994, and they received the Vintage 1995 and later Vintage 1996 with moderate enthusiasm. Demands for Late Bottled Vintage and Single Quinta Vintage Port, Vintage Character and other cheaper port wines at more reasonable prices were more in demand.

But in the United States the hysteria continued. The topic was simply too interesting to just stop at that, so in the New Year edition of the 1997 "The Wine Spectator", a vintage chart indicated Vintage Port at 99 points and the yet to be released Vintage 1995 at 85-89 points. The gap in points was due to the fact that wine had been tasted from casks (!), something that no connaisseur of Port Wine with any respect for himself and for Port Wine would dare give such a verdict upon. But this did not stop "The Wine Spectator" in doing so.

The 85-89 points were a blow to the interested parties in Gaia, for wines with such low points are of no interest to the Americans. But in the old world we should actually humbly thank them for this verdict which ensures that the hysteria is kept well within the editorial walls of "The Wine Spectator".

In the surrounding world life went on. In the first six months of 1999, exports rose to 442,281 hl Port Wine or an increase of 3.7% compared to 1998. But the American imports had fallen by 18.1% - and by 19.5% for Vintage, LBV and better Tawnies!

Port towards the year of 2000

This is where we stand today. October 1999. The final paragraph in this book can be phrased in a few lines.

Port Wine is, as we all are, on its way towards the new millennium. The American buying philosophy and the unstable Asian economy has cooled down the more flighty Port Wine dreams, because naturally some Port Wine people have already calculated that if one Chinese drinks one glass of Port Wine a year, the imperishable glory of Port Wine would persist. At least for the export director. But there is still a long way to go before the Chinese dream is fulfilled. China is not even on the Port Institute's most recent list of Port Wine importers. In 1998 Hong Kong's import share was a mere 0.0% (!) And Japan's 0.3%. It gives food for thought - and should also do so for the shippers - that the old world in Europe covers 91.9% of all Port imports whilst the new world, including the United States, only covers 8.1%.

According to the IVP, the export market figures for the calendar year of 1998 were as follows:

France	36.7%
Holland	18.6%
Belgium/Luxemburg	14.8%
Great Britain	10.8%
Germany	4.1%
USA	4,0%
Denmark	2.1%
Canada	1.4%
Italy	1.4%
Spain	1.4%

Back in the real world, the annual beneficio as usual was published in August. The beneficio for 1999 will be 7.4% higher than in 1998. The price of aguardente will also be higher and is expected to increase by approx. 5% - apart from the price of manpower which according to Christian Seely (Quinta do Noval) will be the most criticised element in future price increases.

Are you suspecting where this will lead to? Vintage 1997 is soon to be introduced on the market. It will hardly be as Vintage 1994 with regard to quality, but the opening prices will be much higher, for the American market not only pays the price for the bottles most in demand but also sets the market price. In Denmark, Taylor's Vintage 1997 is expected to be sold at 70-80 £/100-115 $ a bottle, and the others will follow. Compared to the classified Bordeaux wines, Iranian caviar, and white truffles from Alba, Italy, this does not seem unreasonable. But it might be a problem for the young generation of Port Wine drinkers who in recent years have replaced the old Port Wine drinkers with their podagra and red and blue noses.

Maybe the best Port Wines in the future will be something they will only read about. Well, let them begin here!

In June 1999, the first bottles of Vintage 1997 were ready for shipment on the market. This is perhaps the last Vintage Port of the century. (Photo: HO)

Chapter 2

THE LAND OF SCHIST

The land of schist

This land of Port is dominated by schist. It is an old saying in the Douro Valley that where schist is replaced by granite, there is no more Port.

The major part of the demarcated area dates back from the Pre-Ordovician geological epoch between Cambrium and Silurian whose only characteristic is clay schist which in the Douro Valley is surrounded by granite (by Tua and by Alijó) breaking through the schist in certain places and running along the right bank of the mouth of the Sabor river by Vale do Meão.

"You cannot cultivate Port without knowing your soil", says Bruce Guimaraens, a capacity in this area. Once the ocean covered this land but receded and left deposits, especially schist and granite, not from one day to the other, but at a speed of 1 mm of deposit per 100,000 years! 300,000 mio years ago sudden volcano eruptions compressed the schist so that it stood up vertically. This signifies that the vine roots can only grow downwards, and this is the secret of the Douro Valley's soil - and the reason that there is no other place on the face of the earth where they can make a wine as Port. The barren schist is also the reason that nothing else can grow here other than wine, olives, and maybe almond trees, within the demarcated area.

The first agriculturers must have found out that the rocky ground was just below the surface. To be able to cultivate the land they either had to break up the top layer on top of the rock or distribute a layer of sand or rubble on top of it.

This is why - through intervention of man - there are two kinds of soil in the Douro Valley:

1) Soil which is not tilled by man - or where only the top layer (maybe 20 - 25 cm) is tilled. This is less common within the demarcated area. Here the laying out of terraces results in a tilling of the soil.

2) Soil which is tilled by man when planting the vines. The soil is typically porous down to 1 - 1.30 m with a ploughed-up layer on top and a layer underneath touching the bedrock. Both layers consist of fine sand and small pieces of rock which lie on top of the hard rock. Most of the demarcated area consists of this kind of tilled rocky ground.

Preparing the soil

When Alfred Nobel invented dynamite, it became easier to lay out the vineyards in the Douro Valley, but even with explosives, it is hard work. In other places in the world the first consideration would mainly be about choosing the best grape variety, but on a terrain like the Douro Valley, the biggest consideration is how to lay out the vineyard. There are more or less two possibilities. You

Section of a typical wine lot in the Douro Valley. The top layer of the bedrock is blasted away, or a layer of porous soil is distributed upon the rock. The plant layer is around one metre which is just about enough to hold the vine. The layer of schist has been compressed horizontally after the volcano eruption about 300 years ago. This signifies that the roots of the vine plunge down through the blocks of schist to find nutrition.

can either plant the vines horizontally so that they follow the curve of the mountain, just like when you lay out roads with hairpin bends, or you can follow the shortest road from the top to the bottom and plant the rows vertically. The latter has only existed as an option since the mid 1970'ies because it does require special technical aids.

The man-made vineyards can be divided chronologically into:

1. Pre-Phylloxera terraces ("Geios")

The oldest terraces in the Douro Valley were laid out in the 19th century by Galician labourers. It took them 100 days to build one step and plant 1,000 vines, all by hand. It goes without saying that it was a heavy and labourious task, which took a lot of men, time - and patience. On the other hand, the advantage of making terraces was enormous. You could hold the vines and the water, and it was easier to work horizontally than slantingly all year round, but especially when the grapes were picked.

When the wine louse Phylloxera had raged throughout Douro, many of the terraces fell into decay, partly because the wine growers were afraid that they would never get rid of the wine louse, and partly because they had to admit, that many of the vines were planted quite superficially in badly tilled soil. Many of the terraces also only had one row of vines which was not profitable at all. Around 1900, you could still find approx. 17,000 ha of these abandoned vineyards (mortórios = dead land) within the demarcated area. And today, you can still find pre-phylloxera fields which are being cultivated or at least which have been until quite recently. When Ferreira, at SOGRAPE's purchase of the Port house Offley Forrester, was asked to supervise the Quinta da Boa Vista, even more hectares with pre-phylloxera vines were found which once had been planted all over the place and had been looked after carelessly. This was the result of the easy solution which had now developed into a jungle.

2. Post-Phylloxera terraces (Vinha Tradicional)

Once the Portuguese had collected themselves after the invasion of the wine louse and had to start afresh, they learned from the acquired experience and improved the terraces. So with a little help from experience and even more help from dynamite, they began to lay out more rational terraces with 3, 4, 5, and up to 8 to 9 rows per step. They were called "terraços" or "socalcos".

By using dynamite you could really churn up the soil and thus provide more fertile layers and lay out new terraces on better soil. As with the pre-phylloxera terraces, stone walls were built around the rocks that had been blasted off so that the soil would not cave in. Apart from the blasting, everything was done by hand. This was hard physical work, and the stone walls between the rows made it impossible to use machinery. The only advantage was that all work could still be performed horizontally.

It was very costly to lay out terraces this way, not so much due to the cost of labour than due to the erection of the stone walls. You could plant up to approx. 5,000 vines per ha which is the same as for the more recent method Vinha ao alto (see page 97), but the work was more tedious and more expensive and when there was a shortage in manpower in the 1960'ies and 1970'ies, somebody had to come up with an alternative.

3. Patamares

The biggest disadvantage of cultivating wine on terraces was that it takes a large human effort, both physically and in manpower. Of course, the dynamite does blast the rock, but then all other work has to be performed by hand - from the tilling of the soil to the picking of grapes. With the reduction of labour in the Douro Valley and the introduction of new technical aids, new experiments were carried out in the course of the 1960'ies: patamares where the vines are (nearly) planted horisontally in two rows at a time but without the use of bricks and stones. This means that bulldozers can be used for the initial work and tractors for some of the following work. The vines are planted on slightly sloping terraces at a width of 4-5 metres but without the disadvantages of the traditional terraces. Some choose to let the bare, stoneless ground fill up with weeds; this actually stops erosion, but on the other hand it steals the water. Others keep their land surgically clean, which reduces the problem of water but then there is the risk of erosion. In comparison with the traditional terraces, the patamares have a higher degree of evaporation, as there are no walls to hold the water. On the other hand, a tractor can be applied to gather the grapes in the picking season, and maybe for crop spraying, but not much else. Patamares do not require the same manpower as the old-fashioned terraces, and this was one of the points of introducing the new method. Sandeman, who are one of the largest landowners in the Douro Valley, have planted new plants in 1998-1999 using patamares on Quinta do Vau: two rows of vines on each floor and the patamares laid out so that a tractor can drive up with empty crates and bring back the filled ones in the picking season. Patamares is for the cautious and the only modern solution to very steep slopes. But today, many prefer ...

THE LAND OF SCHIST

4. Vinha ao alto

Ramos-Pinto, who was one of the pioneers of patamares, first introduced Vinha ao alto. The reason was that in the beginning of the 1970'ies José Ramos-Pinto Rosas predicted that there would be a shortage of staff in the Douro Valley and that one would have to come up with a new planting technique mechanizing as many tasks as possible. When João Nicolau de Almeida joined the company in 1976, one of his first assignments was to find a solution to this problem. He remembered having seen a lot with 40 year-old vines where the rows were boldly planted in a vertical position from top to bottom, because the owner, a Swiss engineer, wanted to sell a certain type of tractor. After 40 years, the lot was still in use, but the viticultural experimental station in the Douro Valley had given up using this kind of planting because their only tractor had broken down (!). They had actually obtained quite promising results.

Almeida was sent to Rheingau to study the phenomenon and in 1978 he and Rosas began to plant the first rows ao alto at Quinta do Bom Retiro - on a slope at that! A slope with an inclination of 60-65%. As the experimental station was not interested in any collaboration, Rosas and Almeida chose to continue on their own, and on the remote Quinta da Ervamoira they began to plant vertical rows following the German model. Gradually, others began to plant ao alto, and the results were so promising that today, the whole of Ervamoira is planted vertically.

João Nicolau de Almeida says: "We quickly found out that if the inclination is less than 50%, you should plant with 2.10 - 2.30 m between the rows so that a small tractor can pass through. But if the inclination is of more than 50%, we only need 1.30 m between the rows because we cannot use a motorized tractor then anyway but have to settled with a capstan".

On Ferreira's model property Quinta do Seixo, the patamares and the vinha ao alto thrive side by side - even different versions of both of them. To the left, patamares, in the middle, slanting ao alto, and to the right, the more traditional vertical ao alto.

According to Almeida, the advantages of planting ao alto compared to patamares are the following:

*) By respecting the inclination of the ground we obtain a better result seen from an ecological point of view.

*) Strange as it may seem, a few years after the first trials, less erosion was seen when planting ao alto compared to patamares, and the detected erosion was easier to remedy.

*) As we had predicted, it was difficult to hold the water, but on the other hand we avoided the significant evaporation we experience when using patamares. When you use patamares, you often run into the problem that the row farthest away gets too little water, but the innermost row gets too much. On Quinta do Seixo (using Vinha ao alto since 1992) Joaquim Fernandes has experienced that due to the vertical structure of the schist, pebbles and rain water stay on the ground. By digging a tiny "moat" around the foot of each vine, you can hold the water - which is much better than using patamares.

*) On patamares you can plant 3,000 - 3,500 vines per ha, but using ao alto you can plant 5,000 - 6,500 vines per ha, depending on the conditions of the soil. The close planting reduces evaporation and forces the roots down into the ground.

*) Using patamares you can only apply machinery to a certain extent. With ao alto use can use cater-

THE LAND OF SCHIST

"If the mountain's inclination is less than 35%, "Vinha ao alto" is a first choice", says Joaquim Fernandes (Quinta do Seixo). "But it is important to have 1-2 metres between the rows to make room for the tractors".

pillar tractors with special tracks to crop, fertilize, spray, fetch the baskets and do some of the tilling mechanically, if the inclination does not exceed approx. 50%. This is confirmed by Joaquim Fernandes (Seixo) who uses tractors to plough and spray (against mildew) and send the baskets back and forth during the picking season.

*) The costs are nearly the same when it come to laying out fields using the patamares method or the ao alto method, but it is cheaper to work ao alto. When Ramos-Pinto laid out Ervamoira, which is now 100% ao alto, even though it is quite flat land, the costs were only 1/3 of what they would have been using patamares. This financial benefit is confirmed by Manuel Ângelo Barros, who has noted on Quinta de São Luiz that 30 - 50% of the land would be wasted using patamares but only 5 - 10% using ao alto.

Different opinions

Ao alto was introduced in the 1980'ies when the rumours about the good results at Ramos-Pinto and Ferreira began to spread throughout the Douro Valley. At the same time, the recognized professor Fernando Bianchi de Aguiar from the University of Tras-os-Montes, later President of the Port Institute for several years, spoke highly of ao alto, but he did believe, however, that it would be easier to work on patamares and that patamares would be easier to lay out with cheaper costs for machinery costs too (because the use of machine-

THE LAND OF SCHIST

The land is prepared for planting on Taylor's Quinta de Vargellas. But calcium must be added to the soil before planting, and again every fifth year.

New times have arrived to the Douro Valley. Heavy machinery lay out the patamares on Barros' Quinta de São Luiz, and the tractors will be taking over the day-to-day work.

ry is practically non-existent). On the other hand, the machines do prefer straight lines instead of curves, so for vertical planting, this is an advantage. These reasons were so overmastering that when the World Bank promised to support the laying out of vineyards in 1985, they allowed both patamares and ao alto.

But even with 15-20 years of experience there are still different opinions as to when it is best to plant ao alto or patamares. João Nicolau de Almeida (Ramos-Pinto) believes that 50% is the limit, whilst José Manso on the Barros family's Quinta de São Luiz sets the limit at approx. 45%. Joaquim Fernandes (Ferreira) and Bruce Guimaraens (Taylor's, Fonseca) set a more moderate estimate at 35% and 32%, respectively.

The pioneers Almeida and Fernandes do agree, however, that today they plant ao alto where it is possible and patamares on the rest of the fields. Others are still in doubt.

THE VALLEY OF THE GOD OF WINE

When Pombal's Act of 10th September 1756 (see page 28f) was passed, Companhia Geral da Agricultra das Vinhas do Alto Douro was given the assignment to limit or to demarcate the area for wine growing in the Douro Valley. The general philosophy was that the demarcated area was to produce just the right amount of wine, which at the time went for exports.

When the borders of Lower Douro (Baixo Corgo) and Upper Douro (Cima Corgo) were established and 335 stones hammered into the schist to mark the demarcated area in the period from 4/10-1758 to 4/5-1761, the land within the area was classified according to the same principles as Médoc would be just 100 years later. The soil was classified according to its potential, calculated on the basis of the market price, but the grapes and the wine within the same category could be mixed freely, so the classification did not have the same tight rules as Médoc.

In the top end of the classification scale you found the wine which was called Feitoria wine and which could be exported at the highest price. The list was as follows:

Feitoria   (30,000 - 36,000 Reis per pipe)
Table wine 1 (19,200 Reis per pipe)
Table wine 2 (15,000 Reis per pipe)
Table wine 3 (10,500 Reis per pipe)
Table wine 4 (6,400 Reis per pipe)
Table wine 5 (4,200 Reis per pipe)
Table wine 6 (3,500 Reis per pipe)

Even though the original map is old and difficult to read (see page 32-33), it does give you a good idea about the demarcation limits in 1761. The market prices had set the outline, and when the Company started to function properly, they started to calculate the quality of the wine in three qualities:

SUBREGION	AREA	WINE ACREAGE	WINE GROWERS
Lower Corgo	45,000 ha	13,492 ha	13,338
Upper Corgo	95,000 ha	17,036 ha	13,690
Douro Superior	110,000 ha	8,060 ha	6,052

(Source: Casa do Douro, 1995),

Demarcated Douro Region
Sub-regions

- Murça
- Régua
- Pinhão
- Foz Côa

Baixo Corgo · Cima Corgo · Douro Superior

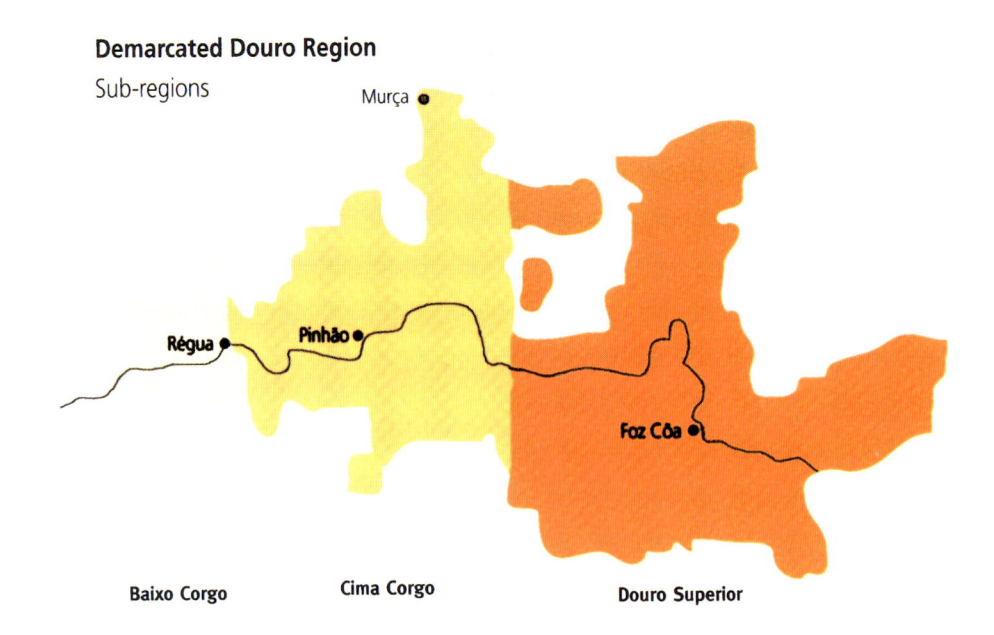

Quality 1: wine for exportation to England
Quality 2: wine for exportation to Brazil and other countries
Quality 3: wine for the home market (vinhos de ramo)

The demarcated area functioned with practically no changes until João Franco's revision of 10/5-1907 when a large area to the east of Cima Corgo towards the Spanish border was included in the demarcated area. After a reduction of the demarcated area in November 1908 and a few minor adjustments in December 1921, the demarcated area for Port has been the same ever since. The demarcated area consists of three sub-regions:

Baixo Corgo (Lower Corgo) is the birthplace of Port, and here you will still find the largest concentration of vines, as one third of Lower Corgo is planted with wine.

Cima Corgo (Upper Corgo) produces the best grapes for the best wine. Here you will find around one fifth of the acreage planted with wine.

Douro Superior is the largest, the most eastern and the youngest part of the demarcated area. It is nearly three times as large as Lower Corgo, but only has 3/5 of Lower Corgo's vines. The landscape is often rough, but here you also have possibilities of extension.

The number of wine growers is now only 29,860 (1998). They own a total of 85,000 lots with around 2 mio vines and produce 98 mio litres of wine a year. Around 2/3 of the wine growers own less than 1/2 ha, corresponding to a production of max. 28 hl.

The demarcated area stretches about 100 km along the Douro river. Of the total demarcated area of approx. 250,000 ha, the 39,782 ha (1998) are planted with vines.

Please note that these numbers often change markedly, and that the sources do not always indicate the same figures (IVP, Casa do Douro, Encyclopedia of the Wines of Portugal).

THE VALLEY OF THE GODS OF WEATHER

I do not think that there is any other wine district in the world where there are such deviations in rainfall, wind and sun within the same Appellation as in DO Douro. But to some extent it seems quite logical that the finest drink of the gods is made from grapes from the Valley of the weather gods.

There are a couple of old Port sayings: "The best wine can hear the tillers creak" and "The best vineyards can always see the Douro river". The river apparently runs from east to west, and the wind apparently blows just as consequently from west to east. But only apparently. At Barqueiros (close to Mesão Frio) where the demarcated area begins, the river makes a few turns and meets the chain of mountains, Serra do Marão, which is often the last resort for humidity and harsh winds, and here you find shelter. If you come up the river, you feel it immediately. The wind blows in your back from Porto to Mesão Frio, but from Mesão Frio and to Régua there is shelter. Between Régua and the demarcation area's eastern border, the river is surrounded by mountains (until 1415 metres on the right bank and until 1382 metres on the left bank). The river is completely closed in, and the cold winds from the Atlantic sea and from Northern Portugal cannot reach you. Neither can the rain. On the contrary, the mountains keep you warm. This is why the rainfall is so unevenly distributed along the Douro river, and it is difficult to understand that you can walk around Porto or Vila Nova de Gaia with its mild Atlantic climate and an annual rainfall of approx. 1300 mm and know that they are having a heatwave or drought in the wine land about 100 km towards the east. But take a look at the below figures. The average temperature and rainfall is measured over a period of 30 years:

	HEIGHT	AVERAGE TEMPERATURE	RAINFALL
Vila Real	430 m	13.6°	1,130 mm rain
Régua	100 m	15.5°	949 mm rain
Pinhão	130 m	16.2°	672 mm rain
Poçinho	150 m	16.5°	407 mm rain

(Source: Nuno Magalhães in "Encyclopedia of the Wines of Portugal". 1998).

WATER PROHIBITED! Irrigation is only allowed in connection with new plantings and for special trials as you can see here at Croft's Quinta da Roêda. A capacity in his field, João Nicolau de Almeida believes, however, that a limited irrigation should be allowed in special situations. "During the long period of drought in 1981, a limited irrigation would have reduced the consequences of stress to which the vines were exposed to", he says to give an example. He also stresses that a limited use of irrigation in exposed areas as well as in periods of a rain shortage could replace around 40% of the water that evaporates. His philosophy is that the vineyard reacts as the human body: it functions much better with a regular supply of water than if it is first flooded and then dries out.

So you cannot indicate one temperature or a certain amount of rain in the demarcated Port region, for it stretches across three different climatic zones: the Atlantic, the Atlantic/Mediterranean, and the Iberian/Mediterranean zones. Especially the border between the first two (at Marão/Montemuro) is important see from a climatic point of view.

The winters in the Douro Valley are usually mild, and the summers usually very hot, locally until 50ºC. The biggest threat in the winter (until April) is the frost which can cause great damage, especially to the vines that grow high up on the mountain sides or that lie sheltered from the wind. If the spring winds are too hefty, a so-called "first harvest" takes place, which means that all the young shoots and buds blow away. Water also plays an important role. April and May should be rainy, but not so much that the vines are stressed. This is what happened in the catastrophic month of May 1992.

The flowering season (end May - early June) is usually cool, often rainy, cloudy with the risk of desavinho (reduced fructification). May often brings very windy weather, on the verge of storms, but you can also experience storms in the summer months. And if the storms bring rain and hail, great damage may occur. Otherwise the weather takes care of itself, as one says. I have heard of Port producers who did not take the weather seriously until they started producing table wines. Which is quite logical. This is partly due to the fact that Port is a mixture of wines, often mixed from wine from different climatic areas, and partly because it is a dessert wine and therefore less delicate by nature.

Chapter 3

GRAPE VARIETIES

Grape varieties

In 1947-48, when Álvaro Moreira da Fonseca designed his ingenious system for the classification of lots in the Douro Valley (see page 116), he listed a total of 76 various grape varieties for Port, 44 blue grapes and 32 green grapes, of which he "only" recommended the 29 grape varieties (15 blue grapes and 14 green grapes).

This was serious business. And a piece of practical Port history, for already in 1531 Ruy Fernandes mentions in a report from the environs of Lamegos that there is an infinity of grape varieties of which some thrive and others fail - and vice versa. He also emphasizes that if you plant different grape varieties together, you are on the safe side, for if one grape type experiences a bad year, the other grape varieties are probably OK, and if the whole vintage is bad, it will most probably be compensated for the year after. Not much changed in the following 400 years - not even after the invasion of Phylloxera, but not many years ago, viticulture was an obscure word of foreign origin in the Douro Valley. Both farmers and producers were busy planting. What they planted and where and when they planted, did not matter much, as long as something was dug into the ground. It was as if some of the magic of Port came from this jungle called a vineyard.

It was practically popular belief in the Douro Valley that the more grape varieties, the better. Ferreira's managing director, "Vito" Olazabal, told me back in 1998 while we were inspecting the mess at Offley's Quinta da Boa Vista that he had been told when he started at Ferreira's in 1965 that it was the number of grape varieties which made Port so complex. There was something quite attractive and mysterious about its heterogeneous maturation and its many-coloured lambency in autumn. Today, we know better. Today, we know that it is certainly no advantage when the lots are planted at random. And we know that it is

GRAPE VARIETY	YIELD	SUGAR CONTENT	TASTE (0-20)
Touriga Nacional	0.8 kg. per vine	13.3 Baumé	17.0 points
Tinto Cão	1.6 kg. per vine	12.8 Baumé	14.0 points
Tinta Barroca	2.4 kg. per vine	14.0 Baumé	15.0 points
Tinta Roriz	2.3 kg. per vine	13.2 Baumé	14.5 points
Touriga Francesa	1.9 kg. per vine	12.0 Baumé	13.0 points

(Source: José Ramos-Pinto Rosas and João Nicolau de Almeida. 1981).

GRAPE VARIETIES

certainly no advantage that the heterogeneous maturation has resulted in clusters of unripe grapes ending up in the lagares. In 1981, when José Ramos-Pinto Rosas and João Nicolau de Almeida presented their important analysis of the grapes varieties used in the Douro Valley, they listed 10 blue grape varieties covering 50-100% of the planted acreage, but what was even more valuable, they had carried out trials over a period of 5 years and found out that there were 5 grape varieties forming an elite and therefore worth focusing on. They presented their results at the University of Vila Real and emphasized the yields of the 5 grape varieties, combined with sugar contents (measured in Baumé) and taste (assessed by a blind tasting).

Today, the "5 noble grape varieties" have been such a success that subsidy schemes in recent years have included a request of only the following 5 blue grape varieties being planted: Touriga Nacional, Touriga Francesa, Tinta Roriz, Tinta Barroca, and Tinto Cão. Those who want to go their own way and who do not present reasons supporting their decision, have had to pay their own way. And you could not even claim that an inferior grape type as Sousão actually is part of the famous Nacional from Quinta do Noval. It was either the "5 nobles" or nothing at all.

This viticultural decision is applauded by the enologists - and these two parties have not always seen eye to eye! But today, many producers pay for their grapes according to sugar content, locality and grape variety, if it can be identified. This identification is naturally possible for all young plants, and you do see more and more lots planted with single grapes, especially Touriga Nacional.

The single grape Ports are however considered as somewhat of a joke by most people. It is the mixture of grapes that counts and the noble grape varieties must supplement each other, not dominate each other. Even young plantations include 2, 3, 4, or all 5 noble grape varieties at the same time, although they are kept separately for as long a time as possible.

The 5 noble grape varieties

Touriga Nacional: As early as in the 1790'ies this grape type was emphasized as being the most valuable grape for Port, and today it is highly recognized as the finest grape for producing Port. It grows solidly - and willingly, but gives a low yield, often just 1/2 or 1/3 of what all the other grape varieties yield. The 0.8 kg of grapes per vine determined in a study in 1981 has risen today to 1-1 1/2 kg grapes per vine by means of cloning, but this is still by far the lowest yield compared to the four other grape varieties. It is reasonably resistant to fungal diseases and thrives on the sunny slopes of Alto Douro. The blue-black grapes are small, but deep in colour, rich on aromatics and tannic acid.

The intensity of the wine is enormous - yielding up to 13% alcohol - but it is perfectly balanced by great quantities of fruit to balance the high extract and the young tannins. Even though the tannin structure is massive, the tannins are quite flexible.

This grape type is sensitive to climatic changes in climate, and according to Bruce Guimaraens it should not be planted to far to the east, as it requires full maturation.

Touriga Francesa: This grape variety (and its close cousin, Tinta da Barca) is more productive than Touriga Nacional and Tinto Cão and it gives both a lighter colour and texture. It is a very young grape, only from 1940, and as you can see on the chart, it has the lowest sugar content of the 5 noble grape varieties and the least number of points in taste. However, it is very versatile, and it is therefore the most planted blue grape in the Douro Valley (around 26% of the total acreage). It undergoes an early maturation, is quite robust and yields a lot of nice clusters, that is if it is planted early in the season, preferably in a sunny spot. It gives a pronounced scented wine, contributing with an intense perfume in the final mixture.

Unfortunately, it oxydizes easily, thus losing its nicest characteristic: the intense and very complex grape aroma. In previous years, there has been a lot of focus on this grape, also on Taylor's exclusive Quinta da Vargellas, but it has now been replaced by young plantings of Touriga Nacional. For João Nicolau de Almeida it is "a wonderful grape, adding body, intensity and a hint af freshness to the mixture."

Tinta Roriz: In Rioja, Spain, Tinta Roriz is better known as Tempranillo, in La Mancha it is known as Cencibel and in earlier times in the Douro Valley it was known as Tinta Monteira or Tinta Aragonêza. It comes from Spain and is the only grape of foreign descent that is of any importance to Port. All the other grape varieties are from Portugal. Tinta Roriz is remarkably resistant to heat, and it gives high yields, 2-3 times the yield of Touriga Nacional. It also thrives on barron landscapes. But it is sensitive to mildew and fungal diseases and does not tolerate a soil with too high a content of minerals. It is the most capricious of all 5 noble grape varieties, excellent in its good vintage years, hopeless in the bad years. In a humid climate it easily produces high yields of a somewhat light must, which contains tannic acid. In warm weather it gives a spicy must, which is rich in colour and contains potent tannins. It produces a masculine wine and contributes to the mixture with a solid tannin structure. It often has a pronounced resinous nose.

Tinto Cão: Tinto Cão has been cultivated in the Douro Valley since the 16th century - maybe even longer. It grows without any problems but produces a low yield, next to lowest after Touriga Nacional. It also has a tendency to oxydate. When it is at its best, it gives a very subtle wine. Contrary to the rich, intense grape aroma of the two Touriga grapes, Tinto Cão contributes to the mixture with its aromatic complexity. The grapes are rather small and loose, but have a high sugar content. This gives a wine with good keeping qualities. It matures slowly, late in the season and must never become overmature. Its quality depends on the climate: hot weather gives the must a peppery aroma and taste whilst the cold weather enhances the floral impressions. Of the 5 noble grape varieties, Tinto Cão is lightest in colour. It is a typical grape for mixing.

Tinta Barroca: This grape variety is considered as one of the "new" grapes in the Douro Valley, as it has only been known in the area for around 100 years (previously under other names: Tinta Grossa, Tinta Vigária, Tinta Gorda or Boca da Mina). It resists the cold weather brilliantly and is therefore often planted on the

GRAPE VARIETIES

northern slopes. It has vitality, gives big clusters and quite a high yield. It produces a robust wine with an aroma, which is often described as "flowery", contrary to the more "fruity" aroma in Port's other classical grape varieties. Tinta Barroca is often used to "soften" a mixture. Some regard it as one of the three most important grapes in the Douro Valley, even though it produces a wine of a varying quality, depending on growth conditions. João Nicolau de Almeida calls it "a useful grape for mixing, as it has a feminine, velvety and elegant aroma". Bruce Guimaraens calls it "quite valuable", as it can be planted far more to the east, contrary to Touriga Nacional. It is lighter in texture and does not require that much sun: "But it is tricky, for if the grapes get too little sun, they will contain too much acid, and if they get too much, they will only be good for jam".

The survival of the fittest

It is difficult to find anyone in the Douro Valley working with other blue grapes than the 5 above-mentioned ones - except for experimental use - even though very popular varieties, such as Tinta Amerela - an excellent grape for Port but rather sensible to oidium - Tinta da Barca and Bastardo are still seen. This concentration on only 5 grape varieties does seem to have resulted in the desired quality improvement, and at least it has stopped the less attractive grapes sneeking into the lagares.

The "5 noble grapes" had their breakthrough when the World Bank in 1985 supported a project for the tilling of vineyards in the Douro Valley granting loans which gave the producers the possibility of planting (or replanting) max. 9.7 ha of their property in the A and B categories on the condition that they would use the 5 noble grape varieties.

These bright colours indicate the historical "spontaneous" planting where many grape varieties were planted together at random and therefore matured at unevenly. Today, as you can see on the illustration on page 105, the grape varieties are carefully separated and usually only these 5 "noble" grape varieties are planted.

Root

Due to the wine louse, Phylloxera, all vines must be grafted (with Nacional as a historical exception, please see page 233f). The most used rootstock is *Rupestris du Lot* which has been popular since the invasion of phylloxera in Douro in the late 1860'ies.

Pruning

Double Guyot is a first choice, and every shoot keeps 3-5 eyes.

Binding

One-sided or (most often) two-sided Cordon.

The Risk

Oidium (in the Douro since 1851): Spraying is carried out several times a year with a Bordeaux mixture against mildew.

Mildew (in the Douro since 1893): Desinfection with sulphur, usually both when the shoots are 15-30 cm long as well as during the flowering season.

Maromba (in the Douro since 1948): This deficiency disease is caused by a deficit of boron in the soil. So boron is added, the dosage of which depends on the content of acid in the soil.

Fungal disease: Some grapes show indications of fungal attacks and are desinfected with sulphur. Noble rot (Botrytis cinerea) is also seen due to the humid winds from the Atlantic Ocean. Most people choose to fight this noble rot, but some choose not to.

The loans were granted at very favourable terms. They were free of interest for 7 years, after which time the loan and accrued interest were to be paid back over the following 10 years under favourable terms which, however, were not disclosed.

The aim was to plant or to replant 2500 ha of vineyards which had either been extinct (due to phylloxera) or which had not been used for wine growing. The qualitative focus on A and B land and the 5 noble grape varieties was based on the fact that less than 50% of Port came from A or B fields at the introduction of the scheme in 1985.

Another major, state-subsidized development programme for farm land in Trás-os-Montes in 1990 and later EU directives concerning young plantations have each time taken the 5 noble grape varieties into consideration, as loans or lower interest rates have only been granted if the 5 grape varieties are used.

The varieties in themselves are not static. There are some attempts to adapt the clones according to climatic conditions. And in recent years good results have been achieved by letting the micro climate decide which grape varieties to use for young plantations.

Ferreira has for example in co-operation with the University of Vila Real carried out trials to promote clones of the 5 noble grape varieties so that they give the best yield compared to quality. At first, the aim is to find a clone of Touriga Nacional, which is more stable and gives a slightly higher yield, and to find a clone of Tinta Roriz, which is more particular and gives a slighty lower yield.

Chapter 4

BENEFICIO

Beneficio

About 10 years ago I was a guest at the house of a Port Wine producer. It was the first Sunday in August. Why I remember this day so well is because my host, on his way to breakfast, practically grabbed the local Douro paper. I thought he might want to see the football results of the day before. But no, it was much more serious than that, he said. He wanted to see that year's *beneficio*. Beneficio is the Port Wine language for offside. Most people in the business know what the word means, but only few can actually define it, and even fewer really understand its significance. Beneficio is Latin and means "to have at your disposal". It is a ration card or book indicating to every single wine grower in the Douro Valley how many of his grapes from a particular year's harvest he may use to produce Port. The rest may only be used for table wine. The quantity of grapes he may use for his Port is his so-called beneficio.

Until the harvest of 1997, a committee from the Port Institute, the *Conselho Consultivo*, calculated the total harvested quantities which were based on the stock of Port in Vila Nova de Gaia, last year's production and exports as well as the export potential. When the Conselho Consultivo had decided how much Port should be produced, they would inform the IVP who would then inform the Casa do Douro, and in the course of June or July - and officially on the first Sunday in August - the public was given notice of the quantities of "beneficiado" for the next harvest. But it gets even more complicated: when the Casa do Douro had calculated the quantities for the total harvest, its clerks would calculate a so-called allocation for every single wine grower, so he would know how much Port to make and thus how much brandy he had to use. You see, until an Order was passed in March 1991, only the Casa do Douro could sell these wine spirits. They lost this privilege from the harvest year of 1992 and do not make these allocations anymore. This is now carried out by the CIRDD (see page 311). However, the actual philosophy behind the concept of benficio has not changed at all.

Points for Port

The calculation of every farmer's beneficio is quite complex. The basis is a subtle point-giving system, which is different for each of the nearly 30,000 wine growers with a total of around 85,000 lots; the philosophy, however, is quite simple and has not changed: the more points a lot is awarded, the more Port may be produced.

The system itself is so subtle that you feel that half a dove's feather on this golden weight of justice could completely change the outcome of the harvest. Some regard the calculation as a kind of work of Wizards, others believe that it is a residue of Casa do Douro's disappearing autocracy from the Douro Valley, which is only partly true, for the seed of the system was sown upon the amendment of the demarcated area, which by decree of 10th December 1921, No 7934, section 2, replaced by decree of 26th June 1986, distinguishes between demarcated table wine and Port Wine for the first time. This new demarcation did not, however, have an impact until after the establishment of Casa do Douro in 1932 when it was decided to prepare a register covering all the vineyards within the demarcated area. It was only a matter of form from a organisational point of view, as all wine producers within the appellation were members of Casa do Douro by definition. Whether the producers were small farmers or large quintas, they all had to indicate the following for every piece of their property:

- the name and address of the proprietor, the parish and residential district;
- demarcation and location of the property;
- number of vines;
- estimated production.

Then this meticulous and laborious work was handed over to the numerous clerks and the even more numerous inspectors. The clerks would calculate the figures and do their theoretical work; the inspectors would carry out the practicalities which took several years and seemed never to end, as the number of lots was forever changing.

The inspectors did not always meet an understanding towards their persistent pacing off the many fields and plots, and their never-ending questions also caused both surprise and indifference. But lines were drawn and finally, by the end of the Second World War, they could prepare a complete register of the entire demarcated area. This register is still updated regularly, and even though many are still sceptical, all proprietors have come to realize the importance of it. For the register is the basis of every year's beneficio.

The grade book of the vineyard

The point system devised on the basis of the register is based on collected and prepared information about soil, climatic conditions and viticulture for every single lot. Minuspoints are also given, and it is remarkable how great a significance is put on the height, yield and soil conditions of the vineyard and that training is counted for more than the choice of grape varieties:

	MIN.	MAX.	SPREAD	VALUE IN %
Altitude	-900	150	1050	20,6%
Productiveness	-900	120	1020	20,0%
Nature of the Land	-600	100	700	13,7%
Locality	-50	600	650	12,7%
Methods of Training Vines	-500	100	600	11,8%
Qualities of grapes	-300	150	450	8,8%
Slope	-100	100	200	3,9%
Aspect	-30	100	130	2,5%
Density	-50	50	100	1,9%
Soil and Degree of Stoniness	0	80	80	1,6%
Age of Vines	0	70	70	1,3%
Shelter	0	60	60	1,2%
TOTALS:	-3430	1680	5110	100,0%

In spite of subtleties, fiddly work and a lot of work on the part of the clerks with regard to the weighting of positive and negative aspects, the system has proved to be sustainable. There is also a fair portion of logic in most of the views and opinions, but some of them have become outmoded. The system is however, so well-rooted that the Portuguese have chosen to keep it and adjust it gradually instead of creating a new system. Some of the more recent changes are, however, somewhat significant:

Density of vines:

It used to be a virtue to have as few vines per ha as possible on the basis of the (false) logic that it was favourable for every vine to have a lot of space to grow on. Therefore plantations with more than 5,700 vines per ha (approx. 1.75 m² for every vine) were given no points at all. Today, we know that the more dense the planting, the more vertical the roots grow thereby giving the grapes a good possibility of obtaining a better quality. Therefore, 50 points are given to a lot with more than 4,000 vines per ha or more. Lots with less than 4,000 vines per ha are not given any points.

Soil and stoniness:

Originally, no points were given for grapes cultivated on granite soil, but now the rules are more flexible so that the soil is evaluated according to the following criteria:

Schist:	100 points
Transition between schist and granite:	-100 points
Granite:	-250 points
More recent deposits (alluvial):	-400 points

Age of vines:

Here, points are given for 5-year periods with annual adjustments. According to the most recent adjustments, only vines that are four years older than the graft (= a total of 5 years) can be used for Port. The evaluation is as follows:

5 - 25 years	30 points
more than 25 years	60 points

Altitude

In the original system, no grapes that were cultivated above 500 metres of the riverbed could obtain a beneficio. But improved techniques, and especially the recognition of the fact the river differentiates by around 90 metres within the demarcation area, has resulted in the Casa do Douro applying a new scale, which just as subtly divides the region into five sections but now allows vines at a height of 150-650 metres.

Productiveness

Originally, productivity was calculated according to produced liters of wine per 1000 vines, regardless of how widespread they had been planted, with 6,000 liters of must/wine per 1,000 vines as the ideal proportion.

When the wine country changed radically in the 1970'ies and the 1980'ies, experience showed that the quality improved when the vines were planted more densely with more vines per ha, and then the basis of calculation naturally had to be changed.

But this took its course of time, and it was not until the harvest of 1991 that Casa do Douro announced that the basis of calculation would be changed from litres of wine per 1000 vines to litres of wine per hectare. I remember that

BENEFICIO

Michael Symington said with some irony that Casa do Douro once again had made a big decision without asking the advice of any of the involved parties, and the very loud protests were even heard outside of Casa do Douro's HQ in Régua, by Casa do Douro's own sympathizers, the small winegrowers, so that the new rule was immediately turned to their benefit and became valid for all vineyards whether they had been classified as A or as F categories.

At first, the maximum yield was set at 5,500 litres per ha, but by decree of 24 December 1996, this figure was raised to max. 6,050 liters per ha.

The altitude of the vineyard is one of the most important aspects when the beneficio is calculated. The limit used to be 500 metres above the riverbed, but with the new planting and cultivation techniques, vines up to 150-650 metres are now allowed. Therefore, you will rarely see plantings at the top of a mountain. (Photo: HO)

Qualities of grapes

The grapes were divided into the following five categories:

Excellent:	150 points
Very good:	75 points
Good:	0 points
Bad:	150 points
Very bad.	-300 points

A total of 76 different grape varieties for Port Wine were approved, 44 blue and 32 green, of which, however, only 29 were recommended (15 blue + 14 green). See also page 106.

Da Fonseca's scale

The honour for conceiving this clever system, which gives points for the location of each lot in relation to the best wind direction, goes to engineer Álvaro Moreira da Fonseca who conceived it in 1947-48. By simple addition, each lot can obtain a maximum of 1680 points, and the quality and beneficio of the lot is indicated by the following scale, which was the basis of the classification of vineyards in the Douro Valley:

From 1200 points:	Class A
1001 - 1200 points:	Class B
801 - 1000 points:	Class C
601 - 800 points:	Class D
401 - 600 points:	Class E
201 - 400 points:	Class F

The lower limit was set at 201 points. Vineyards with less than 200 points could not be classified.

Every year in July the proprietors submit revised information to Casa do Douro (for example about the vines which are a year older), and Casa do Douro revises the register, on the basis of which new allocations are calculated. When the IVP has announced the total harvest of the year, it is a mere formality to allocate the beneficio to each lot.

Each lot is already classified according to points (Ficha Cadastral), and the coefficient is now calculated according to the class of the soil. Well into the 1970'ies, the following scale was applied:

Class A:	600 l wine per 1000 vines
Class B:	600 l wine per 1000 vines
Class C:	550 l wine per 1000 vines
Class D:	470 l wine per 1000 vines
Class E:	400 l wine per 1000 vines

Simple and easy, but a lot of paper work is involved as well as the diligent use of calculators, and as technology and an increasing viticultural awareness have improved the lower classifications, Casa do Douro has since the mid 1980'ies applied an adapted version of the system and given a relatively higher coefficient to the lots in the lower classes. The C/D classes were for example given the same coefficient as the A/B classes already in 1986. The gap between A/B and E has thus been reduced by 33% to 1.9%.

The very theoretical classification of land in the Douro Valley - one almost learns to love it - will have more and more significance on the trade of land in the future and less and less importance on yield and quality.

One could choose to say that the soaring technological development has outrun the dogmatic calculations, but the orthodox legislation has been right in one thing. No more guessing about some unregistered square meters in the corner of a forgotten lot. Thanks to a modern helicopter service, every single vine in the Douro Valley has been photographed from above, so even the most ingenious person can forget about expanding his area without permission.

Chapter 5

FROM GRAPE TO PORT

From grape to Port

Each year in August you can see the young, well-educated oenologist, António Américo da Rocha Graça race along the motorway from Gaia to Ferreira's steel building Quinta do Seixo by Pinhão on the way to evaluate his clones, analyse his polyphenols, correct the acid content and sort the colour pigments.

This is a language that even his mentor, Fernando Nicolau de Almeida, would hardly have understood a word of. For generations, tasting was much more important than measuring, and until the wine was rolled into the cellars of Gaia in the spring, the work involving next season's Port was a problem for the pickers, the quinta manager and the weather. It was said that Port was produced in the cellar. Viticulture and microbiology were just as uninteresting elements as were Web sites and moon landings. Actually, the word vinification was not introduced into the Portuguese language until 1799, centuries after the first bottle of Vintage Port had been sold in London. Why meddle in something, nature was much better at handling!

This attitude started to change during the 1960'ies and 1970'ies, and in the course of the 1990'ies the use of modern techniques exploded. A stale and timeless "bon mot" says: "We have seen a greater development in the last decade than in the past century". I even dare say that wine making in the Douro Valley stayed the same since the Roman invention and until sometime after the Second World War, compared to vinification on the verge of the new millenium.

Almeida's generation became the link between old times and new times. This generation would hardly understand the increased interest in binding, gascromatographic analyses or the use of robots for crushing the grapes, but it did live to accept both autovinification and using means such as tractors for getting the grapes.

But in spite of modern techniques and good intentions, the production of Port is often "full speed ahead" on the spot. If time ever really stands still in a wine district, it must be in the Douro Valley. In comparison with all other technical developement, also in other wine districts - the most important part of Port production is more or less the same today as hundreds of years ago. This is not due to romantic notions but only to the fact that the old methods are the best, the cheapest - or simply all you have at hand.

The world outside the Douro Valley has experienced both technological revolutions and angry machine breakers, but the long-legged tractors and the Italian presses of stainless steel have nothing to fear. Modern techniques have never tempted anyone in the environs of Pinhão to vandalism, for the machines are no threat to employment. On the contrary, the shortage of labour is becoming more and more visible, entailing that a quinta proprietor such as Bruce Guimaraens has been forced to reduce the number of

FROM GRAPE TO PORT

employees on Quinta do Panascal from 33 to 3 in only a few years. The young generation continues to move from the country to the cities, and the older generation chooses to accept the pre-pension schemes offered by the government.

This is why there is no fighting among grape pickers, as you see among the gipsies and young students in the South of France. You just do what you have done for generations when harvest time approaches: you tell the villagers what day the picking season starts, and they all make themselves available, choose a team leader and start working. Just as last year, the year before last, and so on ...

This tardiness of tradition puts a cushion of routines over the whole Port industry. It is a virtue to do as you have always done. And regardless that some technical subtleties may sneak into the approved procedures, the process from grape to Port is more or less unchanged and consists of the following steps:

1. **Picking**

2. **Measuring / Weighing**

3. **Destalking**

4. **Pressing**

5. **Maceration**

6. **Fermentation**

7. **Adding of alcohol**

The critical part of the process from grape to Port is carried out from the moment that the pressing starts and until fermentation is stopped (steps 4-6) which lasts for less than 48 hours. In this period of time, colour, aromatics and tannic acids are extracted, so it is no surprise the development in the vinification process is to be found in these steps. The steps before and after could be taken out of a textbook from the 19th century. They have not changed at all. The complete process looks as follows:

Ferreira's young oenologist, António Américo da Rocha Graça has his own little lab on Quinta do Seixo where he closely follows the development of the grapes before they are picked. One of the modern features in producing Port is that the oenologists have begun to take an interest in viticulture and participate in the winemaking long before the finished Port reaches Gaia. (Photo: HO)

FROM GRAPE TO PORT

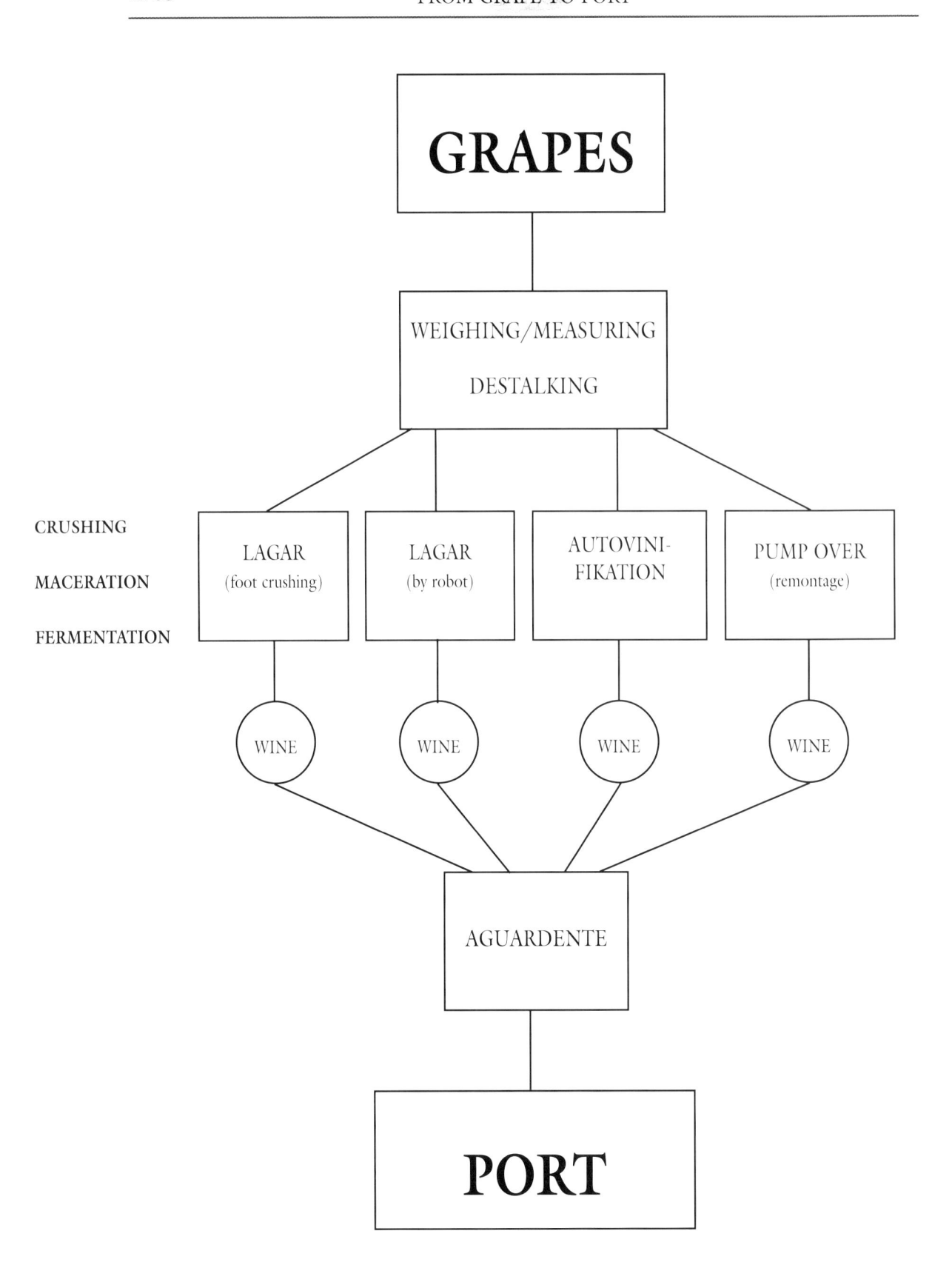

```
                        GRAPES
                           │
                   WEIGHING/MEASURING
                       DESTALKING
              ┌────────┬────┴────┬────────┐
CRUSHING      │        │         │        │
            LAGAR    LAGAR   AUTOVINI-  PUMP OVER
MACERATION  (foot    (by      FIKATION  (remontage)
           crushing) robot)
FERMENTATION  │        │         │        │
            (WINE)  (WINE)    (WINE)   (WINE)
              └────────┴────┬────┴────────┘
                       AGUARDENTE
                           │
                         PORT
```

FROM GRAPE TO PORT

1. Picking

When the quinta manager has given his go-ahead (usually in September), the picking season starts. The best pickers are the women who also pick the largest quantities. They cut off the clusters with a small knife, swiftly and easily, and throw them into small baskets whilst the unripe and bad grapes are cut off and discarded. In the olden days, the quinta manager would request that they sing to their work; this way they could not eat too many grapes while they were working. And if he was not on the lookout, a lot of grapes were eaten!

When the women's small baskets were full, their children would run down to the men with them and tip them into larger baskets which the men carried on their backs. They are called *cestos* and hold 60-70 kg of grapes. When the cestos are filled to the brim, the men walk down to the pick-up truck or maybe directly to the adega (where the grapes are pressed) and tip the grapes into the large stone vessels which in the language of Port are called *lagares*. This heavy work still takes place under song and music, loudly directed by the team leader.

Today, in the modern version the song and music are somewhat subdued - or blasted out from transistor radio - and the heavy cestos have been replaced by smaller plastic baskets, not so much in consideration of the men's backs but more to prevent the grapes from breaking and starting to ferment. Sometimes, a tractor is used to carry the grapes to the adega, and sometimes all the children are at school, so the work is carried out differently, but broadly, the picking is still carried out as it was one hundred years' ago, especially on the old terraces where there is no room for mechanization.

Harvest time. The men carry their heavy cestos filled with grapes to the adega on Quinta do Bomfim. (Photo: Symington)

2. Measuring / Weighing

According to the traditional method, the grapes were simply tipped out of the large cestos and into the lagar, but when foot crushing is applied today, the work is carried out more meticulously.

First the grapes are weighed, especially if they are paid by weight or when the grapes come from other locations. Then the sugar content and the Ph value are measured. This is especially important for the next step in the process when adjustment with tartaric acid is applied. If the grapes have rotted a bit, sulphur is added. The measuring and weighing is a very short process, for the grapes must never start to ferment before they have been crushed. The measuring of sugar content and Ph value is repeated several times during the whole process.

3. Destalking

Regardless of the method chosen, most people choose to destalk their grapes today before crushing, partly to prevent undesirable bitter substances in the must, and partly to prevent the crushers getting scratched on their feet. The destalking is done by machine and is a quick process just as it is in all other wine districts in the world who use the foot crushing technique, for today you can use the smart portable trimmers that relieve the foot crushers hard "corte" so that they can concentrate on the maceration.

4. Crushing

Lagares

The Romans' art of winemaking included cutting large vats of stone for the picked grapes. This practice was also seen in the Douro Valley where there was plenty of granite and clay schist available, and later, when the wine growers appeared in the Douro Valley, they took over the Roman vessels which they named lagares. Soon they had to build their own lagares which were cut into round or rectangular shapes (especially rectangular) so that it would be easier to crush the grapes by foot. For the same reasons they could not be too deep, usually 70-80 cm, sometimes a bit more, and with a capacity of 7,000-8,000 litres. But there are still lagares with a capacity of 5,000 - 20,000 litres. The modern lagares are made of stainless steel and which are very easy to clean and much easier to regulate.

Harvest is over. The grapes have been crushed by foot and the wine has been fortified. The lagares will not be used in the next 11 months until the next harvest. In this period they are used for other storage purposes. (Photo: HO)

5. Maceration

6. Fermentation

Now the waters are divided - as are the grapes. Regardless of the pressing method, you have to "get kicking", for it is vital that the grapes are crushed before fermentation, otherwise you will not be able to extract enough colour from them.

As you can see from the chart, there are four different ways of implementing the next three steps. The first two ways are carried out by means of open vessels (lagares) of stone or steel; the remaining two ways in closed steel tanks:

A. Traditional (foot) crushing

Apart from dreadful folkloric set-ups for the sake of the tourists, the traditional foot crushing of the grapes is used for one purpose only: it is by far the best method. No machine has yet been able to overtake the art of a couple of bare feet pressing and macerating the grapes without destroying them. "The art is to extract as much colour and aromatics out of the grapes as possible without extracting any herb-like or vegetable bitter substances", João Nicolau de Almeida explains and continues: "For that purpose I still need to find a method which is better than foot crushing".

Some producers maintain that they use foot crushing for financial reasons, but when even giants as Taylor's and Fonseca, who hardly need to rummage in their pockets for money, swear by foot crushing, there must be something about it. Nostalgia and romance? "My God", Bruce Guimaraens bursts out. "Try crushing grapes with us for a couple of days, and you'll feel the romance".

Naturally, most producers have adapted the traditional process to local needs, and you will never find two producers working in exactly the same way. But the classical procedure, which is still the backbone of foot crushing, is as follows:

When the lagar was filled up at 20-30 cm from the top, sulphur dioxide was added to prevent an undesirable fermentation. It was important that the lagar was filled quickly, in no more than a day, otherwise the grapes at the bottom of the lagar would start to ferment. And the men had absolutely no time to rest, having worked hard all day carrying the heavy cestos full of grapes to the lagar. They had to throw off their shoes and get to it straight away.

It took two well-grown men per pipe of Port for the first press, the so-called *corte do lagar*. The men formed a line in each end of the lagar with their hands on the shoulders of the man in front of him - so we really can say it was team work, physically hard team work - for the grape pulp was heavy and compact, the grapes were cold, and the stems scratched their legs.

But there was only one way to go - forward: upon the command of the team leader (usually the quinta manager) the rows now approached each other slowly, with their knees high and stepping down hard on their feet, until they met in the middle of the lagar. Then they went backwards again, or perhaps diagonally, lifting their knees up high and setting their feet down hard, again to the recruit-like shouts: left-right-left-right till they reached the back of the lagar again. Again they marched forwards: "Lift up your knees", "Right down with your feet", "Left-right-left-right".

This first destalking/crushing, which can now be executed both quickly and painlessly by means of portable trimmers, lasted for 2-4 hours, and it was extremely hard work physically - mind you after a long and exhausting day in the vineyard.

The "first pressing" was over, when the must started to flow freely, and the grapes had been transformed into a thick pulp. Then the pressing became easier - as well as a bit more fun, for at the command of "Liberdade", the men could let go of each other, and on the command of "Pisa livre" they could tread at their own pace. At this point the music commenced, either a harmonica or maybe a small band - so that the men could keep time with the music. Bottles of young wine were set on the edge of the lagar, so spirits went up and the wine went down their throats.

By now it was nighttime, and the must had to rest till the next morning to be able to maintain the approx. 28°C, which was necessary for fermentation to start. First, the must might be corrected with a bit of tartaric acid (identical to the grapes' own acid) to regulate the acid content in the must, and then the very tired feet could rest too.

The next morning they continued crushing to "Pisa livre" - without the music. The pattern was for example treading for three hours, rest for two hours, treading for three hours, etc. until fermentation was well on its way. A "foot test" of the fermenting must was carried out at regular intervals, signifying that one of the crushers would lift his foot up from the pulp and let the must run down from his heel into a small bowl, the contents of which were analysed in a saccharometre so that the quinta manager could estimate when the fermentation should be stopped.

During fermentation it was vital to keep the "cap" ("a manta") wet. The cap is formed during the fermentation, because carbon dioxide is created causing the grape skin to pop up to the surface and lie there in a 30-40 cm thick layer whilst the heavier grape seeds sink to the bottom of the lagar. If the cap dries out, undesirable bacteria is created. Therefore the cap must either be trodden down or wetted at regular intervals either by crushing ("mexa") or by some of the men walking on planks across the lagar and stirring the cap with long wooden sticks ("macacos") which look like paddles.

Some maintain this process, others shorten it and supplement with mechanical fermentation. They only apply foot crushing until the must is stabilized, then they pour or pump it into a fermentation tank. When the tank is full, the sugar

September 1997: Foot crushing is hard work, as here in the great lagar on Cálem's Quinta da Foz. This is the first hour of footwork, and the grapes are still a thick pulp. The grapes have not been destalked, so the tired crushers get their feet scratched. (Photo: HO)

content, Ph value and temperature are controlled, and yeast may be added.

The remaining dregs are gathered and pressed into segunda wine or used for mixing. Many prefer to pump-over the mixture of wine and aguardente. Under any circumstances, this process must take place as quickly as possible, as the sugar content continues to fall during the entire process. When mixing some oenologists like to add a bit of carbon dioxide.

In any case, the grapes are now reduced to must, which has become wine and is waiting to become dessert wine.

B. Modern pressing (by robot)

No other method is as gentle to the grapes and must as foot crushing. But feet require men, and they are becoming harder to get. Therefore, the major producers have for years experimented with a replacement for human feet, first through autovinification, later by means of robots! This is not a new idea. Renowned John Henry Smithes (Cockburn's) experimented with artificial foot crushing in the 1960'ies. Since then, Taylor's have struggled with a piston system at quinta de Vargellas, and both Barros at quinta de São Luiz and the new team at Quinta do Noval have tried out mechanical replacements of human feet, but it was not until recent years that Peter Symington's and his son Charles' efforts resulted in the Symington family introducing the state-of-art robot system at Quinta dos Malvedos for the harvest of 1998.

The stone lagar has been replaced by a steel lagar, which can pump 17 pipes of Port, and human feet have been replaced by four computerized plungers walking up and down whilst they move forward through the must, exactly like the crushers' bare feet. A hydraulic system tips the lagar so that the contents can be poured out sideways. This signifies that the addition of aguardente is much quicker compared to the traditio-

SEPTEMBER 1998: Robot at work on the Symington family's Quinta dos Malvedos. After a few years' of preparation Peter and Charles Symington introduced their invention which was a great success. Note that the large stone lagar has now been replaced by a smaller lagar of steel. (Photo: Symington)

nal technique when the lagar has to be emptied through the drain plug, and it also signifies that it is easier to empty the lagar of its remains of the "cap" more efficiently.

This advanced robot system is according to James Symington the closest to gentleness and efficiency you can get to human feet. The robot can be used both in the modern steel lagares and in the old granite lagares and will be further developed by Peter Symington in coming years.

Others are also trying out robots. Ferreira is for example planning a new vinification plant for the year 2000 by Quinta de Leda with both lagares and robots of steel.

C. Autovinification

In the 1960'ies, the depopulation in the Douro Valley brought about an improvement called *autovinification*. The depopulation was partly political, for the young men who had not moved to the cities were drafted as soldiers to participate in the Colonial war in Africa so there was nobody left to crush the grapes for the production of Port. Electricity had been introduced to the Douro Valley, but it was still too weak and unreliable and nobody dared invest in modern electrical pumping stations to replace bare feet. Sandeman and Cockburn's tried a makeshift pumping system (movimosto), but it was only adequate for light wines with a limited extraction.

Instead they invested boldly in a new machinery, namely the aforementioned autovinifiers, which I believe originate from Algiers.

Auto means "self". The point of this "ingenious device", as it is referred to in Sandeman's publication of 1990, is that the machine almost makes the grapes vinify by themselves so that a scrupulous maceration may take place avoiding the grape seeds, which contain the bitter oils, being pressed. When the grapes have turned into must, they are pumped up into the fermentation

Brandy or no brandy

There is credible proof from as early as 1678 that the wine from the Douro Valley was fortified with alcohol before leaving on its sea voyage to England (see page 22). This fortification was carried out by the wine merchants in Porto, but about 40 years later somebody suggested that the wine growers in the Douro Valley could stop the fermentation of the young wine by adding brandy.

This proof is written in the first known manual for wine production from 1720, Agricultura das Vinhas. It recommends adding 3 gallons of brandy for each pipe during fermentation to literally "intensify" the wine and improve its quality. However, this amount of alcohol was nothing compared to today. If we assume that the gallons are English gallons and we take a Douro pipe, this corresponds to 13,5 litres of brandy to 536,5 litres of wine, i.e. a proportion of 1:40 against a proportion 1:4 of today. The wine was more or less a "corrected" table wine than an actual dessert wine.

In the course of the 18th century, it became more and more common to add brandy in the wine - either during fermentation or before shipment - or both.

In his book "Vintage Port" (1999), professor Gaspar Martins Pereira quotes the German botanist, Heinrich Friedrich Link, who was doctor of zoology and botany at the University in Rostock and a "professional", the following passage from his travel diary of a trip to Portugal in 1797-99:

"There is no true Port Wine without brandy; this is not really a case of falsifying the wine, as this addition occurs from the moment of the first preparation. Those who cannot stand the taste of

brandy are forced to drink, often excellent, wine from these districts that a connaisseur might well prefer to all the wines destined for export. This, at least, contains no brandy. There is no doubt that the British taste and their preference for intoxicating beverages is the cause for the addition of such a great quantity of brandy."

The sweeter the brandy

Pereira also quotes Baron Forrester harcelating about the enormous quantities of brandy being used, 2-4 almudes (33-68 litres) in the fermentation process, then more brandy after fermentation, typically in November-December, and then more brandy in the spring before the wine was transported to Porto, and finally another shot of brandy before the shipment to England. Forrester wanted to re-introduce the old system and make "genuine" wines without adding brandy.

In the beginning of the 18th century it became common to add brandy during fermentation; in the beginning of the 19th century it had practically become tradition, and by the middle of the 19th century it simply became too much. By then, the producers at Porto had found out that the British market wanted sweet, intensified Port, and it was simply too tempting not to "improve" the Port by adding even more brandy.

Among Forrester's like-minded persons was Dona Antónia, who for Ferreira's Port dictated the use of as little brandy as possible. In Ferreira's archives, there is a letter from Dona Antónia to the quinta manager on Quinta do Vesúvio, dated 1854, in which she gives the following guidelines for the use of the brandy bottle: "Do not add brandy to the fermenting wine (...) this must only be done after the wines have well fermented, unless for strong practical reasons you are forced to do so, as there is no argument to counter to experience."

Professor Pereira estimates that nearly one almude per pipe was used for Ferreira's wines, but not until after fermentation. 40 years later this figure had risen to 3 almudes per pipe, probably upon the approval of Dona Antónia, but by that time Baron Forrester was no longer around.

The word "brandy" was used well into the 20th century to describe the added alcohol, maybe because it by tradition was added a bit of colour. Today, we use the colourless aguardente with neutral taste, so presumably we will never taste the same "hot stuff" as Sandeman's Vintage 1897, which due to a lack of brandy had been intensified with Scotch Whisky!

When the quantities for harvest have been determined, the aguardente is ordered. It is worth a lot of money, not only in utility value, but for every litre of aguardente missing, there would be 5 litres of Port less. That is why the aguardente is well looked after, as here where the full alcohol tank tempts noone to help themselves.

tank of stainless steel and the autovinification may begin. You could say that it is a sort of a mechanical coffee filter. The must is pumped into the tank at 3/4 of its capacity, and the tank is closed.

Inside the closed tank there are two pipes, one leading to the must and the other in a closed chamber at the top. When the fermentation starts, carbon dioxide rises into the top fourth of the tank and presses the must downwards. The must can now only rise up through the two pipes into the top chamber. When the pressure of the carbonic acid gas is released the must only goes down again into the top part of the tank where it is spread over the remains of the grape skin forming the cap (manta) on top of the must.

As long as there is enough carbon dioxide, the autovinification is a kind of time machine signifying that the process starts again and again copying the work of the crushers when they walked across the planks of the lagar and stirred the manta with their wooden macacos.

Price of grapes

If you do not have any grapes, you have to buy them. This is old wisdom for wine producers, so the novelty in the Douro Valley is that the free market conditions have resulted in a more liberal pricing, aiming at free prices for grapes in due course.

For many years, a special council decided the prices of grapes and must. This body consisted of 8 wine growers and 4 shippers, so it all remained on the premises of Casa do Douro. When Portugal became member of the EEC, the first democratization within Casa do Douro took place, and after a few years with "recommended" prices as a replacement for "minimum prices", the CIRDD has since 1997 suggested the annual prices of grapes.

The first autovinifiers were made of cement, but today they are of steel - for the system is still in use and can still lead to hours and hours of discussions at professional gatherings as to whether or not it is ingenious or old-fashioned to use this method.

The Symington family's Quinta do Bomfim also has a historic contribution to make. In 1964, a new adega was erected with modern autovinifiers, and foot crushing was seen for the last time in the great lagares which were removed in 1968, because the Symingtons were convinced that the autovinifiers would become a success. The Symingtons' state-of-art winery (see page 188) is equipped with both pump-over and autovinification systems.

The Barros family's new state-of-art vinification centre at Quinta de São Luiz has no lagares nor autovinification. Instead they use big, cylindric steel tanks with an automatic pump-over system and a piston system.

D. Pump-over (Remontage)

Once the electricity supply in the Douro Valley had been stabilized, modern electric pumps could be used for the significant maceration process. Croft's replaced their autovinifier at Quinta da Roêda in 1989 with a modern pump-over system, but others have kept their autovinifiers, and others again combine the two methods or even several other methods.

The pump-over system (remontagem) is known internationally under the French word *remontage* which means to pull up or to come up again. This is the same word you use about a rose blooming several times a year. It also "comes up" again and again. In the pump-over system, the must is pulled up and sprayed across the "cap" to keep it wet, and a significant extraction takes place. The grapes are pressed by means of slats, pads, plungers, or the like. The main thing is that

It is vital that the "cap" does not dry out during maceration and fermentation. To keep it wet many producers still use the traditional method and let their men "walk the plank" set out across the lagar where they stir the cap with their long sticks ("macacos") as you can see here at Quinta do Vesúvio. (Photo: Symington)

the process is carried out as gently and as quickly as possible. The vertical presses used to be adequate but they required manpower, and they have now been replaced by pneumatic presses (pneumatic means that the propellant is compressed air). The tank consists of an internal system with mechanical stirrers just like a kneading trough. They extract colour and extract from the grape skin and stir the cap, exactly the same procedure as in the lagar. Regardless of which pump-over system you use, the problem always remains the same: it is difficult to render the maceration effective in the short time available.

If you cannot prolong the period of time available, you must make the process more effective. Cockburn's have tried to heat the must to around 70° C for about 15 minutes, the so-called marmalade method, but it is only efficient for poorer qualities, and until today nobody else has tried to use this system. The first tanks of cement were replaced by epoxy tanks, and today the tanks are made of stainless steel. The most advanced tanks have conical bottoms enabling the young wine to be emptied from the bottom, as the skins are held at the top of the tank due to the pressure of the gas.

When fermentation is stopped, the wine is pumped into large vats. Electric pumps work on the fermenting must whilst the aguardente and the finished wine is pumped by means of centrifugal pumps. A regular temperature control is carried out during the entire process.

7. Adding alcohol

When the crushers had done their job, and the quinta manager had tasted and measured the wine to see that the fermentation process had used up the calculated amount of sugar, he shouted "Abrir o lagar". The plug in the bottom of the lagar was pulled, and the fermenting must ran through the hole and was mixed with aguardente and then continued into a lagaretta, which like a pipe contained 550 litres (440 litres of wine and 110 litres of aguardente).

Today, the process is a bit more detailed, but the principle is still the same. You measure the sugar content at regular intervals, and when the fermenting must has reached 6-8 Baumé, you include the remaining period of reduction of sugar from the time the aguardente is added till the fermentation is stopped, and the wine is ready to become a fortified wine. The "stop procedure" can last up to 5-6 days under temperature control and 2-3 days in lagares.

It is important that the fermenting must and the aguardente flow together smoothly. It is just like with mayonnaise. If the aguardente is added too soon, the Port will become too sweet and too dull. If it is added too late, the wine ceases fermenting and will not be sweet enough to become Port.

The Baumé and the time for adding the aguardente all depend on type, character, temperament - and Port house. Cockburn's and Martínez are a good example. They share the same owners, and the same team works behind the scenes, but they follow different philosophies. Martínez is by principle sweeter than Cockburn's, so the must for Martínez must not ferment too long compared to that of Cockburn's.

It all depends on which philosophy to follow, but in all circumstances the fermenting must must be added a colourless, neutral spirits of wine (77% aguardente) so that fermentation can be stopped and the wine and the spirits create a dessert wine with an alcohol percentage of approx. 18.5%. The proportion is still 1:4 with minor variations for the amount of alcohol which may vary with the degree of Baumé. The aguardente is colourless with a neutral taste. And it is therefore today quite misleading to call it a "brandy". It is not until recent years that the quality of the aguardente has been focused upon. Before it used to be the percentage that the producers focused on, and as its distribution was monopolized (Casa do Douro), the producers had no influence whatsoever on its origin or quality. The swindle back in 1973 (see page 70) left many scars, and as relations between the shippers and Casa do Douro were already rather tense, the shippers started to argue that the monopoly should be abolished.

This did not happen, however, until the EEC brought it up, and in 1992 Casa do Douro, and thus the Portuguese state, were deprived of their alcohol monopoly. Since then, anyone can buy freely, but many people have remained faithful to Casa do Douro, especially the small producers, but the shippers have formed their own wholesale society.

8. From fortified wine to Port

Until the Act of 7/5-1986 was introduced, fortified wine coming from the Douro Valley had to be transported to Vila Nova de Gaia's Entreposta to be sold and exported as Port. The absurdity was that all Port had to be produced in Gaia, but the few vines in Gaia could actually only produce Vinho Verde.

Today, the producers may choose if they want to sell and export direct from the Douro Valley or from Gaia. At this point, due to practical and financial reasons only Noval, who is one of the major producers, produce Port in the Douro Valley and sell and export it direct.

All other important producers still send the new dessert wine to Gaia in the spring after harvest. The novelty is that they are now allowed to call it Port even before it reaches Gaia.

Chapter 6

PORT TYPES

Port types

After all the toil and footwork, the grapes had now been transformed into a fortified wine and it was not merely figuratively that this new fortified wine fell into a slumber in the previous chapter on its quinta in the Douro Valley. It was really allowed a beauty sleep during the long winter. Only recent generations of oenologists have begun to visit the place of cultivation and ageing regularly during their long process for more than just curiosity.

Producers who do not who vinify and age Port in the Douro Valley and ship it directly from the Valley have to transport the fortified wine to Vila Nova de Gaia. This is a historical transportation, which for many years was carried out by means of slow oxen, but when the river became navigable from well east of Pinhão in the 1790'ies, the flat-bottomed barcos rabelos became a quicker and easier solution. One hundred years' later they were replaced by the railway which was then replaced by tank lorries using the motorway that is the most common means of transportation today. Somewhat unromantic, but quite efficient.

Today, transportation is merely a banal routine with a driving time of a couple of hours and a regular temperature control all the way. But when the barcos rabelos were used, the navigation time was several days, and it was vital that the pipes with the young wine arrived to Gaia as soon as weather permitted, and especially before temperatures got too high. This required men aboard, men on the banks to pull the boats, and men for the loading and unloading. But at that time, men were available, so it was no problem.

The first impression

When the pipes arrrived to Gaia, they were rolled ashore and placed in the lodges of the Port houses which quite practically were situated close to the river. Here, they were counted and recorded, and when they had been rolled well into place, each pipe meticulously separated from the other, and the wine had rested a bit, the first tastings could be extracted. At this stage, the wine was still young and undrinkable, often quite spirituous with an aggressive tannin. You needed both a good nose and a strong leathery mouth to be able to evaluate it!

But it was important to evaluate at this stage. The wine was now close to six months old, and the responsible taster could easily taste - or especially smell - himself to a realistic evaluation of the quality. It was still too soon to dream about Vintage or Colheita, but from the bottom of the scale, the taster could already sort out the pipes which would only be adequate for the more inferior qualities - and then all he could do was wait and see.

This process has not changed much. Today, modern techniques and measuring equipment signify that the taster (and the lab) can get an idea of

The slim, flat-bottomed "barcos rabelos" were for centuries the most effective means of transportation for Port Wine from the Douro Valley to Gaia. Hundreds of pipes of good Port have been carried safely to the harbour, before the days of the railway and lorries made them redundant. Now they are used for tourism and for the annual Regatta on the Douro river. (Photo: HO)

the potential of the wine quicker and more accurately, just by knowing the sugar content, pH-value and the characteristics of the tannins, but it is still too soon to think about the so-called organoleptic analyses.

And regardless of modern techniques, you will seldom hear a taster pronounce his verdict on the quality of a vintage at this early stage. Maybe experience has made him wary, for one of Gaia's horror stories is about George Sandeman, who in 1866 during an inspection of his vineyards in the Douro Valley was so depressed when he saw how poor the quality of his grapes was that he spontaneously said: "There will be no Vintage this year"!

But then rain fell and hot weather followed, the grapes were harvested, and the vintage was historic and excellent - except for Sandeman's. For a British Port shipper sticks to his word, and Sandeman made no Vintage Port in 1866!

There is a similar horror story about J.R.Wright from Croft's concerning the vintage year of 1868.

A quick decision

The Act on the different Port types more or less pinpoints when the major decisions are to be made. Tawny types first of all require patience. Both the 10-years, 20-years, 30-years, and over 40-years Tawnies can be mixed at any time, and Colheitas (Tawny with year of harvest) can be bottled at any time after approval and ageing.

The Ruby types are more critical. A Late Bottled Vintage is, however, more flexible in it time limits, but Vintage Port is something quite different. First, it has to be forwarded for approval by the Port Wine Institute between January 1 and September 30 of "its second year after harvest" according to law, i.e. when the wine is in its third year. Then, it has to be bottled between July 1 of the second year and June 30 of the third year after harvest. The Act is not crystal clear in its wording, but the meaning is illustrated in the time diagram on page 134-135. It was naturally only realistic to legislate the actual time for bottling (and thus for ageing) when it became mandatory to bottle quality Port in Portugal after 1973.

When I ask capacities in their field, such as Gordon and Bruce Guimaraens, about when they consider a vintage year to be of Vintage quality they both answer: "When the wine is 14-15 months old. And then you have to act quickly - otherwise you will end up with a Late Bottled Vintage instead"!

It sounds more complicated than it actually is. For the responsible tasters/blenders, the time diagram is as follows for the vintage of 2000:

2000 S O N D

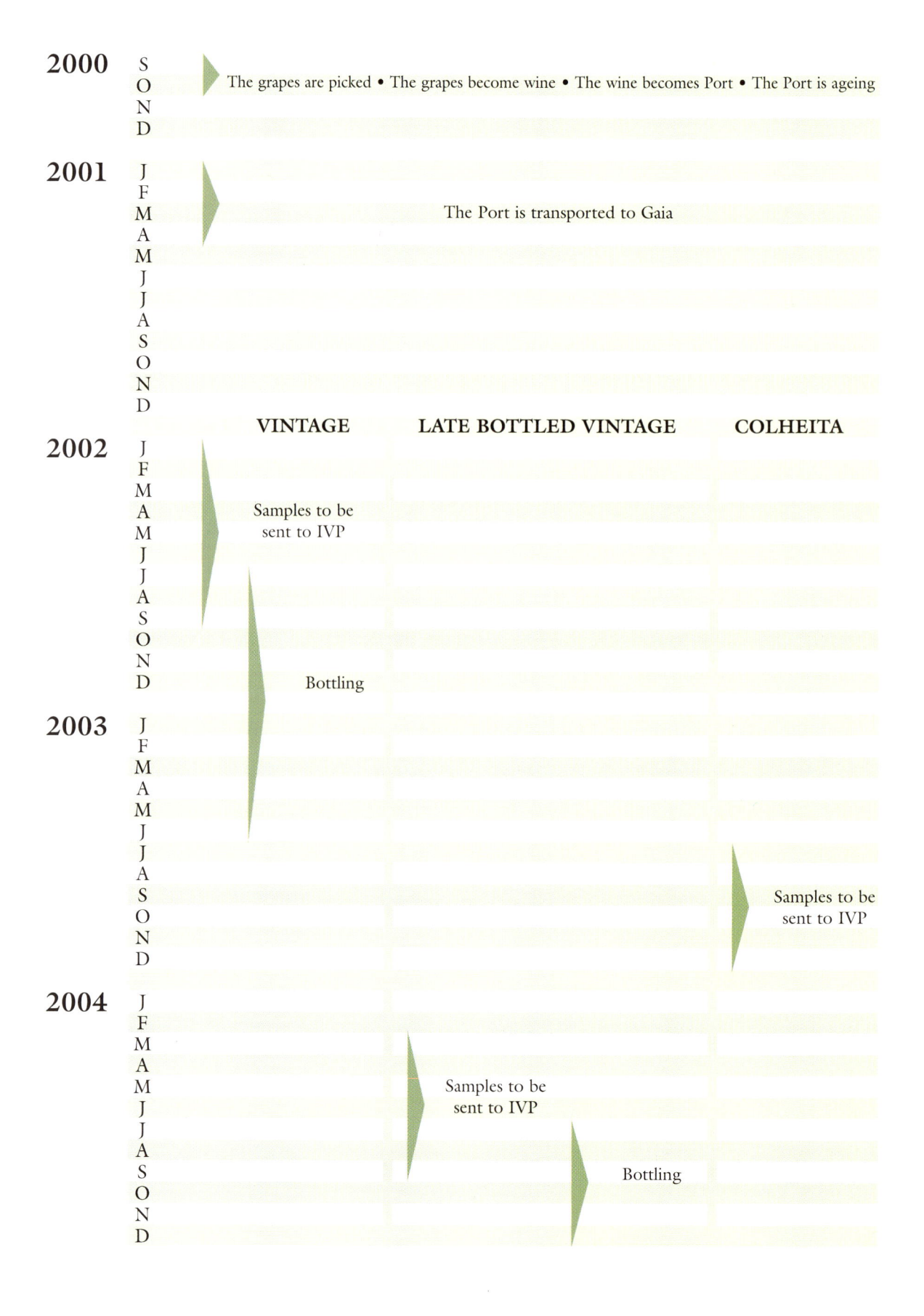

The grapes are picked • The grapes become wine • The wine becomes Port • The Port is ageing

2001 J F M A M J J A S O N D

The Port is transported to Gaia

	VINTAGE	**LATE BOTTLED VINTAGE**	**COLHEITA**
2002 J F M A M J J A S O N D	Samples to be sent to IVP Bottling		
2003 J F M A M J J A S O N D			Samples to be sent to IVP
2004 J F M A M J J A S O N D		Samples to be sent to IVP Bottling	

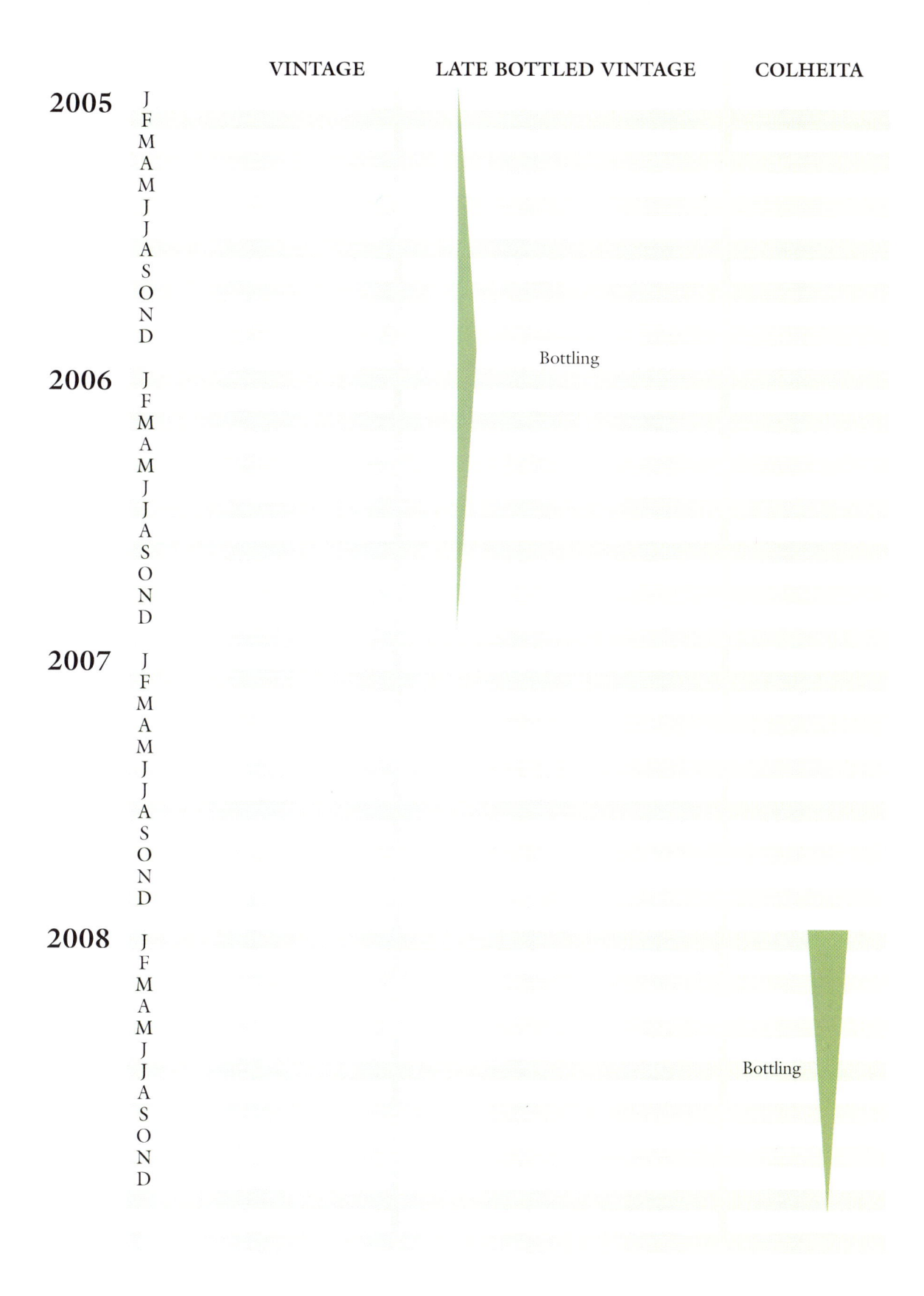

	VINTAGE	LATE BOTTLED VINTAGE	COLHEITA
2005 J F M A M J J A S O N D			
2006 J F M A M J J A S O N D		Bottling	
2007 J F M A M J J A S O N D			
2008 J F M A M J J A S O N D			Bottling

It is practical both for the tasters as for the producers and the consumers to distinguish between the fruity Ruby types, which have a short ageing in wood (Vintage, Late Bottled Vintage, Vintage Character, Crusted Port, Ruby, etc.), and the Tawny types, which have an impression of wood and smoke from a long ageing in casks (Colheita, 10-years, 20-years, 30-years, and over 40-years Tawny, Old Tawny, Tawny).There are four types of Port that are legislated in detail with regard to ageing and bottling and which therefore require samples to be forwarded for approval. These four types are the so-called "Quality Ports": two Ruby types and two Tawny types:

Vintage Port
Late Bottled Vintage
Tawny with year of harvest (Colheita)
Tawnies with indication of age (10-years, 20-years, 30-years, and over 40-years)

All other types, including Vintage Character, Crusted Port, Full Port, White Port, etc., are so-called undefined types entailing no special obligations. They therefore vary a lot in quality and in structure from one producer to another.

Only the aforementioned four types of Quality Ports are defined in detail in the Act and have to be approved by the Port Wine Institute at specific times, but the 10-years, 20-years, 30-years, and over 40-years Tawnies may be approved at any time. But all Ports, regardless of type, quality and colour must by definition be forwarded for approval to the Port Wine Institute (see page 322-323).

The following still applicable Act, approved by the Port Wine Institute's Board on 27 November 1973, and brought into effect on 1 January 1974, entailed that it was no longer possible to store and bottle quality Port outside of the demarcated area (including Gaia). And thus, the vintage year of 1970 was the last important Vintage Port, bottled by wine merchants in Bristol, Glasgow, or Copenhagen for that matter.

Farmer

Blender

Taster

Showman

There is no use for a traditional winemaker in the Port business, for Port is not about the art of winemaking, but about the art of tasting and blending - and about much more. The modern taster/blender must be an expert on theory, but he must also be extrovert, for first he has to prepare and make his Port, and then he has to help sell it.
Here he is photographed in four of his most important functions:

Top left: In the field: Modern philosophy says that without viticulture there would be no viniculture at all. On the photo you can see Croft's John Burnett inspecting the grapes at Quinta da Roêda. (Photo: HO)

Top right: In the tasting room: Whilst the Port maturates, and before and after mixing, samples are extracted at regular intervals, which are stacked meticulously in small glasses and bottles in the tasting room. Ramos-Pinto's João Nicolau de Almeida has gathered quite a collection of samples from the most recent vintage years. (Photo: HO)

Bottom left: In the cellar: Even though he is in his Sunday's best, David Guimaraens knows every drop in the cellar at Taylor's and Fonseca. (Photo: HO)

Bottom right: At the wine festival: Today, the blender's function continues into the sales outlets, for the great Port-drinking world would rather see the oenologists here than sales personnel and representatives. Bruce Guimaraens (Fonseca, Taylor's) is a welcomed guest any time a good Port is presented. (Photo: HO)

7296
612 L
0587
604 L
4932
627
2995
662
3395
645 L
4185
629
4042

FONSECA
VINTAGE PORT
FONSECA
PORT
FONSECA
VINTAGE PORT
FONSECA
BIN 27
PORT

VINTAGE PORT

THE ACT OF 1/1 1974:

DEFINITION

This is a port - Vinho do Porto - of one harvest produced in a year of recognized quality, with exceptional organoleptic characteristics, dark and full bodied, with very fine aroma and palate and which is recognized by the Instituto do Vinho do Porto (I. V. P.) as having the right to the description "Vintage" and corresponding date, within the terms of the following regulation.

REGULATION

a) To obtain approval of the description "VINTAGE" a bottle of the wine must be submitted to the I.V.P between the 1st January and the 30th September of the second year as from the year of the harvest.

b) The stock of this Port must be declared at the time approval is requested and a current account will be duly opened.

c) The bottling of the approved wine must be between the 1st July of the second year and the 30th June of the third year, as from the year of the respective harvest; preferably the classic dark coloured glass bottle should be utilized.

§ - The I.V.P must be informed of the date when the bottling of this wine is completed and two reference bottles must be submitted.

d) This wine will be sold exclusively in bottle, bearing the "Selo de Garantia" and only with the prior approval by the I.V.P of the labels and presentation, within the normal terms governing the use of the "Selo de Garantia"

e) The main label should indicate clearly the brand, the year of the harvest and description "VINTAGE", quite apart from any other supplementary details which may also be duly approved.

f) While this regulation essentially safe-guards the word "VINTAGE", the descriptions "TIPO VINTAGE", "VINTAGE STYLE" and "VINTAGE CHARACTER", or similar approved translations, are permitted on labels or publicity material, but it is expressly forbidden to mention dates or to make any other reference which could cause confusion with genuine "VINTAGE", and even these descriptions are permitted only for wines whose organoleptic qualities so justify.

g) It is expressly forbidden to use the word "VINTAGE" accompanied by the date of harvest for any other Ports which are not referred to in this section, or in following one, which refers to "LATE BOTTLED VINTAGE"-"L.B.V."

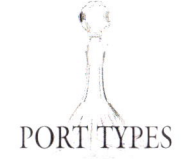

Comments:

To Declare Vintage Port

Any producer has the right to make a Vintage Port every year. No special permissions are needed, and there is no official body advising for or against this issue. But the impulse for too great an activity is reduced in that every vintage year must be approved via analyses and sensory tasting (blind tasting) at the Port Wine Institute.

Origin

As mentioned on page 41, experts are still arguing about the year of the first real Vintage Port. However, this is a fuss about nothing, for a catalogue from Christie's records the year 1765 as the first vintage year, whilst Warner Allen believes that the year of 1775 is the first Vintage deserving the right to be called a Vintage Port.

And the year of 1775 is actually considered the start of a somewhat systematic production of bottled Vintage Ports, but they were presumably 3-4 years' old before they were bottled - more or less as LBV's today. This is documented in a letter from John Croft dated 1788, in which he writes that Port should mature for around four years in casks before bottling. A regular bottling of Vintage Port at around two years after production was not seen until around 1890, but this was a practice without any legislation to back it up.

The first Vintage Port bearing the name of the bottler was sold in 1800 (see page 41), and the first Vintage Port bearing the name of the producer is Warre's 1805, sent to Christie's for sale on 18th November 1812 at 56 shillings a case containing 12 bottles. In the catalogue, you see for the first time an indication of two dates for Vintage Port: the production year and the year of bottling for further ageing in laid bottles.

If we compare a passage from A. Henderson's "History of Ancient and Modern Wines", published in 1824:

"When it [the new vintage] arrives in this country, it is of a dark purple or inky colour, in a full rough body, with an astringent bitter-sweet taste, and a strong odour and flavour of Brandy. After it has remained some years longer in the wood, the sweetness, roughness and astringency of the flavour abate; but it is only after it has been kept ten or fifteen years in the bottle that the odour of the brandy is completely subdued, and the genuine aroma of the wine is developed."

(Translated by the author after Sarah Bradford: "The Story of Port", 1983, p. 41)

some of the characteristics which we still use to define Vintage Port are used in the turbulent years in the beginning of the 19th Century, in spite of the Napoleon Wars and the Continental System: a precise indication of vintage year, the bottle (no more pipes), laid bottles, and keeping qualities.

Vintage - only moderately!

In 1809 George Sandeman called the vintage year of 1797 "the best port vintage ever known", but a wider use of vintage is not seen until the vintage year of 1820 and more systematically as per the vintage year of 1834. At this time, the word Vintage was still a British phenomenon. The Portuguese producers used the word Novidade to characterize the young wine until the 19th Century, some even continued until well after 1900. This word was used for the last time when the Act of 1 January 1974 was put into force. Several Portuguese producers did not think much of the British "young wine" anyway, as it had not laid in casks for very long and was therefore considered as an unfinished product. The prices on the global market made them both accept and even start using the English word for this phenomenon.

When the first legislation had been introduced on the production of Vintage Port (by decree issued 2 March 1932) it was obviously addressed to the British market. The wording of the Act defines Vintage Ports as: "the very best wines from a given superior quality harvest (Vintage), recognised as such by the Viticultural Committee of the Douro, and may be exported to Great Britain with a minimum age of eighteen months". The "minimum age of eighteen months" is also the first exact definition clearly distinguishing Vintage Port from LBV.

Considering the fact that Vintage Port is the most prestigious Port type, as well as the one giving the best price, one should think that a producer would rather make as many Vintage Ports as possible. However, this is not the case. The market situation very much decides how often a Vintage Port is declared, and it is quite common to see potential Vintage Ports be declassified by a producer to avoid overheating the market or to maintain the special magic of Vintage Port.

As an example, Peter M. Cobb, once told me that Cockburn's after the great vintage year of 1994 did not declare the vintage year of 1995 as Vintage Port even though the quality was superb. Instead they settled with declaring their Port as a Single Quinta Vintage Port, solely due to the market conditions. "It is not opportune to declare Vintage Port two years in a row", he told me.

It was the English who started to call the Vintage ports by this name. Far into the 20th Century most Portuguese houses used the word "Novidade", which means the new wine. Burmester's, 1920, on the photo is, however, not a Vintage Port as we know it, but a Reserva, i.e. a Colheita (a Tawny with year of harvest).

PORT TYPES

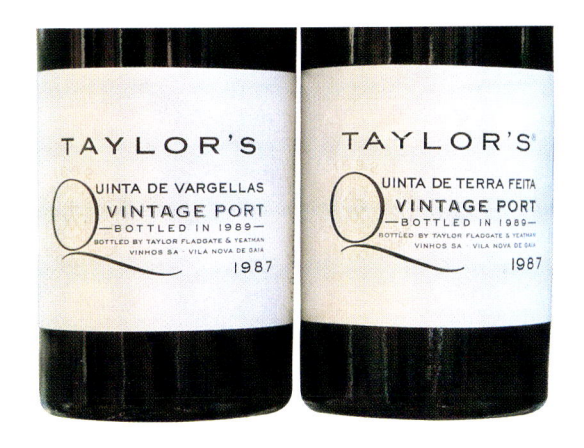

The year of 1987 was a good but not excellent year. Taylor's did not make a Vintage Port bearing the Taylor name but used most of their grapes from their two Quintas, Vargellas and Terra Feita, to make two Single Quinta Vintage Ports, which are excellent wines, and which in quality and development range between LBV and Vintage Port. (Photo: HO)

Single Quinta Vintage Port

A Single Quinta Vintage Port (SQVP) is, as the last two words say a Vintage Port and must abide by the law on Vintage Ports. It is more difficult to explain the first two words: Single Quinta. A SQVP should be made from grapes from the Quinta mentioned on the label - and only from this Quinta - but there is no legislation to cover this issue and not all producers rise to the occasion.

Origin

The first known Single Quinta Vintage Port (SQVP), as we define it, was Taylor's Quinta de Vargellas, 1910. It was presumably produced in a private bottling session for the owners, which was quite common, and was therefore never sold on the market. Old wine catalogues tell us that as early as in 1820 you could buy wines bearing the name of Vargellas on the label, but the content of these bottles is unknown; they might not even contain a Vintage Port, or even be made from grapes from the Quinta de Vargellas.

Instead, according to British tradition, the first commercial, genuine SQVP was Taylor's Quinta de Vargellas, 1958, which was produced after a major production of good grapes, which they did not want to use for a Vintage Port bearing Taylor's name. As there was a lack of Vintage Ports in the 1960'ies, it was only natural to cultivate this type of wine, which with Bordeaux as the ideal was considered a very decent and convenient second-class wine. As some producers chose to lay it in bottles and sell it after 8 or 10 years, it was nearly or completely drinkable by the time it was exported.

Denmark has a humourous contribution to the discussion of the first SQVPs. In one of our oldest Danish books on wine, Peter Bourgogne's "Et godt Glas Vin" (A good glass of wine) from 1935, he says the following: "The Vintage idea has been further developed, i.e. pure, unmixed wine from the same vintage year and from one and the same property. This property is called a "Quinta" in Portuguese. There are not many of them but I have seen Feuerheerd's "Quinta de la Rosa" a few times, rightly called the Château Margaux of the Douro. I have also encountered a few other excellent wines, da Silva's "Quinta Noval" and especially former vintage years of Kopke's "Quinta Roriz".

When Peter Bourgogne says "especially former vintage years" in a book from 1935, we assume that there must have been Single Quinta Ports on the Danish market for quite a few years, and they were most probably considered as Vintage Ports, also by Peter Bourgogne: wines made from grapes from the quinta mentioned on the label and from the same vintage year. But we do not know this, as little as he may know what was in those bottles. The definition of SQVPs is vague and will remain so until legislation sets the guidelines to follow.

Confusion of styles

When the SQVPs started to manifest themselves as prestigious wines "en miniature" in the 1970'ies and 1980'ies, a definition of these wines naturally started to form. In the British wine magazine Decanter, editor Colin Parnell told his readers in 1986: "Graham who own Quinta dos Malvedos are establishing the word Malvedos as a brand, and the word Quinta is no longer visible on the label. Can we assume that this wine is 100% from this Quinta"?

In the October issue of Decanter, W.A. Warre replies that the ideal situation would be that the denomination SQVP or even Single Quinta Port be reserved for wines from grapes which had been cultivated on the quinta itself. In his family they had always used the expression Single Quinta Vintage Port meaning a Vintage Port made from the best grapes of the quinta, the basis upon which the final Vintage Port would be produced. As the quinta's grapes disappeared from the family label, they saw no cause for using the quinta name.

The fog did not clear this time, and exactly the Quinta dos Malvedos has for several years been the most fervid topic of discussion among SQVPs. Certainly, in the Symington family's time the word Quinta has never been placed on the bottles, only Malvedos, but earlier it was only natural to believe that this was a Single Quinta Port from the Malvedos property. You would never have guessed that the grapes from Malvedos were usually of such a poor quality that Colin Graham had to buy grapes for Graham's Vintage Port from Quinta das Lages in the valley of Rio Torto, and that the major part of the grapes for the wine bearing Malvedos' name came from vineyards in The Rio Torto?

The Symington family bought Malvedos in 1970 but regretted this investment a year later, and it was not until a radical re-laying of the fields and the winery that the Quinta dos Malvedos started to yield grapes for Graham's Vintage Port in the mid 80'ies. James Symington tries to lift the fog with the following contribution:

"Graham's has never marketed a wine as "Quinta dos Malvedos" but wine from the quinta has been bottled using the Malvedos name since the 1930s. In the 1950s some wine from the Rio Torto was included in the Malvedos blend because the wine production at the quinta had fallen so much. Grapes were also bought from properties adjacent to Malvedos but which did not belong to the quinta at that time.

Production of the quinta is now [1998] the equivalent of 24,000 cases of Port which is much more than has ever been required for the Malvedos bottling which is normally about 7,000 cases of the best wine produced on the property. Graham's Malvedos is therefore today 100% a single quinta Port."

In another letter to me [1999] he underlines that "all the wine sold under the Malvedos name has been sourced only from the quinta since the middle 1980's and there are no plans to change the successful "Malvedos" name to "Quinta dos Malvedos" on the label."

SQVP - SQ(Estate Bottled)VP

The debate about SQVP became really fervid when the British producers were confronted with the owners of the Quinta-producing wines, especially Quinta do Côtto. Until the amendment to the Act on 7 May 1986, these wines were not allowed for exportation, as they did not come from Vila Nova da Gaia. The wines from these quintas were always SQVPs as they were produced from grapes from the quinta, on the quinta and also bottled on the quinta, so especially Miguel Champalimaud (Quinta do Côtto) was furious with the British shippers and with the system, and he maintained stubbornly that "the first quinta-bottled and exported bottle of Vintage Port came here from the Quinta do Côtto and was our vintage year 1982". However, already in 1978, Quinta do Infantado had produced the first SQVP which was also bottled in the Douro Valley.

But the British shippers, with the Symingtons at their head, were of the opinion that grapes from one single quinta rarely gave an excellent wine. Mixing was necessary so that the grapes from a hot quinta were mixed with grapes from a cold quinta. Michael Symington explained to me that even though a Single Quinta Wine may be an excellent and interesting wine, the ideal Vintage Port is obtained via mixing. When I discussed this issue with Croft's managing director, John Burnett, in the summer of 1998, he put it even more bluntly: "In a SQVP you never obtain the same depth and length as in a Vintage Port".

João Roseira (Quinta do Infantado) did not have anything to mix with, so he understandable said that mixing was not necessary and that the only reliable SQVP was a Single Quinta Estate Bottled Vintage Port, e.g. from Quinta do Infantado.

The amendment of the Act in 1986 has mollified the parties, but a detailed definition and description of SQVP is still desirable, and due to competition and to consumer demands a SQVP should only use grapes from the quinta giving its name to the wine and not as today when you may consider the quinta name as a brand.

In 1999, the Port Wine Institute started to prepare a set of clear guidelines for Single Quinta Ports, including SQVP. The aim is to reserve the quinta name for wines which are solely produced by a given quinta's grapes and to prohibit the use of the quinta name for table wines. But at the conclusion of this book in October 1999 we have yet to see the first words of the new procedures.

Vintage and SQVP in the same year

As the philosophy behing the SQVP is to produce a miniature version of a genuine Vintage Port, because the grapes, in spite of a good quality, are not adequate for a Vintage Port, or because the market conditions are such that the producers do not want to make a Vintage Port, it is absurd to imagine that a producer can make both a Vintage Port and an SQVP in the same year. This does occur, however, as in 1994 when Ramos-Pinto chose to celebrate Quinta do Bom Retiro's salvation from expropriation (see page 270f) by launching both an ordinary Vintage Port and a SQVP from Bom Retiro.

LATE BOTTLED VINTAGE PORT (LBV)

THE ACT OF 1/1 1974:

DEFINITION
This is a Port - Vinho do Porto - of only one harvest produced in a year of good quality, with good organoleptic characteristics, red and full bodied, of good aroma and palate and which is recognized by the I.V.P. as having the right to use the description "LATE BOTTLED VINTAGE" or "L.B.V.", within the terms of the following regulation.

REGULATION
a) To obtain the approval of the description "LATE BOTTLED VINTAGE" or "L.B.V." a bottle of the wine must be submitted to the I.V.P. to be approved, between the 1st March and the 30th September of the 4th year, counting from the year of the harvest.

b) The stock of this Port must be declared at the time it is approved, and a current account will be duly opened.

c) The bottling must be made between the 1st July of the 4th year and the 31st December of the 6th year, counting from the year of the respective harvest.

§ - The I.V.P. must be informed of the date when the bottling of this wine is completed and two reference bottles must be submitted.

d) The sales of this quality are to be made exclusively in bottle under the "Selo de Garantia" and subject to the prior approval by the I.V.P. of the respective labels and presentation, within the general conditions governing to use of the "Selo de Garantia".

e) The main label should indicate clearly the brand, the year of the harvest and that of bottling, together with the description "LATE BOTTLED VINTAGE" or "L.B.V." which description must appear in one line only, and be printed in the same type and colour.

Comments:

As you can see from the calendar on page 134-135, an LBV (Late Bottled Vintage) is a kind of a "Port of Regret" which can be produced from grapes from one vintage year after the deadline for the production of Vintage Port is exceeded - thereby the name Late Bottled Vintage.

On the basis of this philosophy it seems to make sense to use the exclusive name Vintage in connection with a LBV, but opinions vary, as they always have. Vintage signifies prestige, in spite of the late bottling, some say. Others say that the "bastard" ruins the prestige, then rather give it the denomination LB (Late Bottled) or LBP (Late Bottled Port) instead of the prestigious LBV.

Especially in the 1980'ies there were times of fervid discussions, but even though the Port Wine Institute tried to find a compromise in a neutral denomination, the opinions among the producers differed, and the Act has not been amended since 1973.

Origin

There are varied opinions as to whom produced the first bottle of LBV. According to the definition of the existing law text, it was a kind of Vintage Port, which was produced from the 1770'ies up until the 1890'ies, and in some cases into the 20th Century, but was actually an LBV, bottled after 4-6 years of ageing in casks. But as a "Port of Regret" and thus as the type to replace Vintage Port, this phenomenon is much younger. Here are some of the explanations:

Van Zeller's (prev. Quinta do Noval):
"The first LBV was a Quinta do Noval, and it was practically provoked. What happened was that in the beginning of the 1940'ies, i.e. in the beginning of the Second World War, colonel Jack Rutherford, managing director of the wine import company, Rutherford, Osborne & Perkin, which was situated in England, decided to save some unsold Vintage Port on pipe instead of bottling it. The colonel and the colonel's wife were in the good habit of sharing a half bottle of Vintage Port every evening, but it was difficult to procure good Port during the war. After a couple of years in casks, his Vintage Port was much more drinkable with a lot of character.

His company were agents for Noval, so after the war he decided along with Luis Vasconcelos Porto, to make an experiment. This resulted in the Quinta do Noval LBV, 1954. The colonel's idea was the start of a new Port type. But the other shippers were sullen, so in 1965 Noval dropped the "V" and called his wine LB, the first time for his vintage 1961."

Huyshe Bower (Taylor's):
"The first LBV was Taylor's, vintage 1965, which was bottled and released in 1969. Until then, Taylor's had called the same wine for "Vintage Reserve", but others, like Graham's, called it "Late Bottled Port" without the word Vintage.

For more than 10 years, Taylor's were the only ones making LBV, and I believe that if you make LBV and Vintage Port in the same vintage year, it would be easier for the consumers to taste and understand the difference between Vintage and LBV. The vintage year of 1983 is a good example of this.

Taylor's LBV is made from the best grapes remaining after the Vintage Port has been produced either under the company name or as Quinta de Vargellas SQVP."

Paul Symington (in "Decanter", January 1994):
"Dow's produced and exported an LBV back in 1962 (Dow's do not make traditional LBV anymore), and Warre's shipped a traditional LBV 1969,

both bottled after 4 years in casks. These types had been produced for years, so only the denomination was new."

Supplemented by Ian D.F. Symington:
"We know of a Late Bottled Vintage from at least 1945, perhaps even from before the War, and even though it was a reduced production. Back then we called it "Warre's 19XX Vintage", "Late Bottled in 19YY". It had been bottled four years after and not two years after as a genuine Vintage Port. The fundamental difference between Warre's LBV and the others is that Warre's Port is bottled unfiltered as 4-years-old Ports and is then maturated in bottles for several years before it is sold. So it is the lack of filtration and the ageing in bottles which gives the traditional LBV it unique style and nose".

Jorge Rosas (Ramos-Pinto):
"The first LBV was Ramos-Pinto, 1927 which was made for the Brazilian market. Due to the hot weather, they wanted a lighter wine than Vintage so we made it as a normal Vintage but left it to mature for a further two years before bottling it. We still have bottles from the 1920'ies in the cellar and the Port Wine Institute has recognised that we were there first".

The Port Wine Institute confirms that they consider Ramos-Pinto, 1927, to be the first recorded LBV, but this does not exclude the fact that there could have been other LBVs' produced before 1927.

Confusion of styles

In an attempt to handle the new phenomenon, the Port Wine Institute had already in 1965 given a temporary permission to bottle a 3-6 year old vintage wine with the denomination Late Bottled Vintage, if certain requirements as to quantity, control, registration and bottling were maintained, but it was not until the Act of 1 January 1974 that one could distinguish between two types: Vintage Port and LBV. And this is what causes the confusion.

LBV was the result of market demands. In the 1970'ies, a Port type was needed to relieve and replace Vintage Port, especially a type that resembled Vintage, that would be drinkable at an earlier stage, was cheaper and did not need to be decanted.

Even after the Port Wine Institute had prepared the legislation for LBV, the producers have been making LBV's in all possible ways. The Symington family and others aim at the "British" taste with deposit (as Vintage Port and the popular Crusted Port) and skip filtration. Warre's, Smith-Woodhouse, and Ramos-Pinto are good examples of the style that the producers call "traditional LBV". Other producers prefer a friendlier and more unsophisticated style and make cold-stabilized and filtered LBV's which are more drinkable and can be drunk at an earlier stage, for example Taylor's and (partially) Fonseca.

The different styles also signify different keeping qualities. And other things being equal, the unfiltered LBV's have better keeping qualities, whilst the filtered LBV's by definition are drinkable when they are bottled.

The time of bottling also influences the style. As you can see from the calendar on page 134-135, an LBV can be bottled within quite a large time period (30 months), which may cause great variations in style. "And therefore you will find more variety in the producers' LBVs than in their Vintage Ports, and this is very confusing to the consumers", Peter M. Cobb (Cockburn's), says. And he is not the only one. It is also confusing to some consumers that the producers market their products at different times. Some market their LBVs just after bottling. Others keep them in stock for later release.

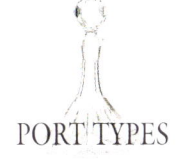

Today, nobody doubts that LBV is a useful medium-type Port, both for producers and for consumers. But even here, the philosophy is different from one Port producer to another. Whilst some maintain that LBV is a supplement to Vintage Port and produce both types in the good vintage years (1983, 1994), others (e.g. Graham's) will not produce LBV in the years they produce Vintage Port.

Traditional late bottled

Most LBVs are filtered before bottling and are drinkable as soon as they are bottled. The year of bottling must be printed on the front or back label. These wines do not profit from keeping. If they do lie for a few years after bottling, they will form a deposit, and decanting is then an advantage.

But some LBVs are not filtered before bottling. The producer actually wants the deposit, as it is a good substance for further maturation in bottles. Warre's is a good example of this feature, and Smith Woodhouse is another. The vintage year on the photo is 1986, but as you can see the bottle was not bottled until 1990 and was not sold until 1999, so the wine has matured in its bottle ("Bottled matured") for 9 years and no doubt has a deposit and should be decanted. The LBVs that are not filtered or only slightly filtered and are launched on the market for maturation in bottles will often have the wording "Traditional" printed on the label, as you can see on Warre's label. If they mature in their bottles by the consumer, they should be decanted before drinking, for example Ramos-Pinto (Vintage 1994, bottled in 1998). Fonseca's most recent LBV from 1994 is slightly filtered, but this is not written on the label.

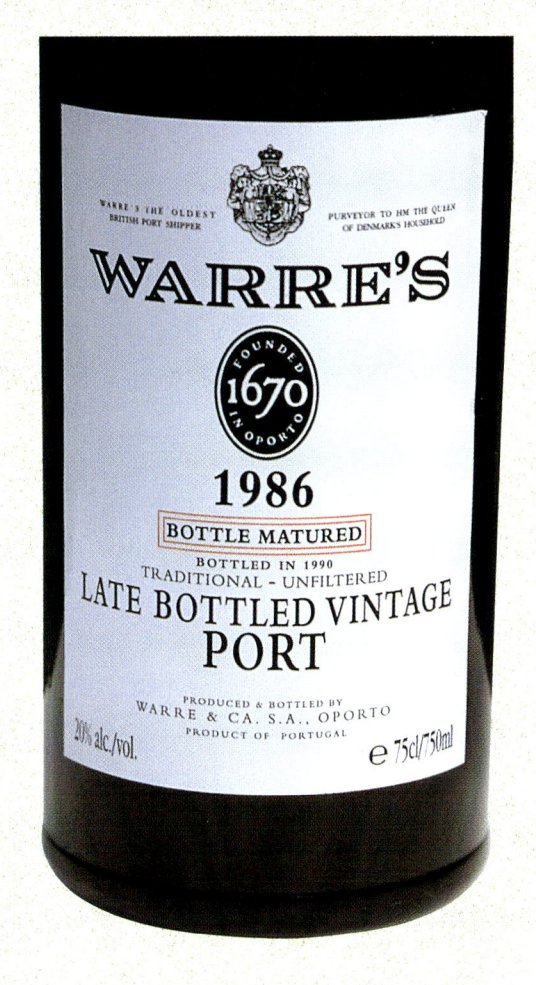

TAWNY WITH AGE

THE ACT OF 1/1 1974:

DEFINITION
This is a Port - Vinho do Porto - of very good quality which is recognized by the I.V.P. as having the right to use an indication of age, within the terms of the following regulation.

REGULATION

a) To obtain the approval for a Port with an indication of age, two bottles of the wine must be sent to I.V.P.

§ -- The indications of age permitted are
10 years
20 years
30 years
Over 40 years

b) The stocks of these Ports will be declared at the time approval is requested, and current accounts will be duly opened.

c) The sales must be made exclusively in bottle under "Selo de Garantia", and with prior approval of respective labels and presentation, within the general conditions governing the use of the "Selo de Garantia"

d) The main label must obligatorily show:
1-The indication of age: - Porto de mais de 40 anos de idade, Porto âgé de plus de 40 ans, OVER 40 YEARS OLD PORT, or any other equivalent description or translation, which is duly approved.
2-THE INDICATION THAT THE WINE HAS BEEN AGED IN CASK - ENVELHECIDO EM CASCO - MATURED IN WOOD - AGED IN CASK - VIEILLI EN FÛT or equivalent description

e) It is also obligatory to show, on the main label or back label, THE YEAR OF BOTTLING, which in principle takes place at the time of sale.

f) Designations with generic reference to the age of the wine, such as: "MANY YEARS IN CASK", "VERY OLD", and equivalent, are not permitted to be used or printed on any label, neck-label, etc.

Comments:

IVP have never clearly defined the meaning of 10-years, 20-years, 30-years, and over 40-years-Tawnies, and I have the feeling that this has been a conscious choice. If you ask IVP, they say that the producers very well know the significance thereof. But if you ask the producers, they say that they are not quite sure about the significance and none of them agree as to the definition. Most of them presume that these Port types refer to a mixed Port, which is more or less 10 years, 20 years, 30 years, or over 40 years old in average. Others maintain that the definition must be that it is a mixed Port which should taste as a 10-years, 20-years, 30-years, or over 40-years Tawny traditionally does with the usual variations from one producer to another. The producers do not have to document what Ports they have used for the blend. The wines are solely estimated on the basis of sensory tastings (blind tastings). One can therefore assume that 10-years, 20-years, 30-years, or over 40-years Tawnies are to be considered as types. As for the other Port types, the style may vary from one Port house to another.

COLHEITA

THE ACT OF 1/1 1974:

DEFINITION
This is a port - Vinho do Porto - of only one harvest of good quality, and which is recognized by the I.V.P., as having the right to use the date indicated within the terms of the following regulation.

REGULATION
a) To obtain the approval of wine with indication of the date of harvest, two bottles of the wine must be submitted to the I.V.P. between the 1st July and 31st December of the third year counting from the date of harvest.

§ -- Wines acquired directly from farmers or the "Casa do Douro", as long as certified by that organization as being of the respective date, can be at any time submitted for the appreciation of the I.V.P. without whose approval they cannot be sold.

b) The stock of this port must be declared at the time it is approved, and a current account will be duly opened.

c) The sales of these wines, which are to be made exclusive in bottle under the "Selo de Garantia" and are subject to the previous approval of the respective labels and presentation, will only be permitted when the wine has reached seven years of age and taken from next 1st January, and will depend upon re-approval, after this date, of the wines the I.V.P. under the normal conditions governing the use of the "Selo de Garantia".

d) The main label must obligatorily show:
1-THE INDICATION OF THE DATE: PORTO... (date) - PORTO DE or PORT OF ... (date) -- ....(date) PORT - or equivalent duly approved; it is also permitted the addition of the description RESERVA-RESERVE - HOUSE RESERVE or equivalent duly approved.
2-THE INDICATION THAT THE WINE HAS BEEN AGED IN CASK: -- ENVELHECIDO EM CASCO - MATURED IN WOOD - AGED IN CASK - VIEILLI EN FÛT, or equivalent.

e) It is also obligatory to show on the label, or the back label: THE YEAR OF BOTTLING, which normally is at the time of sale

e) GARRAFEIRA PORTS, which are dated wines that have been bottled long before their sale, will be subject to a re-approval by the I.V.P. together with the respective labels and presentation before they can be sold.

Comments:

This type of vintage Port is called Colheita (some producers call it Reserva/Reserve). It is a quality Port, which has the longest statutory time of ageing, as it is bottled at least 7 years after the harvest. However, Colheita is also the only quality Port type not to have a so-called last bottling day. If a vintage year has been approved for Colheita, it may be bottled at any time it suits the producer. But to supervise the quality of the approved wine, the Port Wine Institute requires that samples of the pipes of the approved but not yet bottled Colheita are forwarded every three years. If IVP are of the opinion that the wine is too mature, it may only be used for older Tawnies or the like. The Port Wine Institute also check the alcohol percentage, and if it has changed, aguardente must be added.

It is a tradition that older maturing Colheitas can be refreshed with younger Colheitas, but this is not included in the Act.

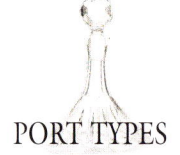

OTHER TYPES

The four aforementioned types of quality Ports are not only the finest and most expensive, they are also the only types that are legislated. Among the other types available, which are not legislated, apart from the fact that they have to be approved by blind tasting by the Port Wine Institute are the following:

Vintage Character: As the name implies, this is a type which resembles a Vintage but is not from a vintage year (it must not indicate a vintage year), and the Act says that it accepts terms as "Tipo Vintage", "Vintage Style", and "Vintage Character" on the label, but as you can see in the provisions for Vintage: "it is expressly prohibited to mention the vintage year or any other reference which could create a misunderstanding compared to a genuine Vintage".

With regard to quality (and price), the Vintage Character is between a normal Ruby and an LBV. Even though everyone more or less agrees that it is less fortunate to use the word Vintage, this is a very popular type both with producers and consumers. Churchill Graham even produces two different versions of Vintage Character.

Crusted Port: This name refers to the fact that this Port is a type with deposit, created for the British market who for some reason adheres to deposit. Some say that they even drink it! Legally, this type has no commitments, and price-wise it is between Ruby and LBV. Only a few producers make it, most of which goes to the British market. Cockburn's is one of the spokespersons for this type of Port.

Full Port: An imaginary type, the word having no meaning. The word "full" just implies that it is more expensive than an ordinary Ruby, and usually also a bit better.

White Port: Ernest Cockburn once said: "The most important thing for a Port is to be red", and this is the general opinion on this matter. Nearly all producers do, however, make at least one white Port, so there must be a market out there somewhere. For many years, white Port with quinine was the cure-all against malaria, but now it ends its days in sauces, snacks and summer drinks. White Port is found in sweet and dry versions. A few producers mature white Port in casks, sometimes with a remarkable result.

White Port is hardly used for anything else: a nice aperitif on a sunny spring day to go with a nice view, as here on Taylor's terrace in Gaia. On the photo, Taylor's managing directors, Huyshe Bower and Nick Heath, enjoying a cigar - and life!
(Photo: HO)

Chapter 7

PORT PRODUCERS

Port Producers/Profiles

Profiles

This chapter is about the most important Port Wine producers. Every presentation consists of two parts: a historical profile of the house and an evaluation of their wines. The latter is of course a subjective evaluation carried out solely by the author of this book and only to the extent that I have a good knowledge of the wines. The length of the various profiles and their evaluation vary, depending on the material I had at my disposal.

The chapter is in alphabetical order. See also the index from page 381.

The text includes an indication of when the wines were tasted and how long they have been bottled.

Evaluation

Evaluating wines with points or symbols is only the second best solution, but as the best solution does not exist this is what I have chosen to do. Out of consideration for the international readers I have used a 100-point scale.

The producers' wines are divided into the traditional categories:

RUBY

(Vintage Port, LBV, Vintage Character, Crusted Port, etc.)

TAWNY

(Colheitas, old Tawnies)

The quality of every category is evaluated on the basis of a certain number of glasses. This evaluation is solely the evaluation of the author and is to be considered as a guideline:

🍷🍷🍷🍷🍷 Perfect

🍷🍷🍷🍷 Outstanding

🍷🍷🍷 Nice

🍷🍷 Decent

🍷 Ordinary

Andrésen
(J.H.Andrésen Sucrs. Lda.).

Founded: 1845
Owner: Familien Flores
Taster/Blender: António Santos.
Quintas: None. Andrésen Port owned one quinta, but it was not included in purchase in 1942

The first Port house in the alphabet is at the same time the only house we can boast of having Danish roots. João Henrique Andrésen, with the Nordic first name Johann Heinrich, was born on the island of Föhr on 29th January 1826 when the island was part of the Slesvig and belonged to the Danish throne.

When he was 14 years, he signed up on a ship and ended up in the merry town of Porto where he felt quite at home with all the other parvenus and where he worked himself up to a certain position in the town. He was even President of the Chamber of Commerce, and in 1845 he founded his own wine house with an emphasis on the export of Port.

One hundred years later, the Andrésen family encountered financial difficulties and had to sell the company in 1942 to a company managed by Albino Pereira dos Santos who was already then a known face both in the Port city of Gaia and among the small growers in the Douro Valley.

The year peace was restored in 1945 was thus also the centennial for the foundation of the company, and this was marked by Santos introducing a *Century Port*, which 50 years later is still the firm's best known Port. Since 1990 it has been marketed as a 10-years Tawny. Originally, it was not called a 10-years Tawny, for it was a mixture of 11-12-years Tawnies and, as Santos says then it would be cheating the wine drinkers to call it a 10-years Tawny.

This philosophy changed when the market was in difficulty in the beginning of the 1990'ies and when is was more profitable to call a Port a 10-years Tawny than a Centennial Port.

Today, the Andrésen's is run by Santos' grandchildren, the Flores family. The daily manager, Carlos Flores, calls Andrésen a consequent Tawny house, which did not launch Vintage Port from 1985 until 1996: "... not because we have anything against Vintage Port, but we are a Tawny house, and we produce what we are best at. Vintage is something you worry about for 2-3 years, then you market it and leave the rest to the consumer. We prefer to complete the wine cycle and then bottle it when it is ready to be consumed." Nevertheless Andrésen are back on Vintage since

Carlos Flores, daily manager of Andrésen's, with the historical "Century Port", which has now been launched as a 10-years Tawny. (Photo: HO)

1996, Vintage Port again in 1997, and LBV from 1994, 1995 and 1996. Andrésen Port does not own land in the Douro Valley but would like to - if it ever becomes financially possible and if it does not shake their status of being "small but good". They have three concepts when dealing with the farmers: they either buy the finished wine, or they advise the farmers and get them to make the wine the company wants, or, they control the process from planting to the crushing of the grapes in the old lagares.

There is a priceless sense of peacefulness and rustic, historical charm over Andrésen Port, and their older Tawnies compel respect. You feel a bit proud of nearly being a co-countryman - even though the surname has been polished by the Porto language and is now pronounced **An**drésen.

RUBY (-)

Andrésen's has developed a new interest for Vintage and LBV, so it is still too soon to evaluate the quality. *Vintage 1985* is a bit too light to keep for much longer, light-bodied, light and fruity, and LBV, 1992, which was a vintage year between the good old times and modern times, is extremely light and feminine. Time will show if *Vintage 1996,* and *Vintage 1997* have or will have personality and character.

TAWNY

Meanwhile I can easily confirm that Andrésen does know the art of making Tawnies. The historical *10-years Tawny* "Century Port" is "massive, slightly smoky, flattering, but especially full-bodied and very potent" (92/100), and the *20-years Tawny* is every better: "Soft brown sugar, delicious, no alcohol, powerful with a delicate sweetness and very fine balance". (96/100). Andrésen does not make a *30-years Tawny* or an *over 40-years Tawny*. But they do make Colheitas. At my most recent visit in the autumn of 1998, I had the occasion of tasting a small selection:

Colheita 1982: "Friendly, drinkable, a bit superficial, but well-made and delicious. Soft, mild, no characteristic impression". (89/100)

Colheita 1975: "Soft, light and refined. Mild, no alcohol, nice substance. The most excellent result from this vintage year". (94/100)

Colheita 1970: "Deep and refined. Sweet and mild style, no sugar, no alcohol. Delicious and harmony with great fruity taste – and character". (97/100)

Colheita 1968: "Brown, light and delicious, again light style, polished and well-made. A bit light-bodied, but nice – as long as it lasts". (89/100)

Colheita 1963: "Full-bodied, convincing, long sweetness. No alcohol. Typical Andrésen style: Light, refined, but with a noble sweetness, complex, well-balanced. A trial of patience. More sweet taste than woody". (97/100)

Colheita 1910: "Incredibly soft and harmonic, complex, slight soft brown sugar, but not sticky at all, but gentle sweetness and great harmony. Still vigorous. Fantastic. Clearly shows Andrésen's and Colheitas' abilities". (99/100)

Barão de Vilar

Founded: 1998
Owner: Family van Zeller
Taster/Blender: Fernando van Zeller
Quintas: None

Fernando van Zeller with one of the brothers' first bottles with the new label "Barão de Vilar"

The family van Zeller sold their Quinta do Noval to the French insurance company, AXA Millésimes, in 1993 with the stipulation that the family could not sell Port Wine on the market for the first five years. Therefore, Fernando van Zeller and his younger brother, Cristiano had to wait until 1998 before they could become shippers under the family title Barão de Vilar. And as they could document the necessary stock of 150,000 litres of Port Wine, they could celebrate the inauguration of the newest Port Wine house in the business. The family has deep roots in the Port Wine business. The brothers' great-great grandfather was Luis Vasconcellos Porto who got Quinta do Noval in shape, and their father, Fernando van Zeller, managed Noval in the period 1963-1982, and in 1970 the Port house was given the same name. Fernando van Zeller (born 1959) also has an experience in the business. He became an independent shipper in 1998. He had worked at Quinta do Noval several times, latest as member of the board from 1987 and until the sale in 1993, he had participated in restoring Osborne Port in 1967, and he had worked for Borges for two years, before the stipulation with AXA terminated, and he could once again make his own Port Wine under his own name. As the eldest male heir, he inherited the Barão de Vilar.

The van Zeller brothers own the vineyard Viña do Vale in Douro but they vinify at Quinta das Aranhas. In 1999, they have built up a stock of 240,000 litres of Port Wine and on the basis of this figure they count on selling 60,000 bottles a year. They had to buy their first Tawnies, because due to the stipulation their first Vintage Port (1994) became to old for Vintage and became a LBV, which is partly made from foot-crushed grapes and looks promising.

RUBY (-)

The above-mentioned LBV 1994 and Vintage 1996 are so far the only quality wines. The brothers also made a Vintage Character, but it is still too soon to evaluate their quality.

TAWNY (-)

This also applies to the brothers' Tawnies. I have tasted a *Colheita 1987* made from purchased wine. In 1999 it was rather sweet and intense, a typical Portuguese product, but this does not say much about its future quality.

Barros
(Barros, Almeida & Ca.).

Founded: 1913
Owner: Barros-Almeida family.
Taster/Blender: António Oliveira/José Sosa Soares
Quintas: The best wines normally originate from grapes from Quinta de São Luiz, owned by the Barros-Almeida family

Of the many Port houses under the charge of the Barros family, the Port house under the family name is the youngest and was founded as late as in 1913 by Manoel de Almeida as *Almeida em Comandita*. When his sister Matilde was married to Manoel de Barros, he become his partner. Their marketing became more direct, and they changed the name to *Barros, Almeida & Ca*.

The new partnership got safely through the two World Wars with Manoel de Barros as the obvious leader, and it was a solid and growing company he left to his two sons, Manuel João Barros and João Manuel Barros. The first is still the nominal head of the company, but in practice, the younger generation has taken over.

The Barros family have quietly and without a commotion taken over other Port houses in the course of the nearly 80 years they have existed, with well-known names such as Kopke, Feist, Hutcheson and Feuerheerd, and always using the same philosophy. Today, the Barros family dominates approximately 5 per cent of the total production of Port, and with an awe towards history, the finest quality is sold under the Kopke name and the second best quality under the Barros, Feist or Hutcheson names. The Barros-Almeida family owns two quintas in the Douro Valley, the large

José Manso has for almost 10 years been daily manager at Quinta de São Luiz, responsible for the many new patamares and ao alto plantings. (Photo: HO)

Quinta de São Luiz (see under Kopke) and the Quinta Dona Matilde, originally called Quinta do Enxodreiro but changed name when Manoel de Barros bought it in 1927 and named it after his wife.

The quinta is so old that it is recorded within Pombal's demarcation and the ravages of time must have left its mark by the time the Barros' family bought it. Now, the neighbouring Quinta da Carvoeira has been included but still no vinification is carried out on the property. The grapes are transported to Quinta de São Luiz and some of them end up on the global markets as 7 or 8-years Tawnies under the name of Quinta Dona Matilde. In 1996 there was also produced a Single Quinta Vintage Port made of grapes from the quinta and bearing its name. Even if the two quintas in 1998 produced 380 pipes (São Luiz) and 76 pipes (Dona Matilde) of Port, it only supplies about 5% af the neccessary amount of wine.

RUBY

It is the family's philosophy to use the best grapes for Kopke; the other brands must share the rest. So it cannot surprise anyone that the quality of Kopke's wines are somewhat better than those of Barros. This especially applies to the Ruby types. Barros' Vintage 1970 was one of the wines of that vintage year with a quick maturation, and my tasting comments of the best vintages are more or less alike. The wines were tasted in 1994 – 1999:

Vintage 1980: "Soft, fruity, incoherent. Breathtaking sweetness, nice but short aftertaste. Fragile".

Vintage 1983: "Raw, aggressive nose. Soft taste, rather sweet, fruity, short aftertaste but still with a certain amount of potency so it should make it past the Millennium".

Vintage 1985: "Slightly aggressive, rather sweet, a touch of smoke. Surprisingly drinkable and will not last for long. Short aftertaste".

Quinta Dona Matilde Vintage 1996: "Nice content of fruit, or berry rather: elderberry, black currant, ripe berries. Very nice wine, quite light-bodied, maybe a bit too decent and drinkable for this stage".

It all stays in the family, but Kopke's Ruby types have more of a backbone and Feist's with a bit more charm than Barros'. On the other hand, there is more volume in Barros' with trade marks such as Imperial (white, Ruby, Tawny), bottled after 3 years, and quite popular in Belgium, Holland and France.

TAWNY

Barros is much better at Tawnies than Rubies. This applies both to the old Tawnies, where the 10-years Tawny is pure and very decent, soft and concentrated with a sufficient amount of sweetness, and the 20-years, 30-years, and over 40-years Tawnies, which are very nice, well-made, rather sweet and very friendly, but it especially applies to Colheitas. The following were tasted in the course of 1995 – 1999, all newly bottled:

Colheita 1983: "Great brown sugar nose. Dense taste, full-bodied, almost creamy. Slightly smoky, good body, not aggressive. Very nice".

Colheita 1975: "The nose is much better than the taste. Nice, slightly aggressive, soft and sugary".

Colheita 1957: "Dark brown, shimmering colour. Light-bodied, with more sweetness than structure. Slides down your throat with no barriers. No great depth, but nice, light taste. Short finish".

The Barros' family's natural domicile in the Douro Valley is Quinta de São Luis that was purchased at the same time as Kopke Port in 1953. The best wines with Barros' own name on the label are also made from grapes from this quinta, which is a very big production quinta with state-of-art technical equipment, but it also has romantic corners like this beautiful chapel. (Photo: HO)

Borges
(Soc. Vinhos Borges & Irmão S.)

Founded: 1884
Owner: Taylor's
Taster/Blender: None
Quintas: Quinta do Junco and Quinta da Casa, now belonging to Taylor's

Borges just managed to celebrate its first 100 years as a Port brand but that was it. When Taylor's in the spring of 1998 took over the ailing Port business of Borges, it was primarily to get their fingers in the old, distinguished Quinta do Junco - an opposite neighbour to Quinta do Noval - and in Quinta da Casa Nova. Taylor's have no intention of using the name Borges, as they do not want to be mistaken with the table wines which are still produced under the Borges name.

Borges & Irmão was founded by the brothers Antonio and Francisco as a bank, tobacconist and wine company in 1884. Eventually, the wine trade became the most important part of the business, and in 1907 they moved their headquarters to Gaia, because the export of table wine, especially to Brazil, had increased drastically. But they also fancied the idea of making Port, and the brothers first bought Quinta da Soalheira in 1904 followed by Quinta do Junco in 1906.

The latter was the company gem, and the quinta underwent improvements and modernizations far into the 1970'ies, new patamares were for example built in 1973.

When both the bank and the winery were absorbed in a financial group under the management of Banco do Formento e Exterior, the quality of the Port became unstable, and the heights of the good Vintages 1960 and 1963 were never to be reached again. From a historical point of view, it is quite sad that the Borges name will disappear from the shelves in the shops, but the good grapes from Quinta do Junco will no doubt get a better treatment in the hands of the experts at Taylor's.

Borges & Irmãos' old coat-of-arms reads "Res non verba", which can be translated into: "Actions not words". The last word on Port seems to have been said, and now the actions must be focussed on the surviving table wines from Douro, Bairrada, the popular wine Trovador, Vinho Verde (Gatão), Espumante, Dão (Meia Encosta), Brandy and Bagaçeira.

Taylor's bought Borges in 1998 due to the high-lying Quinta do Junco, neighbour to Warre's Cavadinha and opposite neighbour to Quinta do Noval – and not due to the parent company or its name. (Photo: HO)

Burmester
(J. W. Burmester & Co. Ltd.).

Founded: 1730
Owner: Burmester Family
Taster/Blender: Jaime Costa
Quintas: Quinta Nova de Nossa Senhora do Carmo

A Port house without a history is like an old Vintage Port without deposit. At least this is what the head of the Burmester family, Arnold Gilbert, confided to me a few years ago. And for that reason he said he had decided to write down the family history from the first generation of Burmesters' and right up to the present day. Hopefully, one fine day this family story will be published to the great delight of all lovers of Port. The following is a commented extract from the clean proof that Gilbert was so kind as to let me read and use. It tells the varied story of a Port family and also notes in a subtle, unresentful way that not alone were there "British" and "Portuguese" Port houses and families; there were also others who, by not being British or Portuguese, had often been in a tight corner due to the international situation.

As the name suggests, the Burmester family comes from Germany. Gercke Burmester is the first known Burmester in the family. He died the mayor (Bürgermeister) of the small town of Mölln situated between Lübeck and Lauenburg in 1550 - which under the Danish king Valdemar had been a Danish fief, frequently used as a war trophy, and until 1864 the Danish king was its duke. In the following centuries the family presumably split up with one or several branches of the family staying in North Germany and one branch seeking its fortune in Porto. And this is where Johann Wilhelm Burmester arrived to in 1834 and the one to lend his name to this Port house. But according to Gilbert there already were other Burmesters in Porto. A family tale tells the story of Heinz "Henry" Burmester who founded the trading company *Burmester, Nash & Co.* in 1730 with the Englishman John Nash, and from at least 1750 they also dealt in Port. Henry Burmester and his descendants settled down in England where the son Henry and his son established H. Burmester & Son in 1806.

The Porto side of the family is easier to track. In 1806 Hermann van Zeller appears on the stage and becomes a partner in Burmester & Co. and the company changes names to *H. Burmester & H. van Zeller.* When van Zeller leaves the company only three years later, the company is renamed H. Burmester & Co. In 1817 the two brothers, Frederick and Edward Burmester, split the activities between themselves leaving the management of Burmester & Co. in Porto to Frederick and the Burmester Brothers in London to Edward.

In the meantime, Rudolf and Johann Gerhard (Rudolfo and João Geraldo translated into Portuguese!) are somewhere in the wings. Well-known as buyers at the auctions in Portugal in 1759, they were presumably relatives of Henry Burmester and contributed towards strengthening the family firm both in Porto and in London.

Henry Burmester died in 1822 as a successful business man with a small estate in Essex leaving a wife and 10 children as well a 16-page testament and a large collection of curios, among others a small snuffbox which the Danish king had given him.

England seemed to attract this German family who had done so well in Porto. Also Frederick Burmester left the city of Porto where he was so highly respected in professional circles that he was made Treasurer of the Factory House. But nevertheless, he left the management of the firm in Porto to the German, Hermann Lukas Soltau, and settled down in London where he became co-founder of The National Westminster Bank and where the mayor of London himself passed his condolences to his widow when he died in 1856.

If it had been up to Frederick, the Port adventure had ended with his generation when the banking adventure got started. In his very detailed will, he asked that Burmester & Co. in Porto be sold to the highest bidder and that the money received along with the rest of the things he left behind should be divided between his widow and his nephews. And this is why the Port house in Porto was sold the very same year to a known local businessman by the name of Manuel de Clamouse Browne who according to Gilbert most probably already had financial interests in the company.

Now things got going. Even though the company in Porto had been taken over by a new owner, Soltau continued the daily management, and it was on his request that a young relative, his brother-in law's brother arrived to Porto on 13th December 1834 to join the company instead of trying his luck in America as most of his peers. The young 24-years-old man was Johann Wilhelm Burmester, born and bread in the large city of Hamburg to which his father had moved from the family town of Mölln.

Presumably, the young Burmester - and maybe especially his worried family - had expected to stay in Porto only a short period of time, but this was not how things went. He began as an apprentice in the bookkeeping department but was promoted, moved in with Hamburg's consul whose sister he married in 1847 and had three daughters and then six sons. Thus he became firmly rooted in Porto.

When Frederick Burmester through his will in 1856 asked for the Port house to be sold to the highest bidder, Johann Wilhelm Burmester was 46 years old and had been promoted to co-director of the company. He was fortunate: Soltau

In December 1991 the family bought its first quinta, Quinta Nova de Nossa Senhora do Carmo, opposite neighbour to Barros' Quinta de São Luiz between Régua and Pinhão. (Photo: HO)

Burmester is a family of German descent who used to be called Bürgermeister, the German word for Mayor. But the name has been adapted so that the Portuguese can pronounce it! Burmester is Burgomestre in Latin, as you can see on the family's barco rabelo in the harbour of Porto. (Photo: HO)

wanted to go back to his native town, Hamburg in 1860, and at about this time the new owner, Manuel de Clamouse Browne died. The entire estate was to be realized which resulted in Johann Wilhelm Burmester drawing up an agreement with Browne's heirs so they each got their share of the company and he himself got 25 per cent of the company's profits. This agreement was so profitable that he was able to buy off the heirs one by one, and on 30th June 1880 the Port house *J.W. Burmester* was a reality with its company address at Rua das Taipas No. 11 in Porto.

Johann Wilhelm Burmester must have been a clever businessman, for he was also a ship owner, he was one of the founders of a glassblower factory in Germany, and among his other activities were banking. He died as dramatically as he had lived. On 2nd February 1885, he drowned just outside of Porto when he was out looking at the new harbour with some friends.

His oldest son with the pompous royal Swedish name, Gustav Adolph, who was already part of the firm invited his younger brother Otto to become a partner. The other brothers dealt in ships, leather, textiles and later in petrol. But dealing in Port was the best asset. All the other values were lost when Portugal was involved in the First World War. Portugal was not bound by treaty to help England in the war, as they had signed a pact of no attack, and the fact was that England had declared war on Germany, but Portugal had become a harbour of safety for the German ships, and pressure from England on the Portuguese become so strong that they accepted to confiscate German property in Portugal and imprison German citizens and their relatives, which naturally led to a declaration of war from Germany.

The Burmester family had to choose between leaving Portugal within 24 hours or being arrested. Most of them chose to leave the country and settled down in Spain. Miraculously, Gustav Adolph managed to transfer the family wines to a good Portuguese friend, at least on paper, until he too had to flee. The friendship lasted, as did the wine, and in 1920 Gustav, his catholic Portuguese wife and their four children returned to Porto where he had the wines re-transferred to the company without any problems, but the family had to borrow money to be able to buy the remains of their property in Porto back from the Portuguese state.

When the family had to leave to Spain a good friend of the family, Teresa de Vasconcelos Porto, took custody of the three children of Gustav Adolph's daughter Maria Luisa, Gustavo, Vasco and Alvaro. Their new "mother" was married to Luis de Vasconcelos Porto, who worked as manager and partner of the well known Port house António José da Silva, who then owned the famous Quinta do Noval.

In 1923 at the age of 73, Gustav Adolph decided how to restructure the Port house for the future: his son João Guilherme was to run the company along with his son-in-law Hans Steinmetz and his nephew and son-in-law Karl Gilbert as co-partner. Gustav Adolph and his wife would keep 44 per cent of the shares.

In these new times, the old Port house looked for a new director. The choice fell on Karl Gilbert who was apparently the best qualified person of the three partners. He had joined the company at the end of the 19th. century and had been consul for the Austrian-Hungarian empire and had been decorated by Emperor Franz Joseph himself.

After the First World War, when the family repossessed their Port, it had matured for four years and prices had risen on the market. And the market did change. Now Scandinavia was Burmester's new main market. In 1925 an exports record was achieved, which was not surpassed until 1980. So even though the crisis in the 1920'ies left its trace, Gustav Adolph was a satisfied man when he celebrated his golden wedding in 1931, and when he died 9 years later, the world was again at war, but this time Portugal was left out. Unfortunately, so was Port. These were difficult times for exports, an often impossible mission, and like the other Port shippers the Burmester family endured financial problems. The British embassy refused to release the necessary navy certificates with the reason that the Burmester family was of German descent. And without a navy certificate, no exportation!

In May 1945, one month after the end of the war, Gustavo's widow, Maria Henriqueta, died, and it was time once again to distribute the shares of the company and make plans for the future. But already when the real estate had to be

Willingness to help has always been a virtue of this family. Without solidarity and willingness to help each other, Burmester would never have survived the long, hard years – and even today, Fátima Burmester Pimenta is willing to help her uncle, Arnold Gilbert, so that his collar sits properly. (Photo: BJS)

divided, the heirs disagreed and things went completely astray when the future of the family Port house was to be decided. Gustavo's and Maria' Henriqueta's daughter Maria Luisa's three sons Gustavo, Vasco and Alvaro proposed that due to the bad, financial times they were not given their share but instead were admitted to the company as shareholders. he older shareholders, João Guilherme Burmester, Karl Gilbert and Hans Steinmetz decided to transfer their shares to their five children which included the author of the family history, Arnold Gilbert. To further complicate the distribution of the heritage, Hans Steinmetz chose to retire and transferred part of his block of shares to his son-in-law Armando Fernandes e Silva. Suddenly the small, solid family firm had at least 9 significant co-owners.

On the other hand, times were getting better, so Burmester avoided the sad destiny of so many others in a battle of heritage, and after a few deaths in the older generation and more allotting of shares between the descendants, the financial and daily management of the Burmester Port house was left to a well-balanced mixture of Gilbert's and Steinmetz', two branches of Gustav Adolph Burmester on the mothers' side. With fewer men at the helm, "the ship", in Arnold Gilbert's own words," had become easier to sail."

With solid hands to manage the financial part of the Port house, there were also solid hands for the production of Port when Frederico van Zeller was employed in 1964 as a consultant and a blender/taster. When he handed over the recipe of a wonderful mixture to António dos Santos Monteiro 20 years later, Burmester had been able to establish itself as one of the finest producers of old Tawnies, but could also boast of making quite elegant Vintage Ports. In the 1950'ies, a new name had even been introduced to the collection. For marketing reasons the "Gilbert's Port" brand was launched, named after Karl Gilbert. According to Arnold Gilbert, Gilbert's Port is in principle the same wine as Burmester, made by the same team, of the same grapes using the same methods, but the stocks are kept separately, and some years Burmester does not make a Vintage Port but Gilbert does. In 1985, Helmut Gilbert died and was replaced in the company by his daughter, Fátima Burmester Gilbert Pimenta, and after Armando da Silva's death in 1989, the company was restructured again. Today, the company consists of Arnold Gilbert, Fernando Formigal, Fátima Burmester Pimenta, Henrique Burmester and Isabel Burmester Formigal.

Since December 1991, when the Quinta Nova de Nossa Senhora do Carmo was bought from the Real Companhia Velha (40 ha of vines - all Class A), Burmester has been self-sufficient in a small part of their best grapes; the rest is bought from small wine growers. But the quinta has also been a costly affair. In Real Companhia's era no vinification took place at the quinta. The grapes were transported to a vinification centre by Pinhão, so Burmester had to discard the decayed and worn-down equipment and install new equipment. Today, the quinta is fully operational and produces about 200 pipes of Port a year but has a production capacity of nearly 1,000 pipes, and this could be realistic when the new plants begin to bear fruit for Port. It already gives about 100 pipes of table wine.

In spite of setbacks and decline, one big family still stands behind Porto Burmester, and their Port is just like the family: German in thoroughness and Portuguese in warmth and elegance.

RUBY

Burmester's Ruby Types are an instructive search with a combination of sweetness and fruit which is carried out to perfection in their Tawnies.

All the LBV's and Vintage Ports, I have tasted, and I have tasted many, have the same compact, solid fruit and characteristic mild sweetness. They are friendly wines that are soft and very drinkable from the 3-years ordinary Ruby to the *Vintage Character*. The LBV's have a uneven maturation period from 4 to 6 years and are all nice and reliable. So is their Vintage Port, which has a much milder style and does not have the same intensity as their Colheitas. I have tasted the following in the course of 1998 – 1999:

Vintage 1985: "Very nice average style with solid fruit, some tannin and a sweetness, which seems to come from cooking chocolate. Nice and decent, good behavious and maybe over the hill already".

Vintage 1989: "Fruity and very friendly. A touch of raw fruit, the rest is nothing but sweetness and amiability. Very pleasant, small backbone".

Vintage 1991: "Very nice, soft and fruity. A Vintage for the golden middle of the road. Surprisingly mature at this stage".

Vintage 1994: "Sweet and spicy, not only peppery but with all the oriental spices. Virile and fruity and very potent. But also with a good deal of sweetness. It will be exciting to follow this wine".

Quinta Nova de Nossa Senhora do Carmo, Vintage 1995: "Soft, ruddy, mild and compliant. Already drinkable and rather sweet".

TAWNY

"Colheitas are our hobby", Arnold Gilbert told me with his convincing smile whilst we were tasting some of the finest Ports in the world. And this is not just some cheap slogan he said: "We make Vintage Port and Colheita from more or less the same quality of grapes, but you must not forget that Vintage Port can be sold at an earlier stage and at a higher price than Colheitas. We can make good Colheitas in weak Vintage years which is to our advantage. But it is very expensive to make Colheitas, and if you look at the profits - then Colheitas are our hobby. But what a wonderful hobby to have"! He digs out a Colheita from the deep dark cellars. It is so old that it is called *Novidade, 1920,* but it was bottled in 1977 because it had stopped maturing in the cask. But it must have further matured in the bottle:

Novidade Reserva 1920 (bottled 1977): "Complex and complete. Lots of sweetness, but subdued and disciplined. Fantastic, mellow wine with depth, finesse and spontaneity. Dreamy when it hits the tongue...but suddenly it is gone".

(99/100)

And to prove that it is no coincidence, Gilbert served the following:

Colheita 1900 (bottled 1972, recorked later): "Hazlenut brown, gentle with a taste of ripe walnuts. It sneaks into you. Polished, nearly fernished with both a disciplined sweetness, long aftertaste and backbone. Overwhelmingly wonderful and well-kept. Velvety". (99/100)

Nostalgy and joy of life on a bottle. Let us follow the more modern "list of kings" in Burmester's tasting premises. First Tawny with age, which by definition is a mixed wine so that the age on the label is an average age. "It is not too difficult for us to find the right age, for we have Colheitas to compare with", the principal taster Jaime Costa explains. The following wines were tasted in the course of 1997 – 1999, all newly bottled:

10-years Tawny: "Intense nose, intense taste. Mild, soft with a taste of brown sugar but not at all aggressive. Virile and well-made, potent and self-confident ". (96/100)

20-years Tawny: "Soft and sneaks into you. Oddly, it seems slightly more aggressive than the 10-

years Tawny, even slightly more robust, but it has the same aftertaste and tastes delicious. Friendly and polished". (95/100)

30-years Tawny: "Soft, mild and friendly. Sneaks into you with its sweetness, very nice and polished". (92/100)

PS. As a curiosity Burmester also makes a 30-years half-dry Tawny.

Over 40-years Tawny (called Tordiz, named after the vineyards by the rivers *Tor*to and Men*diz*): "Soft and polished with nobility and gracefulness, amiable fruit and a long delicate aftertaste of nuts and brown sugar". (95/100)

It is not far to the Colheitas which have made Burmester famous:

Colheita 1989: "Soft, very compliant and friendly with mild fruit, good body and not aggressive at all, still with as intense a fruity taste and woody taste. Young, much too young, but robust and exciting. I'm looking forward to tasting it in 20-30 years". (91/100)

Colheita 1987: "Juicy and dense. A wine you can almost chew – and with great pleasure too. Slightly smoky sweetness, intense fruit with far more sweetness than acidity". (93/100)

Colheita 1985: "Potent fruit, young and virile. Intense sweetness and very full body. Good style with depth and long aftertaste. But much too young. It can keep for years to come". (96/100)

Colheita 1963: "This is Burmester's genuine Colheita spirit: soft, smooth, and deep, dancing with a fairy, a soft, sweet kiss full of magic. Long, long finish and an aftertaste of brown sugar and still with a depth and long aftertaste, full-bodied and woody". (98/100)

Colheita 1955: "Incredibly concentrated, noble and full of disciplined sweetness. Nuts and rock candy. Long, intense, well-balanced taste, nicely matched by a touch of acidity. An excellent Colheita". (99/100)

Colheita 1944: "Noble, elegant sweetness. Very nice structure, long polished taste. Full-bodied and delicious, but with a delicate acidity, which does not make delicious become too delicious. Lovely and well-balanced. Mature and delicious with an exquisite sugar balance so that it feels dry on its way across the tongue. A major challenge". (96/100)

Colheita 1937: "Glossy and slightly burned with concentrated, dark sweetness with a texture practically like syrup. Some orange both to look at and to taste makes this Colheita stand out. Exquisite Colheita with a slight impression of many years in wooden casks, but still fruity". (98/100)

Arnold Gilbert in good company

Cálem

(A.A. Cálem & Filho, Lda.)).

Founded: 1859
Owner: SOGEVINUS SGPS S.A.
(Rogério Leandro da Silva)
Taster/Blender: Martins Alves
Quintas: None, but the new owner has a first claim to purchase grapes from Cálem's Quinta da Foz

Cálem's Quinta da Foz stayed with the family when the company was sold in 1998

It was a sad necessity that forced the Cálem family to sell the 139-years old Port house in 1998 to Rozès' Managing Director, Rogério Leandro da Silva, and his partner, Manuel António C. Saraiva, who owns a transport company and is co-owner of the family-owned property Quinta de Castelinho. The sadness was historical, the necessity vital, as the only candidate of the young generation to replace Joaquim Manuel Cálem, his daughter Maria Assunção, had to give up the day-to-day management of the company due to illness.

Before the sale of the big lodges in Vila Nova de Gaia, production equipment, all the old Port in casks and bottles, brands and rights, the house had belonged to the Cálem family since the beginning of 1859. The family was allowed to keep the charming Quinta da Foz in the outskirts of Pinhão with the clause that the new owners of Cálem have a first claim to buy the quinta's grapes, and they have also taken over the name of Quinta da Foz for marketing purposes. António Alves Cálem had bought the quinta back in 1885, and ever since then the grapes from this property have been the backbone of Cálem's best Ports.

This is also the António Alves Cálem who founded the company in 1859 and who a few years' later took his son, António Cálem Jr., on as a partner. They bought ships so that they could transport the Port to their most important market in Brazil and brought back exotic woods. Affairs soared and Junior gradually became a Port personality. In 1915, he became President of the Chamber of Commerce in Porto and a member of Parliament, and he handed over a prosperous enterprise to his sons, José Joaquim de Oliveira and Joaquim de Oliveira Cálem, who both started working in the company in 1920 and retired in 1974 and 1978, respectively, to make room for the fourth generation, Joaquim Manuel P.O. Cálem, who joined the company in 1972 and was director of the company when it was sold in 1998.

He was also the Portuguese agent for smart Ferrari cars for several years as well as the Dutch consul, so it was only natural that his daughter, Maria, gradually took over more and more of the daily management, especially with regard to exports. It was under his management that the family started to sell off the family silver: first their interests in steel and cars, then land and property, and finally the old Port house and the family name as well as the Ferrari agency.

PORT PRODUCERS

Unfortunately, we only know the broad outline of the family history, for Cálem's archives perished in a fire in Vila Nova da Gaia in 1976. But we do know that the new era started on Friday, 29th May 1998 with the new ownership. Silva and Saraiva split the tasks between themselves so that Silva was to take care of marketing, administration and exports, and Saraiva of the production in Douro and Gaia and well as tourism. However, this partnership bearly lasted a year. In the spring of 1999, Saraiva left the company, and Silva became sole owner.

The purchase in 1998 included Cálem's stock of Port, the 16,000 sq.m large cellars in Gaia fully equipped and including storage space for 4,6 mio litres of Port. At a closer look, neither the cellars, the equipment or the wine fulfilled the expectations of the new owners, so as da Silva says, it was especially the possibilities that were tempting. At the same time, a major clean-up and refurbishment of the cellars was initiated, the new owners prepared an ambitious budget targetted at eleminating bank loans and other obligations over a 5-years period. Furthermore, they set the goal to make Cálem, who at the purchase was the sixth largest Port producer, one of the four largest producers before the year 2003.

A special focus has also been put on tourism. Cálem is the first name the visitors meet on their way across the Dom Luis bridge from Porto to Gaia, and the old offices facing the river are already reorganized as a visitors' centre and a first-class restaurant with Taylor's restaurant as a model is in project.

In 1998, Cálem had more than 97.000 visitors just in this one year. They want this figure to increase so that Cálem can establish itself as the most visited Port house and thus, da Silva hopes, as the Port house selling most bottles of Port to tourists. Things are already looking good.

Not only the equipment and the inventory had been in need of a loving hand for several years, according to the new owners, so did the wine. The old Tawnies were excellent, da Silva told me in the spring of 1999, just after releasing some bottles of Cálem Colheita 1961 which were outstanding. But there were problems with Cálem's Vintage Port and the Single Quinta Vintage Port. "The family has apparently kept the wine much too long in casks at Quinta da Foz instead of sending it to Gaia. This resulted in the Port having an excessive woody taste and a too little fruity taste. But this will change now", da Silva told me. He is not afraid of being short of grapes

A small man facing a great challenge. His partner withdrew from the company in 1999 and Rogério Leandro da Silva is now the sole owner of Cálem's – with a couple of banks, as he humbly says. But the responsibility is his and only his. (Photo: HO)

even though he does not own any land, for from his time as manager of Rozès, he has a lot of useful addresses of small farmers in the Douro Valley, and there will be no problems of getting the perfect grapes from the small wine growers, he says.

It was a tough start for the new owners. They had counted on making 8,000 pipes of Port in 1998, but due to the bad harvest they had to settle with 6,000 pipes. On the other hand, they invested money in refreshing Cálem's vinification centre by Vila Real (São Martinho d'Anta) with a storage capacity of 5 mio litres of wine, including table wine which is sold under the brand name "Quinta de Sá".

The purchase also included the rights to the name Quinta do Sagrado, which might be reserved for prestige Ports, and the name Beira Rio, which the Cálem family had used for various Ports, especially 10-years and 20-years Tawnies. The Cálem family kept the Quinta do Sagrado and a few smaller properties in the Douro Valley.

Amidst the sad, but necessary, change of ownership, it must be a comforting thought that for the first time in many years a Port house has been taken over by Portuguese capital funds. And those, who know Rogério Leandro da Silva's enthusiasm and efficiency remember how he in his 17 years with Rozès put the organisation and quality into shape as well as expanded the export market from 4 to 40 countries. So if anyone can restore Cálem, da Silva can.

RUBY

As at all other important changes of owners in recent years (Noval, Offley, Borges) one should, to be fair, distinguish between the time before and the time after. However, the bottles of the former owner still lie in the cellars for a few more years, so we can only note at this stage that the new owner, da Silva, has big ambitions towards improving the quality of Cálem's best Ruby types, especially Vintage Port. I am fortunate enough to have received an invitation to visit the hospitable Cálem family on Quinta da Foz several times in the last 10-15 years and have thus tasted many Vintages great and small. Especially two Vintages were worth discussing, Vintage 1975 and Vintage 1991. The bottles were very different, and Maria Cálem Assunção confirmed that even the family were wondering about this. But only one assemblage was carried out in each of the two years, and the bottles were stocked in the same way on the quinta so they have no explanation to the phenomenon.

The family does not know either why Vintage 1985 has developed in an unfortunate way and had problems with acidity, for there was nothing wrong with it in its first 10 years. I tasted a couple of bottles in September 1999, and they were more or less the same: a decent, friendly, fruity wine with a sudden dry aftertaste. The wine does not taste bad, but it is not good either.

Cálem's LBV's from the 1990'ies are fresh, fruity types, nice and well-behaved and drinkable wines that are not for keeping. Also Cálem's SQVP's are light-bodied, usually with a very nice fruit content, but they are not for keeping either. Quinta da Foz has produced the Vintages 1982, 1984, 1986, 1987, 1992, 1995, and 1996. Quinta da Cavalheira has only made one vintage, Vintage 1984, and Quinta do Sagrado the Vintages 1988, 1990, and 1994.

At the big tasting, "Vintages of the Century", in June 1999, I had the occasion of tasting some of Cálem's old vintages:

Vintage 1908: "Slightly smoky nose. A Tawny style both in colour and in nose. Tastes like a 20-years or 30-years Tawny with a slightly orange edge. Mild and quite vivid, but not at all the traditional Vintage style".

Vintage 1931: "Light brown. Orange in the nose. And orange in the taste. Much more

Tawny or even more Moscatel than Vintage. Mild and soft".

Vintage 1935: "Dark brown. Slightly acetone nose. Finally a bit of fruit. Soft and decent, meagre but with a nice structure. Still some Tawny in it, but also a bit of fresh fruit".

Vintage 1947: "Deep, smoky nose. Lacks a bit impression, but has a nice depth about it. Light fruit, more Tawny than Ruby".

Vintage 1963: "Very dark brown. Deep nose with a touch of acetone. Good taste, polished, again more like a Tawny than a Ruby. Too much wood? Delicious and very drinkable but lacking typicity".

Vintage 1966: "Rather dark with a deep nose. Distinguished taste with a very nice structure. Impressive harmony, balanced sweetness, very nice fruit. Finally fruit! An excellent wine".

I would also like to add Vintage 1970 to the list – a wine I tasted at Cálem's in 1998:

Vintage 1970: "Nice combination of remaining fruit and aggressive sweetness. Nice balance, soft taste and very friendly. In spite of the sweetness you can still taste the fruit with a dash of stimulating spices. Still nice but it won't be any nicer".

The newly employed taster/blender, Carlos Almeida, who came to Cálem's from Sandeman in 1998 was replaced by Martins Alves in 1999. He now has the difficult job to give Cálem's Ruby types a high, homogeneous quality.

TAWNY

Already in the rather simple Fine Tawny you feel that Cálem's skills are better for Tawny than for Ruby. *Réserve Cálem* is a 6-7-years Tawny, which is really nice with a robust nutty taste. And in the noble Tawnies the quality is even more refined:

10-years Tawny: "Solid, soft, smoky with a nice taste of fruit. Full-bodied, nice and fruity, nice drinkable average style".

20-years Tawny: "Soft, caramel and refined. Light and elegant style, soft with a nice sweetness".

30-years ("WWW") and *over 40-years ("Magnificent")* are produced in very small quantities, but according to da Silva they will be produced in larger quantities in the future. So will the Colheitas where Cálem has been among some of the better producers for several years. Here are a few examples, all tasted newly bottled in 1995 – 1999:

Colheita 1988: "Very sweet, rather light with a nice structure. Silky, graceful but short"

Colheita 1986: "Slightly smoky nose. Long, polished taste ending with a neat explosion in the mouth. Charming and drinkable".

Colheita 1962: "Dark brown. Brown sugar, rock candy and a very light acidity. Nice balance, delicious wine, in which the sweetness is concentrated and actually, It does not seem sweet at all. Delicious".

Colheita 1961: "Taste of brown sugar. Amiable, friendly sweetness. Smoky, polished, dark and sweet with a sinister nutty taste".

When he worked for Rozès, da Silva managed to buy his old Tawnies from small producers and made an excellent over 40-years Tawny of purchased wine. One could very well imagine the same happening at Cálem's, both with regard to the old Tawnies and with the Colheitas.

Carvalho Macedo

(J. Carvalho Macedo).

João Carvalho Macedo made his fortune in Brazil, and when he felt that the former Portuguese colony would become a good market for port wine, he settled down in Porto and founded his own Port Wine house in 1861. The best-seller, "Amadeu", has always been a very popular product in Brazil. In 1927 the house was bought by Ramos-Pinto.

Churchill's

(Churchill Graham Lda.).

Founded: 1981
Owner: Limited Company
Taster/Blender: John L. Graham
Quintas: Quinta da Gricha

Of the handful of Port houses which were founded in the 20th Century, Churchill Graham is among the youngest and the only one with British roots. Churchill Graham was founded by the three Graham brothers, who in 1970 sold the ailing Port house, Graham's, to the Symington family, but they still could not abandon the idea of producing Port under their own name. And that is why Johnny Graham left a good position at Cockburn's in 1981 and gathered enough old Port so that he could found a new family house. The first problem was to find enough Port. The other problem was to find a name, for the Symington family were obviously not interested in a competitive product carrying the name of Graham on its label, so the brothers took the name of Johnny's wife, Caroline Churchill, and decided to use her maiden name as their new brand. This is why the Port house is called Churchill Graham whilst the Port itself is sold as Churchill's.

Ever since he bottled the first Port under his own name, Johnny Graham has been responsible for the mixing and selecting. He explained the modern venture by stating that in a time when one Port house after the other was being taken over by multinational companies, he believed that there had to be a niche for a bona fide producer of traditional-style Port, a style which was not only traditional for the sake of tradition, but because the traditional method resulted in the best Port. In the first years of hardship, he rented a lodge from the Taylor's and convinced the sceptical surroundings that the project was sustainable in the only logical way: by making a series of excellent Ports and forming his own style.

The three brothers still own 51 per cent of the company shares, but the last 49 per cent have since 1994 belonged to a group of American and Canadian investors. They are pleasantly called "Churchill's Wine Club", but their most important task is not to purchase but to invest in the company. They do. More than 50% af the export is sent to USA and England.

Johnny Graham gets his best grapes from two very different properties, one of which is the high-lying Quinta do Água Alta on the north bank of the Douro river and the low-lying Quinta do Fojo in the valley by Pinhão. The two quintas are owned by the Borges de Sousa family, but the Graham brothers nevertheless make their Single Quinta Vintage Port from both properties on the basis of the motto: "Each year has its Single Quinta Vintage", and they also buy the grapes from Borges de Sousa's other properties: Quinta da Manuela and Quinta de Roncão Pequeno. The brothers have for years had one great wish: their own piece of land in the Douro Valley, and in 1999 the wish came true; as they purchased Quinta da Cricha, situated app. 5 km from Pinhão on the left bank of Douro. The 200 ha were by then planted to give 100 pipes, but after new plantations have been made they will give about 250 pipes. The buildings were in rather bad conditions but the old lagares from 1852 were in excellent condition og were used already for the Vintage 1999.

RUBY

After less than 20 years as an independent producer, Churchil Graham can still only give promises but no proof. But they are great promises. Churchill has both ambitions and skills, and Johnny Graham has already proven that he will and can make robust wines with a convincing fruit content and potency. Even his heavyweights are charming.

The following is an all-round evaluation. I have tasted a dozen different wines and I am impressed about the self-confident style:

The Crusted Port (with an indication of the year of bottling) is excellent, and Churchill makes not just one, but two, *Vintage Characters*, a "Reserve Port" and a more exclusive "Finest Port", which is a mixture of two different vintage years and which is drinkable after the bottling. As LBV (I have only tasted the 1992) they are very robust, dry, fruity wines where the stress is put on the fruit. There is even more stress put on the fruit in Churchill's Vintage Ports. They were all tasted in the course of 1998-1999:

Vintage 1991: "Harmonic with an intense taste of berries. Well-structured with a nice sweetness, which is counterbalanced by a taste of fresh fruit. The 1991 is very potent. Very nice but still too young".

Vintage 1990: "Nice, solid fruit. Clean, fruity taste, light and rather short. Dry and decent."

Vintage 1985: "Nice and solid fruity taste. Long, concentrated, fruity taste of berries. A wine, which nicely unites gracefulness with muscle, power and charm. Potency and berries".

The young team behind Churchill's also has a young general manager, Maria Emilia Campos, who shows us a couple of the young vintages. (Photo: BJS)

Quinta da Agua Alta, Vintage 1987: "Dark, intense fruit. Taste of berries, blackberries and elderberries, juicy with a long taste. Well-balanced and very nice".

Quinta da Agua Alta:, Vintage 1996: "Wonderful taste with intense elderberries (like Taylor's). Dense and fruity. Compact, well-made, promising".

TAWNY (-)

Only one Tawny is of a quality:

10-years Tawny: "Nice average style, soft, elegant, fruity with a slightly woody taste".

But as one of the few producers, Churchill makes a very decent good white Port, which has a dry, characteristic taste and is a brilliant apéritif, and which even may be served with food". (See page 348-349).

Cockburn's
(Cockburn, Smithes & Ca. S.A.).

Founded: 1815
Owner: Allied Domecq
Production Team: Jim Reader, Miguel Corte Real og Manuel Carvalho.
Quintas: Quinta do Tua, Quinta do Atayde, Quinta de Val Coelho, Quinta dos Canais, Quinta de Santa Maria, Quinta de Chousa.

As all good Scotsmen, Robert Cockburn had a flair for making money. He had joined Wellington's army in that part of the Napoleon wars which aptly could be called "the battle of the Iberian peninsula" and which the British call "The Peninsular War", and during the British reconquest of Porto was tempted to settle down and live off shipping local products back to England. He carried his thought into action, and when Napoleon had met his Waterloo in 1815, young Cockburn met his fate in Porto and founded the trading company *Cockburn, Wauchope & Co.* with a good friend. They started dealing in wine, dried cod and oil but soon discarded the smelly secondary products and fully concentrated on wine, i.e. Port.

Apart from a nose for business, Robert Cockburn must also have possessed a pipeful of charm, for a certain Mary Duff accepted his proposal of marriage. This was the same Mary Duff whom Lord Byron had worshipped in verse and prose when he was just a young romantic before becoming world famous. But she chose Cockburn and bore him two sons, Archibald and Alexander, who thus secured the line of succession.

In 1828, Captain William Greig joined the company as a financially strong partner and according to usual practice, the company was renamed *Cockburn, Wauchope & Greig*. A few years later, the three partners became four when yet another captain (later admiral), Hugh Dunlop, joined the company. He did not contribute with capital funds but entered the firm by marrying Robert Cockburn's sister. When Archibald and Alexander were of age, there was hardly enough room in the boardroom office, so they were shipped off to London instead where they opened the London office in 1830, and where they succeeded in maintaining Great Britain as far the best market for Cockburn's Port.

When Robert Cockburn died in 1854, Alexander returned to Porto, Archibald stayed in London, and from this point on the company started to shape a sharp sales profile. Shortly after taking over management, the two brothers took on two other brothers as partners: Henry and John Tatham Smithes, and they divided the work at

Cockburn & Smithes among themselves with Henry staying in London and John supervising exports from Porto until the fine vintage year of 1887. John married Eleanor Cobb, sister to the new London-based partner, Charles Davison Cobb, and ever since then there has always been a Cobb in Cockburn's management, until Peter M. Cobb, who succeeded his renowned uncle Reginald as head of the Cobb family in 1985, left the company in 1999.

Kinship was however much more complicated. You see, Eleanor Cobb was not John Tatham Smithes' first wife. He had previously been married to Margaret Teage, so the Teage family also entered the firm through marriage when W. Roope Teage succeeded John Smithes whilst his brother, John Land Teage, ran another Port house, Hunt, Roopes'. John's son, John Land Teage Jr., succeeded his childless uncle, W. Roope Teage, in 1891 and married Alice, a daughter of John T. Smithes, so the number of shareholders was breed true!

When Willie Teage left the company in 1890, William Morphett Cobb was called home from Australia because of the lack of male heirs. After the First World War, when young Fred Cobb was killed, there was a shortage of male heirs yet again, so admirality was looked upon once more and Capt. Frank Rhee made partner. The aforementioned William M. Cobb returned home from the great plains of Australia and drew attention to himself in Porto by not declaring any of the vintages 1917, 1920, and 1924 as Vintage Port, which most of the other Port houses did. He salvaged his reputation with the 1927, the largest and most successful Cockburn's Vintage in history. He was succeeded by his eldest son, Reginald Morphett (Reggie) Cobb, one of the cen-

Peter M. Cobb is the latest Cobb at Cockburn's. Here at work at his favourite address: Quinta do Tua. (Photo: HO)

tury's most outstanding personalities in Porto, taking on as partner Archibald Cockburn (Archie) Smithes, the only son of John Tatham Smithes. Upon John's death in 1939, the partnership was offered to his son, John Henry Smithes, another prominent figure in Porto as well as a legendary taster, who had realized the necessity of producing brands so that the consumers knew what to buy.

When war broke out in 1939, John H. Smithes enrolled in the Royal Air Force and Reggie Cobb had to work alone through the difficult years of war, supported loyally by Frank Nugent and Geoff Sankey. Smithes was appointed the unenviable position as rear gunner onboard a mosquito fighter, but he survived the war and returned to Gaia. Prospects were bright for Cockburn & Smithes, which was one of the houses who gave a first priority to their London office. This was where the partners presided, latest young Peter M. Cobb and Fred Cockburn until his death in 1964.

But times changed, and there was a lack of capital funds again signifying that the families had to sell some of their shares to Harveys of Bristol in 1962. That same year, Harveys of Bristol also bought Martínez Gassiot & Co.Ltd. In 1963, Harveys bought the last shares in Cockburn & Smithes so when Harveys later became a pawn in the game, namely in the Allied Lyons Hiram Walker Group and later again in Allied Domecq, both Cockburn's and Martínez followed the leader.

It was all about capital funds, and Harveys did put fresh capital into the undertaking. More capital than heart! Especially in Great Britain, Cockburn's Port was known as a supermarket Port, and around 1990 Cockburn's was the best selling brand in Great Britain - even overtaking Sandeman's. The annual production had reached a sky-high 750,000 cases, of which 80% included various Ruby types, approx. 18% were Tawnies, and the rest consisted of white Ports and Vintage Port. And when it comes to Vintage Port, Cockburn's have created an image of a house going its own way. Between the giant vintage years of 1912 and 1927, no Vintage Ports were produced at all. Cockburn's did not make a Vintage 1966 either but preferred to produce a Vintage 1967, which they regretted later on, for Vintage 1966 proved to be an outstanding Vintage. They also regretted skipping the classical Vintage year of 1977 - according to Gordon Guimaraens because all the good grapes were, following the wishes of management, to be used for the newly launched Special Reserve. Utter tripe, as Gordon Guimaraens diplomatically puts it, but it did have a positive outcome. Since then management has never meddled in what goes on in the tasting room.

Cockburn's is not like other Port houses either when it comes to land and property. They are one of the largest proprietors in Douro Superior. Their property lies consistently and deliberately on the north side of the Douro river which is much more sunny. Since 1978, Cockburn's has staked heavily and costly on the flat lands which contrary to tradition lie far more north - naturally within the demarcated area.

This adventure began right after the hectic revolutionary year of 1974 when Cockburn's considered to buy land at the present Quinta do Atayde by Vilariça. This was a daring undertaking and could have been a costly affair as the victors of this revolution had proclaimed that they would nationalize the lands. But the newly appointed manager, António Filipe, believed commonsensically that "even communists cannot pocket soil, so let's invest".

And that is just what Cockburn's did - around 1 mio £' worth - and he saw to it that the Assares vineyard was planted with vines in meticulous patches. The idea was to mechanize the flat lands using all kinds of tractors, but the weakness of this concept was that there was nobody in the environs of Assares who could drive a tractor! So they first had to find a tractor driver, build a house for him and his family in nowhere land before the project could be launched. Sandeman and Cruz had also bought land in the same environs but gave up exploiting it because it was too remote.

Luckily, Cockburn's didn't. On the contrary, supervised by the then Vineyard Manager Miguel Corte Real, from 1979 phylloxera-free vines were planted consistently. During planting, both salt dome and springs were found but they were covered up again, for this project was only about vines. Today, the impressive grounds boast the largest total plantation area without terraces in the Douro Superior and have by far proven their value.

The biggest property is Quinta do Atayde with 100 ha and 350.000 vines planted. The grapes are not vinified here but transported to Quinta do Tua which, since its purchase in 1899, has been the magnificent jewel in Cockburn's stoutish royal crown.

Tua used to be a "whistle stop" for the mail coach (Malaposta). People would come down the mountain to the stop by coach, row across the Tua river and walk up to the Quinta do Tua where fresh horses were waiting. Now, the quinta is headquarters for both guests and grapes during the harvest, for after the sale to Harvey's in 1962, investments were made in a new winery with temperature control, cold fermentation system and new fermentation tanks of stainless steel which supplement the old lagares that are still used today.

Since 1978, Cockburn's have invested a lot of money in the eastern part of the Douro Valley,

Early morning atmosphere from the tiny balcony at Quinta do Tua. Before the bridge across the Tua river was built, you had to sail across the river, especially if you took the mail coach from its stop at the quinta. In the background, beneath the sky, you can see a glimpse of a small white house. It is the Symingtons' Quinta dos Malvedos. (Photo: HO)

Quinta do Atayde is not very typical, for it lies far towards the east in the appellation and not by the river, and the vines grow on rather flat land so that they can be planted ao alto. (Photo: HO)

which today consists of around 300 ha so that approx. 20% of the grapes requested come from their own fields. Far east into the so-called "Rabbit Valley", you will also find the Quinta de Val Coelho which is Cockburn's oldest quinta that has been part of the company for more than one hundred years.

Much newer are Quinta de Chousa and Quinta dos Canais. The former was purchased in 1973. Small in size - but the quality of the grapes is so high that Cockburn's is counting on using them for a Single Quinta Vintage Port. The grapes from the latter, Quinta dos Canais, (canais means channel), have been the spinal cord of the house's Vintage Port for almost one hundred years. The quinta has an area of 300 ha of which 150 ha are under vines. The Quinta de Santa Maria in the outskirts of Régua is a popular quinta for guests but yields grapes of a lower quality. There has been a lot of turbulence at Cockburn's since the sale to Harveys' in 1962 - more than what is desirable for this historic Port house where hospitality has always been just as high as quality - and that says quite a lot! The unsettled conditions on the international spirits market might even result in more turbulent years to come, but this does not change the fact that Cockburn's has a fine reputation as being a good place to work.

Renowned John Henry Smithes worked at Cockburn's from 1932, survived the World War and stayed with the company until sometime in the 1970'ies. Frederick Cockburn was there for a lifetime until he retired in 1965. Wyndham Fletcher, a cousin to the Cockburn's, was also around for many years as was Reginald Cobb who lived to celebrate his 50th harvest. And recently retired Peter M. Cobb, undaunted Gordon Guimaraens and Cockburn's invaluable factotum, António Graça have all worked for Cockburn's for more than 40 years.

RUBY ♥♥♥♥

Thanks to Peter M. Cobb's generosity in his time as manager at Cockburn's and good connections to different Danish agents, I believe that I have tasted more of Cockburn's Vintage Ports from recent years than any other brand. What a nice acquaintance, and according to my many tasting comments and my excellent memory there have been hardly any disappointments, even in the more dubious vintage years.

Among Cockburn's more inferior Ruby types you will find the popular Fine Ruby (min. 3 years) in a fresh, fruity, straightforward and very viable style. The Special Reserve is even more popular with the motto: "It is always special, so why reserve it". This wine was a prestige wine from its birth and the best grapes were used for this wine in 1977 to make this brand instead of making a Vintage Port. In spite of its name, Reserve is a Ruby type, almost a Vintage Character, even though it does not have a classification. It is fruity, aggressive, robust and powerful, does not have a woody taste and does not put on airs.

A better quality is seen in the LBV which only consists of a Late Bottled Vintage written in small letters and ANNO and the year written in capital letters. This is due to a certain reluctance of using the denomination Late Bottled Vintage, which could be mistaken for the real thing.

Cockburn's LBV's are nice, correct, fruity wines which often contain just as much potency as Vintage Port, but lack dimension. I really like Cockburn's LBV's which I believe are some of the best around. But naturally, the Vintage Port is the most well-known product. I have good recollections of Vintages 1912, 1927 and 1935 but unfortunately no tasting comments. The wines were served at a fashionable dinner where it was not "comme il faut" to take notes about the wines of the host. But in June 1999, I had the opportunity of tasting the Vintages 1960, 1963, 1967, and 1970 at the "Vintages of the Century".

Vintage 1960: "Tawnysweet. A nice small content of fruit wrestles with a nice overwhelming sweetness so you can easily imagine the result. But the wine is very nice, too nice, pure, clinging with a nice character. But there is no more challenge left in it". (87/100)

Vintage 1963: "Dark brown. Delicate from the first sip with a fine togetherness of nice fruit and a just as nice sweetness. A warm and sweet plum. Delicious, very nice, harmonic with more amiablity than challenge. Polished style with smoke and charm. The fruit wants to be enjoyed now". (96/100)

Vintage 1967: "Soft and glossy, very potent and very, very delicious. The fruit is surprisingly potent compared to 1963, but it is not better, however quite characteristic. Enjoy now. A beautiful combination of fruit and sweetness". (92/100)

Vintage 1970: "Darker and with a much deeper nose than 1963 and 1967. Polished wine with both fruit and charm in an ideal symbiosis. Very nice Vintage with polished fruit. Mild sweetness, friendly and potent taste". (95/100)

Among my many tasting comments from recent years (1995-1999) I would like to put an emphasis on the following wines:

Vintage 1975: "Nice wine from a difficult year. Delicate structure, but the fruit is nice, although somewhat humble. It is, however, one of the most drinkable 1975's – or should I say, was drinkable, for it should have been drunk by now".

Vintage 1985: "Aggressive nose with aggressive fruit content. The taste is characterised by an intense, aggressive fruit content which tastes of black berries. Dense, convincing Vintage with potency, concentrated taste of fruit and a promising structure".

Quinta do Tua Vintage 1987: "Decent and presentable with a characteristic taste of chocolate and lots of nice fruit. Lighter style than the ordinary Vintage, but the fruit is really nice, and the wine has its own flirtatious charm and a surprisingly nice potency".

This Quinta do Tua, 1987, was Cockburn's first SQVP. Vintage 1985 was the first SQVP from Quinta dos Canais, and in the future Quinta de Chousa will be sending SQVP to the American market. And a curiosity: the Vintage 1966 which was not declared but which is found as private bottlings and served on special occasions:

"Vintage 1966": "Fruity, soft, polished, actually rather dry and with a short, straightforward, abrupt and fruity aftertaste".

"Cockburn's style is to make fruity, vigorous full-bodied wines", Peter M. Cobb told me on several occasions. And they have succeeded in doing so.

An anecdote from the dark cellars says that when the British shippers in the 1950'ies and 1960'ies started to bottle an increasing number of their Vintage Ports, Cockburn's chose a very special way to give the wine its "immortal fruit": while some filtrated their Vintage Port before bottling, others chose to bottle with deposit, but at Cockburn's they went even further and rolled the pipes just before bottling so that the wine could absorb as much dregs as possible. The legendary Vintage 1963 is said to have been made this way. The resting wine was rolled violently back and forth in the basement passage just before bottling.

TAWNY

"Cockburn's is a Ruby house, who also makes Tawny, whilst Martínez is a Tawny house, who also makes Ruby", Gordon Guimaraens once told me at the time he was making wines in both houses. Cockburn's Tawnies are some of the most robust wines; the common Fine Tawny however mostly due to its aggressive taste - and their 10-years and 20-years Tawnies can contrary to other houses easily be kept for a few years after bottling.

10-years Tawny: "Extremely fruity, very robust, often slightly aggressive. One of the most solid of its kind but with a much better taste of fresh fruit than of smoke and oak".

20-years Tawny: "Very characteristic taste of berries, robust, fruity and quite without sweetness. Light and nice taste of wood, but dominated by the taste of fruit and berries".

Cockburn's does not make a 30-years and an over 40-years Tawny but a speciality called *PXD* which is only poured to guests and house friends and not sold on the market. It was produced for the first time from Tawnies from 1904 and 1908 and bottled around 1910, but today it is a 12-15-years Tawny, according to Peter M. Cobb, originally made to please the company directors. It is a delicious, slightly smoky and meagre old Tawny, which I really wish some of Cockburn's critics would have the opportunity of tasting.

Croft
(Croft & Ca. Lda.).

Founded: 1678
Owners: United Distillers and Vintners (UDV)
Taster/Blender: John Burnett og Nicholas Delaforce
Quintas: Quinta da Roêda.

Just as the famous pudding, the Croft family comes from Yorkshire, England, but contrary to Yorkshire pudding, Croft did not last forever.

In the beginning, the traditional pattern was followed. As other young people from the landed gentry in the beginning of the 18th Century, John Croft felt a longing to go abroad, and as his mother came from a wine merchant family, who had begun to buy wine in Portugal instead of in France, his trip naturally went to Porto. Here he became a partner in the company *Tilden, Thompson & Croft* with roots in the company Phayre & Bradley that had been founded in 1678, the same year as the first pipes of Port arrived in London.

John Croft was a bachelor, but his brother Stephen had five sons, who all grew up to work in the Port business. John Croft Jr. even became a writer of one of the first books on Port: "A Treatise On The Wines Of Portugal" (published in 1788, but apparentley written several years previously), and is mentioned with awe as one of the first Port historians. The fourth in the line of young Crofts, Thomas Croft, made the trip to Porto in 1759, three years after the demarcation of the Port district by the Marquis of Pombal. He took an apprenticeship with his uncle's, and when John Croft died in 1762, he took over the position on behalf of the family. Thomas Croft was one of the active forces in building the Anglican church in Porto, and once his brother John joined him, they could start the dynasty of Crofts in Porto, even though their English roots were never quite dug up. Thomas Croft's grandchild, John Croft (1778-1862), distinguished himself by becoming Lord Wellington's informer during the Peninsular War, and he must have done a good job, for he was appointed Baron for the job he had performed and received an honourable recommendation, which was signed by Wellington in March 1812.

Sir John, as he was now called, took his brother Frederick's place when he died in 1824, and three years later he could celebrate that *Croft & Co.*, which was now the name of the company, was the fourth largest shipper of Port. After John, his son John Frederick took over, and he had no less than six sons and nine daughters; unfortunately none of them seemed to be especially fond of Port, and the daily management was handed over to Joseph Wrigth who came directly from England to handle this important business. He had a good reputation, was efficient and very easy to recognize when he walked through the British colony, for he had lost an arm in the civil war between Don Miguel and Dom Pedro, presumably due to a grenade, which went right through the ceiling in his dining room whilst he was enjoying a glass of Port.

The Croft's prospered. Their archives tell us that in 1892 6,776 pipes of good Port were stocked in the 140 meter long Terreirinho Lodge in Gaia, and after the Quinta da Roêda at Pinhão was purchased in 1875, the Croft's could also boast of providing their own grapes for their best wines.

The company expanded, and in 1935 it had grown into the largest shipper of Port from Porto. But before reaching this target, the company had reconstructed its London-based administration which now included the powerful Gilbey family who in January 1911 took over the company shares and formed a technical fusion with Croft & Co.

The most important figures of the time were Arthur Dagge and Gordon Gilbey. Dagge was later replaced by the Scotsman Hugh Watson who again was replaced by George Robertson in 1952. It was a company custom that the manager of Croft & Co. in Porto after a few years in the export division, moved to London and took over the position of General Manager there. When Robertson moved back to England in 1955, he was replaced as manager by Basil Kendall who served until 1962, when Robin Reid took over. He had joined Croft's in 1948 and became for the following 40 years one of the most respected personalities in the world of Port. And he fully agrees to what one of the last active family members, Percy Croft, said in 1935: "Any time not spent drinking Port is a waste of time". But technically, the Croft family had actually already left management when the Gilbey's bought the shareholding in 1911, and later this new connection brought Croft into the large wine and spirits family known as the International Distillers & Vintners (IDV).

It might be a coincidence, but on several occasions I have felt that Croft was a company with a special social attitude. I first got this impression during a visit to Robin Reid in the beginning of the 1980'ies when a member of middle management told me that every employee was given 12 liters of wine and 12 liters of olive oil every month on top of their salary or wages as well as a paid lunch every day. He explained to me that this resulted in a special team spirit. Many years later while I was walking through Quinta da Roêda with Reid's successor, John Burnett, I noticed a neat row of mugs in one of the kitchens. They are used every day during the harvest when the 90 drafted pickers enjoy 4 meals a day on top of their wages, and as the wages are not sumptuous, the free meals are a benefit, which is probably also felt in the pickers' efforts in their work.

The aforementioned Quinta da Roêda in the outskirts of Pinhão town is the only property Croft has in the Douro Valley. It changed hands from the Taylor's to the Croft's by marriage in the 1870'ies when Croft's manager in Porto married John Fladgate's daugther. The quinta consists of 113 hectares, of which approximately 60 hectares are planted with vines. They yield 10-15 per cent of the necessary quantity of grapes whilst the remaining 85 per cent are purchased. Even though the quinta lies on relatively flat land, many of the vines on Roêda are so old and entwined that no tractors or any mechanical traction can be used. Instead a mule has taken over the tractor-pulling job.

In the years of glory before oidium reached Portugal, the yield on Roêda amounted to nearly 220 pipes, but when the oidium plague was at its worst, the yield fell to around 2 pipes a year. John Fladgate succeeded in obtaining a yield of 350 pipes a year by mere hard work, but then the wine louse, phylloxera, followed and many years were to pass before the yield again was at an acceptable level. Today, the 60 to 70-years-old vines yield around 500 pipes of Port a year. The old vines are priceless, but for the sake of production the 20 to 40 year old vines are more profitable. The old vines produce a high quality but a low yield; less than one kilogramme of grapes per plant according to John Burnett. On the other hand, the old vines do not absorb as much water as the younger vines that literally gobble up the water.

Croft is still managed with a good mixture of old and new. All the Port is produced mechanically and bottled in Gaia - and you can still find old pipes with old Tawny, even Vintages, at Quinta da Roêda, which are racked and might be bottled here one day - if for no other reason, then for the sake of nostalgia. Also because a good Tawny according to John Burnett should have a bit of "Dourobake", a soft kiss of sunlight at Quinta da Roêda.

Ruby

For many years Croft was known to let their LBV mature for at least 5-6 years instead of the legal min. 4 years. Naturally this resulted in softer and more robust wines. Furthermore, Croft also had a tradition of filtrating their LBV giving a friendly and slightly fruity style.

Robin Reid in Gaia, 1984. (Photo: HO)

Still the style of Croft's Ruby types compared to Delaforce's – which are made by the same team – according to John Burnett by definition a bit more "austere". Another characteristic is that the grapes from Croft's invaluable Quinta da Roêda often has a special aroma and taste of pine. This is due to the fact that a plant called Cum Cistus grows on some of the lots. It is very aromatic, a bit sticky and has a sort of pine needles.

To celebrate Croft's 3rd centennial in 1978, approx. 4,000 non-grafted vines were planted on the quinta as yet another curiosity. Their first grapes were used for the Vintage 1985.

From my tasting comments I can see that I have been more enthusiastic about Croft's matured Vintage Ports than I have been about the more recent vintages. The following wines were tasted in 1997-1999:

Vintage 1945: "Very nice fruit potential. Well-structured, very nice wine with a fine balance between fruit and sweetness. A historical and great glass of wine without any sharp edges". (92/100)

Vintage 1955: "Again a very nice balance between fruit and sweetness. Delicious now, amiable and agreeable with a long, friendly aftertaste. No explosion in the mouth and knotless. Long, clear taste". (92/100)

Vintage 1963: "First great sweetness and a more modest fruit content. Then something happens in the glass: the fruit breaks through the sweetness, the wine becomes more dense and becomes sympathetic and harmonic. There is even a slight explosion towards the end. Very nice wine, well-structured with character. Is at its best now". (96/100)

Vintage 1963 is the best Croft Vintage I have ever tasted. I have not yet tasted the classic Vintage years as 1908, 1924, and 1935 which are said to be monumental. But I do have tasting comments from later Vintages when Croft was not able to live up to bygone days. The following wines were tasted in the course of 1996-1999:

John Burnette at Quinta da Roêda in 1998. (Photo: HO)

V*intage 1991:* "Surprisingly drinkable. Very nice, solid fruit and light sweetness, but no real potency. Well-made, but for Croft's a light style, and a wine to keep an eye on". (86/100)

Vintage 1985: "Nice and decent, and was actually also nice and decent when it was a young wine. Lacks power just as Vintage 1991". (88/100)

Vintage 1982: "One of the light and absolutely nicest wines of this vintage in relation to drinkability. Nice structure, but a Vintage with no ambition and will not win much by keeping". (86/100)

SQVP has been produced on Quinta da Roêda since Vintage 1967. The best one I have ever tasted was (1997):

Quinta da Roêda Vintage 1983: "Seems more virile and more potent than Croft 1982. Taste of wild berries and a bit of madness, liquorice, and chocolate. Very light style in relation to Croft's older vintages. Drinkable now". (88/100)

TAWNY

After the most humble Tawny types, Croft makes the very popular *Distinction*, a 7-8-years Tawny, which like the 10-years and 20-years Tawnies are rather fruity with a substantial nutty taste. Croft do not make 30-years and over 40-years Tawnies, but I must confess that I have never fallen in love with their 10-years and 20-years Tawnies. I feel that the style is too robust and lacks femininity. Croft's do not make Colheitas either.

PORT PRODUCERS

Da Silva
(A.J. da Silva & Co.).

see Quinta do Noval.

Da Silva
(C. da Silva.).

The firm was founded by Clemente da Silva as an export company in the middle of the 19th Century, and he should probably also get the credit for the two most famous brands "Presidential" and "Dalva". The firm has not got any brands of its own, but buys grapes or wine from small farmers. The production is a variegated mixture of light and modest Port Wine for consumption, primarily sold to the French market, and decent and sometimes even really good Tawnies and sometimes even a Vintage. "Presidential" is a good, solid series of Tawnies (10-years, 20-years, 30-years and over 40-years). The full stock is of around 6 mio litres.

RUBY

Even the finest Ruby types are very light in their style with an overwhelming sweetness and no real kick in it. This applies to all Ruby types from *Vintage Character* to *Vintage Port* where vintage year 1985 is on its last straw. The important sales of Ruby types of the most inferior qualities are sold to France and Belgium. And good for them!

TAWNY

Da Silva's Tawny has a light and rather sweet style, but in this wine it is much more legitimate. The following entries were noted in a tasting of "Presidential" in 1998:

10-years Tawny: "Sweet as sirup, lacks attitude".

20-years Tawny. "Soft, delightfully spicy. Very mild".

30-years Tawny: "Raisins, fidele with a very soft touch of sweetness".

Over 40-years Tawny: " Surprisingly ardent with a soft, fine taste of raisins and a more straightforward charm than body".

Da Silva also makes Colheitas. The following were tasted in 1996 as first bottlings:

Colheita 1969: "A bit raw in the taste but with a decent body, sweetness and a slightly smoky taste".

Colheita 1966: "Tastes a bit of medicine, but it has a nice, long taste".

Colheita 1940: "Soft nose, soft taste, both dominated by an intense sweetness without any fruit or structure".

Colheita 1934: "Dense nose. It has vitality, charm and softness. The best da Silva wine I have ever tasted".

Delaforce
(Delaforce Sons & Ca.).

Founded: 1868
Owner: United Distillers and Vintners (UDV)
Taster/Blender: John Burnett & Nicholas Delaforce.
Quintas: None, but since 1980 Delaforce have had a long-term agreement with the owners of Quinta da Côrte, concerning grapes and consultant assistance.

The old, large casks on Quinta da Côrte have to be supported by wooden planks, but that is just an extra charm. (Photo: HO)

When King Louis XIV declared Catholicism as the French state religion in 1685, protestant wine families not only fled to South Africa. Some of the Huguenots fled north via Holland and settled down in England, among others the Delaforce family. More than 150 years would pass, however, before the first Delaforce started to work with Port, but when the 26-years-old John Fleurriet Delaforce arrived in Porto in 1834, allegedly to be a bookkeeper in the company Martínez & Gassiot, the future of the family was decided. His son, George Henry Delaforce, took a huge step and become a shipper in 1868, sensibly married a Portuguese girl and became the supplier to the two Portuguese kings and one of the profiles of the Factory House. You can still enjoy his portrait hanging on the wall to a traditional glass of white Port before lunch.

When George Henry Delaforce left the company to his sons, Henry and Reginald, in 1903, the pioneering company had grown into a respectable Port house, which the brothers led through international crises and two World Wars - in the last years assisted by Henry's two sons, Victor and John.

To the bright side of the story we should mention the introduction in the 1930'ies of the two brands, "His Eminence's Choice" (10-years Tawny) and "Curious & Ancient" (20-years Tawny), as well as a series of solid long-term contracts with the wine growers in the Douro Valley, the last of which was a fine contract in 1980 with Pacheco & Irmão, the owners of Quinta da Côrte by Rio Torte, for the exclusive rights to deliver grapes and the right to use the quinta's name for the Single Quinta Vintage.

The quinta has 25 hectares of A quality grapes. The best grapes (around 15%) are taken aside and crushed manually by foot in the lagares whilst the rest of the grapes are treated mechanically. According to manager John K. Burnett both systems are optimum, and some years the mechanically pressed grapes give an even better product, which is destined for the Vintage Port.

Apart from being used for storing the new wine, the quinta's armazém is also used for casks with up to 25-years Tawny, called the "Family's Reserve". A comparison to a Tawny of a similar age from the Delaforce lodges in Gaia shows that the evaporation at the quinta is approx. 1 per cent higher than in Gaia and that the wine at the quinta is markedly sweeter. There are so many positive aspects of the Quinta da Côrte - and actually only one negative aspect. There is only an average rain fall of 500 mm of rain against 950 mm in Régua and 1400 mm in Porto. This can cause some problems in years of scanty rainfall.

Under David Delaforce, the fifth generation of the Delaforce family, the family company was sold to Croft, and just as Croft's it is now owned by the United Distillers and Vintners (UDV).

RUBY

Among the British Port houses Delaforce has the reputation of making better Tawny types than Ruby types. This is only partly true, but that kind of label gets stuck on you, it is very difficult to get rid of it.

In the many tastings I have organized or even participated in, Delaforce seems constantly to surprise me, both with regard to Vintage Port and to LBV, but to many people, who taste the labels instead of tasting the contents of the glass, Delaforce has become a kind of inferior little brother to Croft's, just as Martínez is to Cockburn's and Dow's is to Graham's.

I have had several pleasant experiences with Delaforce's Vintage Port 1970 which was given - very à propos at the tasting of Vintage 1970 at the Port Festival of Copenhagen in 1988 with probably the most competent tasting jury ever, including 13 prominent producers - much better points than Croft 1970 and even surpassed famous names such as Dow's, Warre's, Cockburn's, Ferreira, and Noval.

Paramount Full Ruby and *Vintage Character* are the basis of LBV which with its 6 years of maturation in casks exploits the wood to a maximum. Delaforce's LBV is drinkable at a very early stage and has a popular, amiable style. My best overall impression of this house's Vintage Port stems from David Delaforce's visit to Denmark in 1995 when he served 5 vintages:

Vintage 1963: "Soft, polished wine, elegant and silky with depth and potency. A bit aggressive, but also fruity enough to last for several years yet in bottle. Full-bodied and very nice".

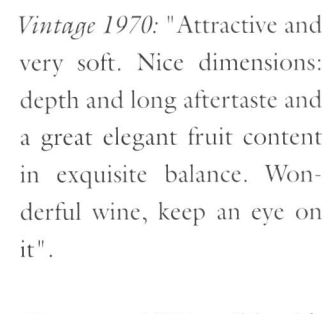

Vintage 1970: "Attractive and very soft. Nice dimensions: depth and long aftertaste and a great elegant fruit content in exquisite balance. Wonderful wine, keep an eye on it".

Vintage 1977: "Torpid, powerful, potent, and a deep sleeper. Don't touch it yet. Promising fruit".

Vintage 1985: "Also a sleeper. Seems unbalanced, very young, still in a transition period, is both very drinkable/fruity and ungenerous. Keep it, and time will tell".

Vintage 1992: "Young and potent wine with dark cherries, a nice body and a dry taste. Is already very drinkable".

In the autumn of 1992 I tasted the capricious 1985':

Vintage 1985: "Fresh and fruity nose. Tastes of young fruit and softness. Polished, already very smoky, dry and young. Nice structure with potent fruit content. Soft, glossy, already drinkable, but will also keep".

I have closely followed the SQVP's from Quinta da Côrte from the early vintages (1978,

Quinta da Côrte is not owned by Delaforce, but Delaforce have a long-term agreement about the grapes. (Photo: HO)

1980) to the more recent vintages (1991, 1995). They are all nice, decent, easily drinkable – and drinkable at a very early stage at that – Vintage Ports, which have been made as mini Vintages quite on purpose.

TAWNY

Technical director, John Burnett, confided in me in autumn 1998 what Robin Reid had only suggested to me: that there is a house philosophy maintaining that the Delaforce style is sweeter than the Croft style. Furthermore, Burnett likes a Douro bake, i.e. a slight oxidation of the Tawny types.

Paramount Medium Tawny is a young, uncomplicated Tawny, very close to the two peaks: "His Eminent's Choice" (10-years Tawny) and "Curious and Ancient" (20-years Tawny). They combine healthy, pure and not very old fruit with finesse, careful maturation in casks and a drinkable style, which is most probably due to the above-mentioned Douro bake.

They both contain a slight richness, and the difference between them is that especially "Curious and Ancient" is longer and milder with a literally more refined taste, as the raw edge in "His Eminent's Choice" has been polished.

Delaforce does not make 30-years and over 40-years Tawnies nor Colheitas.

Dow's
(Silva & Cosens Ltd.).

Founded: 1798
Owner: Symington Family
Taster/Blender: Peter Ronald Symington
Quintas: Quinta do Bomfim and Quinta da Senhora da Ribeira

One of the most British Port houses is actually Portuguese by birth, but is also distinguished in other ways. Bruno Evaristo Ferreira da Silva founded the company in Porto in a humble environment in 1798, and when he found out that the only market was England, as the British were practically the only individuals who drank Port, he realized that he had to find a business connection in London.

As his company was very small in size, he appointed himself to the job, moved to London, married an English woman, settled down in London and stayed here till his death in 1850. There is but one tale to tell: to protect his transportation of Port in the troubled times during the Napoleon wars, he had to buy an armed privateer Fonseca (with a letter of marque!) to accompany him on the long sea voyage, but otherwise his life seems to have been peaceful, fully dedicated to his business.

When da Silva was succeeded by his son and he was succeeded by his son, the latter took on William Cosens as a partner in 1862 which gave the company the name of *Silva & Cosens*. In 1868, George Acheson Warre became co-owner, and according to family history, he is the one to take credit for the company surviving the phylloxera. In 1877 Silva & Cosens purchased Dow & Co. which had such a fine reputation that the Dow brand was adopted as the main brand of Silva & Cosens as it remains today. James Ramsay Dow, who joined the company on this occasion, was more well-reputable as a flute player than a Port producer, and at times he was feared in the business for he was a bad-tempered salesman.

The new partners ran the business well carrying it gracefully into the new century, until in 1912 Andrew James Symington became a partner in Silva & Cosens and the Warre family became partners in Warre & Co. which he had purchased in 1905. This complicated arrangement was brought about by an exchange of shares and A. J. Symington ended up owning one third of both Warre & Co. and the much larger Silva & Cosens Ltd. From that time onwards Warre & Co. and Silva & Cosens Ltd. were managed in Oporto by A. J. Symington and his three sons. Today it is part of the Symington family's business empire with a special bond to Michael Symington and his son, Paul.

Michael Symington has always had a warm relationship with Dow's and with Quinta do Bomfim. Here he is seen in good company. (Photo: BJS)

Quinta do Bomfim is in the outskirts of Pinhão, just by the water's edge and neighbour to Quinta da Roêda.

Dow's own the Quinta do Bomfim in the outskirts of Pinhão. It was purchased by George Acheson Warre in 1896 at a time when the vineyards had been abandoned after the violent attack of phylloxera. It might have been an act of resignation that led to the erection of the main building a year later, as a copy of a Ceylonese tea planter's bungalow (!) But the quinta picked up again, even though it was not till the 1920'ies it was regarded as good as George Warre's other purchases in the 1890'ies: do Zimbro and Senhora da Ribeira. Both the latter were sold in the 1950'ies due to economic troubles. Even Bomfim the family only kept by a hair's breadth.

In the 1930'ies, Bomfim was carefully planted, and since 1963 when a new adega was built with a modern autovinification centre - entailing that foot crushing had taken place for the last time in the large lagares - things have picked up with regard to Bomfim's reputation and quality. In 1968, the last lagar was pulled down and replaced with modern techniques and after another rebuilding in 1972, Bomfim has produced 6,500 pipes of Port in its adega each year since 1973, of which the 300 pipes come from the quinta's own grapes. Under Dow's auspices a new, high technological winery was built to manage the harvest in 1996. It lies in connection with Quinta do Sol between Régua and Pinhão and according to James Symington it cost at the time the tidy sum of £ 2,000,000. It is a state-of-the-art winery. All the fermentation tanks are made of new, sparkling stainless steel and specially designed for remontage and autovinification. Naturally there is an advanced temperature control, and even the aguardente is cooled down before it is added to the wine. This way the must does not become heated during the addition of aguardente, and the finest aromas are maintained in the wine.

In the spring of 1999, Dow's repurchased the Quinta da Senhora da Ribeira which lies across the river from Quinta do Vesúvio. The quinta was purchased in 1890 by George Warre, but it was sold again in 1954 due to the financial crisis. For some years - and ever since 1988, the Symingtons had a contract for the grapes and the wine from this quinta, and today it is part of the family collection once more.

RUBY ♦♦♦♦

When Dow's Danish agent for many years, merchant Flemming Karberg, in the 1980'ies was able to by Château Fombrauge in Saint-Émilion by selling nearly all his stock of Dow's Vintage Port, he was so grateful that he served from the golden vintages to the Danish wine journalists. It goes without saying that this was a wonderful and very useful. Here are my tasting comments on the best wines from autumn 1998. All bottling was carried out in Denmark:

Vintage 1947: "Brown edge, soft nose. Soft and fruity taste, supple, seems ageless. Soft, long, deep and great. Seems rather dry. A great challenge and far from the end of its lifetime". (96/100)

Vintage 1955: "Colour: mahogany. Soft, supple, slightly smoky and deep taste and quite powerful. It sneaks across your tongue, is flirtatious and self-confident. Drinkable now, but is actually still too young. Dries out in the glass. Exquisite and excellent". (97/100)

Vintage 1960: "Colour: tawny with a glimpse of darkness. Light and decent, slightly polished, very nice, not at all aggressive, very polished, but surprisingly more drinkable than 1947 and 1955 and without the same challenge in the glass". (91/100)

Vintage 1963: "Intense nose. Soft, persuasive taste with a hidden powerful taste. Soft and delicious with fresh, dry fruit with a light sweetness to go with it. Drinkable but can easily keep". (94/100)

Vintage 1966: "Intense fruity taste, quite rich and wonderfully smoky. Slightly tawny in its sweetness and richness, but the fruit gives a solid challenge. Elegant wine, convincing structure". (92/100)

Vintage 1975: "Smoky, friendly, mild and a rather short aftertaste. Nice wine from a difficult vintage year, a small copy of something big, for it has a nice structure. Delicious taste for as long as it lasts". (88/100)

The Symington family quote with pride George Saintsbury's note in his famous "Notes on a Cellar book" (1920): "There is no shipper's wine that I have found better than the best of Dow, '78 and '90 especially". They can supplement these gracious words with the words from a capacity as Michael Broadbent who remarked the Vintages 1912, 1927, 1945, 1947, and 1955.

Dow's is the driest and most potent of the Symington Vintage Ports. They provide a special robust style, which requires a lot of patience. This also applies to the young vintages which confirm Dow's position as one of the most reliable Vintage brands. Oddly enough Dow's is underestimated compared to Symingtons' other brands, even though Graham's were the only ones who were able to compete with regard to quality and reliability for many years.

To support this, take a look at my comments when James Symington opened the following bottles for me in the tasting premises at Gaia:

Vintage 1977: "Very nice fruity nose. Potent, dry sweetness (!). Compact fruit with a taste of berries. Great potential. Very nice, confident structure. After Graham's the best 77' from the Symingtons". (95/100)

Vintage 1980: "Rather light nose. Soft and amiable taste with characteristic fruity sweetness. Potent, gusto, exciting – just wait for 5-10 years. More potent and more unpolished than Graham's 80'ies." (92/100)

Vintage 1983: "Dense, potent fruit taste. A fruit bomb, equally fruit and bomb. Dry, patient and promising". (94/100)

Vintage 1985: "Dark berry nose. Powerful, dense berry taste. Muscle. Intense juice, dark and with a fine disciplined sweetness. Potent and closed. The most potent wine of all Symingtons' 1985's". (95/100)

Vintage 1991: "Young, nice fruit. Soft, round taste, Fruity and nice, a solid medium style". (88/100)

Vintage 1994: "Intense berry nose and intense fruit. Masculine and rather dry. Seems more undeveloped and more durable than the other 1994's from Symington. Promising. But has to keep yet for many years". (93-96/100)

In the good vintage years, Quinta do Bomfin makes SQVP. I have a recollection of a nice and dry wine with a short aftertaste (1979) and a decent and amiable wine (1984).

Dow's LBV's are rather fruity and rather dry as Vintage Ports. Vintage Character ("AJS") made from 4 to 5-years-old wine is dry and solid with a nice fruit content. The more common Ruby types are robust and straightforward.

TAWNY

I have tasted Dow's 10-years and 20-years Tawnies many times in the course of the 1990'ies, also at many blind tastings, and they always end up in the low end for my taste. Oddly enough, they seem to be produced according to another philosophy than the best Ruby types.

The 10-years Tawny is semi-rich and glossy, oily, not fruity and rather sweet, i.e. contrary to Dow's Vintage Ports. The 20-years Tawny is much better, also with a rather light style, darker in colour and taste, but like the 10-years Tawny somewhat lax. The 30-years Tawny has the same dark tone as the 20-years Tawny with the same light and rich taste as the 10-years Tawny. But again no backbone.

Feist
(H. & C.J. Feist Vinhos S.A.)

Founded: 1836
Owner: Barros-Almeida Family
Taster/Blender: António Oliveira/José Sosa Soares.
Quintas: The best wines normally originate from grapes from Quinta de São Luiz, owned by the Barros-Almeida family

Feist is one of the few Port houses, which was not established in Porto, but in London when the two cousins, H. and C.J. Feist, came from Germany to England in 1836 and opened offices in London. It was not until 1870 that the company could enjoy a profit so that C.J. Feist could settle down in Porto and see to the wine being shipped off to London. In 1921, Carl Feist left the management of the offices in Porto to his son-in-law, J.H. Speich, and 13 years later he himself was assisted by Carl Feist's grandson, who was also called Carl Feist. During the Second World War, the office in London was damaged so badly during the German Blitz that it had to be closed down, and as times were not ripe for any new building activities, all interests were concentrated under the name of *H. & J.C. Feist* with company address in Porto. In the 1930'ies, the family business was taken over by another family-run company by the name of Barros-Almeida, and the wines with a Feist label are now produced and marketed now by the same team who handles Hutcheson, Barros and Feuerheerd.

RUBY

Feist's Ruby types are very light. Even their Vintage Port is remarkably soft and friendly. Usually, they are small, nice and sweet lightweights, which should not be kept for too long.

Quite by chance, I stumbled across Feist's Vintage 1970. When an old merchant in Copenhagen died in 1986, his remaining stock was sold very

Just as the other top quality wines from Barros-Almeida, the best wines carrying Feist's label are supervised by Manuel Ángelo Barros. (Photo: HO)

cheap and included a few cases of Feist Vintage 1970, which I naturally got my hands on immediately. They were Danish bottlings, bottled by the merchant, and had been treated carefully.

I still have a few bottles left. And they are still drinkable - well, I hope so, for if I am to summarise the 58 sensations in one word, it would be "unreliable". The bottles are characterised by an indifferent lightness and by a great wine with charm and a good concentration of fruit. And if I am to give them points they would range from around 70 points to 95 points - and this is not due to the time factor, for sometimes the difference is noted in two bottles which were opened – and drunk - at the same time.

TAWNY

Feist's Tawny types are much better than their Ruby types, as are the other brands from Barros-Almeida. Both the 10-years Tawny and the 20-years Tawny are mild, sweet and semi-rich with a more nutty taste and a taste of rock candy than a fruity taste. These wines should be enjoyed in good company. The best wines are their Colheitas. The following was tasted at Quinta de Sao Luiz in the course of 1995-1998, all newly bottled:

Colheita 1977: "Very mild caramel, soft taste, nice aftertaste, quite charming".

Colheita 1965: "Slightly smoky nose. Soft, long aftertaste, maybe too soft, but with a small explosion at the end".

Colheita 1975: "Fragile, but pure and refined. Nice nutty taste. Not aggressive at all".

Colheita 1963: "Rather dark, dense colour. Caramel taste, a bit crude, but with an intense sweetness and a slight acidity. Not completely balanced, but otherwise quite nice"

Ferreira
(A.A. Ferreira Succrs.).

Founded: 1751
Owner: SOGRAPE
Taster/Blender: José Maria d'Orey Soares Franco
Quintas: Quinta do Porto, Quinta do Seixo, Quinta da Leda and Quinta do Caêdo

When you look at all the hopeful British adventurers who settled down in Porto as business men, it's refreshing to visit Ferreira which is the only Port house founded by wine growers from the Douro Valley - and the only Port house with royal ancestors. Ferreira is also the only Port house not to owe its history to a man of enterprise, for just as the stout-hearted widows Clicquot and Pommery who dominate the history of Champagne, Dona Antónia Adelaide Ferreira thrones the history of Port. She took the helm at A.A. Ferreira's in 1844 and steered it steadily until she was carried to her grave on 26th March 1896. Apart from leaving money in the till and an inestimable reputation, she left her heirs 33 quintas in the Douro Valley. This information was passed on to me by her great-great-great-grandson, Ferreira's now residing director, Francisco Javier de Olazabal, better known as "Vito".

Ferreira sets the year of foundation as Port producer as 1751, but the first reliable written piece of evidence dates from 1772 when an invoice dated 22nd April of that year was issued by Companhia Geral da Agricultura do Alto Douro to the wine grower José Ferreira for the shipment of seven pipes of wine. However, Ferreira's breathtaking archives also include references to a much earlier relative, namely to Manuel Ferreira, who baptized his daughter in March 1630 in the small wine village called Travanca. From this point on, the genealogical tree branches out vigorously each illustrating a child and with the practical tradition within this business of cousin marrying cousin.

The José Ferreira mentioned on the invoice from 1772 was succeeded by his son Bernardo Ferreira, and all we know about him is that he was a cultured man who lost his life for being a man of breeding. On 22nd June 1808, he was on his way across the Jugerios bridge in Godim when he was approached by French soldiers. They asked him where he was going, and when he answered in perfect French they thought he was royalty fleeing the country and shot him - just to be on the safe side! This, at least, is what the family history tells us.

His sons, António Bernardo and José Bernardo Ferreira, were so well-informed of what was going on by their agent in London, Joaquim Máximo Virginiano (see page 49) that they could closely follow the Peninsular war from Porto. Virginiano's letters are kept in Ferreira's archives and tell part of the invaluable contemporary history, so posterity may appreciate what the publishers of "Um Português em Londres" (1988) objectively claim, namely that he was better at writing than in doing business!

António and José also had a third brother, Luís - there were actually 11 brothers and sisters all in all - and the three brothers ran the company side by side and took care of its different interests from 1808, all the way through the troublesome years following the Napoleon wars, and up to 1835 when António I died and his son, António Bernardo Ferreira II, and his wife, Dona Antónia, the daughter of José Bernardo, inherited the firm. They were first cousins, and this might explain the fact that even though they were even-keeled, they were at the same time very incompatible people.

The emu is Ferreira's trade mark. According to managing director "Vito" Olazabel, seen here with the emu, because it never runs backwards! (Photo: HO)

This was you see a marriage of convenience in which the convenience consisted of all the properties and the values, which belonged to the two branches of the family, were now united. Dona Antónia bore the three expected children accordingly, one son and two daughters, but they cannot have enjoyed their life together, for while António enjoyed the merry life in Porto, Dona Antónia enjoyed the peaceful life in the countryside of the Douro Valley.

At the time when António and Dona Antónia entered the company, Ferreira boasted a significant exportation to both England and Brazil as well as a couple of quintas in the Douro Valley, among others Quinta das Figueiras, later known as Quinta do Vesúvio, which António Bernardo Ferreira had purchased back in 1823.

Apart from the three children, the son, António Bernardo Ferreira III, and the daughters, Maria da Assunção Ferreira and Maria Virgínia Ferreira (who died at the age of 4 in 1841), the marriage seems rather platonic, so when Dona Antónia's husband died in 1844, everybody expected the grieving widow to retire slowly, but apart from the fact that António Junior was only 9 years old at the time, she possessed the same dynamic personality and ambitions as the Champagne widows, so she simply took over management herself. And not only did she take control, she took such a firm control of the company that it expanded, so when her husband died - on a trip to Paris (!) - shortly after signing a 5-years contract with Sandeman regarding that they would buy all their grapes from the Quintas Vesúvio and Vargelas, she also had lots of time to plan for the future.

The happy days in the Douro Valley abruptly ended in 1854 when Dona Antónia precipitately had to flee to London with her daughter, Maria da Assunção. This was the reverse of the medal, for Portugal's Prime Minister, Duque de Saldanha, had become so fascinated by Dona Antónia's wealth that he wanted his son to be married to 12-years-old Maria. Dona Antónia felt that he would not accept a refusal of marriage, so she fled via Vigo to the British capital where she very practically met with Francisco José da Silva Torres, who was responsible for managing her quintas.

What he was doing in London, nobody knows. But family history objectively states that she married him in 1856 and that they did not have any children. He got a first class life, she got a contract on the man who knew all about the land and vines. They both seemed happy, maybe even happier than young Maria who married a good match - at least in title - in 1860 at the age of 18. Augusto de Mendoça brought with him the title of Conde de Azambuja, and his grandfather was the João VI who was King of Portugal from 1816 to 1826.

It was Dona Antónia's own merits, skills, ingenuity and head for money matters that meant that from being the mother of her children and her husband's wife she became the Queen Victoria of the Douro Valley. Her energy and ambitions seem enormous for a posterity who is used to raising the flag every time a Port house buys a new quinta. Even though the demand for land and property in the Douro Valley was not as high a hundred years ago, you can only be impressed. And even the Symingtons' and the Barros-Almeidas' impressive association of Port houses today seems tiny, compared to the empire that Dona Antónia left in 1896 to her only son, António Bernardo Ferreira III, who did not even have to sit down and count his fortune, for his mother did it for him before she died.

The statement is found in Ferreira's archives and shows that Dona Antónia - apart from a wine cellar of nearly 13,000 pipes - left 33 quintas in the Douro Valley, of which the 22 contributed towards an annual production of approx. 1,500 pipes of Port. Upon her death some of the quintas produced next to nothing, but this was only due to mildew or to the fact that production was included in one of the other quintas. Thus Dona Antónia's last accounts read the following:

Name of Quinta	Production in 1896
Vesúvio	106 pipes
Vargelas	0 pipes
Granja e Per-o-Couto	9 pipes
Nogueiras e Lodeiro	138 pipes
Caldas	123 pipes
Lourentim	88 pipes
Travassos e Quebrada do Porto	176 pipes 28 pipes
Casal de Soutelo	36 pipes
Santinho	0 pipes
Serro	0 pipes
Arnozelo	1/2 pipe
Moncorvo e Sampaio	21 pipes
Pego	36 pipes
Pousa	73 pipes
Coalheira	20 pipes
Porrais	80 pipes
Valado	25 pipes
Vila Maior	23 pipes
Rodo	82 pipes
Mera e Caucela	62 pipes
Vale do Meão	389 pipes

Posterity's mention of Dona Antónia is as expected somewhat variegated ranging from grovelling admiration to smearing her good name and gossip, especially with regard to her relationship with Baron Forrester. But even her greatest competitors mention her with respect and posterity's greatest reproach against her seem to have been that she would not donate money to any good purpose that was presented to her.

She spread myths, and it was therefore a daring and unpredictable project when the historian Gaspar Martins Pereira, in co-operation with Vito's wife, Maria Luísa Rosas Nicolau de Almeida de Olazabal, started to expose the myths and presented the results in the ambitious works "Dona Antónia" in 1996. The book was initiated by Ferreira, and not without some remorse, Vito told me, during the unravelling of the dust of the archives.

Afterwards, he was both relieved and joyful: "I am very happy that we wrote the book, for there has always been a lot of myths about Dona Antónia - both within and outside of the family - about how fantastic she was, but at a certain point I simply did not know what to believe. But now I see that it was all true. She really was a fantastic person."

And she must have been. She had even planned her own funeral, so when she died at Quinta das Nogueiras on 26th March 1896, it was the end of an era. She was called Ferreirinha - the little Ferreira - when she was young and was just her husband's wife. She died as the most important Ferreira in history.

There is not much to be said about her daughter, Maria, apart from the fact that she married Augusto de Mendoça, the count of Azambuja, who had royal ancestors, but she is said to have been the one who in 1899, just three years after the death of Dona Antónia, sold the unproductive Quinta da Vargelas only because it was in a terrible state and unsuitable for the production of Port. Considering the fact that it was immediately bought by Taylor's and that it today yields the best grapes for Taylor's Vintage Ports, one can only conclude that this was a misjudgement, which would not have pleased her mother.

Her brother does not seem to have inherited Dona Antónia's skills either. He was 61 when he finally, like the Prince of Wales, was allowed to take over, and it was not his son, António Bernardo Ferreira IV, who led the company through the First World War, but first Francisco de Lima and Jorge Viterbo Ferreira, and then his niece's husband, Ramon de Olazabal, whose grandchild is Francisco Javier de Olazabal, better known as "Vito", who has been with Ferreira's since 1965, for the last 20 years as director of the company.

The family tree has really been split into several branches with all the problems this entails. The more the family members, the more who wanted to see money. This is the same tune we hear in the great châteaux' of Bordeaux and which could well be a signature tune in the Portuguese wine sector. In Dona Antónia's time, problems were solved by letting cousin marry cousin, but these practical marriages of convenience are no longer acceptable in the 20th Century.

As mentioned (see page 66f), Ferreira's other great personality, Fernando Nicolau de Almeida, solved the acute problems of sales after the Second World War by introducing his Barca Velha, but in the course of the 1960'ies and 1970'ies the number of family shareholders had attained 150 and the already heavily reduced hereditary estate and inheritance were shrinking rapidly. One of the branches of the family owned the Quinta do Vesúvio, the other branch of the family the Quinta do Vale do Meão (the Barca Velha quinta). But this was not enough. Both Seagram, Allied Domecq and SOGRAPE manifested their interest of taking over Ferreira, and as SOGRAPE gave the best bid Ferreira stayed in Portuguese hands. In 1988 the family at length decided to sell and A.A. Ferreira was taken over by SOGRAPE who bought 99.5% of the shares as well as 4 quintas, among others Quinta do Porto and Quinta do Seixo. Thus SOGRAPE became Portugal's largest wine producer. Mateus Rosé swallowed up Barca Velha.

The sad part of the adventure about Dona Antónia's descendants even ended worse when the

Ferreira's two quintas are opposite neighbours a bit west of Pinhão and are complete opposites: Here the poetic Quinta do Porto. (Photo: HO)

PORT PRODUCERS

branch of the family who owned Quinta do Vesúvio, the grand old lady's favourite quinta, was tempted by a big bag of money and accepted an offer from the Symingtons in March 1989. So it was not Ferreira but the family who sold the largest quinta in the Douro Valley. The Barca Velha quinta, Quinta do Vale do Meão is still, however, in the hands of the family, since 1996 owned by "Vito" who is going to leave Ferreira in the year of 2000 to settle at the quinta, making wine together with his son Francisco, who is an enologist.

SOGRAPE's take-over of Ferreira did not only mean money in the hand and thereby delight in the family, but also more positive visions for the future. Money was invested immediately, and if anybody had some doubt as to the intentions of SOGRAPE, they do not any longer. Especially the two most important quintas, do Porto and do Seixo, which lie across from each other a bit west of Pinhão, have enjoyed a bit of fresh capital.

Quinto do Porto is the beautiful and romantic quinta while Quinta do Seixo is the practical and steely quinta. And I must say that I do have a very special relationship to the Quinta do Porto that was the first Port Quinta I ever stayed on and which I have been allowed to enjoy on other visits waking up to a heavenly view of the blue Douro river from "my" room, and I even consider the

And here the prosaic Quinta do Seixo where vinification and all practical issues are handled – seen from Quinta do Porto. (Photo: HO)

Douro river as "my" river - even though I do not have the documents to confirm it! This is the quinta where I suffered the stifling heat waves of the Douro Valley, this is the quinta where I sailed boldly through the night with the good skipper, Fernando, after a couple of bottles of Quinta do Porto (10-years Tawny), and this is the quinta where I have climbed the steep mountain slopes in the morning with tired feet, and this is where I have enjoyed the calm early evenings with a glass of Quinta do Porto in my hand on the green terrace overlooking across the river. This quinta is my Nirvana - the Paradise of total surrender.

   Back to reality: the 25 ha of vines all face south and yield some of the finest grapes year after year ever since Dona Antónia bought the quinta in 1863. Until 1988, the grapes were vinified in this cellar's lagares, but since then the grapes are for practical reasons transported across the bridge to the opposite neighbour, Quinta do Seixo. Ferreira bought Seixo as late as in 1979 - about the same time that the less known Quinta da Leda was purchased - and under the management of Joaquim Fernandes it became the display window of the Douro Valley in the years thereafter with its bold new vertical rows of vines (ao alto, see page 99).

Today, the Quinta do Seixo houses one of the Douro Valley's most advanced vinification centres where all the grapes from the quintas: do Caêdo, do Porto and do Seixo are vinificated - whilst the grapes from the quintas: Leda and Meão are vinificated at Meão. Most of Seixo's 60 ha's of vines are plantet ao alto and are a model of the use of modern techniques in the Douro Valley.

Whilst Ferreira's guests are relaxing at the Quinta do Porto the oenocologists of Ferreira, led by José Maria Soares Franco, have designed the Quinta do Seixo as their command centre. Here, especially young António Américo da Rocha Graça, who has built a clone centre and is involved in new trials in co-operation with the University of Vila Real, should be mentioned. One of the objectives is to clone a vine with Touriga Nacional in a more lucrative and stable version than the existing one as well as to create a clone of Tinta Roriz giving fewer but better grapes. He and his team do all the grafting themselves taking shoots from old plants. Of course, this requires a special technique, and there is no lack of techniques at this modern steely quinta where all the grapes are fermented and mature on stainless steel. Ferreira's best Ports never see wood until they reach Gaia. Today, Ferreira is self-sufficient up to 35-40%, including all the grapes for their quality Ports, and including the grapes from the quintas owned by the family. When Ferreira bought Seixo in 1979, 90 pipes of Port were produced annually here. Today, this number has increased to more than 500 pipes, including however what the three small quintas contribute.

There seems to be centuries between Seixo's modern industry to Dona Antónia's artisan production, but only slightly more than 100 years have actually passed. But there is a solid link that has created a fantastic continuity - called Almeida. When Fernando Nicolau de Almeida was employed at Ferreira's in 1935, he succeeded his own father, who have been with the company for more than 40 years and had lived to experience Dona Antónia. When he died in the spring of 1999, he had been with Ferreira for 62 years, and his daughter, Maria Luísa, had married Ferreira's director, "Vito" de Olazabal. When Fernando Nicolau de Almeida, this charming and skilled live wire, filled with all the kindness of the world, the

Dona Antónia, the "yellow widow" of Port took over the management of the family firm Ferreira at the age of 33 in 1844 when her husband died. And as the Veuve Clicquot she not only managed to save money, she also made it multiply, so upon her death in 1896 she left her heirs 33 quintas and a prosperous Port house. The photographer is unknown. His historical work is on the family's Quinta do Vale do Meão.

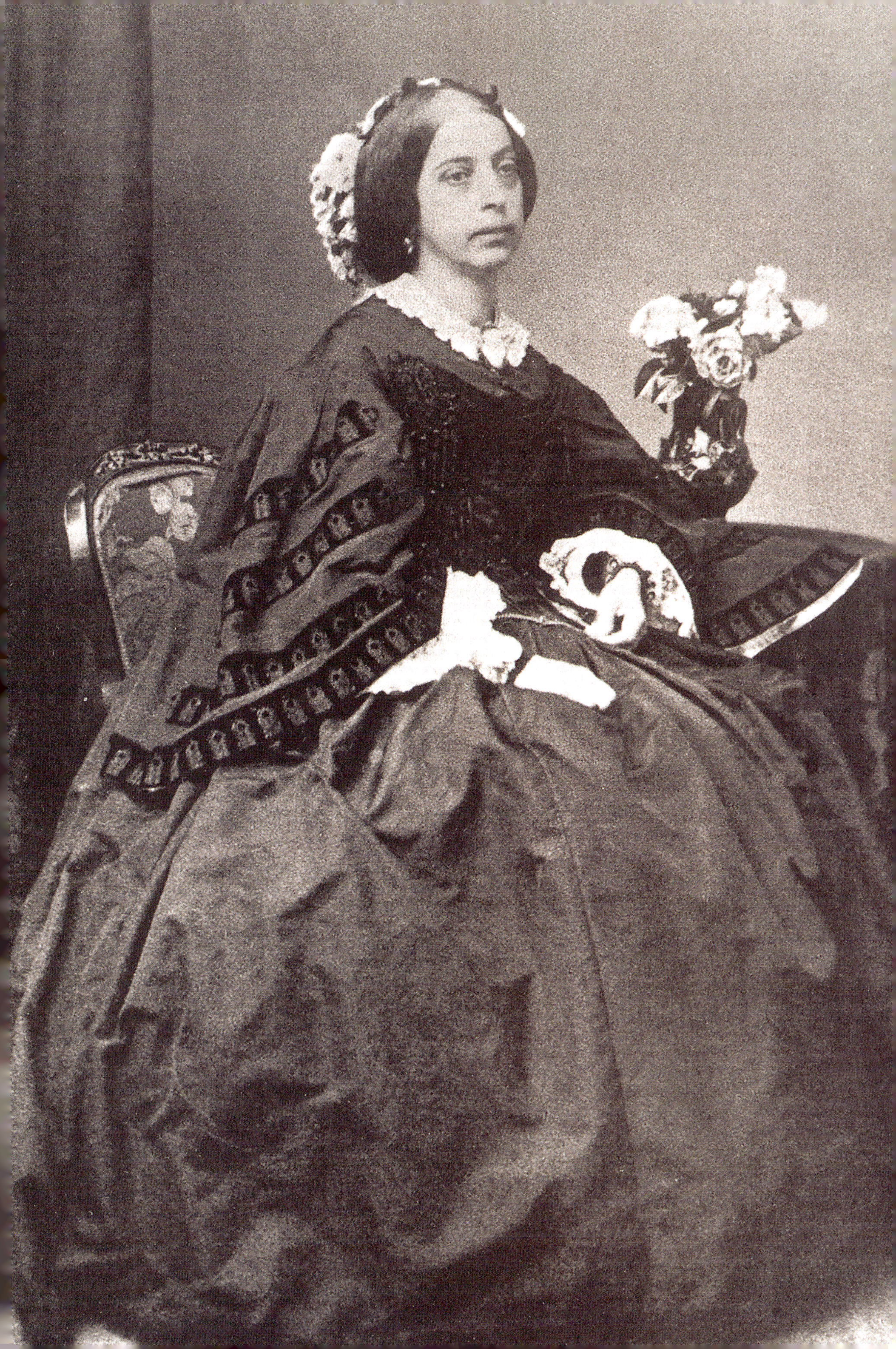

Barca Velha's inventor and the leader of the Confraria began to slow down in the late 1980'ies, his major responsibilities were handed over to his apt pupil, José Maria Soares Franco, who began his apprenticeship working for Almeida in 1979. Soares Franco is still sitting firmly in the chair. Three men in this important position in 100 years. Nobody can say that the staff-turnover at Ferreira's cellar is high!

RUBY

Of all the Portuguese houses only Quinta do Noval has obtained a greater international success with its Vintage Ports than Ferreira. If you look at reliability, Ferreira's Vintage Ports can be compared to Château Figeac in Bordeaux, but even in the small vintage years these wines are very reliable. 1978 and 1980 are good examples of this.

Ferreira also makes other more inferior Ruby types, for example *Vintage Character* and *Late Bottled Vintage*, but not of the same quality as the more inferior Tawny types. The LBV's are in a transition phase. Almeida originally did not want to make LBV's, but was persuaded to do so when the other Port houses proved to be successful, and they made their first LBV in 1980. However, they were so-called inferior wines, and Soares Franco wants to change this. "Until 1987, our LBV's were solely commercial wines. Now we want to bottle as early as possible and give them more fruit. The fruit is a secret. But we do know more today, and we make better plantings. We want to enhance fruit content, sweetness, tannin and structure", he says.

But the above-mentioned José Maria Soares Franco is only the third chief taster/blender in 100 years, so one must say that there is a certain continuity in the production. Soares Franco does not mind admitting that he has continued the "Ferreira style", which he in a moment's eagerness mentions as the "Almeida style".

His even more intense caring about the fruit and the fruity taste than his famous predecessor is

Ferreira is one of the few Port houses that can write its history on the basis of loads of archive material. Maria Luisa Nicolau de Almeida de Olazabal keeps the archives updated. She has her surname because she is the daughter of renowned Fernando Nicolau de Almeida and married to "Vito" Olazabel (to the right), Ferreira's managing director, who has a history of his own. (Photo: HO)

already seen in *Vintage 1994* and is perhaps even more characteristic in *Vintage 1995*, which is just as unimpressive in its structure and potency than the more famous 1994'.

The first Vintage Port from Ferreira that I ever tasted was *Vintage 1863* which Almeida poured me in the cellars in Gaia after I had travelled through rain and snow on a bold sea voyage from Quinta Vale do Meão in December 1984. So this wine was even from before the Almeida era, but it has no doubt set the course. I remember it as being historical, tasted in a monumental moment, very sweet and very Tawny like.

The Tawny characteristic of the old Vintage Ports was confirmed during the big tasting of Vintages of the Century in Porto in June 1999 when I had the opportunity to taste the following:

Vintage 1900: "Dark brown. Tawny sweetness with the same refined taste as an old Colheita. No fruit left, but very charming. A dream wine, if only it had been a Colheita. That's how dense and intensely sweet it is".

Vintage 1912: "Rather light style with an orange edge and a rather short aftertaste. Tawny character, short and decreasing aftertaste".

Vintage 1945: "Dark brown – also in the nose. Intense sweetness – of a Colheita, but also a touch of very nice fruit. Again more a Tawny than a Ruby type, but delicious, full-bodied and smoky. The slight fruit content completely disappears in the glass".

Vintage 1947: "Looks like a 1945, but contains an even more characteristic sweetness and no fruit at all. A lovely glass of wine, which should have been served as a Colheita or an over 40-years Tawny".

You really feel the change of style from these Vintages to the Vintages of modern times.

The following wines, which contain far more fruit, and this is not only due to age, were tasted in the course of 1998-1999:

Vintage 1977: "An equal amount of fruit and future. Passed the dry matter stage, but still closed. It has Ferreira's characteristic taste of lacquer, combined with a long aftertaste of liquorice. It should be kept for at least 10 years, during which it will be polished".

Vintage 1980: "Soft as velvet, homogeneous with a touch of liquorice towards the end. Flawless and very friendly. Soft, sweet with a stable course towards sweetness and friendliness. Maintains a good style. Drinkable now, but will also keep".

Vintage 1985: "Still youthful with potent, spicy fruit. A lot of sweetness, but still solidly wrapped in a dense, muscular fruit. Very nice balance. Will be exciting to taste it in 15-20 years".

Almeida tried to make SQVP, but stopped. Quinta do Porto's name has always been used for a 10-years Tawny, but both Quinta da Leda (Vintage 1990) and Quinta do Seixo (Vintage 1983) have also made a SQVP. And this type may very well be brought to life again, Soares Franco says, but emphasises than Ferreira considers the SQVP as a "second-class wine", as many other do, so they will only make this type in the really good vintage years.

TAWNY

Ferreira, as many other producers, but maybe especially Ferreira, has many small Tawnies with different names and content of sweetness to give money in the till, but only a few of them are quality wines. As Ferreira does not make Colheitas, these wines show three different characteristics:

"Dona Antónia" (6-7-years Tawny): "Robust, solid type with a nice balance of fruit and sweetness, slightly woody taste and a long aftertaste. The prototype of a young, fruity, soft and masculine Tawny".

"Quinta do Porto" (10-years Tawny): "Soft and mild, creamy and slightly smoky. Fruit content and full-bodied. Complex and a great 10-years Tawny".

"Duque de Bragança" (20-years Tawny): "Full-bodied, smoky and creamy. Great, well-made 20-years Tawny with fruit and backbone. Very sweet, but the sweetness is under control".

"Quinta do Porto" is made from 8 to 15-years old wine, and only from the grapes of this quinta. "Duque de Bragança" is made from 15 to 40-years old wine. Soares Franco seeks the fresh fruity taste in these wines: "I seek a balance between the fruit content and a slight oxidation, and only a touch of wood. I want a long and complex aftertaste. We use younger wines in the old Tawnies contrary to the days of Almeida to procure more fruit and sweetness. We want to make full-bodied, complex wines and not burnt Tawnies".

Sometimes he also makes some bottles of 30-years and over 40-years Tawnies, but there is not much interest on the market for these wines – not due to quality, but due to price. Also, according to Soares Franco's opinion the 30-years and the over 40-years Tawnies have a tendency of being too alike. He has also experimented with a Colheita 1979, but he has the same opinion as Alemeida that "a mixture will always be better than a Tawny from one year". Soares Franco is also responsible for the Barca Velha, which is not only the Douro Valley's most popular red wine but also the most popular red wine in Portugal. Today, it is made from grapes from both Quinta do Vale do Meão and Quinta da Leda – approx. 50% from each quinta. After the harvest, the wine is immediately transported to Gaia where the malolactic fermentation takes place.

In previous years the wine stayed on large and small casks on Quinta do Vale do Meão, but today maceration is an important factor, and the wine has to be under constant supervision. The grape varieties are separated, and only new casks are used for the process. In the first 6-8 years after harvest, when the wine has been bottled, a decision is made whether to put Barca Velha on the label or if the wine is to be a "second wine" under the name of "Reserva" (former Reserva Especial). The latter is considered the next best Douro red wine by many people.

Feuerheerd
(Feuerheerd Bros. & Ca. Lda.)

Founded 1815
Owner: Barros-Almeida Family
Taster/Blender: António Oliveira/José Sosa Soares
Quintas: The best wines are usually from the grapes from the family Barros-Almeida's Quinta de São Luiz

In the turbulent years following the Congress of Vienna in 1815 when the European borders were opened again, the young German adventurer, Dietrich M. Feuerheerd, came to Porto where he started dealing in wine. He was more prosperous than his successor, Albert Feuerheerd, who due to Black Friday and the following world crisis in the late 1920'ies was forced to sell the Port Wine house. His last vintage was Vintage 1931 which was never introduced on the market. He died shortly after, but his daughter, Claire Feuerheerd-Bergqvist, succeeded in keeping the family gem, Quinta de la Rosa, and it still remains the property of the Bergqvist family. Feuerheerd is now part of the Barros-Almeida group. They make both Ruby and Tawny bearing Feuerheerd's name, the latter being by far the best.

Fonseca

(Guimaraens Vinhos S.A.R.L.).

Founded: 1822.
Owner: Same groups of owners as of Taylor's.
Taster/Blender: David Bruce Fonseca Guimaraens.
Quintas: Quinta do Panascal, Quinta do Cruzeiro and Quinta de Santo António

Fonseca, one of the most renowned Port houses today and the only Port house producing a Vintage Port of a quality and at a price competitive to Taylor's - was so insignificant in 1822 that 27-year-old Manoel Pedro Guimaraens joined João dos Santos Monteiro as a partner of the company at a very modest price. From the beginning, the new company, now *Fonseca, Monteiro & Guimaraens* continued to trade under the name Fonseca, that of an earlier, senior partner whose name has been traditionally handed down to this day by MPG's descendants.

MPG, as he is still affectionately known in the family, was not to enjoy peace in Portugal for long. Magdalena Gorrell Guimaraens, married to Bruce Guimaraens and the historian of the family, explains why:

"An ardent Liberal, he was actively involved in supporting the cause of Queen Dona Maria and her father Dom Pedro against Dom Miguel in the civil war (see page 47ff). In 1828, as repression of the Liberals took a decidedly nasty turn, MGP was forced to flee to England - according to family legend, hidden in an empty pipe of Port. (Already in 1822 he was taking steps to protect his family from persecution as by then he had changed his name from Gonçalves to Guimaraens).

Soon after he arrived in England he opened his office in a lovely old Georgian building in Crutched Friars in London, where all principal wine shippers were established, and continued trading as successfully as before. Nothing much had changed except that the Porto offices were manned by his cousin, Manoel Gonçalves and the Altona/Hamburg offices, by João Gomes Monteiro, one of his partner's relatives. In 1927, the firm closed its offices in London and the family returned to Porto.

It was from here and from his home in Maida Vale that he worked tirelessly to assist his countrymen who sought refuge in England and France until the political storm had settled. Working through his commercial agents in Belgium, Holland and Germany he developed an ingenious way of obtaining funds from Portugal for fellow Liberals in exile - he issued "fake" invoices to their families back home! As an eminent member of the Portuguese community, both in political and literary circles (he was a close friend of Almeida Garrett, one of Portugal's most famous writers of the period and whose wife had also taken refuge in London for the duration), he was one of the select guests at a reception for the future Queen Dona Maria upon her first visit to England to raise money for her cause. In fact, MPG wrote a hymn in her honour that was sung on that occasion. Queen Dona Maria did not forget his dedication - in 1834, MPG was appointed a member of the most noble Portuguese Order of Christ and raised to Knight Commander of the same order six months later.

A very knowledgeable botanist in his own right, MPG made the acquaintance of some of the principal English botanists and became one of the earliest members of the Royal Botanical Society at Regent's Park. His favourite flower was the pelargonium and from experiments with this plant he produced some splendid specimens. He never forgot the flora from his native country; correspondance of the period relates to his ordering potted fully grown orange trees from Porto - no mean feat at the time! The mind boggles! No sooner had the siege been lifted, that MPG settled down to the more practical business of creating a family. He was now 39 years old and time was passing. A copy of his marriage licence from the Vicar General of the Archbishop of Canterbury reads: "On 29 October 1834, Manoel Pedro Guimaraens, of St. Olave, Hart Street, in the City of London, a bachelor, aged 21 and upwards, to Georgina Frances Pearson, of the district of St. Luke, Norwood Surrey, a spinster, aged 21 and upwards, at St. Luke, Norwood".

Georgina, whose father was a solicitor from Greenwich, Kent, bore him a daughter and three sons. All three of sons were to enter the firm: his eldest son Manoel Fonseca Guimaraens who was only 20 when his father died succeeded him as head of the company; Pedro and Frederico joined after his death."

When MPG died in 1858 at the age of 63, the firm had changed its name to *M. P. Guimaraens & Sons* and was now trading almost exclusively in wine. It grew rapidly in repute and importance and, by 1840, was the second largest Port shipper. Fonseca Guimaraens's first shipment of Vintage Port to England in 1847 set the seal on the firm's prestige.

Pedro Gonçalves Guimaraens joined the firm in London in 1862 and then moved to Porto to establish Messrs. Guimaraens & Co. In Porto, Pedro married Helen Florence Fladgate, daughter of John Alexander Fladgate, Baron da Roêda (see page 296f), co-owner of Taylor, Fladgate & Yeatman. Little could he imagine that some hundred years later, when as a result of the economic hardships affecting the entire Port trade as a result af World War II together with the burden of heavy death duties, the Yeatman family's purchase of Guimaraens & Co. in 1948 would again unite the two families, albeit only commercially.

Although he headed the firm for 26 years, his family can only say little about Manoel Fonseca Guimaraens other than he sired six children and died in 1885 when he was replaced by his oldest son, Manoel Pedro Guimaraens who moved to Porto but preferred to write poetry instead of dealing in Port. He gradually retired, dedicating himself to his books and leaving the well-established Port house to his uncle Frederico Alexandre Guimaraens who, by that time, was known to all by the more English version of his name - Frank.

MGP's direct line in Guimaraens & Co. skipped a generation as his only son Charles Bruce Fonseca Guimaraens broke with tradition to work with W. & J. Graham where he rose to the position of Managing Director shortly before his retirement, when the firm was sold to the Symington family. Charles married Kathleen May Allott in 1930 and they had two sons who would grow up to produce more great Ports than most families. Gordon Guimaraens was born in 1934 and Bruce in 1935, shortly before the Second World War, which made life a hassle for so many Port houses - also for the Guimaraens'.

Future Port lovers undoubtedly will admire Bruce and Gordon Guimaraens, so alike in their expertise yet so different in appearance and personality, with the same historical admiration with which we recall past Port notables such as Dona Antónia, Frank "Smiler" Yeatman, George Sandeman, John Henry Smithes and Reginald Cobb.

The elder, John Gordon, born in 1934, tall, slender and possessed of typical British reserve, joined Martínez Gassiot & Co. in 1952. After this house merged with Cockburn's, he was appointed Production Director for both firms.

"Please ring" the sign says, and many people do. Quinta do Panascal is open to visitors, and is worth a visit even though Bruce Guimaraens rarely shows people around. Bruce fills out the Port landscape well, both physically and humanly. He is one of the biggest personalities in the business. (Photo: HO)

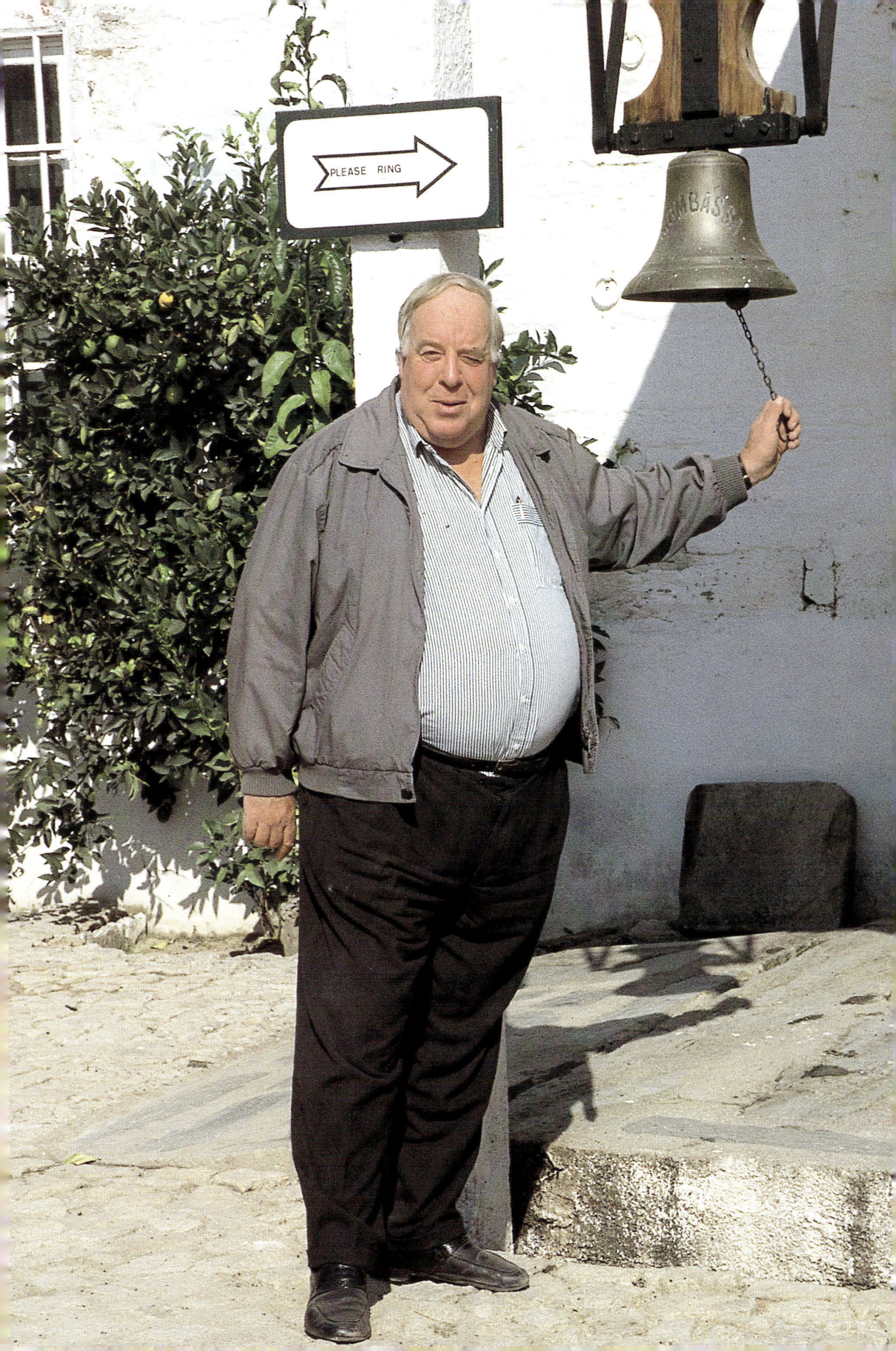
PLEASE RING

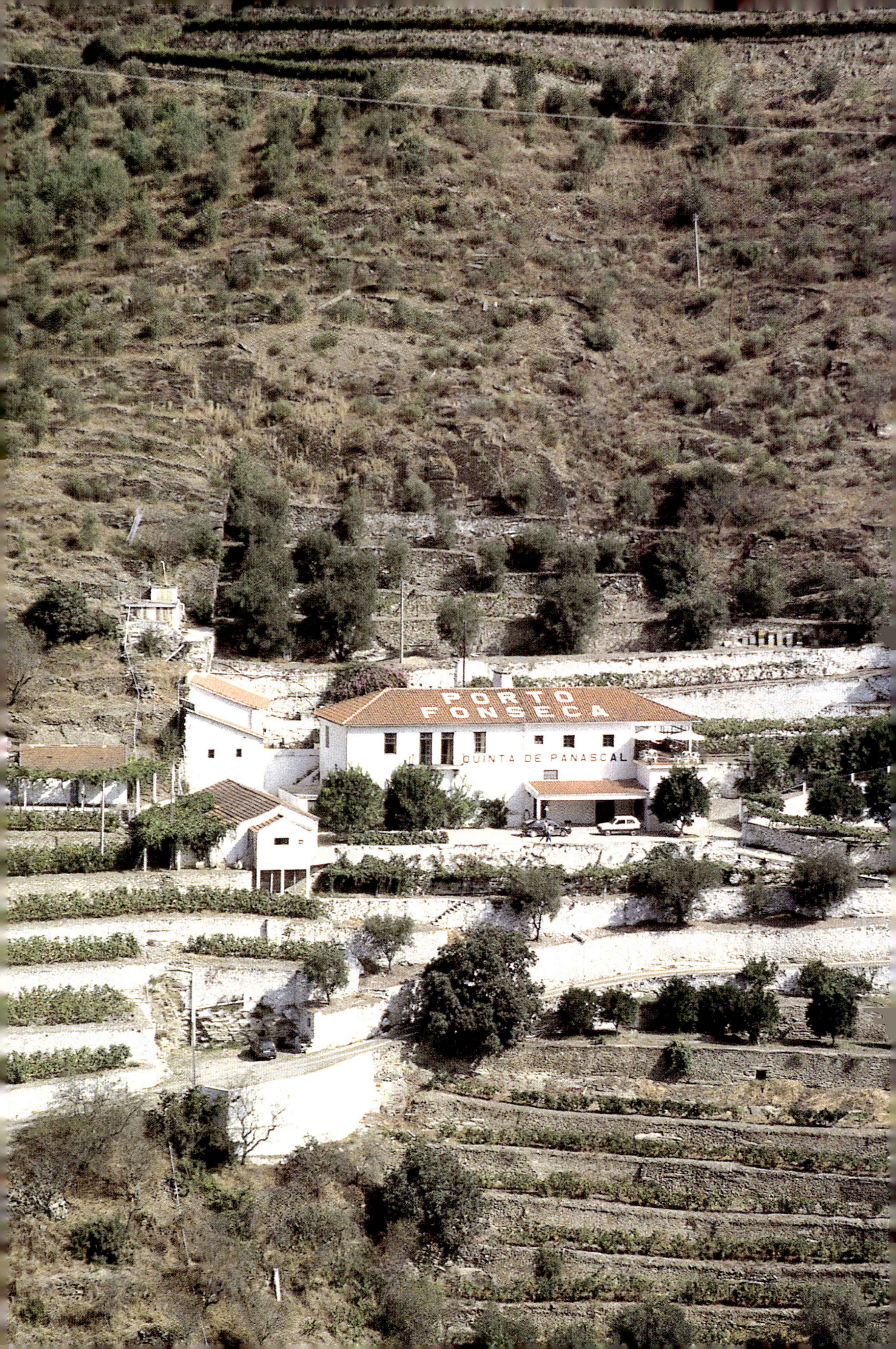
PORTO
FONSECA
QUINTA DE PANASCAL

He retired in 1996 after more than forty years as Senior Winemaker. The younger, Bruce Duncan, born in 1935, also tall but more full-bodied and with an open jovial manner, joined the family company in 1956 after returning from Africa where he had served as a Royal Berkshire Officer in Ghana. 1956 was his first vintage year at Fonseca Guimaraens. It was a terrible time, he recalls. "It poured cats and dogs and worse still, I didn't know the first thing about the making of Port!". He would, eventually, under the expert training of Frank Guimaraens' daughter Dorothy whose talent in the tasting room, until her untimely death from polio in 1963, would shape his entire future as a winemaker.

Unique in the annals of Port, all the Fonseca Guimaraens Vintages from 1896 to 1991, with the exception of 1955 that was made by Dorothy Guimaraens, were made by one of two people: Frank Guimaraens from 1896 to 1948 and Bruce Guimaraens from 1960 to 1991. Bruce retired as Director and Winemaker (the term he uses) for both Taylor's and Fonseca's in 1995, to be succeeded by his son David Bruce Fonseca Guimaraens, the 6th. generation of a family with an enduring tradition in making quality Port.

From his country estate and its spectacular view over the Minho River across to Spain, in Vila Nova de Cerveira in North Portugal, where he enjoys a semi-retirement advising his younger son Christopher Tilton Guimaraens in the latter's horticultural enterprises and occasionally travelling abroad to give tutored Port Tastings, Bruce reminisces fondly over his years supervising the Douro quintas. The apple of his eye will ever remain Quinta do Panascal that Fonseca Guimaraens purchased in 1978 from the Pacheco family, from whom they had bought wine for more than 20 years. It is located on the south bank of the Douro River, just outside Pinhão in the Tavora River Valley. The quinta dates to the 17th Century and after years of improvements and new planting, it produces 300 pipes of quality wine. 43 ha of its total 74 ha are under vine.

When it was purchased, Panascal produced 3.000 bottles of Port a year, citrus, fruit and almonds. Today, all but a few trees have been dug up and everything is gone except for the vines - even the quinta manager has moved to a neighbouring village. The main building and the outhouses no longer serve as permanent dwellings but remain ready to welcome visitors. Panascal was the first Port Quinta in the Douro Valley to set up a tourist office and offer cellar door sales of its own products (see page 376ff).

A model of mechanisation and modern techniques, the number of permanent employees at Panascal has dropped from 33 to just only 3. Most of the daily work is performed by tractor. On occasions when more human resources are needed, such as during the pruning season and at the vintage, Fonseca Guimaraens contracts a roga of some 30 men and women. These are groups of itinerant workers from villages often many hundreds of kilometres from the Douro, whose family tradition in working the Douro vineyards dates back many generations.

In pursuit of the Guimaraens family's commitment to producing fine wine, care is taken to continue with man's all-important role in the winemaking process. At the vintage, each bunch of grapes is hand-picked and carried to the lagar where the grapes are crushed by foot. Both Bruce and David firmly believe that this is still the best method for extracting the most colour from the skins and for producing the highest quality Port, as can be attested by the Single Quinta Vin-

Quinta do Panascal that Fonseca Guimaraens bought in 1978 has always been the apple of Bruce Guimaraens' eye. The quinta is situated by Rio Távora, a tributary to the Douro river.

tage Ports made at Quinta do Panascal. Also the new planting is approached seriously. Shoots are cut from the vines and sent to France for grafting on virus-free rootstocks. After remaining in France for an entire year to gain in strength, they return to the Douro for planting out. In addition to Panascal's extensive new planting, in 1985 Fonseca Guimaraens purchased the adjacent property of Quinta do Val dos Muros whose 15 ha are almost entirely planted in patamares.

Besides Quinta do Panascal, the grapes from two other Fonseca Guimaraens quintas form the backbone of Fonseca's Vintage and Guimaraens Vintage Port: Quinta do Cruzeiro and Quinta de Santo António. In lesser years, the wines produced on all three properties are used in the blends for "Fonseca Bin 27" and its Tawnies.

Already in the 1870ies, Fonseca Guimaraens was purchasing wine from Quinta do Cruzeiro. One of the previous owners, having fought with her relatives, was insistent on selling the property to the Church; Taylor's Dick Yeatman persuaded her to sell it to her quinta manager instead. After his death in 1973, his daughters sold it to Fonseca Guimaraens. At the time of the purchase, the property was small, but extremely well kept, as it had been for many years by the dedicated old man. A major restoration program followed and the vineyards were re-shaped, modernised and re-palnted. In 1988 the property was extended with the purchase of 3 ha of adjoining land. Today, Cruzeiro produces 150 pipes of top quality wine, all trod by foot.

Quinta de Santo António was purchased in 1979 from the Freitas family from whom Fonseca Guimaraens had been buying wine since 1912. A smaller, less spectacular property in that its original house lies in ruins, this quinta produces, according to Bruce Guimaraens, some 30 pipes of superior quality wine form superb grapes that are trod at Quinta do Cruzeiro, just 3 kms. away.

It is interesting to note that all these three quintas were purchased in the 1970'ies: Cruzeiro in 1973, Panascal in 1978 and Santo António in 1979. This is a consequence of the development in the 1950'ies and the 1960'ies, Bruce Guimaraens explained to me: "In the 1950'ies there was no good reason to spend money on land and quintas, for we could buy all the best wine we could ever wish for from small farmers - and we had a tough time selling Port back then as well. But in the course of the 1960'ies, due to the abuse af chemical fertilisers, we were offered more and more grapes of a poorer quality until eventually, we could not buy enough grapes or wine of the desired quality, so we had to invest in land for ourselves. Also the price of grapes was forever rising. Whilst prices had remained somewhat stable from 1956 to 1962, in the 1960'ies they began to increase every year. Lastly, it is a well-known fact that if you want to make Port of the most superior quality, you have to have your own vineyards.

As Bruce looks back to the past, David looks to the future. Born in 1965, he always dreamed of following in his father's footsteps. A graduate of Roseworthy College, Australia's finest school for winemakers, he was trained in the latest winemaking methods which he brought to the Douro Valley, yet never disdaining the value of the centuries old art of making Port.

David stresses that yes, he has learnt to make wine, but Port is less about making wine than it is the art of blending - and the art of blending cannot be learnt from books. It can only be gained through experience and when you have the experience, you can blend anything. His father could not have put it better!

David has tackled the challenge with great respect. "I knew that when I came back, this would be the first thing I would have to learn: to learn!" To learn from the older generation, to ensure that his ancestor's skill and expertise are transmitted to future generations. Maybe his son Samuel Fonseca Guimaraens, now only 6 years old, will some day represent the 7th. generation of the family in the Port trade! On his father's recommendation, David has become very interested in viniculture, something which according to both father and son has always been neglected in the Douro but which more and more people are focusing on today.

Like his father, David is the Senior Winemaker (he prefers to call himself "Portmaker") for both Taylor's and Fonseca Guimaraens. Like Bruce, he sees no problem in making a Vintage the same year for both houses, "for Taylor's and Fonseca are not made according to my choice but according to the conditions of the grapes. I just have to make the most of them!"

Like his father also, David is fortunate enough to have the resources to make the world's greatest Port without having to worry about the financing. So he does not have sleepless nights and can

David Guimaraens had a flying start as the responsible person for the best wines at Fonseca's and Taylor's with the expensive Vintage 1994. Here he is showing what Fonseca Guimaraens has to offer in the genre: Fonseca Vintage, Guimaraens Vintage and SQVP from Quinta do Panascal. (Photo: HO)

adhere to Bruce Guimaraens' exclusive philosophy which he expressed to me one late night at Quinta da Vargellas: "I have dedicated my whole life to Port and to making the best Ports possible. I cannot accept second best. But you cannot buy quality. The most important thing is quality, then money - not vice versa!"

As you may have already guessed, I cannot hide the fact that I am a great admirer of Bruce and David's - and of Fonseca. And if I believe strongly enough in quality - which I do - sufficient money is sure to come my way so that I can afford to buy it ...!

RUBY ♥♥♥♥♥

The banal secrets behind Fonseca's Ruby types are: extreme high-quality and reliable products.

It all begins with the common Ruby (approx. 3 years) and already with the rather famous "Bin 27" (approx. 5 years) you feel their skill. According to David Guimaraens it is a Vintage Character type. It is always the same and is one of the best non-quality Ruby Ports that exist.

The Guimaraens' have a subtle relationship to LBV. Bruce simply did not like the name, and maybe not even the type, but in the end he was persuaded to produce it, because the market just could not get enough Vintage. But if he was forced to make this type, he wanted to make a robust and therefore unfiltered wine living up to Fonseca's image, but that meant that it was not easily drinkable, as the market required it to be. David has a more pragmatic point of view and only makes a slightly filtered type, which is – at least to a certain extent – easily drinkable. It is marketed just after bottling:

Fonseca, LBV 1990: "Dark and juicy, light, nice dryness, soft juice, liquorice. Nice and mature".

Fonseca, LBV 1983: "Powerful, not quite harmonious, but improves with some oxidation. The power seems to grow in the glass. Should be oxidated. Seems like an old-fashioned crusted Port with an extra layer of muscle".

Bruce and David also have their special list of kings in the upper Ruby region which is quite different from the other Ruby Ports, also from Taylor's. They make two different Vintage Ports so the hierarchy can more or less be described as follows:

1. Fonseca Vintage Port
2. Fonseca Guimaraens Vintage Port
    Quinta do Panascal Vintage Port
3. Fonseca Late Bottled Vintage

The definition is quite simple: Fonseca Vintage Port is only produced in the classic vintage years. Fonseca Guimaraens Vintage Port is produced in the good vintage years, which are not classic vintage years. Therefore Fonseca Guimaraens is always a small impression of Fonseca Vintage. The difference is found in the depth and length, and not in the style, Bruce explains: "Fonseca Vintage must be kept for 30 years and then lasts for another 20 years. Guimaraens must be kept for 20 years and then lasts for another 10 years".

Whilst the Guimaraens Vintage is a miniature version of Fonseca Vintage, the SQVP from Panascal goes its own way. It is produced in the good vintage years when the grapes are not used for Fonseca Vintage, but it follows its own style as well as the style of the vintage year. "It has its own profile", David says. He also says that he would very much like to make one of the three Vintage Ports every year, if the climate and the grapes promise well. They did not in 1993.

Fonseca Guimaraens Vintage Port is lighter than Fonseca Vintage Port, but it is still a Vintage Port which many producers would be very happy to have as their best Port. It even looks good in the bad vintage years, as for example in:

Guimaraens Vintage 1976 (tasted 1995): "Fruit and body, young and not aggressive with a nice, long aftertaste. Potent". (89/100)

Guimaraens Vintage, 1984: "Intense elderberry nose. More elderberry in the taste and a long fruity taste. Nice body, but not too much. Lots of fruit and berry. Seems to have a light structure, because the fruit/berry taste is so dominating". (93/100)

Guimaraens Vintage 1991 (tasted 1999): "Dense black currant nose, elegant taste of black currant, short and great finish, delicious and drinkable, potent with a rather sweet fruity taste". (93/100)

It can be surprisingly durable, its inventor, Bruce Guimaraens, tells me: "I made a Guimaraens Vintage in 1965, the year David was born. Unfortunately it was not very promising, always closed, stand-offish and inelegant, but then it woke up in the 1990'ies! It started as a small boy wearing a sailor's collar and grew into a great man. I have never tasted a wine, which could change its character to such a degree".

In conformity with the Guimaraens family's philosophy there is a marked difference between Guimaraens Vintage and the SQVP from Panascal:

Quinta do Panascal Vintage 1986: "Liquorice and pepper, then berry. More charm than power. Rich taste, tempting, but a rather short aftertaste". (87/100)

Quinta do Panascal Vintage 1987: "Very soft. Lots of dark berries, but macerated and manageable berries. Friendly taste – and then suddenly ending off with dryness". (89/100)

And now let us take a look at King Vintage himself. When it comes to Fonseca Vintage Port, I could write a long story about all the excellent Vintage years that I have not even tasted. But I am sure that you can read about them elsewhere. Instead let me summarise the Vintages I tasted in the course of 1996-1999:

Fonseca Vintage 1963 is rightly considered as a classic vintage and one of the best vintages of this vintage year. I am looking forward to tasting it someday. It was such a success that Fonseca's importers were not interested when Vintage was declared in 1966. But thank goodness: Vintage 1966 was produced!

Fonseca Vintage 1966: "Dark in the glass. Soft on the tongue. The fruit seems incredibily young. An encounter of natural sweetness and ripe fruit in an embrace of potency, passion and gracefulness. Chocolate and liquorice. It is not only decent, it is not only nice – it is excellent. Excellent now and it will be excellent for years to come". (98/100)

Fonseca Vintage 1970: "Very dark, obscure as a bottomless forest lake and with the potency of the mermen who probably live there and tempt mermaids and mortals every day. A super potent wine of temptation, a red Ferrari of Port, a fruit time bomb of fruit, which already now, long before the final blast, strike sparks and is a never ending sensation". (99/100)

Fonseca Vintage 1977: "When it was a young wine, it was very friendly, but now (in 1998) the friendliness has changed to sweetness, intense fruit, then body and potency. The sweetness is so dense that the potency has difficulty in emerging. An obvious deep sleeper not to be awakened yet. Massive and promising". (95/100)

Fonseca Vintage 1980: "At first it seems very, very friendly with only a touch of liquorice to challenge the tongue. It is more soft than sweet with a deep and long ending. But what a cheat! It is like the firecrackers you think have fizzled out, but it keeps on fizzling with a forever lasting soft, potent taste of liquorice. An incredible long aftertaste". (90/100)

Fonseca Vintage 1985: "Coal-black. Deep nose: liquorice and tar. Exciting, rich and plump baccate fruit: black currant and elderberry. Concentrated, long, soft, dry taste with dry matter and depth. Very friendly and very fruity with a dash of liquorice and tobacco. But an eruption is on its way". (97/100)

Fonseca Vintage 1994: "Dense and thick with an intense taste of black currant. Self-confident structure, impressive balance. Lots of dry, potent juice, intense baccate fruit, warmth, softness, dry matter, not aggressive at all. Thick as oxen blood, friendly as a calf with its tongue stuck out, a swelling bull in a bottle". (97/100)

"One of the most important elements is the maceration and the extraction of colour. Colour is a very important aspect. The colour pigments give the body colour", Bruce once said. You can see and taste very distinctively that there is a lot of colour in Fonseca's Vintage Ports - also in the very promising Vintage 1994, which was young David Guimaraens' first vintage. What a start!

I have no further comments. The points and the words speak for themselves.

TAWNY

Bruce Guimaraens has never been very interested in Colheitas and in new casks for Tawnies. "I don't like new casks. Even the old Tawnies should have just a hint of wood". This is his philosophy. And even though I seem to have noted a slight change of style since David joined the company towards a bit more of a woody taste and a bit more raw fruit, the general philosophy of Fonseca has not changed at all.

The following series was tasted in the autumn of 1998:

10-years Tawny: "Soft and powerful. No time to lick off the fruity taste - full speed ahead! Fruit"! (93/100)

20-years Tawny: "Intense nose. Delicious, fruity taste, soft and creamy, caramel, very nice". (95/100)

30-years Tawny: "Soft, nearly as pastry with brown sugar, but not sweet as sweets. Harmonic, refined, polished. Still more fruit than sweets". (96/100)

Over 40-years Tawny: "Soft, long, mellow taste of cream caramel and brown rock candy. Delicious with a well-balanced fruit and an elegant sweetness. Still fruity and some power". (94/100)

In earlier tastings the 30-years Tawny has always been the weakest of the four Tawnies, but not this time. Either there has been a change of style - or my taste has changed. But no matter what, Fonseca is also among the best producers of Tawny, and they are always reliable, just as Fonseca's Ruby types.

Gilbert's

see Burmester

Gould Campbell

Founded: 1797
Owner: Symington Family
Taster/Blender: Peter Ronald Symington
Quintas: None

In 1797, a year dominated by wars and revolutions all over Europe, George Clode defied the harsh times and settled as a Wine Merchant in Bishopsgate Street, London. The following year a young Irishman, Garrett Gould, literally flew from the revolution on his native island and sailed from Cork to Lisbon where he established the firm of *Messrs. Gould Brothers & Co.* The Irishman had luck and in conjunction with the important merchants and bankers, Messrs. James Campbell & Co., he also established a Port company in Oporto under the name of *Messrs. Gould, James Campbell, Jones & Co.*

According to Charles Sellers ("Oporto Old and New", 1899), during the Peninsular War, Garrett Gould and his partners "amassed a considerable fortune, and, after all the foreign troops had been withdrawn from Portugal, Mr. Gould founded the house in Oporto under the style of Messrs. Gould, James Campbell, Jones & Co. On the retirement of Mr. Jones from the Oporto firm, Mr. Gerald Gould, son of Mr. Garrett Gould, became a partner, and the firm was Messrs. Gould, James Campbell & Co." In 1851, George Clode's company, Clode & Baker were appointed agents for Messrs. Gould, James Campbell & Co. in the United Kingdom, and two years later, in 1853, as the senior partner Mr. Callanane died and nobody in the Gould family wanted to enter into Port business, Messrs. Clode & Baker purchased the stock and the right to use the brand name, eventually abbreviated to the present Gould Campbell. Nathaniel Clode was succeeded by George Baker as the senior partner of the new company, the latter settling in Oporto. He died in 1885, acknowledged as a gifty businessman, as well as an expert on roses. His son, George Baker was more of an adventurer who had to fight with new war times and revolutions.

For many years the company kept a rather low profile, until it was purchased by the Symington family in the 1960'ies. Since then its name has been closely linked to the reputation of good Vintage Port.

Gould Campbell has never owned a quinta, but some very fine quintas have supplied its wines for very many years. In particular the Vintage Ports, which are the most distinguished wines of the company, are based on two small superb quintas in the Rio Torto both of which are long time suppliers to Gould Campbell. These Vintage Ports are especially appreciated in U. S. A. and Canada.

RUBY

Gould Campbell make the traditional series of Ruby types from Fine Ruby, an uncomplicated, fruity average style, to LBV and to Vintage Port. As Gould Campbell has no quinta, they do not produce a SQVP under the Gould Campbell name.

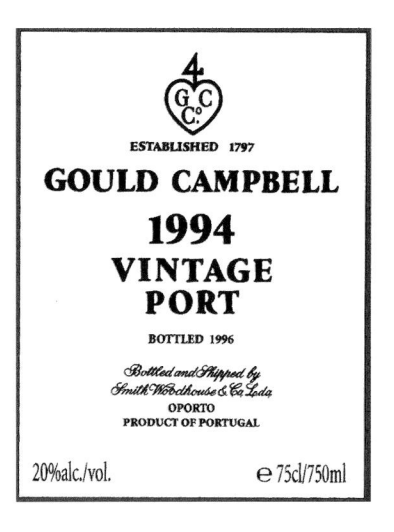

```
ESTABLISHED 1797
GOULD CAMPBELL
1994
VINTAGE
PORT
BOTTLED 1996
Bottled and Shipped by
Smith Woodhouse & Co Lda
OPORTO
PRODUCT OF PORTUGAL
20% alc./vol.          e 75cl/750ml
```

In 1999, I had the occasion of tasting all six brands of Symingtons' *Vintage 1970* in one tasting with the surprising result that Gould Campbell came just after Warre's and closely after Dow's and Graham's. In 1998, Gould Campbell *Vintage 1977* was still a young and potent wine. *Vintage 1980* is milder, drinkable now and elegant, *Vintage 1991* is surprisingly potent and self-confident in a somewhat unpredictable vintage year, and the very young *Vintage 1994* has "an impressive combination of power, potency, and fruit".

I have especially had several good experiences with Vintage 1983 which have impressed me every single time and, which are one of this year's most well-balanced and most fruity wines, and with *Vintage 1985* which I had the possibility of comparing to two other "minor" Symington wines, Quarles Harris and Smith Woodhouse, in August 1999.

It was an instructive comparison. Gould Campbell quickly opened but took a long time in opening completely. It was definitely more potent than Smith Woodhouse and had more length and tenacity than Quarles Harris. After three days in the decanter, Gould Campbell was the only wine that was still alive, and kicking quite well. A potent and decent Vintage Port, which should lie for at least 10 more years.

According to the Symintons, Gould Campbell's Vintage Ports are very popular on the American market, because the Americans like the pulpy taste.

TAWNY

Gould Campbell's Tawnies are nice and well made – but they are no match to the Ruby types. They have a fruity and "British" style with no excess richness and smoke. The 10-years Tawny is robust and rather light with no character of significance.

Graham's
(W. & J. Graham & Co.).

Founded: 1820
Owner: Symington Family
Taster/Blender: Peter Ronald Symington
Quintas: Quinta dos Malvedos

It was not due to Port that the two Scottish brothers, William and John Graham settled down in Porto in the beginning of the 19th Century, for they had come here from Scotland to deal in textiles. But in 1820, they had to accept 27 pipes of Port as an installment from a debtor, which was probably all he owned, and one can easily imagine that their particular Scottish noses preferred the bouquet of an old Tawny too textile fluff.

Naturally, there were some problems in the balance of the cashbooks back in Glasgow, and the two brothers were reprimanded for their rash settling of accounts, but the Port was easily sold, so they were told to put the textiles aside and go look for more good casks of Port.

This is how the Port adventure started, and in 1826 the brothers shipped their first pipes of Port under the Graham family's name. These pipes were also quickly sold and the success of Port rolls through Scotland just as quickly as the pipes of Port rolled on board the ships in Porto.

From the first busy days and till late in the 19th Century there are pages missing in the private family album, but the Graham's hardly made a fuss when a young Scotsman by the name of Andrew James Symington was employed as a clerk in 1882. They should have kept a better eye on him, for he marched forward in the firm and in the world of Port whilst the Graham family did not move, and as a historical à propos, young Symington's descendants bought the well-renowned Port house in 1970, which at the time had more of a reputation than capital.

The purchase included the Quinta dos Malvedos that the Graham family had purchased back in 1890 but it was in such a terrible state that the Symingtons wanted to get rid of it right away. However, the Grahams had neither the urge nor the money to repurchase it, and at some point there were serious discussions about its possibilities as a lemon farm instead of a Port quinta. Thank goodness, the vines were left in the soil, and the Symingtons made a deal with the new owner to vinify the wine here. But in the long run, this solution was unbearable and expensive for the perfectionist family, and in 1981 they bought back the quinta and immediately started restoration. Two years later, electricity was installed and the tumble-down buildings were transformed under skilled hands into a wonderful villa, which is the gem of James Symington today.

According to James Symington, the quality of the wine from Malvedos had always been excellent while the production grew smaller and smaller. After the repurchase very substantial new planting was undertaken from 1982 and furthermore a considerable number of mature vineyards were bought from neighbouring farmers and incorporated into the much enlarged quinta.

In 1987, more than 100 pipes were produced from the quinta's vines for the first time. All wines sold under the Malvedos label had been sourced only from the quinta since the middle 1980'ies, and the family have no plans to change the successful Malvedos name to Quinta dos Malvedos

Good stuff is waiting for better times. Already now, Graham's Vintage 1977 is one of the mastodons of the vintage. The photo was taken in Graham's cellars in Gaia. The Port houses on the quintas rarely have more than a few bottles for "everyday use" and for visitors. (Photo: HO)

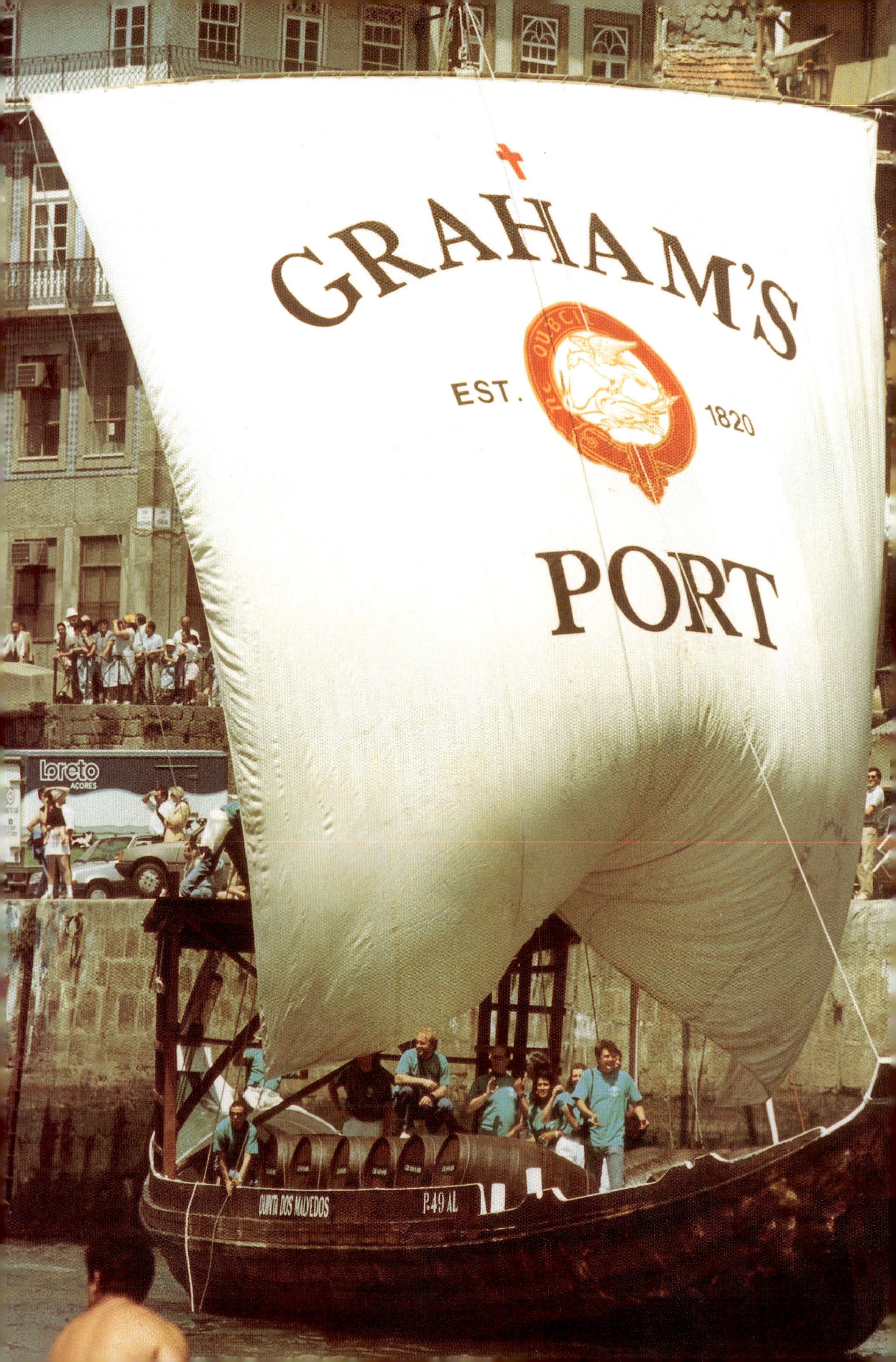
GRAHAM'S
EST.
1820
PORT
Loreto
QUINTA DOS MALVEDOS
P-49 AL

on the label. The 100 pipes of Port in 1987 have now grown to nearly 400 pipes a year, and the grapes from this quinta are of such a high quality today that they are the backbone of the Graham's Vintage Port in the good years. The cellars have also undergone a miracle since the electricity grid was installed in 1984. And since the harvest in 1998, a new and homemade robot has been used for the foot crushing of grapes. It is, as the lagar, made of stainless steel, computerized and according to James Symington by far the best replacement of human feet.

The trick is that its plungers move up and down while it moves forward in the lagar. After fermentation and when the wine has been run off and had aguardente added to it, the lagar is tipped automatically, exactly as a tipping waggon full of sand so that the fermented cap slides out.

The advanced robot was constructed by Graham's staff under the management of Peter and Charles Symington. In 1998, it was used as an experiment with great success, according to James Symington. And its versatility is especially delightful, as it can be used both in the modern stainless steel lagares as well as in the old granite lagares.

The robot will naturally be included in the new winery which will be ready for the harvest in the year 2000. As a kind of compromise, the new winery renders three kinds of crushing possible: the traditional foot crushing in the lagares, robot crushing and autovinification on stainless steel.

It is only symbolic that Graham's does not move. In reality Graham's catch the wind, especially i USA where every bottle of Grahams's Vintage Port is well paid. The photo is from the annual boat race in Porto. (see page 316-317)

RUBY

Vintage Port made Graham's famous all over the world, but you can sense their clever skill and the good raw material in the fruity *Six Grapes,* a cherry-like, young Ruby with tiny impression of Tawny, which is not so strange, as the wine is bottled after 2-3 years and has matured in casks for 5-6 years before bottling takes place.

LBV

I do not know if the Symington family acknowledges a special "Graham style", but at least I do. A harmonic experience of fruit, healthy fruit, softened gently by good oak and wrapped in a delicious sweetness. Completely cultivated in the LBV which is bottled after 6 years, i.e. after the longest possible maturation in casks. Its long maturation in casks would be fatal if the fruit were not convincing, but luckily in Graham's LBV it is and it is also produced in the big Vintage years as 1985.

Vintage Port

But the Vintage Port is Graham's greatest feat. Graham's is the reliable, polished, classic Vintage Port of the Symington family's groaning jewel case. Dow's can be wilder and drier, Warre's can be more sensual, but none of them are as complete and complex as Graham's.

Unfortunately the Symingtons have always had a hawk's eye on England as a seller's market, but James Symington did visit Denmark once and with him he brought a big armful of Graham's Vintage Ports to persuade the Danish market. I can see from my comments from the event (September 1987) that Vintages 1945 and 1970 were two highlights and that James Symington called Vintage 1970 "the best overall year".

In the spring of 1999 I tasted a series of Vintage Ports from the 1960'ies at a private session, including Graham's:

Vintage 1966: "Soft, clingy, elegant. The fruit sneaks into you and explodes after a long time in your mouth. Semi-rich, delicious and still potent". (95/100)

When James Symington organized a monumental tasting for me in Gaia in the autumn of 1998 consisting of Dow's, Graham's and Warre's different vintages, I noted the following about Graham's:

Vintage 1977: "Intense nose, a real Port Winenose. Luscious, subtle taste. Juicy, smiling, polished sweetness. Elegant wine, which could use another 10 years of peace and quite – and polishing". (96/100)

Vintage 1980: "Liquorice nose. Very nice fruity taste with a considerable sweetness. Actually drinkable now with well-balanced fruit. Soft, elegant and still durable". (92/100)

Vintage 1983: "Intense elderberry, lots of sweetness, juice and youth (!). A rather sweet, fruity and refined style. Young and promising". (92/100)

Vintage 1985: "Dark elderberry nose. Full of sweetness and charm, muscle and potency. Well-structured, still a remarkably young fruity taste. Polished fruit with a great future potential". (95/100)

Vintage 1991: "Intense, dominating sweetness of berries. Lacks backbone. It will be exciting to see what is hiding behind the sweetness – if there is anything at all". (84/100)

Vintage 1994: "Intensely luscious, elderberry-like, full-bodied sweetness. Friendly, massive fruit. Seems very mild and forthcoming - surprisingly forthcoming. Evaluation at this stage is a disappointment, but I would not mind tasting it again sometime". (90/100)

Unless something has changed in the vinification process in the last decade – and I do not think so – it looks as if it is a special trait of Graham's Vintage Ports that they have a characteristic, fruity sweetness from birth and that this sweetness for many years "over-sugars" the other qualities of the wine. Through maturation the sweetness buckles under to fruit and power, and when the three elements meet on the thin line of balance, Graham's Vintage shows a potent charm that no other Vintage Port has.

Graham's Vintage Ports are usually surprisingly drinkable as young wines, even as very young wines (Vintage 1994!), but do not let this fool you: they may be firecrackers covered in a sugar coating.

Graham's also make their famour SQVP Malvedos from the quinta bearing the same name (see page 142), and if you want to know how a producer's classic SQVP develops compared to a traditional Vintage Port I recommend that you buy a bottle of Graham's Vintage Port 1977 and a bottle of Malvedos 1978. This is what I did in September 1999, and it was a sensational experience.

After decanting the wine, the two wines were surprisingly heterogeneous, both soft and juicy with a slightly ripe taste of liquorice and both with the same long taste. But after 15-20 minutes something happened. It was as if the 1977 only let out some of its charm whilst the Malvedos 1978 just let go of its own charm.

Every half hour that passed the difference grew bigger and bigger, especially in depth and length, and Malvedos' fruity sweetness gradually lost more and more of its fruit. Two day later,

Quinta dos Malvedos lies on the north bank of the Douro, a bit west of Cockburn's Quinta do Tua. Compare this photo with the photo on page 175 and with the cover photo. (Photo: HO)

Graham's 1977 had developed an impressive, liquorice-polished style whilst the Malvedos stayed mild and creamy with a much shorter taste but with a delicate sweetness drying out more and more. No doubt a decent wine, that just had to surrender to the 1977.

Graham's Vintage 1977	(96/100)
Malvedos, 1978	(87/100)

In young vintages, such as 1979, 1982, and 1984, "Malvedos" seems to have a lighter style than 1978, and even a young Vintage as Malvedos 1984, which I tasted in August 1999, I would not even keep any longer.

James Symington calls Graham's Vintage 1980 the most underestimated vintage and Vintages 1970 and 1994 the two best vintages in his time. As to the first statement I fully agree. When I had the pleasure of organising a tasting of Vintage Port 1970 in November 1988 before the Port Festival i Copenhagen, 23 wines were evaluated by 24 tasters, and I dare say this was the most competent tasting jury that has ever been gathered, and including 13 producers of this noble drink – and they chose Graham's Vintage 1970 as a sure winner in front of Fonseca.

TAWNY

Graham's do not make Colheitas, but the whole series of old Tawnies. The four wines were tasted in the autumn of 1998 at Graham's in Gaia:

10-years Tawny: "Sweet but not sticky. Mild, semi-rich, a dash of smoke, very nice body and nice length". (92/100)

20-years Tawny: "Extremely sweet fruit. Friendly and soft with a taste of brown rock candy and brown sugar. Seems quite light but consistent in its mild, luscious style". (93/100)

30-years Tawny: "Thick and brown, almost a Colheita. Dense structure, oily, tastes of brown sugar and is delicious. A very potent 30-years-old". (94/100)

Over 40-years Tawny: "Dark colour with brown sugar consistency and a well-balanced, intense sweetness. Rich, clingy, complex with an irresistible and slightly fruity sweetness". (92/100)

Graham's is no doubt the family's trump card in the art of making old Tawnies.

Gran Cruz

Gran Cruz' wines are rarely seen in Scandinavia, but in France "Porto Cruz" is the best sold brand. Especially the very ordinary, cheap Port Wines are sold in France, and this is one of the reasons why Gran Cruz can present more than 4 mio litres of Port Wine that have aged in casks for more than 20 years in its lodges in Vila Nova de Gaia. The owners also present other impressive figures: stainless steel containers for 32 mio litres of wine situated on 16,000 m², and a state-of-the-art winery bottles 13,000 bottles an hour. So the first bottle in 1926 has surely been followed by millions of other bottles since. The best wine I have tasted from this house is a 20-years Tawny.

In 1901, the firm was named after its best-known brand "Gran Cruz", and when the firm was sold to the French group "La Martiniquise" in 1972, the name was slightly changed to Gran Cruz Porto (1975). Since then large quantities of old wine of a dubious quality have been purchased by Casa do Douro to satiate the French market.

At a census in 1998, Gran Cruz disposed of 24 mio litres of Port Wine in Gaia, and another 22 mio litres, which are still in stock at Casa do Douro. Since 1996, Gran Cruz has been the largest exporter of Port Wine with regard to volume, of which the major part ends up in France

Hunt, Constantino

(Hunt, Constantino - Vinhos Lda.).

See also Ferreira.

Old and new found each other in the beginning of the 1990'ies when Hunt Roope & Co. (with roots from 1650) merged with Porto Constantino (founded 1877). Among the wines of different houses you will find once very prestigious Tuke Holdsworth and Morgado and Antino. In 1893, Hunt Roope bought Quinta da Eira Velha which provided the best grapes to Tuke Holdsworth's Vintage Port, but in 1907 it was taken over by one of the company's directors, Cabel Roope, in exchange for his shares in the company.

He became one of Port's many colourful personalities, a dandy and a cosmopolitan who never learned to speak a decent Portuguese and therefore was had to take many jokes about his personality. He died in 1911 of a disease of the liver. Hunt, Roope & Co. bought back the quinta in 1938, but when Hunt, Constantino was taken over by Ferreira, the quinta was sold off to the Newman's who were the co-owners of Hunt Roope.

Ferreira has toned down the production of Hunt, Constantino's wines which are no longer on the market today after a period when they were used as alternatives on the various export markets.

Hutcheson

(Hutcheson, Feuerheerd & Associados Vinhos S.A.).

Founded: 1881.
Owner: Barros-Almeida Family
Taster/Blender: António Oliveira/José Sosa Soares.
Quintas: The best wines normally originate from grapes from Quinta de São Luiz, owned by the Barros-Almeida family

Hutcheson, Feuerheerd & Associados was founded in 1881 in Porto as a traditional Port house by two British citizens: Thomas Page Hutcheson and Alexander Davidson Taylor. Even though they worked under humble conditions, they managed to profile their wines brillantly at major exhibitions, but unfortunately the company dissolved in the 1920'ies when Thomas Hutcheson retired and Taylor died without leaving any heirs. Augustus G. Bouttwood carried on the Port house, until it shortly after was taken over by the Barros-Almeida family. A rationalization in 1986 resulted in Hutcheson merging with Feuerheerd Bros., Vieira de Souza and The Douro Wine Shippers & Growers Association. This new constellation is behind brands such as Hutcheson, Feuerheerd, Santos Junior, Souza, Rocha and Almeida.

RUBY

I have not written down many comments to Huchesons's Vintage Ports and LBV's, but the few comments I have noted are very much the same: wines with a mild, light taste, some sweetness and very amiable, but without any special traits of fruit or potency. *Vintage 1985*, which I tasted in August 1999, had a rather hard fruit content and seemed uncouth. After a few hours the alcohol emerged and put its heavy imprint on the fruit. The wine became more hard and aggressive than weak.

TAWNY

Tawny is no doubt Hutcheson's forte. Both the 10-years Tawny and the 20-years Tawny is rather sweet, although with a concentrated taste, full-bodied and charmingly soft. They have a tendency towards being a bit "burnt" and obtaining a taste of burnt caramel, but I believe that this only enhances the charm.

I have only tasted a few of Hutcheson's Colheitas, the recent one being *Colheita 1979*, which I call "a Colheita with a good body, very nice sweetness and a nice structure. Fine texture. A Colheita with a long, straightforward taste".

Hutcheson is rightly famous for its older Tawnies and Colheitas. Some of them are seen here in very good company. (Photo: BJS)

Kopke
(C. N. Kopke & Ca. Lda.).

Founded: 1638.
Owner: Barros-Almeida Family
Taster/Blender: Alonso Cid
Quintas: Quinta de São Luiz

Kopke is the oldest, still-existing Port house. Unfortunately, Kopke's archives burned down in a big fire in 1882, so all we know today is what history has passed on from one man to another and from scattered notes.

Previous history is however certain: after the Hanseatic towns by the Baltic Sea had been imposed a double Baltic taxation in the 1580'ies and the Portuguese seafarers had conquered the great world and all its wealth, the Hanseatic people signed a commerce treaty with Portugal in the beginning of the 17th Century. As their first Consul General in Lisbon the Hanseatic towns chose Nicolau Kopke, and his son, Christiano Nicolau Kopke, travelled further north and established his own company in Porto in 1638 under his own name, but at the time he simply dealt in "vinho", not in Vinho do Porto or Port.

The ownership remained in the hands of the Kopke family until the late 19th Century when the family first formed a collaboration with the British Bohane family who took over the company in 1870 (Mason Catley & Co.). The big fire in 1882 and Joaquim Augusto Kopke's death in 1895 meant the end of the Kopke influence. The Bohane's owned the company until 1953 when it was taken over by the Barros family.

Unfortunately, we do not know much more about the oldest existing Port house, but we can open a small window to its history through Quinta de São Luiz which belonged to the Kopke's and later to the firm which now supplies the best wines to the Barros family. When Barros bought Kopke in 1953, the Barros family already owned some of the quinta's neighbouring properties, quinta de Dom Pedro and Quinta da Fonte Santa, which were purchased in 1937.

Quinta de São Luiz was not included in the classification in 1757 (Feitoria), contrary to some of the neighbour quintas, and from the records prepared after the revision in 1761, it does not seem as if São Luiz existed as an independent quinta at that time at all. The name does appear towards the end of the 19th Century when the lots were changed. C.N. Kopke took over the company in 1922, after which it became part of the package which was sold to the Barros family.

Until 1973, the grapes were crushed by foot in the old lagares, but then new techniques in the form of steel and cement were introduced, and recently these techniques have been replaced by a state-of-the-art technique so that the quinta's vinification equipment now stands proudly among the most modern equipment in the Port industry. From foot crushing to computerized control of all vital processes in 25 years! A major achievement, which also says something about the ambitions of the Barros family!

The quinta's assignment is quite large. It delivers grapes and vinifies the best of the grapes for the family brand wines. It does help improve yields, however, that the Barros' have been buying up the neighbouring plots since 1972 so that the quintas: da Lobata, da Galeira, da Alegria and da Mesquita are all now part of the Quinta de São Luiz that disposes of 90 hectares of vineyards of a total area of 124 hectares.

São Luiz is the family's most prestigious brand. The best Kopke wines are always made from the grapes of Quinta de São Luiz and are vinified on the spot, and the Single Quinta Vintage from São Luiz is estimated by the Barros family as being more exquisite than Kopke and Barros Vintage, which is made from grapes from both São Luiz and the warmer Dona Matilde. As

Quinta de São Luiz was purchased by the Barros-Almeida Family together with Kopke's in 1953. It is one of the most versatile quintas in the Douro Valley, containing both habitation, guest rooms, its own church and one of the most modern vinification plants in the valley (the long building in the middle). (Photo: HO)

an example, the best grapes in 1995 were used for the Single Quinta Vintage carrying the São Luiz name. According to Manuel Ângelo Barros there is also a distinct difference in the styles of Barros and Kopke - Kopke having more depth and structure, both as a Vintage and as a Colheita.

The grapes and the most are carefully selected during the vinification but it is only the blend of the finished Port that decides what is going to be sold under the label of Kopke - or the label of Barros, Feist, Hutcheson or Feuerheerd.

RUBY

You realise very quickly when you drink Kopke's Ruby types that this producer is a Tawny house, not because they are inferior or thin, but because the fine, natural sweetness and the touch of refined fruit are the characteristics of a Tawny. These wines are quickly drinkable, even young vintages as Vintage São Luiz 1995 and 1996. As a curiosity, they are not marketed as São Luiz but as St. Luiz.

The ordinary Kopke Bridge Ruby is a quite ordinary, and in my opinion the Kopke Vintage has had difficulty in lasting for more than 20 years even in the great vintage years. This does not have an impact on quality but says something about the style.

Of the old vintages, which I have tasted in the course of the 1990'ies, I was mostly impressed by *Vintage 1952* for its straightforward and refined soft fruit and by *Vintage 1966* which is the best Kopke Vintage Port I remember.

In 1999 I tasted some of the more recent vintages and made the following comments:

Vintage 1985: "Elderberry and sweet liquorice. Great, unsophisticated charm. Very amiably, nice and fruity, but a bit too developed".

Vintage 1994: "Fruit, elderberry, lightness. Nice and fruity, sympathetic, but lacks dimension".

Vintage 1995: "Elderberry and a bit of liquorice. Soft, fruity style, rather mild and amiable, a bit superficial and already drinkable".

TAWNY ♛♛♛♛

If Kopke's Ruby types are among the average types, their Tawnies are among the best types. Try tasting their (white!) Muito Velho Branco which has been aged in casks for more than 40 years. This will give you an indication of a producer who knows his oak.

In the autumn of 1996, Manuel Ângelo Barros visited Denmark bringing with him an impressive collection of Kopke wines. I have also visited Kopke in Gaia and at Quinta de São Luiz three times since then, so my impression of Kopke's wines is based on a vast experience.

The following evalutations are from 1996-1999. All Colheitas were new bottlings:

Colheita 1900: "Rich brown sugar. Beautiful, concentrated, soft taste. Juice and intensity. No sign of age, but mild and vivid. Complex, wonderful wine". (97/100)

God himself can witness this old contract from 1760 and you also faintly see the name of Kopke as the middle signature. The contract, hanging at Kopke's in Gaia, unfortunately is one of the few curiosities that survived the fire in 1882.

Colheita 1915: "Delicious, soft taste of brown sugar with a touch of acetone. Wonderful and still virile". (93/100)

Usually everything in the Douro Valley is 100 years behind Gaia, but at Kopke's it is vice versa. State-of-art technology on Quinta de São Luiz, but still the Middle Ages in Kopke's cellars in Gaia that have not yet seen modern machinery and ergonomists. (Photo: HO)

Kopke is rightly famous for its Colheitas. Here is some good, old-fashioned evidence.

Colheita 1927: "Complex and powerful (!) with a fine youthful charm. No signs of age. Vivid and delicious, just as vivid as delicious". (97/100)

Colheita 1935: "Deep brown colour. Dense, compact wine with a touch of acetone and more brown sugar. Delicious, long-lasting taste with a fine, intense sweetness". (89/100)

Colheita 1938: "Full-bodied and elegant Colheita with a touch of smoke. Short but very nice. (89/100)

Colheita 1940: "Deep dark brown, elegant, depth, dark and polished". (92/100)

Colheita 1947: "Dark, very dark. Soft nose, slightly smoky and very subtle. Enormous body, power, density. Intense, agile wine even though it is more than 50 years old. An undertone of acetone is sensed somewhere in the background, but is of no importance. The sweetness grows towards the end. Elegant wine". (96/100)

Colheita 1951: "Dark brown caramel. Great sweetness, character, smoke. Mellow and elegant. Long caramel taste that does not fall into the trap of sweetness". (94/100)

Colheita 1952: "Clingy, sweet, rather light with a touch of orange going well with the sweetness. Delicious and well-balanced". (93/100)

Colheita 1960: "Smoky and rich. Clinging soft taste with richness and substance. Harmonic, very nice wine with body and character". (94/100)

Colheita 1966: "Dense and slightly spicy without an intrusive sweetness, more refined brown rock sugar than brown caramel, harmonic, full of character and fine explosion in the mouth". (95/100)

Colheita 1968: "Soft, juicy, very pure, elegant structure and taste. Dense, refined, well-balanced". (92/100)

Colheita 1974: "Nice, dense, smoky nose. Nice taste of brown sugar. Nice but lacks a bit of character". (87/100)

Colheita 1978: "Fine, smoky nose. Soft, smoky taste. Rather light structure. A hint of sharpness in the glass". (86/100)

Colheita 1980: "Very nice, stylish Colheita with a fine measured sweetness. No richness, masculine, nicely balanced and charming". (93/100)

Colheita 1982: "Very young with a slight acetone nose. Polished and sugary taste with a very nice robustness and distinct alcohol in the background. Potent – but too young". (89/100)

Colheita 1985: "Dark brown, rich and sweet. Woody taste and raw power, but much, much too young". (90/100)

I seem to have noted a slight deviation of style in the 10-years Tawny in the last decade. I have a feeling that this type has become more fruity and less smoky than before. But it is still a wonderful wine.

Krohn

see Wiese & Krohn.

Martínez

(Martínez Gassiot & Co., Ltd.).

Founded: 1790
Owner: Allied Domecq
Production Team: Jim Reader, Miguel Corte Real and Manuel Carvalho
Quintas: None, but via Cockburn's, Martínez gets part of the grapes from the privately-owned Quinta da Eira Velha

Extremes meet and there is music in the air - as well as heavy tobacco smoke! For when Sebastian Martínez arrived in London around 1790 to trade in Port, Sherry and Havanese cigars, he met John Gassiot in 1822, and this new partnership was an immediate success so that they could buy their own company in Gaia, including a good stock of Port and good cellars.

John Gassiot had three sons: John, Charles, and Sebastian, who all became partners in name more than in fact for they all had other jobs to take care of, and the practical part of the work was thus carried out by William Ones and John F. Delaforce.

When Sebastian Gassiot died in 1902, the firm was put up for sale and oddly enough the later partners at Cockburn's recommended John Teage in Porto to buy the well-renowned company, which he never did.

Instead, fresh capital was put into the undertaking, and until 1916, Arthur Nugent handled the daily management, followed by Donald MacLean until his death in 1939, and since by Gilbert Eastaugh. In 1962, Martínez was bought up with Cockburn's by Harveys of Bristol who later sold the two houses to Lyons Hiram Walker Group who later sold both houses to Allied Domecq.

As you can see, Martínez has led a stormy life and had the same owner as Cockburn's. Gordon

Guimaraens who began at Martínez in 1952 has had a lifetime responsibility for the best wines of both houses. But the lodges of the two houses are closely separated, and there is a noticeable difference in the two styles. Martínez is (in relation to Cockburn's) known as a producer of "Buyer's Brands" and whilst Martínez is profiled via its Tawnies, Cockburn's is most famous for its Ruby types, especially its Vintage.

Martínez benefits (with Cockburn's) from wine from the Newman family's Quinta da Eira Velha. In good years it is used for Single Quinta Vintage Port with Martínez' name on the label. In less good years it is blended into Cockburn's and Martínez' best Ruby Ports.

RUBY

Martínez is one of the Port producers who is much better than they get credit for. To many Port Wine drinkers, even some of the best, Martínez is just a little brother to Cockburn's, like Delaforce is a little brother to Croft's. But this is not at all fair. Martínez and Cockburn's are made by the same team, for many years under the supervision of Gordon Guimaraens, but first of all the special Martínez style is sweeter than Cockburn's, so they are not at all comparable, and secondly Martínez gets its grapes in the best years from the privately-owned Quinta da Eira Velha whilst Cockburn's gets its grapes from other localities.

Since the 1970'ies Martínez has been supplied with grapes from the Newman's Quinta da Eira Velha lying majestically far above Pinhão looking down at the small Douro train and the famous blue tiles of the railway station. (Photo: HO)

Martínez' sweet tooth is best tasted in the standard wines and in the *Vintage Character,* which contains more sweetness than fruit. The *LBV* has a sympathetic medium style with a slight inclination towards sweetness whilst both Vintages bearing Martínez name and the SQVP, which is sold at Quinta da Eira Velha but is marketed by Martínez, is a solid medium style, which is always reliable and always worth its price. They are a bit sweeter than Cockburn's and lack Cockburn's depth and length, but they have their own, berry-dominated charm. The following Vintages were tasted in the autumn of 1999:

Vintage 1982: "Light colour and actually also light style. So mild and sweet that you are afraid than it will disappear in the sugar coating on your tongue, but a bit of power emerges as sweet liquorice and results in a dry, spicy ending. Delicate fruit, short charm, but great friendliness. Keep a good eye on it". (86/100)

Vintage 1985: "Much darker than the 1982. Again aggressive sweetness, but it gives way to a lot of power behind it. Well-balanced and harmonic. Glossy and amiable style, but a far more interesting structure than in 1982. Promising balance. Sympathetic development in the decanter". (92/100)

Vintage 1987: "Dense, dark colour of cherries. Intense elderberry taste, which is both soft and sweet and powerful. Harmony between sweetness, fruit and power. Well-balanced and well-made Vintage with a dry ending. Delicious and promising". (92/100)

Vintage 1991: "Mild taste of malt and jam, a lot of sweetness and friendly fruit. But this is an adolescent and not a man. No muscle. Short taste, very friendly but no challenge. The pleasure is short-lived, but the development in the decanter is significant. Better the next day". (87/100)

Quinta da Eira Velha 1995: "Overwhelming rich sweetness, abruptly replaced by a dry, short ending. Practically no aftertaste. Just like elderberry juice added alcohol and with the intensity of alcohol. Over-fruity middleweight without backbone". (81/100)

Martínez' Vintage Ports have their own nice and sweet personality. They become friendly and drinkable at a very early stage, but they can also be quite durable. Every time we have a blind tasting, Martínez and Delaforce have the ability of ending up much better than expected, i.e. usually in the middle somewhere and usually in front of several Vintage Ports with more exclusive labels!

This confirms that Martínez can often be quite a good buy! To celebrate the 2nd centennial in 1990, a special anniversary wine was produced: "Anniversary Port", which was bottled in 1990 for maturation in bottles for further years. The wine is a mixture of wines from the quintas that have supplied grapes to Martínez, and apart from being a festive anniversary wine, it also shows how excellent Port, Gordon Guimaraens and his assistants could make if they were given the opportunity. Here Martínez' usual sweetness is gone with the wind and replaced by a masculinity, which resembles Cockburn's.

TAWNY

The natural sweetness is best seen and profiled in the Tawny types. Especially the 10-years Tawny is much sweeter than the similar types carrying Cockburn's name, but they also have a richer structure. The 30-years Tawny seems less sweet with a more svelte style and rich on fine nuances. These Tawnies have a far more "Portuguese" style, a bit like the "British" style, but are always in balance and with a very nice fruit content.

As for the Vintages, Martínez' Tawnies are always reliable and usually a very good buy.

Gordon Guimaraens was responsible for more than 40 years for the best of Martinez' and Cockburn's wines. In the same period his brother, Bruce, was responsible for the best wines bearing the Fonseca and Taylor's labels, so the two brothers had an impact on some of the finest Port Wines. (Photo: BJS)

Messias
(S.A. Vinhos Messias)

Founded: 1926
Owner: PLC
Taster/Blender: Not reported
Quintas: Quinta do Cachão by Ferradosa

The religious name of Messias refers to Messias Baptista, who founded the Sociedade Agrícola e Comercial dos Vinhos Messias in 1926 and was the manager of this house until 1973. Since 1934 Messias, with headquarters in Bairrada, also produces and sells Port, but the table wines are still the most important asset of this house. Messias' only property in the Douro Valley, Quinta do Cachão by Ferradosa, is also the name of a red wine, a Single Quinta Vintage Port, a LBV and a Vintage Character.

I do not remember any bottle of Messias Port that has impressed me. The Ruby Ports are very light, the Tawnies very sweet.

Montez Champalimaud
(Quinta do Côtto)

Owner: Champalimaud Family
Taster/Blender: Miguel Champalimaud
Quintas: Quinta do Côtto

Port Wine is a drink for the patient, and most Port Wine producers do not have to make very many big or quick decisions. They just have to choose if they want to make Tawny or Ruby, and maybe if the Ruby should be a Vintage, LBV or something else - but even these decisions do not have to be made rashly. They have months to think about it in.

But at least one producer in the Douro Valley has to make a quite a different and a much quicker decision. When fermentation has started - at the latest, but usually before the grapes are picked - Miguel Champalimaud at Quinta do Côtto must decide whether to make red wine or Port from the grapes, and whether the must should complete fermentation or stop the fermentation with alcohol.

You see, this family produces a unique product: red wine and Port Wine from the same grape substance. However, Port Wine is only produced in the good vintage years (1982, 1989, and 1995) (Single Quinta Vintage Port) - whilst the other vintage years are used for red wine, most often red wines with the name of the quinta on the label, and is especially in excellent vintage years as *Grande Escholha*, the only Douro red wine that nearly lives up to Ferreira's Barca Velha in quality as well as reputation.

Their choice is often a dilemma. For the recognised great Port Wine Vintage 1994, Champalimaud used all the grapes for Grande Escholha, but a year later they produced both Port Wine and Grande Eschoha. But the decision about making

Port or red wine is not only based on intuition and a spontaneous decision. The market has something to say too. Port Wine also brings on another problem as soon as the decision of making Port Wine is taken, namely that the Port Wine must be approved - red wine may be produced freely.

Unfortunately, the Champalimaud family has to pay for having such a atypical wine. Contrary to the other producers, Miguel Champalimaud cold-stabilises all his Port Wines, as well as his red wine, and filtrates them so that there are hardly any dregs, and without this having any effect on the keeping qualities the family says. However, the Port Institute does have a problem because Champalimaud's Port Wine due to the atypical vinification are atypical and not "characteristic" which they should be according to the weakly defined guidelines.

The consequence is sometimes, as in the vintage year of 1986, that Champalimaud's Vintage Port is rejected by the Port Institute and does not get the necessary seal. Instead the family made Tawny from the rejected Port Wine - without marketing it.

Before 1976, the family sold its grapes to other producers, but when Miguel Champalimaud became responsible for the wine at the take over of the new generation, this strategy was changed. At that time it was not yet possible to export Port Wine direct from the Douro Valley, and as the family had no buildings in Gaia, Miguel Champalimaud chose to make a prestige red wine from the best grapes instead. It was introduced on the market in 1980 and was called Grande Escolha.

When the new Act of 7 May 1986 was passed, the Champalimaud family had been ready for many years and proved that producers other than the producers from the lodges in Gaia could easily make quality Port Wines. In the autumn of 1986, Miguel Champalimaud challenged the British Port Wine producers in a heated debate about the blessings and limitations of Single Quintas, in which he claimed that the classic Vintage Port in the course of a few years would have to be a Single Quinta Vintage Port, and in which the British maintained that the finest Vintage Port always would be a mixed wine from different properties (see also page 141ff). And until now they have been right.

Miguel Champalimaud had produced a Vintage Port 1982 which he called the first "Quinta produced and Quinta-bottled Vintage Port", and which he repeatedly regretted not being able to export due to the unjust law. After 1986 he was able to export, but he did not deem his own Vintage to be good enough until Vintage 1989 - as did the Port Institute. Vintages 1989 and 1998 (with a new design) did not promote the quinta name on the label; it was launched as Champalimaud Vintage Port.

Apart from the 50 ha of vineyards on the Quinta do Côtto, the family owns a property in Vinho Verde (Paço de Teixeiró). They have re-planted at Côtto and now focus on the three most important grape varieties: Touriga Nacional and Tinta Roriz for Vintage Port and Grande Escolha and Touriga Francesca which are used as the third Port Wine grapes. The vinification equipment is state-of-the-art and very practical. They do have the old lagares, but they are no longer in use, as they are, according to Champalimaud, used for tourism and for the wine journalists! He would not dream of making a Tawny Port, as he believes that oxidation damages the wine and gives it a weak quality. He also believes that there is too much alcohol in Port Wine – at least in other producers' Port Wine. The alcohol in his Port Wine is at 19%, and he would like to reduce this figure to 17-18%, for his motto is: "I am the wine man. Other producers are liqueur people!"

The Champalimaud name and some of the fiery, self-confident personality signals France, and actually the family does have French blood from the time when a daughter of the old Portuguese family married a French general with a Portuguese mother and French father.

And there is something pompous about the

quinta that resembles an old château more than 90% of the real châteaux' in Bordeaux. The quinta lies far to the west in Baixo Corgo, but was included in the original demarcation in 1757 and is mentioned in documents as far back as in the beginning of the 14th Century. The buildings are, however, from the 15th and 16th Centuries and the main building is from the 18th Century.

Lagares or no lagares: Champalimaud does not mind the tourists visiting Quinta do Côtto, so in the coming years the château will be modernised, the yard will be elevated, and a hotel with 12 rooms will be built. If the wines of Champalimaud cannot go to the world, the world can come to the wines of Champalimaud!

RUBY

Fruity and freshness. These are the keywords from a man, who does not normally lack words. Miguel Champalimaud would like to make Vintage Port with less alcohol and less sweetness and put more of an emphasis on the fruit. He makes Port Wine like he makes red wine; only the maleolactic fermentation and the addition of alcohol is different. Only Vintage Port is produced, and only in special vintage years (1982, 1989, and 1995). The following Vintages were tasted on Quinta do Cotto in 1998:

Vintage 1998 (demi-bouteille): "Fruit intensity, easily drinkable, soft and friendly, but by no means weak. Resembles a muscular red wine".

Vintage 1995 (demi-bouteille): "Young, pure taste of berries. Fresh and full-bodied, aggressive fruity taste and a very nice sweetness. Already drinkable".

Miguel Champalimaud - a man of his own opinion with very personal wines. (Photo: HO)

Morgan Brothers

Morgan Brothers was founded by a certain Mr. Haughton around 1715. The name comes from a clerk, Aaron Morgan, who fought his way to the top and ended up as the owner of the company in the late 18th Century. In the 19th Century Morgan was known for its "Dixon's Single Diamond" and "Dixon's Double Diamonds" that was so well known that it is even mentioned in Charles Dickens' novel "Nicholas Nickleby".

In July 1898, the company re-organised as a private company under the name of *Morgan Brothers Ltd*. The name and its delicate products were bought by Croft in 1952, but today, the Morgan name is only used for the more inferior qualities on selected markets.

Nacional

see Quinta do Noval

Nacional is not the name of a Port house, but the name of a special brand from the Port house of Quinta do Noval, and it is such a special brand that exquisite vintages of Nacional, especially the vintage 1931, are most expensive bottles of Port around. Apart from their reputation, the quality and being a collectors' item world wide is due to the fact that the lot on Quinta do Noval, that produces grapes for Nacional, is planted with ungrafted vines as they used to be before the time of phylloxera. When this hungry louse had eaten its way through the fields in the 1880'ies and 1890'ies, the wine growers in the Douro Valley had to replant with vines that were grafted on American root-stocks. This also included António José da Silva, who had bought the Quinta do Noval in 1894. For some reason or other, he disinfected a small lot with a powerful sulphur solution, most probably to see what would happen to the vine lice. Unfortunately, the archives of Noval were lost in the fire in 1981, but according to the story which is passed on in the family from one generation to another, the first vines in more recent times were planted on the lot in 1925.

The soil consists of shale with a low content of nutrients as on the rest of the quinta, but it is rich in potash and also has deposits of nitrates and phosphates. The vines more or less reach the same age as on the rest of the quinta, which is max. 50 years, and the approx. 6,000 vines which are to become Nacional are at this point (1999) around 35 years old in average.

The grapes are Touriga Nacional, Touriga Francesa, Tinto Cão and Sousão. The latter is a obscure grape which is known from Minho and Dão but which is not counted for much in Douro. However, it has always been of interest to Noval where the opinion is that it gives the Nacional a special, intense colour and backbone. According to Christian Seely it is dark when it is young and has a reputation of becoming weak upon ageing, not however at Quinta do Noval where it manages to keep its virility.

The yield from the Nacional lot is about half of that of Noval, because the yield of ungrafted vines is somewhat less, but it amounts to 15 hl/ha for Nacional and 35 hl/ha for Quinta do Noval's Vintage. Nacional is only produced as a Vintage Port and is vinified and treated exactly as Noval's Vintage and by the same team. It also has the same maturation process and comes from the same grape varieties so that only *le terroir* is different - to the great satisfaction of the French owners.

Nacional is the result of faultless workmanship, except for the foot crushing. The grapes are somewhat smaller than Noval's other grapes and have a solid skin. They are usually picked very late in the season to ensure maturation, but the picking is over and done within a few hours. After picking, the grapes are transported to the adega. The smallest lagares (5 pipes) is used. The grapes are pressed immediately and are then, depending on their temperature, cooled down or slightly heated so that the must keeps a temperature of 28° Celsius. 4-5 men now foot-crush the grapes in the lagar for the entire period of fermentation which is about 2 days. This slow maceration process results in a good estraction of polyphenols. When the wine is ready for fortification, it is a full-bodied wine of a deep red colour - and full of tannic acid. The addition of aguardente takes place as on Noval. The fortified wine then lies in wooden casks until February-March of the following year and matures about 1 1/2 years in used pipes. If the Vintage does not reach a Nacional Vintage, the wine is used for mixtures. Nacional can easily be declared a Vintage independently of Noval. As an example, Noval was declared three times in the 1980'ies: in 1982, 1985 and 1987, whilst a Nacional was produced in 1980, 1982, 1983, 1985 and 1987.

When replanting on the Nacional lot, cuttings are planted directly in the soil, or an effort is made to try to get an adjacent plant to take roots. Only ungrafted vines are planted, but naturally none of the existing vines are from before the phylloxera era - contrary to what many people may think. The ungrafted vines still thrive on the Nacional lot even though there is still phylloxera in the soil on every other inch of the quinta. That's just how it is, and according to Seely there are no plans of analysing the soil to try to find an explanation to

Christian Seely at work – decanting the precious drops of a Nacional 1970. Nacional is a typical "lawyer's wine" – not only because you need a small fortune to buy it, but also because you have to be good at reading the small writing on the label. (Photo: HO)

this weird fact. If there is one, it might stifle the mythe. The production from the 2 1/2 ha is a limited one. A maximum of 250-300 cases of Vintage Port is obtained, and they are becoming more rare than in earlier times, for during AXA's management a decision has been made not to produce as many vintages as before. This means that no Nacional was produced in 1995 because the grapes were not good enough, or as Christian Seely points out, "The grapes were excellent, and went into the Noval Vintage 1995, but the wine was simply not outstanding enough in our opinion to merit a Nacional declaration."

The distribution policy has, however, changed. When the van Zeller's were in charge, Nacional was used as a sales prize so each agent who sold well of Quinta do Noval's wines was awarded a special permission (!) to buy a few bottles of Nacional. Under the management of AXA, Christian Seely explains, "there is no longer a direct link between allocations of Nacional and purchases of Noval Vintage. It is no longer logical as the Noval Vintage itself is also sold on an allocation basis, and not necessarily to the same people."

The name of Nacional has got nothing to do with the grape called Touriga Nacional. Nacional refers to the fact that the ungrafted vines are in direct contact with Portugal's soil. This is the genuine product, the last of its kind from the time before the world and the vine phylloxera fell!

Nacional has always been an innocent victim of becoming a collector's item. The most expensive bottle of Port which was ever sold/traded is therefore also a bottle of Nacional from the legendary year of 1931 - a bottle of which was sold in 1988 for 5,900 US dollars (3,470 £) at a dinner for business men in the Bahamas. The price included a bit of charity and a lot of prestige.

Nacional also holds the record for a young Vintage Port, after a case of Nacional, 1994, was sold for 5.250 US $ at auction at Sotheby's in New York in 1997.

RUBY

As for Quinta do Noval, one should distinguish the time before and after the purchase by AXA. Not all Nacional vintages from the 1970'ies and 1980'ies are convincing, and some of them should not have been declared at all. After AXA's take-over, the philosophy behind Nacional has been shaped up – not so much in the vinification process as in the launch of the product. Nacional is only produced in the best vintage years, only top quality products are made, and not too many bottles.

Vintage 1995 is a good example of the new ambitions. In Christian Seely's own words the grapes were "excellent" and used for Noval Vintage, but they were not "outstanding" enough to carry Nacional's name. An intriguing comparison can be made in the vintage year of 1997 when both Noval and Nacional were declared.

The following vintages of Nacional were tasted during Christian Seely's Europe tour of 1995, a couple of years after AXA had purchased Quinta do Noval:

Nacional, 1987: "Dark red, almost black. Fresh and fruity nose, slightly aggressive, dry, reluctant with slight taunted taste of liquorice and black currant. The taste is intriguingly sweet and deep with an explosion in the mouth. Lots of (soft) fruit. Immature but compact taste. Great development in the glass. Wait for at least 10 years".

Nacional, 1982: "Reddish brown colour, just like a Tawny. The nose is a bit hard, straightforward, fruity. Soft taste, very soft, with black currant and a long, sliding taste. Characteristic and long, wonderful taste of black currant, long and complex with no flaws. Develops a deliciously soft, fruity richness in the glass. Delicious now. And delicious is the right word to use; it has a rich, soft coating, but it is not mature yet. Wait for another 5-10 years".

Nacional, 1970: "Dark red. Nose of fresh fruit, strawberries, raspberries, and is in a transition period between a young fruit and a noble nose. The taste is at first very soft, almost rich, then a bit of lacquer, and then an explosion in the mouth. Seems divided into three at the moment, disharmonious, but will no doubt concentrate. The taste is long and compact. Great development in the glass".

Nacional, 1966: "Deep, sweetish nose, resembling more to a dessert wine than a vigorous wine. Velvety taste, sweetish, clingy, the nose is more or like a noble Tawny than a noble Vintage. Smooth, delicious, soft and hardly durable".

Nacional, 1963: "More red than brown. Deep, deep nose: liquorice, tobacco, a hint of smoke (?), depth, berries, more depth, and then again liquorice. The taste is extremely soft, fruity, both very friendly, clingy and explosive. Enormous fruit and great potency behind the softness and elegance. Great, classic Vintage. To be enjoyed now, but keep some, for this is a sleeping beauty, a great, great Port Wine".

Nacional, 1962: "The same colour as Malmsey Madeira: dark brown sugar. The nose is a bit passive, but opens reluctantly after 5-10 minutes with a touch of liquorice. The taste: dense, finely structured liquorice; this wine contains structure and dry matter for many years to come. Oddly as it may seem: it expands deliciously in the glass, but it also seems to be a deep sleeper. In the glass the nose develops into an old Oloroso Sherry: smoky and deep. Wonderful wine with still some years to go".

The following vintages from Nacional were kindly opened by Christian Seely during my visit to Noval and to Porto in 1997-1999:

Nacional, 1967: "Dark red as a red wine, impressive dark colour. Almost youthful with a very fruity nose. Youthful in its taste too, fruity with a lot of liquorice, no signs of age, fruit rather than sweetness – and potency. No age, no aggressiveness, but a lot of fruit and charm.

Nacional, 1970: "Opens slowly, velvety with a nice and light explosion, but rather mild taste, does not keep to long in the glass with only a lot of sweetness left. A bit too short, but refined and sensuous as long as it lasts".

Nacional, 1966: "Dense, intense, very juicy, incredibly friendly with richness and tannin, but potent – and unfortunately also with a short taste. A quick and intense experience".

Especially Nacional 1970 has changed markedly in the last 3-4 years, and the 1966 has got an even shorter taste. In general, Nacional's special character is, or at least has been, in its refined structure rather than in its power and keeping qualities. It goes without saying that it will be exciting to follow Nacional in the years to come. I still say it – just to be on the safe side!

Here it is: 2 1/2 ha of ungrafted vines providing grapes to Nacional. For some reason there is no phylloxera in the soil here, but on all other lots on Quinta do Noval there is. (Photo: HO)

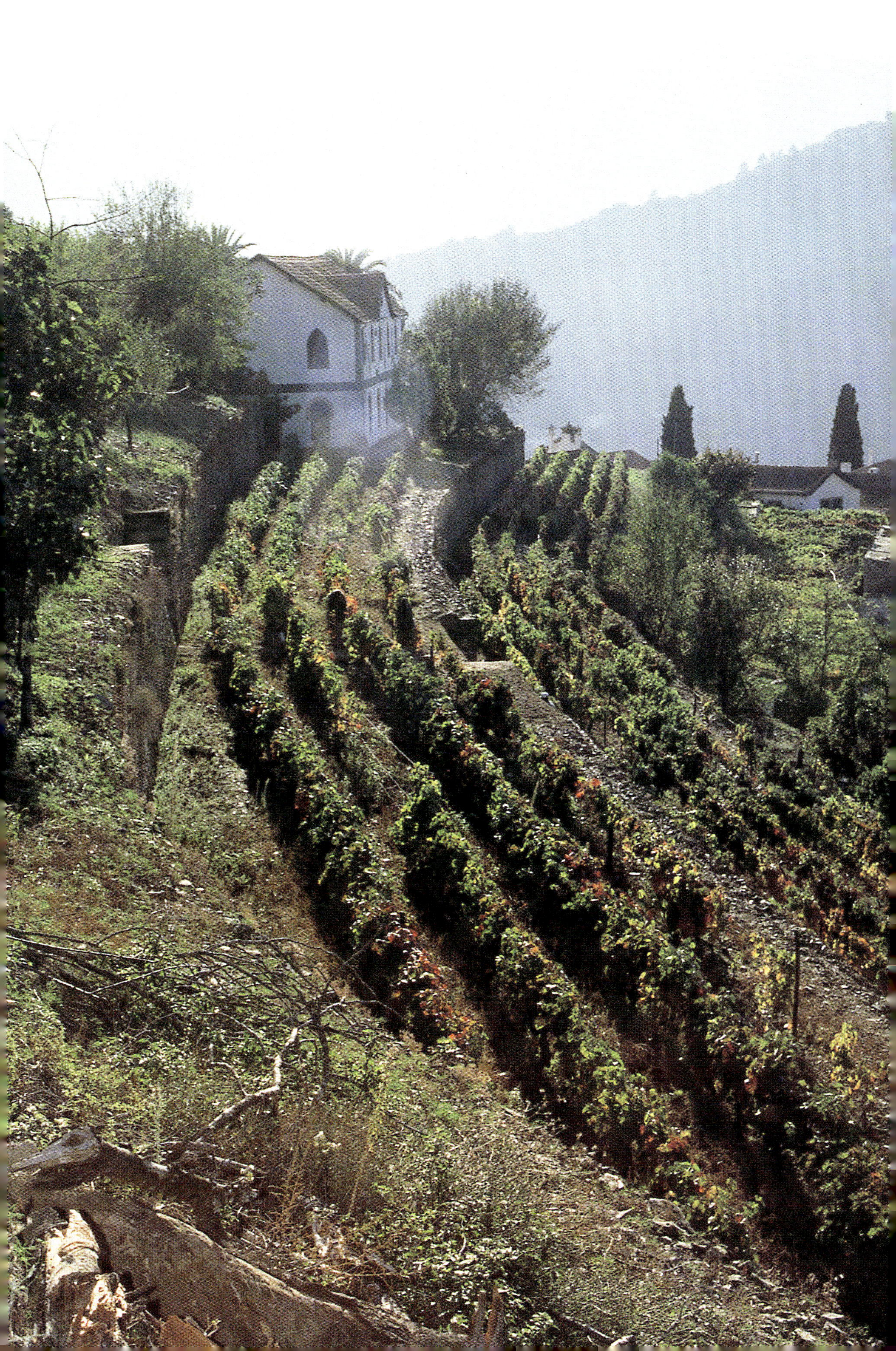

Niepoort
(Niepoort Vinhos S.A.)

Founded: 1842
Owner: Family van der Niepoort
Taster/Blender: Dirk van der Niepoort & "Zeze" Nogueira
Quintas: Quinta de Nápoles and Quinta do Carril between Régua and Pinhão. Dirk van der Niepoort is co-owner of Quinta do Passodouro in Vale de Mendiz

The official family history has never been written down and is therefore quickly recited: Eduard Kebe founded the company in 1842 and took on Dutch F.M. van der Niepoort as a partner five years later. When Kebe died in 1858, van der Niepoort became sole owner and changed the company name to its present name. In 1873, his son, E.C.J. van der Niepoort, entered the company, and after his father's death in 1897, he too become sole owner, until his son, Eduard M. van der Niepoort, became co-owner in 1908.

The same pattern continues: After his father's death in 1912, Eduard M. van der Niepoort's son took over, and in 1965 his son Eduard Rudolph ("Rolf") joined the company as a partner. The long waiting time was presumably due to "Rolf" not having a great desire to join the company, but eventually he did follow his father's command and footsteps. The father had already introduced a special Port (bottled in 1941) in 1927 produced from this great vintage year and "reserved for my son, Eduard Rudolph ("Rolf") van der Niepoort, born that year". Do not even start looking for it. Only 360 bottles were produced, of which glasses have been poured to friends of the house for many years - by the drop.

The young Dirk also followed his father's wishes when he, still wet behind the ears, started working for Niepoort's in 1987 and had his international debut at the large Port festival in Copenhagen in 1988. Since then, things have been going according to plan: Rolf van der Niepoort has more or less withdrawn to enjoy his beloved veteran cars, and Dirk is keeping up the good work in the company.

One must say that Dirk is a controversial person. He never took a degree in oenology, but in economy, but he is not interested in money at all - instinctively he is of the opposite opinion of any other people in the business, by which he follows his father's lines perfectly. When all others agree that a Vintage quality cannot be evaluated until 16-18 months after the wine has become a dessert wine, he believes that he can do this after 2-4 months, as it then will close and not open again until after a couple of years, i.e. when it is bottled as a Vintage Port. As the curve for the opening of wine is on the rise towards the last possibility of bottling, he must bottle as late as possible, which he does when it comes to Vintage Port, but he bottles the LBV as early as possible to keep the wine's natural freshness.

And freshness is his mantra. "I want to make a fresh not a fruity Port", he says cheerfully, but when we are tasting bottle after bottle in the humble tasting room - this is what an alchemist's chambers must have looked like in the Middle Ages - I find out that he rather means freshness instead of laxity, because there is a lot of fruit in the closed young wines. But now it is the fruit he focuses on. "If it were fruit, I wanted, I would make strawberry wine", he utters whilst his persevering co-taster, "Zeze" Nogueira, fourth generation in the alchemist chambers, looks upon with a worried look on his face.

At the same time, Dirk is a peaceful rebel and a good boy who follows family traditions - also the part of being a peaceful rebel. He also inherited his ancestors' love for the fat glass flasks which in the table wine language are called demijohns. According to family tradition, Dirk's great-grandfather

Rolf van der Niepoort, 1989. (Photo: HO)   *Dirk van der Niepoort, 1999. (Photo: HO)*

bought them in the late 19th Century, but they date from the 1780'ies and were manufactured in Flensburg where they most probably were used originally for storing beer. Nobody can tell. But what everybody in the Niepoort family can tell is that they know from experience that Port likes to mature in the demijohns, and their Garrafeiras is proof hereof. These apparently forever-young wines have matured for 3-6 years in wooden casks and then for several years in Demijohns. They are produced in 1931, 1933, 1940, 1948, 1950, 1952, and 1967, and Dirk has put the wine aside so the "list of Kings" may continue. The wine oxidizes differently in the demijohns, slower and better he tells me - as his father once has said. But naturally he would not dream of using the demijohns for Vintage Port.

Rolf van der Niepoort's philosophy is that you do not have to own land and property to make great Ports is fully accepted by Dirk, but he does keep a door slightly ajar to new and modern times. Whilst the father never meddled in what his grape suppliers did, Dirk has begun to advise them to obtain a better raw material. But he does not have fixed contracts, just as his father did not, but buys spontaneously what according the tastes he enjoys the most. He does not care if the wines come from grapes from A, B or C fields. But he does care about the taste of the wines, and that is also what sets prices. He has found good wine from small, new farmers, and like his father he lets them make the wine themselves, no matter how antique their equipment is. He believes in many, small vinification plants instead of only a few big ones.

And in spite of the fancy philosophy, the Niepoort's have also become land owners. In 1987-88 they bought the old, decayed Quinta de Nápoles between Régua and Pinhão and the adjacent Quinta do Carril. This gives them a total of 15 ha of young vines and only 10 ha of old vines. Furthermore, Dirk has a co-operation with German Dieter Bohrmann for the Quinta do Passodouro, which they both own, situated in the Vale de Mendiz where Niepoort also has access to a small and rather old-fashioned vinification centres. They have made Vintage Port under the name of the quinta since vintage 1992 and LBV since vintage 1995 - only from the grapes from this quinta.

Dirk and "Zeze" Nogueira in the "alchemist den" at Gaia. A Nogueira and a Niepoort have tasted wine together here for four generations. (Photo: HO)

In accordance with tradition, 40 per cent of Niepoort's wines comes from grapes which have been foot-crushed in lagares so the only new element is that there is now a winemaker in the Douro Valley, Jorge Serodio Borges, who produces the wines that Dirk and "Zeze" taste in Gaia.

Such is life at Niepoort's. Rolf van der Niepoort's passion for cars has been replaced by Dirk's passion for the cellular phone, and to quote the poet: "only by rebellion and protest can the young generation follow tradition in the best possible way". So does Dirk. He is the man behind Niepoort's modern, closed and pruny LBV's - a type his father for many years refused to touch because there were too many bad LBV's around. "I want to make a Rolls Royce or nothing at all", Rolf van der Niepport once said. But he finally surrendered and eventually made a LBV in 1981. Since then, one impressive, powerful and juicy vintage after the other has followed.

As his father, Dirk goes his own way, but so far he has been successful. The joke of the year in Gaia back in 1996 was that the Niepoorts had to send samples of their Vintage 1994 to the Port Institute seven times before it was approved, but their obstinacy bore fruit. However, Dirk prefers freshness, so he hopes that the Vintage 1997, his first, will be approved the first time around.

As you can see in my tasting notes, Niepoort's is one of the few Port houses which manages all types of Port - and they do it to perfection.

RUBY 🍷🍷🍷🍷

Considering the fact that Rolf van der Niepoort started to make LBVs because he was provoked to do so, it is unbelievable that the family's LBVs have become some of the best in the business. They are consistently pure, juicy, and potent.

I have recently tasted three of the more recent vintages in the tasting rooms at Gaia in February 1999:

A masculine *LBV 1990* with prunes and liquorice in a wonderful style, a darker and more massive *LBV 1992*, again with a characteristic taste of prunes, and a dense, muscular and very potent *LBV 1994*. Impressive wines where especially the 1990 reflects Niepoort's masterly Tawny skills – also seen in the Ruby types. Everything considered, I know of no other producer whose best Tawnies and best Vintage Ports, especially after some 20 odd years or so, are so similar in style and structure. Could it be the small, plump demijohns. I just cannot say.

I put a stress on Niepoort's excellence with regard to Vintage 1994. It this is not so weird as one could imagine, because there is a special Niepoort style which clearly distinguishes itself and makes their wines atypical. In Rolf van Niepoort's time because they resembled the Tawny style in purity and richness of fruit, in Dirk's time because they go in another direction and maintain what is written in their manifesto in the year 1999: "Our LBVs and Vintage Ports put an emphasis on freshness and not on fruit. These wines should contain a lot of tannin - the Vintage Ports supplemented with some oxidation, just a drop"

Whether he obtains his objectives time will only show. His ancestors had other objectives, which I tasted during the "Vintages of the Century". The following were on the wine list:

Vintage 1927: "Dark brown like brown sugar. Dense, solid nose with a touch of acetone. Extremely sweet taste like a Colheita in both sweetness and structure. Delicious, wonderful, but far more Tawny than Ruby".

Vintage 1955: "Great nose with lots of fruit and slightly smoky. Elegant taste, polished, just as when you polish the floor, and refined. The development in the glass is more towards a great Colheita than a Vintage. Super Tawny – but that was not the idea"!

Vintage 1970: "The only Vintage of these three vintages that is red in colour and Ruby in taste. Lots of delicious, very nice fruit. Very amiable taste, affectionate and embracing, no resistance or hooks. Delicious, with Ruby's nice fruit and Tawny's mild sweetness".

Of the more recent vintages, I have good recollections of *Vintage 1982*, which found a fine balance between fruit and acid at a very early stage, as well as other vintages which I remember only sporadically, and my conclusion is that if you stick to Niepoort you will never be disappointed.

When Rolf van der Niepoort was around, Port Wine were made according to a sort of planned economy when you made the Port Wine you just had to made and not necessarily the Port Wine which was in demand. This gave a free rein between types and styles which were something quite special for the Niepoort family. Rolf was also very sceptical towards restaurants. One of his doctrines was: "You should never sell Vintage Port to a restaurant". And if you did, only a half bottle, which he produced, for example in the excellent Vintage 1987. He also produced a small 2-person bottle "Retinto", a young Ruby Port, for restaurants. But I do not think it was especially popular.

TAWNY 🍷🍷🍷🍷

I cannot come close to a bottle of Niepoort's Tawny, or even a Tawny, without thinking of Rolf's definition from the 1980'ies: For a Port

Wine drinker Vintage is not a real Port Wine. Vintage is a dinner jacket and a hangover the next day. Real Port is an old Tawny"

Vintage is a good weather, harvest at the right time, mixing, bottling, sealing and then it's all up to the customers. Tawny is all about nursing the right casks, mixing, tasting, maturation and waiting until the wood has set its impression.

This is naturally reflected in his 10-years, 20-years, 30-years, and over 40-years Tawnies, which have always been among the most pure and refined wines – and still are.

And this is best seen in the best of the old Colheitas which were nurtured and had an edge and were made in a special soft and smoky style, which did not resemble other Colheitas. It aggravated him of course that the quick Vintage Ports always resulted in the highest prices instead of the slow handicraft, but: "The big producers have no patience and do not want to wait 7 years to make a Colheita, so they all agree that there is nothing special about a Colheita. To them a Vintage is the only acceptable wine"

After tidying up my old comments – never do that! – my tasting comments on Colheitas from Rolf's time are gone, but I still have the experience cemented in my head where they are stored in a safe, soft spot.

For the sake of good order, we should include the minor Tawnies, of which the most popular types are "Junior", made from approx. 3 1/2-year-old wine, and "Senior", made from approx. 8-year-old wine.

When Rolf was in charge, Niepoort also produced a monumental white Port, for example 1917, bottled in 1927, re-corked in 1973 and still drinkable today – with great pleasure. Rolf also made a luscious Moscatel, well actually, he made anything he felt like making, and then everything went by the heart, so it was always well made!

The future belongs to Dirk. He will be closely followed with high hopes.

Demijohns, the secret behind Niepoort's special style. Dirk's old grandfather bought them 100 years ago, and they are still in use. (Photo: HO)

Offley Forrester
(Forrester & Ca., S.A.)

Founded: 1737
Owner: SOGRAPE
Taster/Blender: José Maria d'Orey Soares Franco
Quintas: Quinta da Boa Vista

Just as colourful and glorius as the first chapter of Offley's history was, just as dull was the second chapter. This house was purchased by Sandeman in 1962, but only a few years later Martini bought 50 per cent of the shares, and in 1983 the remaining 50 per cent, without however, showing much interest in Port, and when Martini again a few years later purchased 20 per cent of the shares in SOGRAPE, it was paid by handing over the failing Port house. Offley Forrester was then under the command of Ferreira, which has already proved to be very favourable for Barão Forrester's reputation.

The Offley name is due to a British family whose whitest sheep reached the fine position of Lord Mayor of London. But it was the seventh William Offley who settled down as a wine merchant in Porto in 1737. In 1803, the Scotsman Joseph Forrester was made a partner, and it was his nephew, Joseph James Forrester, who came to Porto to sell Port but ended as a cartographer in the Douro Valley and as one of Port's history grand old men (see page 50f).

Some time in the late 19th Century the company had yet another partner and was renamed *Offley, Webber & Forrester*, and there was enough money to buy the Quinta da Boa Vista, next-to-neighbour to Ferreira's Quinta do Porto. When the company's last Forrester, by the first name of John, realized all his values to emigrate in 1924, the quinta was sold. It was a strange deal for British interested parties bought 75 per cent of all the values, the Portuguese interested parties bought the remaining 25 per cent, but the quinta remained in the hands of the Portuguese investors.

After some turbulence, the company Offley Forrester, which as mentioned had been sold in 1962, managed to repurchase Quinta da Boa Vista in 1979, but until SOGRAPE's take-over of this historical quinta only tinkering and small repairs were carried out and the vines are not doing well.

The years of non-commitment have worn down Offley Forrester's equipment and reputation. These were the years of "easy solutions" when grapes were bought from cooperatives and when no money was used on vinification and the necessary improvements and reparations.

Apparently Offley Forrester and Quinta da Boa Vista are looking at new and brighter times. Ferreira's director, "Vito" Olazabal, has great plans of making the quinta into a tourist attraction furnishing 10-12 small rooms and make paths in the vineyards. The small winery is to be reinstalled and many loving hands are to put it to work.

"Vito" promises us that the name of Boa Vista will sparkle once again. The quinta lost so much of its reputation that until 1979 it was only used as a common brand and gave a name also to low quality wines from Offley Forrester. Since then, the name of the quinta has been reserved for a Single Quinta Village whose quality can only improve.

Osborne
(Osborne & Ca. Lda.)

Founded: 1967
Owner: Osborne Portugal
Taster/Blender: Francisco Barata de Tovar
Quintas: None

Ramos-Pinto's lightly clad nymphs, Sandeman's Don and Osborne's black bull are the direction finders of the Port landscape, even though the bull is far more known in its own country, Spain, where Osborne makes its Sherry.

The Port adventure is actually quite new. "Osborne Portugal" was founded in 1967 by António Osborne Vasquez and only gained a foothold when they bought a lodge in Gaia in 1988 from the family van Zeller who was moving all their production to the Quinta do Noval. During this time, Osborne bought some pipes of Port and had a close co-operation with Noval until AXA purchased Noval in 1993. Now, Osborne has to learn to cope by itself, but since 1988 the company has invested heavily to be able to stand on its own two feet. Osborne owns no property in the Douro Valley but buy many of their grapes and some ready wine here vinifying it on their own modern plant situated at Pinhão and Moncorvo. Their quite impulsive stake on quantities and cheap wines has now been replaced by a more particular eye for a better quality, - today this area of business covers approx. 25% of the total sale of quality wines. Unlike the bull, this Port house has had quite some problems in profiling themselves, but their ambitions are very positive aspect.

RUBY

"We consider ourselves to be a Vintage house, who also makes Tawny", manager José Teles Dias da Silva explains, and he should be the one to know. The Ruby types I have tasted have always

Osborne's famous bull is on every bottle of Port. (Photo: HO)

been nice in a rather light style, a pure berry taste and somewhat ordinary but solid. The following were tasted during my most recent visit to Osborne in October 1998:

LBV 1982: "Light colour, light fruit, light taste, easily drinkable. Soft and nice, short and quick".

Vintage 1985: "Soft fruit, rather light style, almost a Tawny in its mild sweetness. Friendly and drinkable, but not especially durable".

Vintage 1994: "Berry taste, very fruity with an explosion ending in a friendly sweetness. Nice and amiably, but not especially durable".

Vintage 1995: "Intense fruit and nice sweetness, but also a nice taste of berries, hardly any power. Friendly and decent".

TAWNY ♥♥ ~ ~

Osborne focuses on mildness, softness and lightness, both for their Ruby types and for their Tawnies. They expect to make a Colheita from their 1994, which is still in casks, but also offer the regular types:

10-years Tawny: "Rather light, nice and friendly, not aggressive at all, mild and short".

20-years Tawny: "Nice sweetness. Again a very light style, slightly rich, more youth than power. Lightness is the key word. More harmonic than the 10-years Tawny".

Osborne does not produce a 30-years or an over 40-years Tawny but several other common types, such as "Special Reserve" Master of Port that is a young Tawny made in a light style. It got its name because it is used for a Sommelier competition about "Who knows most about Port ?"

Poças
(Manoel D. Poças Jr.)

Founded: 1918
Owner: Poças Family
Taster/Blender: Jorge Manuel Soeiro e Silva Pintão
Quintas: Quinta das Quartas, Quinta da Santa Bárbara and Quinta de Vale de Cavalos

On the 15th August 1918, one week after the allies' breakthrough on the Western front, but while half the world was still at war, 30-year-old Manoel Domingues Poças Junior put his shaky hand solemnly on the contract to sign a partnership with his uncle, Manuel Francisco Gomes Jr. From this day he could call himself co-owner of the Port house, *Poças & Comandita*, which he was to manage all by himself, as this uncle mainly contributed with money.

Manoel knew a thing or two about Port. He had roamed the harbour of Porto and he talked to the farmers in the Douro Valley. He started his long career as an errand boy and ended in the responsible position as principal at the Port house of Ferreira. Here he encountered an international atmosphere every day, and it must have been a cold douche for the young hothead to find out that a Port house does not automatically have a network of exports and incoming orders.

The beginning was difficult. The First World War did finally come to an end, but there were many people involved in the exportation of Port, and Manoel and his uncle had to find something else to deal in as a supplement. The solution seemed simple - not table wine, as it was only two generations later they got that idea - but the just as obvious: Brandy.

The figures show that the demand for brandy for producing Port doubled between 1911 and 1918, and in the course of a few years Poças & Comandita had established themselves as one of the largest brandy producers with their own premises in Gaia and three distilleries.

Manoel's 18-year-old little brother, António, was taken on to look after the distillation process, and progress continued with a peak in 1921 when the company sold more than 150,000 litres of wine. Then came the crisis, and just two years later, in 1923, Poças export orders totalled a mere 77 litres of Port. Something had gone wrong, because the total exports of Port were still on the rise, just not at Poças who shut down the exports department in 1924. The emergency lamp was not only blinking, it was shining ominously. Before the adventure fell completely to the ground, the uncle left the partnership. Manoel Poças remained with an empty till and a very small production which he could not sell. He began to enjoy other pleasures of life. The company was renamed to the more realistic: *Manoel D. Poças Junior,* and he began to spend more time with his family and in his garden. His grandchild, Manuel Poças Pintão has told me that one of his grandfather's problems was that he had to take care of all the financial aspects alone. He had two daughters, but no sons, and even though his marriage with his childhood sweetheart, Maria Alves dos Reis, was a happy one, you did not discuss economy with your wife. He even maintained his childhood modesty and always took his shoes off before entering the big family villa. It was all a question of order and discipline.

In the beginning of the 1930'ies, things started to pick up a bit, but just as the production of brandy has begun to stabilize again, Salazar decided to introduce a monopoly on brandy for Port

Harvest time on Poças' Quinta das Quartas sometime in the 1930'ies. The women are picking the grapes and throw them into the baskets which the boys carry to the men's large "cestos". They are carried to the quinta's adega and thrown into the lagar. Note the pickers' "foreman" to the left with the cane. (Photo: Poças)

in 1934. António was out of a job, and Manoel Poças had to sell his distilleries suffering great financial loss. Once again he had to decide for himself if it was profitable to continue. And once more he decided to stick to Port.

He was blessed with two daughters and suffered the great loss of losing two sons, twins, who died in childbirth. But in 1937, his eldest daughter, Cacilda, finally bore a son, which any leader of a family firm needs, and from his birth, Manuel Poças Pintão was predestined to play an important role in the company, which he has done and still does. When Manuel a year later had a little brother, Jorge, the heritage was 100% secured.

Finally, the exports of Port boomed again. New markets opened up, when the financial crises of the 1920'ies were surpassed, and Poças' exports rose from 277,000 litres in 1936 to 504,000 litres the year after. Now it was no longer enough to just sit in the office in Gaia and send Port all over the world. Manoel had to go out there with his little suitcase to get personal contacts, but just as things were going well, the international doors slammed in his face once again.

The Second World War broke out, and Poças' exports fell to one third from 1940 to 1942, of which only 25% went to the new market in Colombia. Most of the other markets had closed down due to the war. And thus only the home market remained and an increasing lack of bottles.

The company ran at half speed, and so did Manoel, it seems. On top of everything, Manoel was ill most of 1944, but the year before he had gathered all of his staff and the family to celebrate the company's fragile 25th anniversary.

When he was younger, Manoel had taken many big decisions all by himself, especially with regard to financial interests. And he kept on doing so, even when his two brothers joined the company. And often things did go well, but sometimes they also went badly, for example in

Quinta das Quartas was purchased for some brandy and some unpaid bills. Here the quinta seen from above in 1999. (Photo: Poças)

1944 when he took over the remains of the Port house J.P. Gouveia, which proved only to be remains! The wine mentioned in the purchase contract was simply non-existent. The cellar was empty and the small office only contained a chair. "The most expensive chair in the world", his grandson, Manuel Pintão calls it. And it wasn't even that comfortable. It was to reflect the dark times with shortage of funds and instalments for the new and rather unnecessary debt.

In 1952, Manuel Pintão Poças joined the company at the age of only 15. With him came the new blood which the company so badly needed. He had wanted to be a diplomat, an assignment he would have handled brilliantly, but instead of marble floors he walked the trodden-down wooden office floors. He started out as an apprentice in the family firm, "for the best school is the school of life". This is what his grandfather told him time and time again. In 1954, his brother Jorge joined the company, so Porto

Poças now included 7 family members, all closely and lovingly followed by "Godfather" Manoel or "padrinho" as he liked to be called.

I once asked Manuel Pintão how long his grandfather had kept on having the last word in the company. "Until a couple of years after he died," Manuel Pintão answered. The young generation first had to settle with the stiff patriarchal stubbornness. Manoel Poças partly retired in 1959 and pronounced the two sons of his daughter and their father as partners, but this only part retirement was what everyone knew would go on forever and had to accept.

Still, the new partners did not for a second believe that they would just be obedient subjects. They voted against Manoel's will and decided to make a Vintage Port in 1960: "We usually let the British Port houses do that"! But this paid off and became a great success, and the young generation kept going and enjoyed yet another success, so Manoel began to speculate in plastic, just to pass the time, an area he knew absolutely nothing about.

On the company's 50th anniversary in 1968 he held a speech about the good and bad times of the company - not a theatrical event as at the 25th anniversary - but a sad one. He had just turned 80 and was happy that the young generation had not only lifted the company but had also set a new and safe course for it. In the course of the 1960'ies, exports had tripled and quality risen. Manoel had become superfluous on management level, and when his wife, Maria Alves dos Reis, died in June 1970, he rapidly grew feeble. His health weakened and his last year was a long series of heart attacks before he finally found peace in January 1975, according to Manuel Pintão without perceiving any of the socialistic revolution the year before, and perhaps that was only for the best.

In 1974-1978, after the revolution, the company noted another tripling of exports, and in 1980 a state-of-the-art bottling plant was launched. In 1987, Jorge's son, Jorge Manuel Soeiro e Silva Pintão, returned from the University of Bordeaux with a new and modern education in oenology and took over the responsibility for the family wines.

To ensure a stable quality of the grapes, the family bought the Quinta de Santa Bárbara in Valdigem in 1980 after years of buying wine from this quinta. But the new motorway ruined 40% of the quinta, so in 1998 the family sold the quinta and instead bought 10 ha by Vale de Cavalos, a quinta the company owned in Numão since 1988, and named the place after its predecessor, Quinta da Santa Bárbara.

For Denmark Poças and especially their "Pousada Port" has had a very special ring to the name for many years, partly because Poças' Danish importer is the supermarket chain FDB, Denmark's largest wine importer, and partly because no Port producer has ever visited Denmark as often as Manuel Pintão Poças, who for many Danish Port drinkers simply represents Port.

"We have many names for the things we love". So does Poças. The same wine is sold in different series to different markets. The series "Pousada" is very popular in Denmark.

RUBY

Poças made its first Vintage in 1960, then in 1963, 1970, 1975, 1977, and 1978 but the first successful one was produced in 1985 – and 25 years is not so bad for learning this difficult art. Since then the style has obtained a more self-confident and substantial structure, of which 1991, 94, 95 and 96 are the most recent evidence:

Manuel Pintão Poças is the family profile towards the surrounding world, world famous for his commitment to the family's port wines – and for Port in general. (Photo: BJS)

Vintage 1985: "Fruity and concentrated, almost rich with a sweetness ending in a dry and straightforward taste. Characteristic taste of berries with a bit of pepper".

Vintage 1991: "Concentrated berries, very nice and juicy with a long, intense sweetness that enhances the taste of fruit. Seems friendly but also resolute. Very fruity style. Exciting to follow".

Vintage 1994: "Soft and round with a nice fruity taste and self-confident, discrete muscle. Well-built with a fine balance. Sweet without being too sweet. Promising style. Seems far drier on the second day after opening, still with a fine balance and still promising".

Vintage 1995: "Fruit and sweetness, semi-rich structure with a characteristic taste of berries (black currant and blackberries). Potent, sweeter and richer than 1994".

Vintage 1996: "Dark with a sweetness turning in the glass and drying out. Peppery fruit. Compared to its age it has a light structure and is more pleasant than durable".

The LBVs have also improved in the course of the 1990'ies. More flesh and blood so to speak, and the delicate style characterising the first LBVs has changed. *LBV 1994* is probably the best Poças has produced since the first LBV in 1967.

You will also sense that Poças has improved its Ruby types, if you taste the special "Vintage Character 2000" which has been produced to celebrate the new millennium. A robust, non-aggressive wine with a nice fruit structure and a harmonic sweetness.

Of the more common types Poças produces a series of "Pousada Port" with "Old Days" Ruby and Tawny as well as the series "Two Diamonds" as both Ruby, Tawny and white Port.

TAWNY

The two classic 10-years and 20-years Tawnies always do very well in blind tastings and are often found to be among the best wines. I have a feeling that the style has been modernised and revived in the course of the 1990'ies. I have tasted the following in 1999 from fresh bottlings:

10-years Tawny: "Light, chestnut brown. Soft and creamy, like real cream, with and aftertaste of nuts and dry mushrooms. Not aggressive at all, delicious, tastes of more than a 10-years Tawny. Delicious initial taste and delicious aftertaste". (92/100)

20-years Tawny, "Quinta de Santa Barbara": "Rather light colour but not a light taste. Smoke, softness, mildness. Glossy, sentimental and delicious, more polished and self-confident than the 10-years, but without the 10-years's irresistible boyish charm". (94/100)

30-years Tawny: "Feminine style, mild and friendly taste. A bit of smoke mixing well with the characteristic woody taste which makes the fruit seems frail. Refined, almost delicate". (89/100)

Over 40-years Tawny: "Even more refined and even more thinned out fruit than in the 30-years. Also seems delicate with feminine fruit and straightforward woody taste. The richness is light but matches the taste that has a nice length but lacks depth". (90/100)

Colheitas are naturally a matter very near to the heart for a family house who is known for its old Tawnies. These wines have always been reliable, for example:

Colheita 1985: "Very nice, intense nose. Muscular taste with more fruit than wood, robust, adolescent, and naturally much too young. But the cask is promising. It will be exciting to bottle it in 20-30 years' time". (92-95/100)

Colheita 1967 was very popular on the Danish market because it marked the Danish Queen's silver wedding in 1992 and the Tivoli Gardens' 150th anniversary a year later:

Colheita 1967: "Soft, mild brown sugar with a dash of acid helping the wine to maintain its balance. Smoky and creamy. Good length. Ends in a long, soft aftertaste. Very nice dimension, especially nice length". (93/100)

I do not know why the older Colheitas are so much better than the 30-years and over 40-years Tawnies, but they are. In the other end of the scale "Pousada Old Days Tawny" is made from 6 to 8-years-old wine, an excellent and sympathetic little brother to the 10-years Tawny. You never go wrong with Poças' Tawnies.

Produtores Associados
(Produtores Associados de Vinhos Progresso do Douro Lda.)

The owner of the company with its long name has a name, which is even longer: Cooperative Vitivinícola do Peso da Régua - Caves Vale do Rodo. The co-operative situated close to Régua was founded in 1982 and exports 1.2 mio bottles of port wine annually, mainly to the Benelux countries and to France. The most well-known brands are Cedro (young Tawny), Cortez (young Tawny), and Réggua (10-years Tawny). The wines are light, sugary and rich.

Quarles Harries

Founded: 1680
Owner: Symington Family
Taster/Blender: Peter Ronald Symington
Quintas: None

Quarles Harris' history is - if not non-existent - then just as short as its description, even though it is old in years. The company was founded by the British Dawson family who did business with Brazil and therefore also started to deal in and carry Port. In 1680, Thomas Dawson felt that they did not have to go beyond Port, and he founded the Port house *Dawson & Harris* with a partner. The Port house was, in 1791 renamed to Harris Stafford and Sons, eventually becoming *Quarles Harris & Co.* In 1792, the house became the second largest Port Shipper, but in the early years of this century the company had some difficulties and shipments were considerably reduced. In the early 1920'ies a direct descendant of the original Mr. Harris, Reginald Quarles Harris, sold the company to his cousin's husband, Andrew James Symington, and curiously enough it is the only Port company in the Symington possession to whose family name they are linked.

RUBY

In the course of 1998-1999 I had the opportunity of comparing some of the vintages from all the Symingtons' Vintage Ports with a most confusing result: Quarles Harris was the weakest of all six wines of Vintage 1970, but seemed to be one of the wines with the most potent fruit in Vintage 1985. Unfortunately, some of the potency disappeared from the decanter after a couple of days, and the remaining power was concentrated in a short, intense fruity taste. Of the more recent vintages *Vintage 1991* is: "Like chocolate, friendly, fruity with a short, violent fuse, but also with a tendency to burn out".

Vintage 1994 has much more backbone, more berries and more length. Nice potency, nice promises but it is not among this vintage year's heavyweights.

Many producers would be proud to make a Vintage Port as Quarles Harris, but in the Symington's wide range it only ranks as a No. 7.

TAWNY

Quarles Harris' *10-years Tawny* has got not a very nice aroma (and sometimes taste too!) of a painter's workshop. But their *20-years Tawny* is more aggressive and more dominated by acid and fruit than of wood. It is feminine on the verge of a-norexia. The more common types are characterised by alcohol, acid and aggressive fruit.

Quinta da Casa Amarela

This quinta, which lies between Régua and Lamego and that since 1885 has been owned by the same family, only makes one Port Wine for marketing purposes, namely a 10-years Tawny, which Laura Regueiro started producing in 1979 and introduced on the market in 1994. And what a wine: the richest, creamiest pure and noble 10-years Tawny you could ever imagine. Apart from this Tawny, the quinta sells its wine "elsewhere" without their label. The family has planned to supplement with a 20-years Tawny. The quinta has 8 ha of quite old vines (45-50 years) according to Laura Regueiro they are planted with Touriga Nacional, Touriga Francesa and Tinta Barroca.

Quinta da Romaneira
(Sociedade Agrícola da Romaneira S.A.)

Founded: before 1757
Owner: Limited company
Taster/Blender: José Manuel Soares de Costa
Quintas: Is a Quinta

Until the new Act of 7 May 1986 was passed allowing the quintas to sell and export Port Wine direct, Quinta da Romaneira had to settle with the historic pleasure of having produced the first Single Quinta Port Wine sold on Christie's auctions in London.

This took place as early as in 1872 when a significant number of bottles of Romaneira Port, Vintage 1861 and 1863 were put up for sale - and were sold. It was not a Vintage Port in the modern sense of the word, but more likely a Late Bottled Vintage Port, for the wines had been bottled 4-5 years after harvest.

But they gave Quinta da Romaneira a personal profile, which was not changed until 1986 when the Act was passed and the Romaneira's were one of the first to take advantage of the situation.

The quinta goes back to Pombal's early registrations, but it was not until the end of the 19th Century and the beginning of the 20th Century it became significant. Then the quinta expanded. Adjacent land was purchased, and from a historical point of view the quinta consists today of 13-14 other properties, which could even be called quintas in their own right. It is by far the largest property in Costa de Roncão by Pinhão and a genuine country house with more than 50 km of access roads and exit turns.

In modern times, the limited company of Quinta da Romaneira was founded in 1942 by Monteiro de Barros who expanded the already large property. Through marriage and heritage it became the property of the bank Borges & Irmão but after being a victim of an unfortunate family feud, António Borges Vinagre bought it in 1967. At that point it was run down and parts of the quinta are still not operational.

Today the quinta is run by the António Borges Vinagre's son-in-law José Manuel Soares de Costa.

RUBY

Both the regular Ruby and *Vintage Character* are rather mild with a characteristic taste of fruit and berries. Vintage 1985 is in 1999: "Very sweet and mild, a wine which runs deep down the throat with pure, polished fruit, no dryness at all, no resistace and with an almost rich aftertaste". After 24 hours in the decanter it opens even more, but apart from the sweetness and richness you will only find a small moment of explosion in your glass. After three days it is almost gone. In some vintage years, Romaneira also produces Vintage Port under the name of one of its sister properties, such as *Quinta das Liceiras Vintage, 1982,* an extremely mild, tender and toothless Vintage which was drinkable very quickly.

TAWNY

The mild style with a short, friendly taste suits the Tawny types much better. They are light and nice and drinkable - to my taste quite sugary and fidele, but there are Port Wine drinkers for this style. Both the old Tawnies and the Colheitas are very, very nice.

Quinta de la Rosa

Founded: 1988
Owner: Bergqvist Family
Taster/Blender: Raymond Reynolds & Pedro Correia
Quintas: Is a Quinta

Perhaps it is the Quinta de la Rosa's unique location on the right bank of the Douro between Pinhão and Régua, spread out like a fan with small and middle-sized buildings on the 55 ha, that have inspired the Bergqvist's to do more for the future tourism than for Port Wine.

The quinta belonged to the Port Wine house Feuerheerd, and when it was sold to the Barros-Almeida family in 1933, the heir, Claire Feuerheerd, née Bergqvist, managed to keep the quinta. She had been given the quinta as a present at her baptism by her generous father, Albert Feuerheerd, in 1905 during the golden times. In the years 1933-1988 the family sold grapes and wine to the major producers, such as Croft, Delaforce, and especially Sandeman, but when the Act of 7 May 1986 was passed, and it was possible to sell and export Port Wine from the quintas in the Douro Valley, Sandeman's interest in using the quinta's grapes declined, and the family decided to make their own Single Quinta Vintage Port. Tim and Sophia Bergqvist have made their own wine from their own grapes from 1988.

It was a lot of hard work and took some capital, but so far the project has been a success, and today, around 200 pipes of Port Wine and table wine are produced on an annual basis - as well as olive oil. Everything takes place on the quinta, also tourism. You can rent one of the small cottages and live off the quinta's produce.

Quinta de la Rosa lies idyllically on the right bank of the Douro a bit outside of Pinhão. (Photo: HO)

Quinta de Val da Figueira

The quinta is famous for planting the first vines on American roots in the Douro Valley, which after the phylloxera era were planted here in 1878. In 1936, the quinta was bought by the Cálem Holzer family who are related to the famous Port family, Cálem, and for many years Cálem got all the grapes from this quinta, until the new Act in 1986 made it possible for the quinta to produce and sell wine themselves.

Now-retired Alfredo Cálem Holzer supervises the two types of wine that are produced on this quinta: a 10-years Tawny and Vintage Port (1987, 1989, 1991, 1994). Especially the quinta's 10-years Tawny is quite remarkable.

Cálem Holzer's Quinta de Val da Figueira lies between Quinta de la Rosa and Ferreira's Quinta do Porto on the right bank of the Douro river.
(Photo: HO)

Quinta do Castelinho

Founded: 1990
Owner: Saraiva Family
Taster/Blender: Joaquim Anacleto & Ana Miquelino
Quintas: Is a quinta, but also owns Quinta de São Domingos

The new Act on direct sales and exports of Port Wine from the Douro Valley ensured that the Saraiva family on Quinta do Castelinho could not only sell their own wines with their own labels instead of selling it to the major producers - it also gave them the financial possibility of purchasing Quinta de São Domingos which lies in the outskirts of Régua. They bought it in 1994 from Ramos-Pinto, and thus the quinta became a quinta proprietor. Quinta do Castelinho lies on the border between Cima Corgo and Douro Superior and has been in the Saraiva family for generations. And they have most probably made excellent Port Wines for generations, we will never know, for they either disappeared in the mixtures of the other producers, or the family drunk them themselves. After the amendment to the Act in 1986, a company was founded in 1990 for the production, sale and exportation of Port Wines from this quinta, and since then things have been going well.

The family-owned port house is run by Manuel António Saraiva, his daughter, Elisa, and his son, Manuel António Cruzio Saraiva. The latter became co-owner of Porto Cálem in 1998, but withdrew again in the spring of 1999.

Today, the quinta's production from the 50 ha is used as 95% for Port Wine and 5% for table wine, and of the overwhelming quantities of Port Wine 70% goes to the production of Tawnies. The Port Wine is made in the traditional way in Lagares and are matured on Quinta de São Domingos.

RUBY

After the Act of 1986 it was suddenly fun to make Vintage Port, so it is no surprise that Castelinho wants to have a Vintage profile. The following vintages were tasted at Castelinho's in 1998:

Vintage 1986: "Fruit and berries. Dominated by juice, lots of berries, but it has a weak backbone. Time will only show. This wine is, however, not to be kept for too long".

Vintage 1991: "Strong taste of elderberries, rich and sweet and well-balanced. Potent juice that practically drowns everything else. Needs time and development".

Vintage 1994: "More elderberry, not as intense as 1991, and both lighter and milder. Seems incredibly friendly for the vintage year. Nice, but not to be kept for too long".

Vintage 1997: "Dark, intense taste of berries: elderberries, elderberries and more elderberries. Full of juice. Very promising".

Castelinho's Vintage Ports are, as are the best of their Tawnies, very fruity and with a bigger impression of fruit and berries than of wood. Personal style. It will be very interesting to follow these wines in the coming years.

TAWNY

The newest product is "Millennium Reserva", a 7-8-years Tawny, which is nice, robust with not much alcohol, and which signals that Castelinho is best at the Tawny types. Robust style with a dash of sweetness and a nice fruity taste. The following were tasted during a visit at São Domingos in 1998:

10-years Tawny: "Soft, rather light with a nice, somewhat non-sugary sweetness".

The parent Quinta do Castelinho in Cima Corgo, east to Pinhão, lies high above the blue Douro river. What a beautiful view from the quinta's terrace! (Photo: HO)

20-years Tawny: "Weak, dull fruit, inanimated, but with a nice sweetness".

Bottled in 1993! but the wine benefited from maturation in bottles, Romaneira's man on the spot declared. I did not think so.

Colheita 1961: "Dense and mild with a fine Douro bake. Nice balance, vigorous and sweet".

Colheita 1962: "Full-bodied, nice structure. Solid style with a good, refreshing sweetness giving it a refined balance. Very nice".

The major part of the production consists of Tawny types, namely 70%, whilst white Port, LBV/Vintage and more common Ruby types both cover 10% each.

Quinta do Côtto

see Montez Champalimaud

Quinta do Crasto

Founded: Is mentioned in 1615
Owner: Roquette family
Taster/Blender: David Baverstock & Dominique Morris
Quintas: Is a Quinta

This is a classical locality, for they say that Crasto comes from the Latin word Castrum, which indicates that there was once a Roman fortified settlement here. The quinta is also mentioned in some of the oldest records of Douro Valley's properties, but not for its Port Wine. In the 19th Century the quinta belonged to Ferreira and did not get its own identity until after 1910 when Constantino de Almeida (Constantino Port) purchased it. Today, his granddaughter and her husband, Jorge Roquette run the quinta.

After the Act of 7 May 1986 was passed and it became possible to sell and export Port direct from the Douro Valley, new Patamares were laid out and planted ao alto so that the owners could aim at making good Port Wine more efficiently. The production of the Quinta's 48 ha of vines yield an average of approx. 15,000 of cases which only approx. 10-20% are used for quality Port Wine (Vintage and LBV) bearing the quinta name whilst the rest is sold as bulk wine to other producers. The year 1994 was a memorable year for the new quinta exporters. On 1 January, the family employed Cristiano van Zeller (former Quinta do Noval) as a consultant for Port Wine and later that year they hired the Australian-born winemaker David Baverstock (former Symington family) to make red wine, which he did so efficiently that the first quinta red wine was launched in the autumn of that same year.

Vintage Ports from 1927 are in stock in the Quinta's cellars, but the first commercialized vintage, sold as SQVP, was Vintage 1978. Since then, Vintage Ports have been produced in 1985 and 1987, while 1988, 1989 and 1990 have "only" been LBV's. My knowledge of Crasto's wines is very modest, so I have not given my evaluation.

Quinta do Crasto, seen from the terrace at the opposite neighbour, Quinta de São Luiz. (Photo: HO)

Quinta do Infantado

Founded: 1816
Owner: Roseiro family
Taster/Blender: João Roseira
Quintas: Is a Quinta

Terroir is the code word for this pleasant Roseiro family on Quinta do Infantado. Here the Port reflects the character of the soil on the around 40 ha, and they only make Port from the grapes of their own quinta where all the land is classified as A fields. António Roseira likes to emphasize that the soil is the most important element, but so is the traditional treatment of grapes, which are naturally foot-crushed in the old lagares. Another important factor to the quinta profile that all bottling has taken place on the quinta since 1979.

The quinta dates from 1816. It once belonged to crown prince Pedro, later King Pedro IV, thus the name: Infante means crown prince in Portuguese. At the turn of the century, the quinta was bought by João Lopes Roseira, father of the present owners, Luís and António Roseiro. He had lots of Port Wine grapes in the neighbourhood and could use an extra 5-6 ha of grapes which were then planted on this quinta. When he planted the new plants, he suddenly died, and his widow had to take over the daily management and raise three sons. She did a good job, and when she died at the age of 93 in 1984, she could pass on a well-functioning quinta to her sons, António and Luís.

Luís got the idea of making a "genuine" Quinta Port in 1979, the first Estate Bottled SQVP (Vintage 1978), instead of selling the wine or the grapes to other producers (especially to Taylor's and Sandeman), which was common for quinta owners who did not own buildings in Gaia. The new image and the first sales to the home market were followed by the purchase of several lots around Pinhão so that the modest range of offers from 1979: Ruby, Tawny, and 20-years Tawny, could soon be extended.

As soon as exportation from the quintas of the Douro Valley was possible, a new era started at Infantado - also workwise. Here, Antonio Roseira and his daughter Catarina are on a promotion tour to present the till then unknown quinta's wines. (Photo: BJS)

Today, António's son, João, has taken over the daily management of the quinta, but it is still run in the traditional way. As much as possible is handicraft with foot-crushing and hardly any chemicals. From Vintage 1994 the family even produces an organic Vintage Character. The quinta is a production quinta. The family does not live there. They still live in the little town of Covas do Douro.

RUBY

Infantado is first and foremost a Tawny producer, even though especially *Vintage 1985*, which is an excellent wine with an intense elderberry taste and a refined sweetness in an aftertaste that changes its character the day after opening the bottle and becomes almost dry. In a difficult vintage year as 1989 Infantado managed to make a very nice *Vintage 1989*, which is quite light but still very good. *Vintage 1982* is a light vintage with a nice fruity taste of berries but with a short dry taste. *Vintage 1991* was made only on Touriga Nacional, and both this wine as well as *Vintage 1992* have a characteristic impression of berries and fruit and are quite dry behind the natural sweetness of the product. The organic Vintage Character is fruity and solid.

TAWNY

Infantado's Tawny style is rigid. The sweetness is not too characteristic but keeps a sober balance between a fruity and woody taste, especially their 20-years Tawny. The family's best product is *Colheita 1977* known as "Reserva da Familia" It is surprisingly dry considering its natural sweetness, as if the consistent dry style was a family trait.

Quinta do Noval

Founded: 1715
Owner: AXA-Millésimes
Taster/Blender: António Agrellos
Quintas: Is a quinta itself

Some brands outgrow their inventor, such as Dow's, and some quintas become more famous than their owners, such as Quinta do Noval which grew so famous that Fernando van Zeller in 1970 chose to rename the Port house A.J. da Silva & Co. after its quinta, and while only a few well-informed people today know the name of da Silva, anybody who can lift a glass of Port knows the name of Quinta do Noval.

The Quinta do Noval is an old property. It was registered under the name of Noval in 1715 for the first time. It was owned by the renowned Port family Rebello Valente for more than one hundred years, to whom it had been given by the Marquis de Pombal, but as so many other quintas it suffered under the phylloxera in the late 1880'ies resulting in the soil losing its value. As the Rebello Valente family did not believe that the soil could ever be cultivated again, they sold the quinta to António José da Silva in 1894. After a lot of hard work he managed to get the vines to root again, and in 1920 he convinced his son-in-law, Luis Vasconcelos Porto, to abandon a promising career as a diplomat and become a partner in the firm.

This turned out to be very fortunate for Quinta do Noval. Luis Vasconcelos began restauring the quinta, and in the course of the 1930'ies he carried out a renovation that has made the quinta just as famous and photographed as the old cedar tree on the terrace. He had noticed that only the first row of vines on the old pre-phylloxera terraces were giving fully-ripened grapes, so he began to break down all the old terraces and build new and broader ones. They were even whitewashed, and the name Noval was printed beautifully on them and could be spotted from miles away. This work was carried out so scrupolously that the bright terraces of Noval are considered among the Douro Valley's attractions today and are unofficially considered a local and national monument worth preserving.

The new owners, AXA Millésimes, have respected this work and have not for a minute been tempted to molest the monument, although that could have boosted production, Christian Seely explains, "When we decided to replant a large procentage of the vineyard of Noval we took the deliberate decision to replant and mechanise the old terraces, rather than bulldozing them to make patamares. This was of course partly for aesthetic reasons. The ownership of a great historic vineyard like Noval implies a responsibility for maintaining its heritage, and it would have been unthinkable for us to have bulldozed Noval's terraces. But also we believe that by replanting the old terraces we achieve a perfect harmony between old and new: We keep the aesthetics of the old, we replant with separated noble grape varieties, we render the terraces mechanisable, and we maintain a good density of plantation that keeps yields low and thus quality high."

Through Luis Vasconcelos' daughter, Teresa, the Quinta do Noval came into the hands of the van Zeller family, and did not fair at all, for Fernando van Zeller was very much against his son, Cristiano (1900-1937), marrying the young Miss Vasconcelos, to such an extent that he disinherited his son - at least with regard to the quinta. The Quinta do Roriz was left to the two other sons, Rolando and Pedro. Teresa got her Cristiano, and

Working on the famous terraces. To the left the vines in February. To the right the vines in October at harvest. (Photo: HO)

their three sons, Fernando, Cristiano and Luis as well as their daughter, Isabel, were made heirs to this famous quinta. It was the oldest son, Fernando, and the youngest son, Luis, who together took over the daily management when Luis Vasconcelos Porto retired in the Vintage year of 1963. Fernando and Luis were successful in the beginning, for the Quinta do Noval had already gained international fame so that in 1970 the family could approve to abandon the old producer's name of da Silva and sell and market their best wines under the name of the quinta.

The good times of prosperity and fame were suddenly put to a stop when a fire broke out in the autumn of 1981 and Noval's stocks burnt to the ground in Vila Nova de Gaia. 350,000 litres of Port in casks went up in flames along with 20,000 bottles of Vintage Port 1978 and the family archives containing a long family history. This resulted in a slight family crisis and when Fernando van Zeller's two younger brothers, Cristiano (deceased 1980) and Luis (deceased 1981) died within a year, he chose to retire himself in 1982.

It was time for the next generation to take over, even though they were very young. Luis Vasconcelos Porto's great-grandchildren Cristiano and Teresa were only 22 and 23, respectively, when they had to take over the daily management, but they tackled the situation head on with an optimism only the young can own - and with a bit of imprudence only they can have. Osborne took over the lodges that had not burned down, and instead Cristiano and Teresa started to restructure the Quinta do Noval from being a vineyard to a production farm. They built an impressive plant by the quinta which they called the "Cathedral" and which was inaugurated in 1985, ready to hold 6,500 pipes, boasting all state-of-art equipment - strangely enough except temperature control, which was installed by AXA in 1994 - so that all Noval's wines (and stocks) could be assembled here in the future. The permission to export directly from the Douro Valley was lurking around the corner and was approved by law in 1986. At this point, no other major producers were as ready as Quinta do Noval. But the many projects and investments emptied the money box, and as Teresa Vasconcelos and Cristiano van Zeller had been so imprudent as to have four children, which in the world of Port is the same as four new co-owners, who also had children of their own, and as they could not all sit at the place of honour in the boardroom, the bad times immediately led to disagreements about small matters - and on a long term an increasing desire to see money on the table.

When Noval entered the 90'ies it was in need of capital to be able to keep up with development and keep the quality standards of their bottles. A few years of bad accounts made the unrest smoulder beneath the surface, just as a camp fire ready to burst out in flames. When Noval unofficially had been up for sale for a few years, the French insurance company, AXA Millésimes, bought the quinta in May 1993 with all its fixtures: buildings, equipment, names and stocks, 145 ha of land, with the only exception of a lodge in Gaia.

On a national basis it was a great sorrow to see Portugal's most famous quinta becoming French property, but it was reassuring to know that the man behind AXA's investment was no other than Jean-Michel Cazes whose genuine love for wine and viniculture had already been seen on several occasions in Bordeaux, France. As daily manager of Quinta do Noval, he appointed the young and then unknown Englishman, Christian Seely.

At this point the Noval Nouveau project was launched. First, the new owners discovered that there were so-called "grey spots" on Noval: lots on which the vines did not produce the required high quality of grapes, but which had not been replaced because the van Zeller family had lacked capital. The vines were now replaced by only 5 noble grapes varieties and planted in straight rows with a platform at the very end of each row so that a special tractor manufactured in Switzerland could be used, at least partly. But as mentioned previously, the old whitewashed terraces were to be left untouched, so all the work had to be carried out carefully. Since 1994, a total of 28 ha has been replanted and newly planted, of which the first acceptable grapes were yielded in 1998.

Under Christian Seely's management the redirecting of Quinta do Noval continued, from the quay in Gaia to the plateau above Rio Pinhão. This was naturally a copy of the château principle where everything is kept in one place so that you avoid spreading the workplaces, and especially the oenologs and the tasters avoid having to run from lodge to quinta in the busy periods.

Thus Noval became the first Gaia-based Port house to move all its wine out to the Douro and only kept one office building in Gaia. This was a clear departure from tradition, but as Christian Seely says: "Earlier on there were three reasons to produce Port in the Douro Valley and then transport it to Gaia for maturation. First of all, it was too hot in the Douro Valley. Second of all, Gaia was very close to the ships and the sea. And thirdly, nobody wanted to live as far away as the Douro Valley. But today, we have full temperature control, we do not sail the Port anymore but transport the wine via the new motorway and a completely new infrastructure, which signifies that more and more people choose to live in the Douro Valley". He is one of them.

As for AXA's other wine investments, either in Pauillac, in Sauternes or in Tokaij, there is no saving on investments. In the spring of 1994, a

The view from Noval is quite fantastic, and the view towards Noval is quite fantastic too. Here is the quinta seen from the west. (Photo: HO)

new vinification plant was constructed at the quinta, with revolutionary stainless steel vinification tanks incorporating mechanical treading "feet" on pistons inside the vats. The lagares were also extensively renovated, incorporating temperature control, new horizontal Vaslin presses, and the machine treader in the lagares. All this was ready by the harvest of 1994, which looks like it is going to become a classic vintage, and this is a good omen.

There are now two centres by Noval. At one of the centres, all the wines bearing the quinta name are produced, and they are only made from grapes from the quinta. Half of all Noval's wines are made from foot-crushed grapes in the old lagares: 1/2 mio of a total of 1 mio bottles a year and all the quality wines are only produced in the lagares. This is not about romantic notions and the joys of the country, but simply the fact that foot-crushing gives a far better extraction and a far better quality, Christian Seely tells me. And that is why the lagares are used, even though this production method is much more costly.

The costs especially relate to manpower, and it is becoming increasingly difficult to find volonteers, as it is very hard work. Foot-crushing takes place for six weeks in a row, day after day, and most of the volonteers only feel like doing such work for a day or two. But in spite thereof and in spite of the improved technical equipment, Noval's best wine will still continue to be produced in this old-fashioned way. A special cooling system has been built so that the temperature can be regulated accurately and the different lagares are separated from each other for the vinification of small quantities.

From the harvest of 1994, a special character has been part of the production process: a robot which is still used for foot-crushing - but only as a supplement! 18 men times two feet is still the best method when the crushing is to be done, but the robot is useful as it does not get tired and can work at any given time and in any given place around the clock. It does not smoke and it does not ask for an increase in wages. A new bottling plant and warehouse at Alijó were opened in 1995 approx. 12 km from the quinta which will completely separate Noval from Gaia. No wine is vinified here. All the superior category Ports are made in the lagares at the quinta, all the others in the new winery at the quinta. They are all bottled in the new bottling plant.

Since AXA took over Noval in 1993, the strategy of the company has changed in emphasis, with a much greater concentration on the production of superior category Ports, which now account for over 60% of the sales, as against less than 20% in 1993, according to Christian Seely. Today only Vintage Port and Colheita wines are made form 100% quinta grapes and for these wines the name Quinta do Noval is used. LBV, 10-years, 20-years and over 40-years old tawnies are 100% trodden in the lagares at Noval, and will be made from a very high proportion of quinta grapes, but grapes from high quality suppliers will also be used, so for these wines the label Noval only is used. The LB is made from a blend of wines vinified in the lagares and in the new winery, while the tawny and ruby are made in the new winery. These wines are also sold as Noval.

Until the harvest of 1999 Noval has also bought grapes from Quinta de Roriz, which is still owned by a branch of the family van Zeller. However, the wines were so promising that the proprietors have decided to go it alone as independent producers. Quinta do Noval is the only Portuguese Port house that has had a real impact on the British market and that can be compared to Taylor's, Fonseca, and Graham's when it comes to reputation. The breakthrough came with the exclusive Vintage 1931, which might have become exclusive because only three shippers declared a Vintage that year whilst all others were deterred by the international crisis and the many bottles of 1927 which were still on the market. Even though the quality of Noval's wines was not always credible in the course of the 1970'ies and the 1980'ies, the name has kept its ring of quality and patina, and from 1993, which was the year AXA took over Noval, under the direction of Christian Seely, new times have come to the quinta. The year 1994, the first under AXA's auspices, may prove to be the beginning of a new era with the same golden lustre as in 1931.

RUBY ♥♥♥♥♥

When it comes to the quality of the wine in the bottle there are three important years to remember for Noval: 1920, when Luis Vasconcelos put all his energy in rebuilding the quinta and its wines; 1982 when his great-great grandchildren Cristiano and Teresa of 22 and 23, respectively, took over the company with great enthusiasm and used their young strength to restore the name and reputation of; and 1993 when AXA bought out the family and launched its new project with Christian Seely as daily manager. Especially the year of 1993 is an epoch-making year, because AXA proved to be able to combine ambition with a sound economy.

The new "Noval LB", which is a Vintage Character, contains fruit and a wonderful straightforward freshness. Noval LB has changed its style since the time of van Zeller, and from the vintage year of 1992 it has launched a firmer fruit structure and a potent, straightforward sweetness. History's ups and downs are especially noted in their Vintage Port. Luis Vasconcelos gets the credit for the notorious and famous 1931 and for

Christian Seely in Noval's new domicile in Gaia. The production has been moved to the Douro Valley, but for practical reasons Noval still has an address in the centre of the Port Wine city. (Photo: HO)

the incredible wines in the difficult vintage years of the 1940'ies and 1950'ies. In the1960'ies, however, the quality is not as good. *Vintage 1996* (tasted in 1999) has great charm and length, but there are metallic flaws in the polish and it is more robust than good. *Vintage 1970* (also tasted in 1999) is one of this great vintage's medium wines, nice without being flamboyant, and as 1966, made by Frederico van Zeller.

Vintage 1982 was Cristiano van Zeller's first vintage. In 1999 it has an "intense sweetness, wrapping around the delicate fruit. It seems dull, makes a tentative effort, but falls back and has nothing to offer. The fruit is too weak, the sweetness too dominating". *Vintage 1985* does not live up to the possibilities this vintage offers, and I have noted that when it is included in a blind tasting of 1985s, it always ends up in the middle.

New times for Noval, the AXA period, began in 1993, and Christian Seely and his team launched two promising Vintages in 1994 and 1995 - and what a beginning:

Vintage 1994: "Nose with depth. Intense sweetness and fine power. The sweetness is almost violent, but the fruit is powerful too. Well-built. Very promising. Dense nose and taste. In spite of the sweetness in the beginning, the fruit seems dry and very potent. Ends in an explosion of liquorice. Patience is required for many years yet"!

Vintage 1995: "Intense fruit – and berries, lots of elderberries. Concentrated and very potent with a refined combination of natural sweetness and a fine dryness in the fruit. Very promising".

In 1996 Nacional was produced, but not Noval. In 1997 both were produced, as was "Silval", named after a lot on the quinta, but made from grapes from other corners of the quinta and in Seely's words: "from high-quality grapes that are not used for Quinta do Noval Vintage". Although it is much too soon to taste these three wines, they do give an indication of style and potential and were tasted in September 1999:

Nacional Vintage 1997: "Intense elderberry nose. Impressive, dense structure with characteristic taste of blackberries and a lot of dry fruit. Starts off as concentrated juice from black berries but ends up as crisp sweet liquorice. Stubborn, reluctant, more dry than sweet, especially in the long, dry aftertaste. The length is prolonged further in the glass. The day after: still great concentration of blackberry and again the intense sweetness changes into a dry, straightforward dryness. Wonderful explosion in the mouth. Super potent".

Silval Vintage 1997: "More dull in the nose than Nacional, but with nearly the same dryness in the end. Also more impressive taste of liquorice in the end than Nacional, but not as snappish and unfriendly. The first mouthful is the most complex of the three wines with more taste nuances, what a thrill. The day after: still milder than Nacional and Noval, and the mildness just continues to increase. Juicy, berry-like, mostly elderberry, and sweet. Same length as Nacional, but not the same depth".

Noval Vintage 1997: "Closed nose. Mild and smooth, the sweetest of the three wines, dense structure with the least dry ending. Softer in the berry taste than the two other wines. Lacks the dimension and the power in the beginning that the two others have, but in the glass it expands from its middle and begins faster and faster and ends later and later. It has the nicest development of the three wines in the glass The day after: the nose has woken up. More substance, denser structure, but without Silval's mildness in the fruit. Dominated by liquorice in the long aftertaste, but it is still less dry than the two others. But potent".

Having drunk the last drops, my conclusion is that Nacional has the most explosive taste, Silval the softest and mildest, and Noval the longest. All three wines are exciting encounters - and convincing encounters. Great promises - and great expectations! My high opinion of Noval's future is also due to the fact that I know Jean-Michel Cazes and Christian Seely very well and know that they will avoid any compromise with regard to quality, and as they also have the means, we can expect many fantastic vintage years of Noval, Silval – and Nacional. About Nacional, see also page 233ff.

TAWNY

I was thinking of what the master of the tasting room, António Agrellos said about a year ago when we were tasting an old Colheita: "Just because a wine is old, it does not have to be weak"!

This is a very fine philosophy, but unfortunately it does not always apply to Noval's old vintages, but is very characteristic for the time span of the oldest ones I tasted:

Colheita 1937: "Rich, delicious chocolate fudge nose. Richness, refined smoky taste, big smoky nose. Delicious, long taste, pure and very nice. A super wine with flaws and with enormous inner qualities".

Just as the following Colheitas, which were tasted in the course of 1996-1999 in very nice company with Christian Seely, the above was a first bottling. In the following the list of kings with capricious deviations as to style and quality:

Colheita 1967: "Soft, light and fine sweetness. Somewhat rich, but light style. Light and nice. Nice and serene".

Colheita 1968: "Nice taste of brown sugar, but only slightly rich. Rather short taste, a bit aggressive with a blunt ending. Disappointing".

Colheita 1971: "Sweet, very fine brown sugar powder and decent, but rather short taste. Then a bit of acetone, then nothing. No richness, no charm, no finesse".

Colheita 1974: "Acetone nose. Nice taste, slightly rich, but far from convincing. Slightly aggressive, fragile with a weak character".

Colheita 1976: "Fragile and rather aggressive. Very light-bodied, slim on the verge of meagre. Acetone! Short and rather anonymous".

Colheita: 1984: "Slightly aggressive nose. Soft, nice taste, a bit aggressive, slightly smoky with a very nice potency. Young and vivid".

Colheita 1987: "Pure medium style, pure fruit, short taste. Nice and pure, rather anonymous, but Noval also makes this style".

After AXA's take-over in 1993, a fresher style was applied to the 20-years and over 40-years Tawnies, so these two wines, as well as the 10-years Tawny, establish Noval as a prominent Ruby producer who also masters the art of making Tawnies:

10-years Tawny: "Rich and delicious, almost a Colheita structure, with a light taste of nuts".

20-years Tawny: "Dense and elegant with an intense nutty taste and lots of wholesome fruit potency. Excellent 20-years".

Over 40-years Tawny: "Dark brown, like treacle, rich and superb, with nuts and figs, chocolate fudge and a very nice body. Elegant and wonderful".

Quinta do Portal

Founded: 1989
Owner: Branco Family
Taster/Blender: the Branco brothers
Quintas: Quinta dos Muros, Quinta da Abelheira, Quinta do Confradeiro and Quinta do Casal de Celeirós

The Branco family had been producing wine in the Douro Valley for many generations and selling it by tradition to the major producers, but when a new generation took over in 1974, Eugénio M. Branco and João M. Branco inherited the Quinta do Portal and began to put the wine in stock instead of selling it off immediately. When the Act on direct sales and exports from the Douro Valley was passed in 1986, they decided to become producers with their name on the label in 1989. In 1991, they bought two quintas from Sandeman and became shippers. 1993 was the first vintage year, in which they vinified their wine, and their wines have been marketed since 1986 and thus became visible, so this is a true adventure story.

The family's "parent" quinta, Quinta dos Muros by Pinhão has been in the hands of the family for more than one hundred years. Here, all the best wine is put in stock. In 1978, the family bought the neighbouring Quinta da Abelheira, and in 1991 the Quinta do Confraderio and Quinta do Casal de Celierós, which today is both a vinification centre and works with tourism. The family owns a total of 95 ha with vines distributed on the four quintas. An LBV, 1994, is produced under the name of "Rupestre" which is sweet, slightly fruity and very drinkable. The 10-years and 20-years Tawnies are called "Parador". The 10-years Tawny is "dense, sweet, nice, not rich but pure and clear", the 20-years Tawny is "rich and intense, and very Portuguese in its straightforward, sweet style".

Quinta do Roriz

The millennium will signify new times on Quinta do Roriz. The co-operation with Quinta do Noval ceased in 1999, as the van Zeller family, who owns this quinta, has decided to produce under their own label in the future. In the hands of Noval, both the LBV and the Vintage with Quinta do Roriz' own name was somewhat lighter than Noval's and was sweeter.

The quinta, which was famous in the time of Pombal belonged to the Kopke family for many years and has until now had a tradition of selling wine to the major port wine houses and for several years to the Sherry house, Gonzalez-Byass, who once had a brief encounter with Port Wine.

Quinta do Vesúvio

Founded: Mentioned as early as in 1565
Owner: Symington Family
Taster/Blender: Peter Ronald Symington
Quintas: Is a quinta itself

The Quinta do Vesúvio is not only the Douro Valley's largest Port quinta boasting 408 ha but also the only quinta to be run consistently according to the French Château principles. It therefore produces a prestigious wine (Vintage Port) from its own grapes every single year, apart from disastrous years as 1993. While the quinta was owned by Dona Antónia and her descendants (see page 194ff), the grapes were used for Ferreira's best wines, but when the Symingtons took over the quinta in 1989, it became its own master,

Quinta do Vesúvio is the largest quinta in the Douro Valley and has a fantastic location. The 67 ha of vines sweep the background beautifully. (Photo: HO)

and the year 1989 was the first vintage carrying the quinta's name. In the beginning of the 1990'ies, an extensive planting was carried out (30,000 of vines in 1990 and 50,000 vines in 1991) so that the quinta now disposes of 300,000 vines on 67 ha. Today, the family only aims at four of the five classical grapes varieties, namely Touriga Nacional, Tinta Roriz, Touriga Francesa, and Tinta Barroca, and strangely enough the two latter varieties are the ones mostly applied. Of an annual production of approx. 240 pipes, only about 50 pipes carry the quinta's name as a Single Quinta Vintage Port - this gives around 30,000-36,000 bottles of Port - whilst the rest is used for the Symington family's other Ports.

Vesúvio is situated far East into the Douro Valley (120 km from Porto) with very hot summers, and the Symingtons have therefore equipped the quinta with modern temperature control and a special cooling system of stainless steel which is lowered into the lagar so that the temperature does not run out of control during fermentation. The system was designed by Peter R. Symington who is responsible for the vinification. The eight granite lagares still remain in use and all the grapes are crushed by foot. This is how the past and the present are silently linked on the quinta whose history dates back to 1565 when it was first mentioned under the name of Quinta das Figueiras. It was not until 1830, five years before it was inherited by Dona Antónia and her husband, that it was renamed Quinta do Vesúvio. After the dams began to block Douro's natural reaches, it has experienced several floods, the latest one in 1989, just after the Symington family had taken over the quinta. But it was a thing as banal as a family dispute that made a majority of the shareholders sell their shares to the Symingtons.

RUBY

The first Vintage was Vintage 1989. The following was tasted in the course of 1998-1999:

Vintage 1991: "Lots of juice and power, black berries and an intense, juicy sweetness. More juicy than fruity. Very nice 1991". (92/100)

Vintage 1992: "Sunny disposition, natural juice. Well-structured, pulpy and characterised by berries and a good tannin. Still very young, but promising". (91/100)

Vintage 1994: "Young elderberry nose. Dense, intense elderberry taste, added a bit of chocolate. Virile and personal, still stand-offish, potent and promising. Good keeping qualities". (93/100)

Vintage 1995: "Intense and juicy with elderberry and cacao. Dense fruit, enormous juice content with potency and calories. A body-builder with enormous fruit muscles". (94/100)

Vintage 1996: "Intense baccate fruit. Closed and still under lock and key, but very fruity and very promising". (90-93/100)

Vesúvio, or Vezuvio, as it was once called, was in its days of glory when Dona Antónia was alive, and this label comes from that time. Vesúvio will be in days of glory again under the Symingtons.

Ramos-Pinto Port
(Adriano Ramos-Pinto Vinhos)

Founded: 1880
Owner: Louis Roederer Champagne
Taster/Blender: João Nicolau de Almeida
Quintas: Quinta do Bom Retiro, Quinta de Urtiga, Quinta dos Bons Ares, Quinta da Ervamoira

The old Brazilian colony was only too tempting for the 20-years-old greenhorn, Adriano Ramos-Pinto so that he dared to send his first bottles of Port by ship the long way across the Atlantic Ocean in 1880. He called his wine "Adriano" and eventually it became such a success that after 15 years he dominated 50% of the South American market, and in 1896 the company could afford to take on his brother, António, as partner in the *Ramos-Pinto Brothers*.

They did not lack courage nor did they lack good ideas, as one can see from the Ramos-Pinto imaginative posters from the turn of the century and right up to the 1920'ies. And when Ramos-Pinto's competitors closed their bottles of Port firmly, Adriano popped the corks and let the bottles breathe freely among Bacchus' subjects and graceful and lightly clad young nymphs. This very avant-garde advertising paid off, for both sales and exports rose, and the brothers had no problems in sharing the pleasures. António was the practical person who kept an eye on finances whilst Adriano was an art-lover, who was crazy about Paris and modernism and very outgoing. This gave the young company a lot of free publicity in the press.

Adriano and António Ramos-Pinto saw the advantages of owning property in the Douro Valley, and this is one of the reasons why Ramos-Pinto is approx. 80% self-sufficient today and is the Port house who obtains most of its grapes from own vines. The four present quintas cover a large area: Quinta do Bom Retiro and Quinta da Urtiga lie in Cima-Corgo, Quinta dos Bons Ares and Quinta de Ervamoira lie in Douro Superior.

The finest quinta is the Quinta do Bom Retiro which was purchased back in 1919. It has around 60 ha of vines (including the neighbouring Quinta da Urtiga). The name means "A good place to retire" and according to sly tongues the name hints that Adriano had a good time here with many a young lady who arrived by the express train from Paris - and there really was an express train from Paris!

The quinta boasts of having the first swimming pool in the Douro Valley and was for many years just as much a country estate than a wine estate. But in José António Rosas' time in the 1970'ies, a major new plantation and re-plantation took place with the epoch-making commissioning of patamares and later on vertical ao alto planting. (see page 96ff)

Upon refurbishing Bom Retiro, Rosas was aggravated by the fact that the vinification here was not efficient enough and that there was not enough room for mechanisation - at least to the extent he desired. So he looked around for a place by studying old military maps and outlines of the old hinterland and thus found a remote area by the Côa river where he found a quinta by the name of Santa Maria. At the time, it was used for cultivating corn so the soil had not been exhausted by vines. And as the two old sisters, who owned the quinta, wanted to sell it, the deal was concluded in 1974.

When Rosas heard that the name Santa Maria was already a registered name by Cockburn's, he realized that he could not use this name for his Ports so he found inspiration in a French novel about a Port family and a small white flower growing by the Douro river: Ervamoira, and this became the new name of the quinta. Quinta dos Bons Ares, not far away, was purchased in 1989 to produce grapes for table wine, and today, its modern vinification plant produces table wines and Ports from Ervamoira. According to now-deceased Rosas, Ervamoira was the first quinta in the Douro Valley to scrupulously follow a micro climate plan, planting grapes in blocks according to grape variety, and only the five classical grapes were used. Ervamoira is also the only quinta in the Douro Valley which is planted only ao alto (100 ha.). By the way, according to Jorge Rosas, later on the five classical grape varieties have been supplemented by a few other varieties which João Nicolau de Almeida found useful.

The quinta holds other records. Not only is it one of the youngest Port quintas in the Douro Valley, it also has the dubious historical fate of being a fine water line that could have completely disappeared from the map. You see, it is situated close to the Côa river, and in 1989 the State-owned electricity company, EDP (Electricidade de Portugal), planned to build a gigantic dam which signified that 2/3 of the quinta, including buildings and vineyards, would be expropriated and flooded.

The engineers might have been up against the forces of nature, but Ramos-Pinto's were up against just as powerful forces, namely the Government. But the Quinta da Ervamoira was worth fighting for, and the family made several attempts to avoid its sad destiny. But even though many remains worth preserving were found in the excavations, this was not enough to stop the flooding. But fortune favours the brave! During the scientific analyzes of the quinta and its sur-

Jorge Rosas (to the left), the son of renowned José António Ramos-Pinto Rosas, and João Nicolau de Almeida (to the right), the son of the just as renowned Fernando Nicolau de Almeida, are responsible for exports and wine-making, respectively, at Ramos-Pinto. (Photo: HO)

roundings before the expropriation, a Portuguese archeologist found some obscure engravings on the rocks in 1994. At first he kept the discovery to himself, but then he saw João de Almeida with tears in his eyes on a TV programme asking for a miracle, which would save the quinta, and then he reacted. The building of the dam was suspended until further notice until the drawings had been examined, and in 1995 the Portuguese government announced that the rock drawings were so unique that the dam would not be concluded. Instead an archeological park has been projected (see page 379f).

Ervamoira had been saved, but what was even better: in December 1998 Ramos-Pinto received the message that UNESCO had classified the area with the rock engravings, including the Quinta da Ervamoira, as "specially worth preserving" (World Heritage). This makes the 100 ha of vineyards the only vineyards in the world that are officially classified as such, and Ramos-Pinto celebrated this rescue operation in 1994 by declaring both Ramos-Pinto and Quinta da Ervamoira for Vintage Ports. The irony of fate willed it so that in 1999 the quinta had electricity laid in - at a very high price. The planned large-scale power plant, which was to reduce prices, had stopped, so electricity had to come from afar ...

The Quinta da Ervamoira, which according to João de Almeida, lies on the driest spot in Portugal and is therefore perfect for wine growing was not Rosas' only wild idea. He had many more - but for some years he had been in need of a competent sparring partner and finally, in 1976, he employed his sister's son, João, who had just returned from the Universities of Dijon and Bordeaux. It was not an easy task, however, for João's last name was Nicolau de Almeida, son of the Fernando Nicolau de Almeida who had invented the Barca Velha and had substituted his own father as Chief Winemaker at Ferreira's, so it was in the air that this young Almeida - and he is still called that in Gaia even though he is in his fifties

A piece of nostalgic history from Ramos-Pinto's office. Not many years ago, the typewriter was transfered to the museum! (Photo: HO)

- should also choose a career in Ferreira's tasting room. But uncle Rosas was shrewd. 23 years later João tells me: "He said that he had something to show me and asked me to come and see him. And I agreed, of course, even though I knew every corner in his laboratories and cellars. But I went there and he dragged me off to the Douro Valley and showed me all his dreams. And I was hooked".

He began working for Ramos-Pinto in 1976 and has never left. He also has many honorary offices and is regarded as one of Gaia's finest wine tasters as well as owning a good sense of humour. The partner race between João and his uncle resulted in a great period for Ramos-Pinto, both with regard to quality and ingenuity, but financially they suffered by the fact that too many family members were small shareholders who wanted to see cash on the table, so at a certain point they had to look for fresh capital.

It turned up in August 1990 when the Champagne house, Louis Roederer, bought 55% of the shares and has since then taken over the remaining 45%. "This is of course a little sad but necessary and useful and the best solution to give continuity to the production of top quality Port," says Jorge Rosas, the young generation in the old family firm. He is responsible for exports.

With Louis Roederer's help João de Almeida can now live according to his good philosophy: producing quality instead of quantity. He is fully supported by the new owner, Jean-Claude Rouzaud, in his views: that it is better to be beautiful than big!

The Champagne people do not meddle at all, but confirmed a five-years investment plan just after the take-over in 1990, which would first consider the quintas, the wineries and the vineyards. In 1996, the turn came to the buildings, offices and cellars in Gaia.

Things are still blooming at Ramos-Pinto from the great lodges in Gaia with the many old casks to the faraway flowers on the preserved Quinta in the Côa Valley.

RUBY

"We are fed up of being called a Tawny producer. We want to be the best at all what we do, but we got the label because we sold so much Tawny to South America and had no tradition of making Vintage", Jorge Rosas says, when I asked him how it feels to be called a Tawny house.

But things will probably stay this way, until the day when Ramos-Pinto's Ruby types become as reliable as their Tawny types.

"Fine Ruby" is at the bottom of the chart. "Quinta da Urtiga" is a *Vintage Character* with a nice robust fruit but rather light. Late Bottled Vintage is unfiltered. It is bottled after four years and is potent and exciting, the latest is Vintage 1994.

It is very exciting to compare LBV 1994, Vintage 1994 and Quinta da Ervamoira 1994 (SQVP) where the LBVs are softer and smoother, and there is quite a difference between the two Vintage Ports:

Ramos-Pinto Vintage 1994: "Self-confident, peppery fruit. Slight sweetness, long aftertaste. Lots of potency and a nice depth. Consistent and well-made Vintage with many good years to go. Put it aside and keep it for at least 10-15 years".

Quinta da Ervamoira Vintage 1994: "Very soft, mild, friendly – without being too sweet. Personal style that seems self-confident behind the mild face. Definitely feminine. Somewhat shorter keeping qualities than above".

Vintage 1995 is "dark blue, sinister and dense. Impressive potency with lots of black berries, chocolate and pepper. Fruit potency and promising".

I have the feeling that the quality of Ramos-Pinto's Vintage Ports has improved in the last decade. The style seems to be more concentrated, more fruity, tighter, so it is different from the Tawny style that Ramos-Pinto follows by tradition. But there are discrepancies between the different old Tawnies, as you can see from my tasting comments from the "Vintage of the Century" in 1999:

Vintage 1921: "Intense nose: brown sugar coated pastries, syrup, pines (!). A bit of orange in the sweetness keeps the richness at bay. Delicious wine, as a delicious Colheita with an intensity and a structure, dense, sweet and fascinating".

Vintage 1931: "Again a touch of orange, giving a slight taste of Moscatel, and reducing the impression of sweetness. Smoky and rich, but also elegance. Colheita – and a very nice Colheita at that – but almost no fruit".

Vintage 1960: "Enormous variety of colours form the golden brown of the 1931 to the rusted red of 1966. Fruit, yes, but even more sweetness, more richness and more orange – most sweetness and richness. Once more a Tawny-like Vintage".

Vintage 1970: "Glossy and polished, but embracing, friendly fruit and considerable charm. Wonderful, delicious wine, somewhat fruity, but with a natural sweetness. Very amiable, a bit too amiable to be durable".

TAWNY

After the more common types, the next in line is the 5 to 6-years-old "Adriano", which is rather sweet, like a puppy licking your hand. But not at all embracing, on the contrary strict confidence in the best Tawnies where the *10-years Tawny* ("Quinta da Ervamoira") is "delicious, rich, with a character and clingy and semi-rich without being too sweet", and the *20-years Tawny* ("Quinta do Bom Retiro") is an "elegant, lighter style than the 10-years, softer, finer, more refined, but more or less a lightweight". The *30-years Tawny* is "more masculine than the 20-years Tawny with a great body, smoke, a very nice structure, and has a wonderful nutty taste". No doubt one of the best 30-years Tawnies around.

Ramos-Pinto does not produce over 40-years Tawnies, and they have not produced Colheitas since 1937, which on the other hand has a wonderful concentration of raisins. A bottle of 1890 with the inscription "WWW" - where one "W" means: very old (!) - contains even more raisins and is incredible, just like a desiccated Tokaij essence. But João Nicolau de Almeida will not make Colheitas, and neither would his father actually: "There are too many problems with Colheitas, and so many bad ones are being produced today, so we don't have to make yet another one. I am a mixer, and Colheita is not a mixed wine, so it is better to let things be the way they are"."The art of mixing wine is the most important issue", he continues. "An unmixed wine is just a natural product. My father used to say: Vintage is a wine, Tawny is a Port Wine. And I quite agree".

The secret behind the old Tawnies which is still the strength of Ramos-Pinto is, according to Almeida, that he keeps 1/3 of every type every year as a basis for the finished wine, i.e. a kind of Solera system. This way, the style and taste can be maintained, and this is better using your nose and tongue. And the style and taste must be maintained. Techniques, tradition, teamwork, and patience are the means. Every taster is a link in a chain, which is more important than the taster. Almeida's uncle taught him this, and it has become his own philosophy.

"W" means very old, "WW" means very, very old, and "WWW" means very, very, very old, and this is what this 100-years-old Tawny is. It is incredible, dark, with a concentration of raisins. (Photo: HO)

Real Companhia Velha
(Royal Oporto Wine Company)

Founded: 1756
Owner: da Silva Reis Family
Taster/Blender: António Santos
Quintas: António SantosQuinta: Quinta das Carvalhas, Quinta de São Gonçalo, Quinta do Carvalhal, Quinta dos Aciprestes, Quinta do Casal da Granja, Quinta do Sibio, Quinta do Sidrô

Real Companhia Velha is not very popular with most of the other Port producers. Born with the state as its mother and monopoly as its father, always scolded and often disliked, not without a reason and often they were to blame.

Actually one should distinguish the Real Companhia before and after the time of state monopoly, but things are never that simple. Since Manuel da Silva Reis bought the ailing Companhia in 1960 he has run it as if it were still a state monopoly and has in the forever smouldering, at times flaring, conflict with the rest of the Port Wine industry grown stronger standing alone - and he has also had a powerful supporter in Casa do Douro.

The battle among the enemies culminated in 1990 when Casa do Douro made its not very intelligent purchase of 40% of the shares in Real Companhia Velha (see page 84ff). The Shippers' Association, including all Port Wine exporters, except Real Companhia Velha, feared the dumping of prices and dishonest competition, and even after the deal had been annulled a few years late, the rest of the business was still busy expressing its contempt for Casa do Douro and its disrespect for Silva Reis. But even though they were criticising Casa do Douro for their clumsiness, Silva Reis could hardly be criticised for much more than having been a bit too smart. Casa do Douro ended by being disappointed, but the matter further isolated Real Companhia.

The old royal company that Manuel da Silva Reis took over in 1960 had been established by King José I upon his famous royal decree of 10 September 1756 with the blessing from Marques de Pombal and personified by a combination of the most important wine growers in the Douro and the most important people in Porto. Companhia Geral da Agricultura das Vinhas do Alto Douro, as it was called, was to settle the dispute between the small wine growers and small farmers on the one hand and the shippers, especially the British shippers, on the other hand via its control and indication of prices.

To maintain a balance, the Company often had two support both parties at the same time, for example during the French occupation of Porto in 1809 when it sold Port Wine to both the French troops and to Wellington's army. This may be smart on a short-term basis, but was strenuous on a long-term basis, and this describes very well the Company's future strategy. It also abused its monopoly by selling wine to Porto's small bars and taverns in the 19th Century, and in the period 1834-1838 its was actually dissolved. When it was reconstructed, it had lost its former power.

Due to the Company's own incompetence and changing times, King Ferdinand finally took away the Company's privileges in December 1865 and declared the free trade of Port Wine. Real Companhia Velha thus began the life of a normal Port Wine producer who had to comply with rules and regulations, which some of the later owners of the Company have had difficulty in accepting. Its days of glory in modern times started in 1960 when Manuel da Silva Reis took over the company. His father had worked in a Port Wine cellar in Gaia, and the family was far from well off.

When Manuel was 13 in the mid 1930'ies he got a job in the Port Wine industry at a daily wage of 1 Escudo, but he was hard-working and stubbornly and diligently worked his way up, sometimes with a bit too smart ideas which brought him into difficulties with the other Port Wine producers already in the late 1940'ies. But due to his ambitions he managed the situation, and in 1956 he was appointed general manager of the Souza Guedes Port Company, which he took over later on. In 1960, he bought the ailing Real Companhia Velha, and in 1963 he bought the table wine company Real Vinícola.

Sky was the limit for da Silva Reis. In the course of the 1960'ies and in the beginning of the 1970'ies he bought a total of 13 different wine companies, but the Carnation Coup of 1974 signified that he had to go into exile - as one of the very few in the Port Wine business. He had to stay in Brazil for four years before he could return to his empty director's chair.

In his dynamic, uncompromising style he has always been a loner but also a pioneer. As the first Port Wine producer he introduced stainless steel tanks for vinification in 1959. He stood alone but was strong, always criticised and scolded, but also respected for his efficiency. However, it was not before his son, Pedro, entered the company in the beginning of the 1980'ies that the old state monopoly finally found a modern and more sympathetic profile.

Real Companhia Velha distinguished itself in Manuel da Silva Reis' times of glory as being the largest Port Wine producer and the largest landowner. The domicile in the Douro Valley is the first thing you lay your eyes on: the round Casa Redonda lies high above the large Quinta das

Quinta das Carvalhas by Pinhão is the Real Companhia's most important quinta and a small town in the big town. (Photo: HO)

Carvalhos overlooking Pinhão and the Douro Valley. The quinta is mentioned for the first time in 1759, but did not begin to produce Port Wine before Miguel de Sousa Guedes bought it in 1880. When Manuel da Silva Reis bought Sousa Guedes in 1975, the quinta was included in the bargain. The entire estate is of around 600 ha, and around 500 pipes of Port Wine are produced here annually.

Real Companhia also owns Quinta dos Aciprestes which was created by joining several small properties in the 1860'ies. It lies along the southern bank of the Douro river by Tua and is 2 kms long. In recent years nearly all the vines have been removed and all new plantings are ao alto. The family also owns Quinta do Casal da Granja by Granja de Alijó, 520-640 metres above the ocean, and Quinta do Sidro, which was purchased in 1972 and is being renovated. The two latter quintas only yield grapes for white Port Wine and table wine, including Marques de Soveral and Evel - once so popular in Denmark. Real Companhia has always been a two-headed dragon.

Feared, scolded, disliked. Now Pedro da Silva Reis has been given the difficult task of giving the dragon a humane touch.

RUBY ♥♥˅˅

If I am to summarise my experiences of the Real Companhia's Ruby types throughout the last 20 years, I can only use the word "unreliable". Many of them, actually most of them, have been modest and quick, such as *Royal Oporto Vintage 1982*, which is a "light, nice, simple and slim in style. Drinkable immediately, not for keeping".

The same wine in the *Vintage 1963* was superb and a great sensation, while other Vintages have been labile. *Vintage 1985* is also remarkably well developed for its vintage, full of sweetness and light in taste with no muscle and tasting more of oak than of fruit. *Vintage 1987* is also remarkably were developed, light and simple with no keeping qualities whatsoever. *Vintage 1994* is fairly well developed, but has a nicer structure than 1987 and 1985. The consistency of fruit is more solid, characterized by elderberry and a mild taste, but this wine has no keeping qualities either. *Vintage 1995* has a stronger taste of elderberries and was already drinkable after 3-4 years.

Real Companhia also makes a modest Ruby under the name "Quinta dos Aciprestes" and also produces a modest Tawny under the quinta name: "Quinta das Carvalhas" and a white Port under the name "Quinta do Casal da Granja".

TAWNY ♥♥♥˅˅

Tawnies are a much better product for Real Companhia. A classic Portuguese style, smoky and rich on the expense of the fruit content. The *10-years Tawny* is somewhat aggressive, characterized by youth and aguardente, but in the *20-years Tawny* you can sense a calmer style, richer and sweeter and with less alcohol. This is a light wine just as the over *40-years Tawny* which is nice and clarified.

Real Companhia also makes Colheitas which in my opinion are light in style, smoky and soft, friendly and quite drinkable, as are the old Tawnies.

Robertson
(Robertson Brothers & Co.)

Founded: 1847
Owner: Seagram's
Taster/Blender: Carlos Silva
Quintas: None

Say Robertson and you might as well have said "Pyramid Port", for this uncomplicated, light 10-years Tawny is the company's profile. We are now in the light, popular end of the Port scale. The name derives from James Nisbet Robertson who bought his way into the Port shippers, Burdon & Gray, as a partner in 1847, and after eight years took over the whole business. In 1953, *Robertson Bros.* was bought by Sandeman, and today it is a very discrete member of the Seagram group.

Robertsen is used as an alternative on various export markets, but Sandeman does not do much to profile the name nor the wines from this house, nor the name of Rebello Valente that Robertson Bros. purchased in 1881 and which is used for the best wines, including Vintage Port.

Romaríz
(A. Romaríz E Filhos)

Founded: 1850
Owner: Limited Company by British shareholders
Taster/Blender: Rui Lameiras
Quintas: Quinta de Romarigo

The old Brazilian colony was such an attractive market for exporting Port that Manoel da Rocha Romaríz founded a family company in 1850 with Brazil as their main target and England as an extra asset. Today, the tables are turned. After the British investors, of which some of them are the principal shareholders of Taylor, Fladgate & Yeatman, took over the shares in the company in 1987 and employed the dynamic Albino Jorge da Silva e Sousa as general manager, England has become the most important export market, and now Brazil is merely an insignificant clause.

Until 1966, the company was owned by the Romaríz family, but there were no heirs, and via Guimaraens & Co. Romaríz was taken over by Taylor, Fladgate & Yeatman.

Romaríz disposes of one farm, which - with a certain embarrassment - is called a quinta. The Quinta de Romarigo by Régua comprises 24ha's planted with vines and in the old lagares 150 pipes of Port are produced each year, which in the best vintage years become Vintage Port with Romaríz' name on the label. The vines are old, and no fertilization is applied. Close to S. João de Pesqueira, Romaríz owns an even larger and very modern plant with new and renewed barrels with enough space for 4 mio litres of wine giving enough capacity to nurture the purchased grapes which by tradition are paid for according to sugar content and classification. Albino Jorge and Rui Lameiras draw on Romaríz' excellent "consultants", especially on Bruce and David Guimaraens, and with their assistance Romaríz manages to produce better and better wines here every year. The wine goes through 2-3 days of fermentation for a full extraction. Then alcohol is added. This is done automatically from a steel tank, and when the alcohol and the part of the wine that runs down itself has mixed and become dessert wine, the rest of the grapes is pressed to give more colour and tannin.

The unity of wine and alcohol must take place as quickly as possible, and the entire process only takes 30-90 minutes, depending on the quantity of grapes. An Australian rotation tank is applied instead of pumping. This gives a better flavour, Jorge and Lameiras say, and they do not used steel but only wooden casks for the following maturation. Albino Jorge's convincing philosophy is: "If quality is more important than money, you use wooden casks". And luckily there is enough money to maintain that kind of philosophy - and quality.

Albino Jorge and Rui Lameiras take a break at one of the old casks at Quinta da Nogueira. (Photo: HO)

After the gentle treatment, Romaríz' wines are bottled - as are the bottles from Taylor, Fonseca and Rozès - in Fonseca's cellars where their bottles are carefully cleaned with water and brandy (!) So it does not seem so strange that the best wines from Romaríz have established themselves more and more clearly in recent years due to both quality and special characteristics which not alone apply to the small fat bottles but to a consistent effort on "personality!. With the purchase of Borges' stock, Romaríz seems to be even better equipped to challenge the rest of the Port industry. Possibilities are enormous and are only exceeded by ambitions.

RUBY

Romaríz has not got a wide range of wines, but it has made up its stock in an optimum way. The foundation is the "Superior Ruby", then LBV and finally Vintage Port in a selective range:

Vintage 1985: "Dense nose with lots of fruit and a bit metallic. Powerful taste of berries and liquorice. More muscular than charming which indicates durability. Seems closed and hesitant, but promising".

Vintage 1994: "Black currant nose. And black currant taste. Soft and a rather friendly type, but muscle and fruit behind the friendliness. Juicy and slight peppery. Well-made with a self-confident structure. Power and baccate fruit".

TAWNY

"Superior Tawny" is a very straightforward Tawny, solid and honest. "Reserva Latina" is an old, undefined Tawny with a nice smoky sweetness. It resembles the series of old Tawnies that Romaríz has purchased and mixed. Following wines were tasted from first bottlings in the course of 98-99:

10-years Tawny: "Soft and mild, a bit sugary, not aggressive, friendly, a bit tame". (88/100)

20-years Tawny: "Concentrated, nice and pure. Very good behaviour, not aggressive at all, actually not sweet at all either, but overall nice and easily drinkable". (91/100)

30-years Tawny: "Intense brown sugar. Sweetness, softness, mildness. Slides down your throat without any resistance and with no challenge. But a well-made 30-years wine". (91/100)

Over 40-years Tawny: "Soft and friendly, sober and mild, nuts and chocolate fudge. Rich and amiable, slightly smoky and very drinkable". (90/100)

Colheita 1963: "Soft and friendly, clingy and sugary, with a very nice finish and an explosive aftertaste. Very nice and very friendly disposition, delicious". (90/100)

Colheita 1944: "Dark brown. Velvety, virile and delicious with a very nice sweetness, smoky and nutty taste. Well-balanced with a nice explosion in the mouth. Very decent, and still vivid, old Colheita with both juice and power. Delicious".

(97/100)

I had the good fortune of tasting a gem with Albino Jorge: a Reserva 1897, which had been lying deep down in a humid and cool cellar for many years before it was found by chance. But the Port Institute will not allow it to indicate its age, so it was poured as a clandestine thimbleful of wine: "Black as Fernet Branca. Dark, intense nose with treacle and brown sugar. Very, very elegant, concentrated and challenging thick as boiled-down stock. Delicious, beautiful and timeless", and if points were given, it would be 100/100!

Rozès

Founded: 1855
Owner: Vranken-Lafitte Champagne
Taster/Blender: Manuel Louzada
Quintas: None, but the Quinta de Monsul provides grapes and the name to a table wine and to some secondary Port on certain markets

For many years, Rozès was associated with cheap Port providing the French market. And why the French market? Well, it not so strange, for Ostende Rozès founded the company in Bordeaux in 1855, the same year that the historical red wines received their famous classification.

Sales went so well that Rozès shortly after could open a company in Gaia, and Ostende Rozès' son, Edmond, was handed over the responsibility of following the production of Port in Porto. He introduced the small, fat bottle which since then has been a special trait of Rozès. The export markets also grew in his time - even though not nearly as much as what Rozès' general manager, Rogério Leandro da Silva, achieved in his 17 years in the company, from 1981 to 1998, when he managed to expand the export markets from 4 to 40 countries. A turning point in Rozès' history came in 1977 when the company was taken over by the fancy group of companies, Vuitton-Moët-Hennessy (LVMH). The new capital funds led to an improvement of the quality of Port and to the investment of a fruitful co-operation with Taylor, Fladgate & Yeatman. They have serviced the company for several years as consultants and bottling Rozès' wines. Rozès own approx 5 ha's of vineyards in the Douro Valley, but they do not own any quintas and have to manage with grapes and wine from six permanent producers in Douro. After da Silva left Rozès in 1998 and took over Cálem, this Port house seemed to be in a waiting position for a new buyer - and this new buyer apeared in the summer of 1999: Vranken-Lafitte Champagne.

RUBY ♥♥♥ ～ ～

Rozès is one of the Port producers whose quality has mostly improved in the last 8-10 years. The breakthrough with the Ruby types came with Vintage 1985 and 1991 which have been followed by several very nice Vintages and potent, pulpy LBVs. The following was tasted in the course of 1998-1999, partly on the premises of Rozès and partly in Denmark:

Vintage 1985: "Powerful raw fruit. Soft, slightly peppery juice and a very nice length. Rich without being fatty, sweet without being too sweet".

Vintage 1987: "Intense elderberry nose. Rich taste, soft and a touch of berry and with a late, straightforward tannin. Drinkable now, like black currant juice containing alcohol and tannin. Promising with a nice structure".

Vintage 1991: "Elderberry and black currant. Incredible soft taste that is rich and well-built. Lots of berries, mildness, softness – and tannin. Self-confident structure. Will be exciting to follow".

Vintage 1994: "Dense, dry fruit. More dryness than in the 1991 and 1987, less unsophisticated charm, but more potent. Lots of fruit and straightforward tannin. Seems more closed and stand-offish than the berry bombs from 1987 and 1991, more severe and tense. Give it time".

Vintage 1995: "Soft and mild with a dense berry taste. Very nice, smooth and agreeable, drinkable now. Does not have the same berry development of 1987 and 1991 but has a nice structure and convincing fruit content".

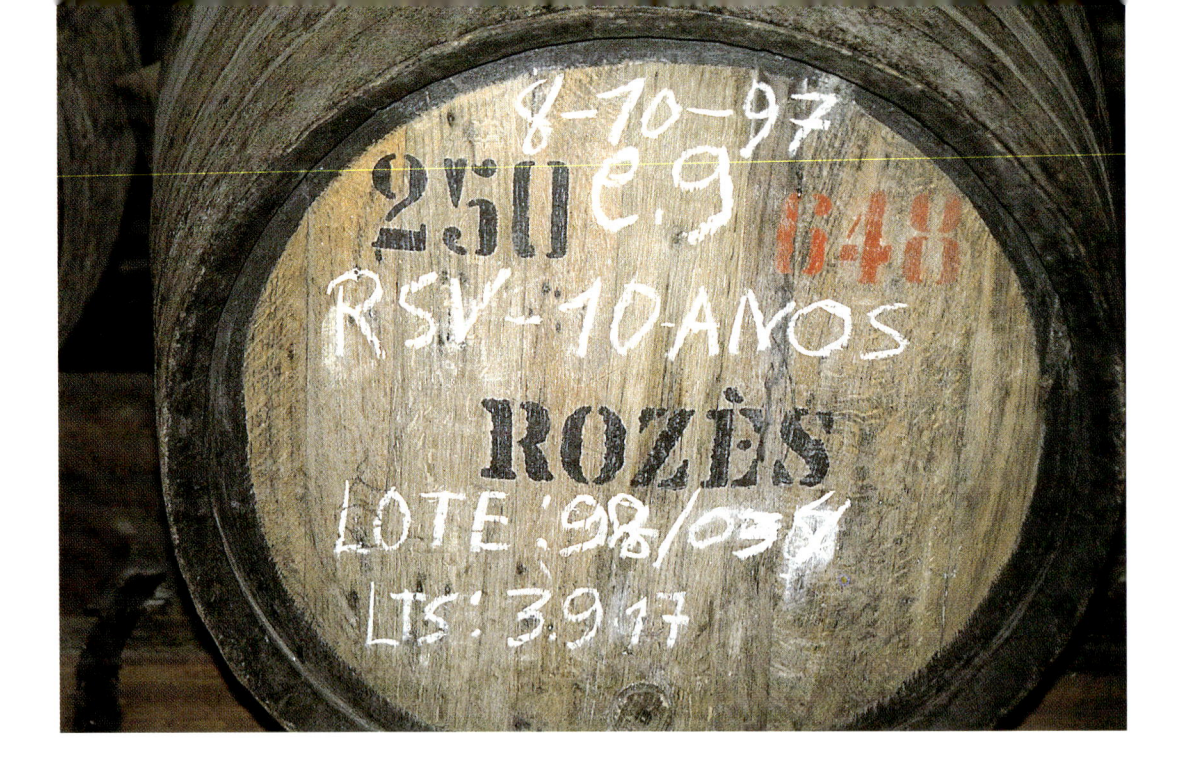

Rozès became renowned with their 10-years Tawny called "Infanta Isabel". Since then other fine wines have followed. (Photo: HO)

Also Rozès' LBVs have become more straightforward and more fruity. The successful LBV 1994 is produced as an unfiltered and muddy LBV with the title: "Reserve Edition". Rozès' more inferior Ruby types are solid, fruity wines.

TAWNY

As it is easier to purchase old wine in casks than in bottles, Rozès did not distinguish themselves with a confident series of old Tawnies until the 1980'ies. This category has also undergone a change of style and improvement of quality in the 1990'ies to a more self-confident fruit content and a surprisingly great Over 40-years Tawny, which was not launched until 1997. The following was tasted in 1999:

10-years Tawny ("Infanta Isabel"): "A strong touch of fruit, very robust and hardy with more fruit than richness, more berry than smoke. A solid 10-years Tawny, not too sweet and no other flaws".

20-years Tawny: "Same intense nose, same robust fruit. Refined and solid 20-years Tawny without being clingy, but self-confident style, fruity and muscular".

Over 40-years Tawny: "Beautiful brown mahogany. Almost youthful in the nose and the first Tawny to have a sweetness of sweets in the taste. Soft, fine and slightly smoky, clingy, like a Colheita in its structure, no signs of age. Wonderful, long taste, like butterflies in the stomach, slightly smoky and delicious".

This Over 40-years Tawny used to be manager Rogério Leandro da Silva's product. He bought the pipes he needed from the small farmers in the Douro Valley which had been set aside for children and grandchildren, but either there were no grandchildren, or the grandchildren would rather see the money than have an old Tawny in the cellar.

When da Silva presented the first bottle in 1997, he said that it was made from approx. 50% 1951s, approx. 45% 1955s and approx. 5% 1935s.

He also had a dream of making a 30-years Tawny and tried to make Colheitas, but since the new owners took over Rozès in the autumn of 1999, future will show what they offer us.

Sandeman

Founded: 1790
Owner: Seagram's
Taster/Blender: Carlos Silva
Quintas: Quinta do Vau

What a terrible story, H.C. Andersen would have said, for the Sandeman family might not live up to their name at all when they persistently claim that they come from Scotland. You see in Danish, Sandeman actually means a man who tells the truth. Former chief librarian at the University of Copenhagen, Dr. Sofus Larsen, says: "Sandeman is mentioned in the Law of Denmark of 1241, Valdemar Sejrs Jyske Lov (Vol. II) as a court of 8-10 truthful lay assessors who are appointed by the King to hold a court under oath and judge criminal cases. On the thingsted of the town of Viborg, the Sandeman sat high above on a seat placed on four girders resting upon large stones, and in the 14th and 15th centuries it became common to add a man's position to his family name, so we can easily imagine that the Sandeman family originally came from the peninsula of Jutland and then were sent to either the Orkney or Shetland islands which were Danish at the time. They had been given as dowry at princess Margaret's wedding to the King James III of Scotland."

The possible kinship with the Danes is something we can only be proud of, for if continuity and stability in the Port business was to be pronounced in one word, it would be Sandeman. Ever since the first Sandeman emerged in the Port business in 1790, a Sandeman has always occupied the managing director's chair - today well occupied by George Thomas David, a 9th generation Sandeman with his replacement already waiting round the corner: young Christopher who was born in 1978.

So, directly or indirectly there is Scottish blood in the Sandeman's veins, but there is a great difference between the well-bred David and George of our day and David's great-great-great-grandfather George who according to his own great grandson Walter Albert was short in height but large in ego and who founded the company at the age of 25 in 1790 explaining in a letter to his sister back in Perth, Australia:

"I shall remain where I am, till I shall have made a moderate fortune to retire with, which I expect will be in the course of nine years; which to be sure is a long time, but some lucky stroke may possibly reduce it to five or six."

He did not lack self-confidence when he rented his first wine cellar in London and started out on the Sandeman Port adventure. He also had many other good qualities, at least according to his own beliefs. In the same letter he says to his sister: "People stand out of my way as they see me bustling along the streets. I have a good word to say to everybody I meet, and, as I am informed, I frequently laugh in my sleep."

George also tells his sister that he has only recently decided to become a wealthy man. A bold decision, yes, but he had seen his father make his fortune as a cabinetmaker, and according to the Sandeman family history, George built his empire on equal parts of ambition, his father's money and the moral support of his brother. There are some wonderful letters in the family archives, in which he tries to convince his father that he will only accept his father's money to avoid his brother taking any risks. A noble thing to do, which resulted in 300 pounds from his father, and this was his initial capital. He himself did not seem to have a penny to his name.

He bought the aforementioned wine cellar for the 300 pounds and started to work as a wine merchant, wine dealer, wine importer - one has many names for the things one loved to do - but without offices, for according to tradition most deals were concluded with a handshake in one of the coffee houses in London - in Sandeman's case it was Tom's Coffee House in Birchin Lane, Cornhill.

Why he chose to deal in wine, nobody knows. Nor do we know why it was Spanish and Portuguese wine. It could have been a coincidence which led to the family's long and good fate. But already in 1792, the firm's second year in business, accounts show that he sold 127 1/2 casks of Sherry to England plus 25 1/2 casks to Scotland.

The Sherry was soon supplemented by Port. According to Sandeman's archives, George Sandeman must have ordered a few casks of the 1790 Vintage, which he then bottled himself at a very early stage in 1792 and labelled with his own name. The cylinder-shaped bottle had already seen the clear light of day making it possible for a wine dealer like George to buy the Port in casks, bottle it and then sell it by the bottle. If the first true Vintage Port really is a 1775 vintage then he was a very early starter.

These were the golden years of Port, both for the shippers in Porto and for the wine dealers in London. In 1792, around 50,000 pipes of Port were shipped to England, and the fact that the British Prime Minister, William Pitt Jr., was said to consume 6 half litres of Port a day boosted sales. This was not all pleasure. Port had been prescribed to him when he as a weak child was told to drink Port instead of taking medicine. Those were the days of real doctors ...

However, the revolutionaries in Paris did not waste their time drinking Port, and Napoleon was too busy making war instead of making love, so when George Sandeman celebrated his company's 25th anniversary during the Congress in Vienna in 1815, it had taken him much longer than he had

George Thomas David Sandeman, 9th generation in this historic firm looks as if he is having a good time keeping his balance on the water's edge. To the left Sandeman's export manager, Manuel Maria de Magalhães Ferreira. (Photo: HO)

predicted to make his fortune. This fact is confirmed in letters which he sent to his father. He had been about to give up many times, because selling wine was not an easy task. But he kept at it in spite of low sales figures, and in the spring of 1794 he had made enough money so that he could purchase a small property in London for his business.

The Napoleon wars resulted in increased sales of Portuguese wine to England, however, but also in a much higher risk and thus higher prices. The shipments of Port out of Porto reached a sky-high record in 1798 with 64,402 pipes even though the whole of Europe was at war, for the Port was there to be shipped, and luckily the seas were controlled by British ships. Things were picking up fast now, and George Sandeman had to find a contact in Porto and chose a shipper by the name of Campion Offley Hesketh & Co., whom Warre & Co. eventually joined. At the same time, Sandeman also got a contact for his Sherry, but it was difficult to deal with Spain who first sided against France, then with France, and then against France again.

In the turbulent years, George Sandeman had formed a partnership with Samuel Sketchley Robinson, and when he passed away, James Gooden entered the scene in 1809. When George was in need of risk-bearing capital again, his cousin, John Carey Forster, became co-owner in 1812. At the same time, the business was extended to include table wine, and since then everything, including woollen clothes, silver bars, and in the course of a few years, the company was so well-consolidated that a bank failure did not influence George Sandeman who merely moved his money to the more secure Bank of England. All merchandise, especially imported goods, rose by around 100% between the time of the Napoleon wars and the Congress of Vienna in 1815, but this only seemed to have a positive influence on Sandeman's, and an overview from Real Companhia Velha of the shipment of Port for the year 1813 shows that Sandeman's had its own lodges in Gaia, for according to Sandeman's own archives, they were purchased in 1813.

With all due regard to the partners, the company was named *Geo. Sandeman, Gooden & Forster* until James Gooden's death in 1828. The company was then called Sandeman, Forster & Co. until John Forster's retirement in 1856. At that point, George Sandeman had also retired, first to Brussells where he lived until his death retiring to the happy Port grounds on 2nd February 1841 at the age of 76 with a career which turned out differently than he had ever imagined as a young man when he wrote to his sister, but it was no less successful at that. And he did become a wealthy man, even though it did take slightly more than his planned 5-7 years.

Apparently, he was obstinate till the end. He did not make his son, George, his companion and his successor, even though George worked for the company. Instead he chose his sister's son, George Glas Sandeman. Shortly before his death, Sandeman's founder could rejoice in the fact that his London-based company had grown to become the largest shipper of Port with 4,580 pipes in 1835.

George Glas Sandeman was the sole proprietor in the difficult oidium years in the mid 1850'ies when production fell to one tenth of normal production, but he died exactly at the time when phylloxera came to the Douro in 1868, so his eldest son, Albert George, took over the company assisted by his younger brothers, John Glas and George Glas, and the company name changed again, this time to *Geo. G. Sandeman Sons & Co.*

The years following the phylloxera were difficult, but fortunately, the family had no property and no fields in the Douro Valley. Instead they had invested in the pompous lodges which still dominate Avenida Diogo Leite in Gaia, and in 1870 shipments had risen to 3,781 pipes of Port which signified that Sandeman's were still by far the largest shipper of Port - and one of the most creative with regard to direct advertising and smart marketing methods, long before these concepts were to become common in America and Europe. When Sandeman's celebrated their Centennial in 1890, they also celebrated their great success in shipping Port from Sandeman's in Porto to Sandeman's in London, bottling the Port in London and re-exporting it to France with the Sandeman name on the label.

In 1902, the family firm turned into a limited company with Albert George Sandeman as President until he turned 90 years. His life is a story of its own. He began his career by leading the company well through the phylloxera crisis and ended it by leading it well through the First World War. In 1923, his son Walter Albert was to become the fourth Sandeman in the red chair, and his son, Henry Gerard Walter Sandeman who replaced his father in 1937 and ran the Sandeman company through the Second World War and through the hard times in the late 1940'ies. Upon his death, his younger brother, Patrick Walter Sandeman, took over the leadership of the company (1952), and with his sons, Timothy (7th managing director, 1959-82) and David Patrick (8th managing director, 1982-90) we reach the present day and the aforementioned 9th head of family, George Thomas David, who was born in 1953.

In 1952, Sandeman's had bought the small Port house, Robertson Bros., and were now getting prepared for the industrial development which first led to the mechanical bottling plant in 1959 so that the vintage year 1955 would be the last hand-bottled Vintage Port.

In 1962, Sandeman's bought the Port house, Offley Forrester, which was sold off again in 1973, but Sandeman apparently had enough property in London and Porto, so he did not purchase his first quinta until 1988: Quinta do Vau by São João da Pesqueira. At that point Sandeman had been launching TV spots in colour and exporting Sherry to the Soviet Union for more than 20 years. The giant leap into the future, however, was made on 28th November 1979 when the spirits giant, Seagram's, took over the Sandeman shares and Tim Sandeman's title changed from being managing director and president of Sandeman's to Chairman of the Board. The new ownership meant fresh capital and fresh ideas, even as far away as in Bordeaux where Sandeman's old business connection, Barton & Guestier, who was also owned by Seagram's, introduced a "Sandeman Claret" in 1981.

The following year, heavy investments were made in equipment in Gaia. Among other things, a completely new and very advanced bottling plant was erected, which can fill 12 mio litres of Port a year. Quite a large number, you might say, but not large enough, for only a few years later Sandeman's were selling more than 15 mio bottles of Port a year - so modern technique simply could not cope!

Vau is one of the least romantic quintas I have ever come upon. There are no lagares and casks here, just stainless steel, pumps and tankers. Alcohol is added the wine, and the dessert wine is immediately pumped into the awaiting tankers which drive direct to the vinification centre in Celeirós - one of the two large centres which the Sandeman's own in the Douro Valley. In Celeirós, immense wooden casks are ready to store the Port until it is driven off once more, this time to Gaia.

It is true, however, that one should not only measure success according to the number of pipes. For many years, quantity was Sandeman's philosophy, and the black Don was the company's brand logo. George Sandeman admitted this upon his return from the U.S.A. in 1990, his head full of new ideas for a Port house "with a reputation for Tawny, with good to excellent Vintage Ports, and with a whole lot of wine of a more dubious

Sandeman's Quinta do Vau lies remotely on the left bank of the Douro river a bit east of Pinhão. (Photo: HO)

And as the train only runs on the opposite bank, there is only one way to go to Vau: by boat. (Photo: HO)

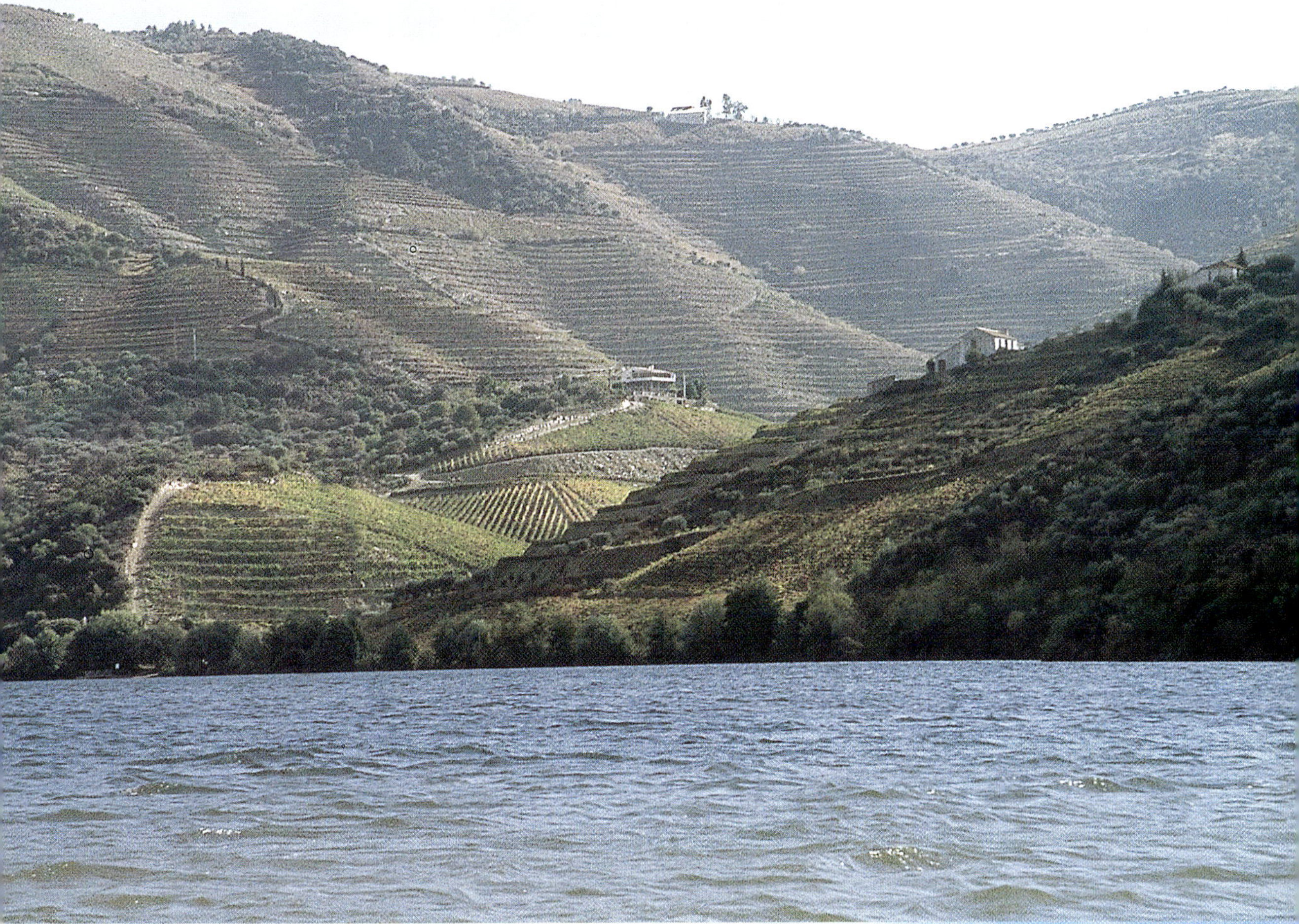

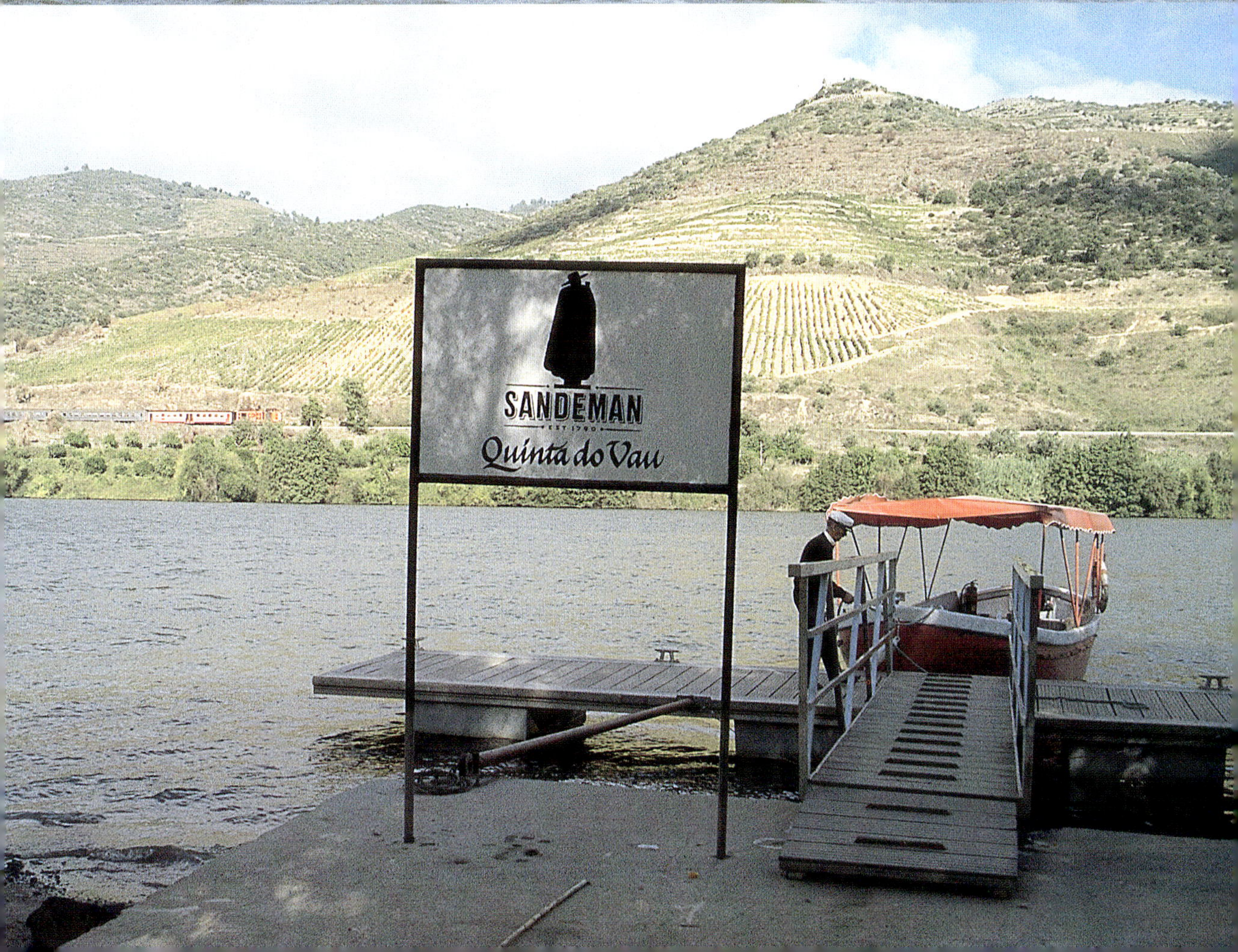
SANDEMAN
EST 1790
Quinta do Vau

George Sandeman, founder of the family house, drawn by his son, Edwin.

David Patrick Sandeman, 8th head of the family, retired in 1990.

quality, which was only produced to maintain the position as the largest producer on the home market". These are his own words!

In the beginning of the 1990'ies under the auspices of George, the strategy was changed from quantity to quality. This was soon reflected in the change of grape suppliers. Previously, Sandeman had depended on more than 1,200 small and middle-sized farmers, all of which did not produce the best quality of grapes! Now, the 1,200 operators were rapidly reduced to approx. 600, and all grape suppliers from the categories E and F were discarded, and only grapes from A, B - with C as backup - were accepted.

Finally, the recipe of the Vintage Port was improved so that only grapes from the Quinta do Vau would be used in the future, supplemented with good grapes from handpicked farmers. New plantings were immediately laid out in block parcels at Vau, and the new ownership of the quinta was rewarded by being able to produce the first Single Quinta Vintage Port in 1998. Better quality and better customers are the future visions for George Sandeman. The better customers for the better quality are found by for example spreading the knowledge of Port, especially to the great lodges in Gaia where Sandeman's is visited each year by around 100,000 guests, where there is a small museum and tasting premises, and where you can frequent the Port business' only "Port School" - even choosing your own grade!

Those days are over when it was enough for the Sandemans just to be the biggest in the business ...

RUBY

Is there a Sandeman style? "Yes", George Sandeman says: "It is dryer than most other styles. We do our utmost to maintain the right balance between tannin and fruit". The practical sales philosophy is: few but easily identifiable brands, has nurtured the Ruby type "Founder's Reserve" which was launched in 1982 and has a dark-coloured label – contrary to "Imperial Tawny" that has a light-coloured label. This way, it is easy for the consumers to see what is what, and they also know that "Founder's Reserve" is a young, fruity, aggressive Ruby, the foundation of which has sometimes been declared a Vintage Port.

Sandeman's LBV 1994 is very decent wine with an impression of fruit and some friendliness. There is a bit more structure in the SQVP from Quinta do Vau that was marketed for the first time in 1988 and that has now been followed up with Quinta do Vau Vintage 1996: "Attractive with young fruit and red cheeks. Again, almost a lightweight, which is light without being thin".

Sandeman was an important supplier of wines at the tasting of "Vintages of the Century in 1999: 45 vintages! And funnily enough, the oldest was the best:

Vintage 1900: "Rather dark brown. Aggressive, fruity nose. Soft and delicious with polished fruit and a noble taste of an old, well-made Vintage. Stays for a long time in the mouth in the most delicious way – but then suddenly disappears, just as when you let the water out of your tub. But a delicious, Ruby-like Vintage, which is still vigorous. A fantastic greeting from the year of 1900".
(98/100)

Vintage 1912: "Light brown. Characteristic Tawny nose. The taste is also more Tawny than Vintage: soft, sugary, like a 30-years or 40-years Tawny. Very manageable". (88/100)

Vintage 1917: "Delicious, really delicious, but seems more like an old Tawny than and old Ruby. Gentle and affectionate, short and amiable taste".
(86/100)

Vintage 1927: "Intense sweetness. Colheita taste with weak fruit, sugar candy and treacle. Very pleasant, but not as an old Vintage, much more as an old Colheita". (85/100)

Vintage 1931: "Medium brown. Extremely rich taste and creamy consistency. Syrup and dark honey. No fruit, but a large concentration of sweetness. Soft, rich, very nice and much more Tawny than Ruby". (86/100)

Vintage 1935: "Sweet nose with a touch of acetone. Very soft and intense taste, the first vintage since 1900 with fruit. Nice development in the glass. The fruit is enhanced, the richness is repressed. Well-structured Vintage, still vivid and will enough power to last for several years". (96/100)

Vintage 1945: "Intense, almost youthful nose. Concentrated, polished sweetness, but also characteristic, pleasant fruit. Even though the fruit is not massive, the wine almost seems to be hesitant. But it lacks the virile fruit of the 1935". (90/100)

Vintage 1946: "Tawny nose. Soft, soft and sweet, sweet, sweet taste. Subdued fruit, pure and nice taste. Small, friendly and easily drinkable wine. Soft, sweet and more than mature". (84/100)

Vintage 1947: "Medicine-like nose. Sugary taste with a hint of nice fruit somewhere but also a nice length and a nice, explosive ending. Great development in the glass: the fruit is enhanced – without, however, overpowering the sweetness. Nice, with many Tawny features". (91/100)

Vintage 1948: "Same medicine-like nose. Sweetness, no real fruit. Unfinished as a wine, but finished as a Vintage. Resembles a good, old, jolly Tawny. Light and drinkable now". (84/100)

Vintage 1955: "Finally – again an intense nose with everything else but sweetness. The taste is, however, so sweet, a delicious, sugar-free sweetness, but also has a very nice potent fruit content. Perfect now, in total harmony. Drinkable without being over-mature". (96/100)

Vintage 1963: "The nose is more intense than pure. Remarkable and remarkably sweet, a sweetness lying as a coating around the self-conscious fruit. A very nice wine, but the fruit is disappointingly tame of a 1963. I would not keep it for long". (90/100)

Vintage 1970: "Nice fruity nose, nice fruity taste. Well-made and well-structured, but a subdued style lacking ambition. Dominating sweetness, the fruit is the fellow passenger. Nice and decent now – I would not keep it for long". (89/100)

To this abundant selection I have the following tasting comments. All wines were tasted at Sandeman's in the course of 1997-1999:

Vintage 1985: "Ether nose. Fruity, light taste. Thin skeleton with soft, light fruit. The fruit is disappointing compared to the other 1985s". (88/100)

Vintage 1994: "Intense nose. Great fruit, power, nice sweetness that does not overdo it. Personal and very promising. Potent and fruity. Towards the light and fruity, but very nice". (92-94/100)

I was confirmed in my impression of a rather light style with a subdued fruit content, but according to George Sandeman, a deliberate change towards a more fruity structure has taken place. It will be exciting to see – or taste – the results. I, for one, bet my money on Sandeman's new style.

TAWNY

A very limited selection – very conscious one. "Imperial Aged Reserve Tawny" is a mixture of 7 to 8-years-old wine and is a reliable, nut-brown and delicious young Tawny. Sandeman's is different from the other producers in that they do not make a 10-years Tawny, but a 20-years Tawny instead, which is "deliciously clingy with a soft, nutty taste, semi-rich and overall wonderful".

Silva & Cosens

see Dow's

Skeffington

This brand was introduced on the market in the 1980'ies to satiate the British market especially. Belongs to Romaríz and is produced by Romaríz.

Smith Woodhouse

Founded: 1784
Owner: Symington Family
Taster/Blender: Peter Ronald Symington
Quintas: Quinta da Madalena

Smith is the name of many British families, but the Christopher Smith who opened offices in Porto in 1784 to ship Port to England was no common Smith. He was a member of Parliament and later became Lord Mayor of London. At that point, his two sons has already joined the company along with the brothers, William and James Woodhouse, who were already well-established as importers of fine wines. The company naturally changed its name to *Smith Woodhouse Bros. & Co.* in 1928, and ever since then, Smith Woodhouse has been known for its "Fine Wines", especially its Vintage Ports, and that image was solidly manifested after the Symingtons took over this house in 1970 by the purchase of Graham's who had bought Smith-Woodhouse in 1960.

In 1976 the company purchased Quinta da Madalena in the Rio Torto Valley. Today the wines under the Smith Woodhouse label are especially popular in U. S. A. and Canada.

RUBY

The Symington family likes, very understandingly, to quote professor George Saintsbury who wrote in his famous "Notes on a Cellarbook" (1920): "I don't think I ever drank – I certainly never had – a better '87 than some Smith Woodhouse".

This was in a 1887 Vintage, tasted in the beginning of this century, long before the family could add more brands to their noble list of Ports. But where it belongs today, I do not really know. The Symingtons' three heavyweight brands: Dow's, Graham's and Warre's are all built up around their own special features and have each their quinta. They are somewhat easier to look at and take apart than the three "minor" brands: Gould Campbell, Quarles Harris and Smith Woodhouse, of which only Smith Woodhouse disposes of grapes from their own quinta.

To be able to convince me that there really is a difference between styles and characters James Symington organised a comparative tasting for me one day in October 1998 to taste the different Vintage Ports from all six houses. And I must admit that especially my experience with the three minor houses was instructive - but naturally also the relationship between Smith Woodhouse and the three "biggies":

Vintage 1977: "Eucalyptus nose. Soft, characteristic elderberry taste. Seems rather youthful, nice, drinkable and very fruity". (88/100)

Vintage 1980: "Dominated by fruit, nice and with integrity. Rather light style, no explosions or surprises, but all in all very nice". (88/100)

Vintage 1983: "Nice fruit, dense structure, nice length, nice, nice, nice. Very nice medium style with a good balance". (90/100)

Vintage 1985: "Liquorice nose. And liquorice taste, also a taste of berries and eucalyptus. Nice and decent, rather light and probably not very durable". (89/100)

I use the word "nice" quite a lot, and it is hardly a coincidence. My overall impression is that Smith Woodhouse represents a nice, good behaviour, the reliable and expected and therefore sets itself as the practical medium.

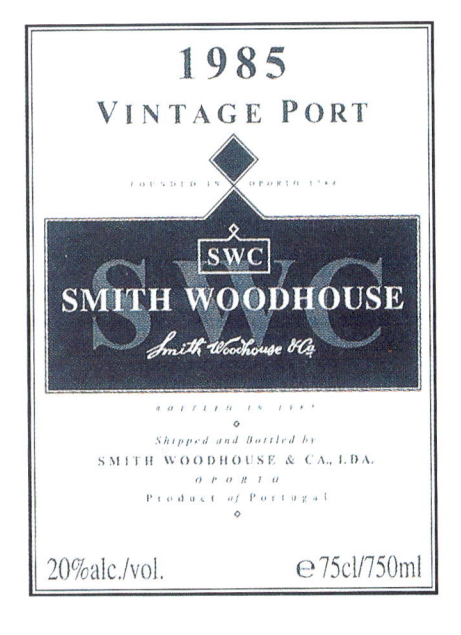

Smith Woodhouse's LBV, like Warre's, is unfiltered. "Lodge Reserve" is a tasty Ruby, which is supposed to resemble a Vintage (and is often compared to a Vintage Character), but it has matured in casks for 5-6 years before a light filtration and then bottling. LBV is called "Traditional" to underline the British style with an emphasis on fruit and deposit.

This is also why it is matured in bottles before it is sent in the market. The Vintage has a stable, fruity style, from the solid, robust 1977 to a more recent series of impressive, very fruity and durable vintages whose secret it is said to be the fine and very masculine grapes from Quinta de Vale Dona Maria. Combined with the recognisable niceness!

TAWNY

Nice, excellent, solid Tawnies with no real profile. The best Tawny is the 10-years Tawny, a polished, fruity and easily drinkable Tawny, not too rich.

Symington Family

When the Symingtons gather around the dinner table, they must all be in a nice dilemma as soon as they reach dessert, for what should they pour in their glasses! The family wine, of course, but should it be a Port from Dow's, Graham's, Warre's, Smith Woodhouse, Gould Campbell, Quarles Harris or from Quinta do Vesúvio - or perhaps even an old Madeira from Blandy's, Cossart Gordon or from Leacock's. No matter what: it is all in the family. You see, they own them all!

Andrew James Symington was not born with the golden touch. He left his Scottish homeland and reached the harbour of Porto in 1882 where he got a job in a textile company, owned by the Grahams. But it is no surprise that he acquired more taste for Port than he did for yarn, and little by little he passed over from textiles to Port. As his flair for Port, he must have also had a flair for business, for in 1894 the Portuguese government asked him to handle a shipment of Port consisting of 20,000 pipes to be sold to the British market. And he was only 31 years at the time! The pipes derived from a bankruptcy estate, who owed the State some money. AJS, as the family called him, sold the 20,000 pipes of Port, and he continued to prosper. In 1905, he took over Warre & Co., and in 1912 he became co-owner of the major company, Silva & Cosens (see page 187). His Port empire grew to such proportions that he had to involve his sons, Maurice, John and Ronald in daily management.

The family managed to survive the two World Wars, the depression of 1929, as well as the difficult export problems in the years following the Second World War, and soon the third generation was ready to take over; first Michael in 1947, then Ian, and a few years later, James, Peter and Amyas.

Michael has told that from the very first day he was "apprenticed" to his uncles Ron and John in the tasting room. They were twins but had separate sorts of taste so that one of them could find a "wonderful flavour of melons" in a wine, but the other one a "horrible flavour of melons" in the same wine. It was a bit confusing, but young Michael learnt from it, and especially he learnt to create his own opinion.

Among the first assignments for the 22-years old Michael was to participate in the family council to decide how to handle the Port of vintage 1945. Today we know that the vintage was both historical and outstanding, but in 1947 the export prospects were rather gloomy. The British market was still closed and times had changed. Even the fashionable families had cut the wellinformed butler and nobody could afford to store Vintage Port for their children. The casting vote told them to make

120 pipes of 1945 as Vintage Port. They never regretted that decision. But it was hard days. Ian Symington joined the daily business in 1949 and experienced the difficult 50'ies when the family seriously considered to give up Port, sell everything and return back to England. But then happy days were there again, once more people got interested in Port, and when James Symington joined the company in 1960 things had changed.

Exactly 1960 became a most memorable year. When the Vintage Port of that year was declared two years later, the family shipped more than had been shipped any year since 1896 and three years later when they celebrated the even greater Vintage 1963, the last Vintage with all grapes trod by foot, they decided for the first time to bottle a considerable part of the Port themselves and store the bottles instead of shipping all the pipes abroad.

Altogether the 60'ies was a hectic time. In 1961 the Warre family, who had been partners with the Symingtons since 1912, sold the rest of their shares to the Symington family, who also bought W. & J. Graham & Co. along with its sister company, Smith Woodhouse, in 1970. Gould Campbell was purchased in the 1960'ies and the small company of Quarles Harris had been in the family's possession since AJS' rule.

Since then, the heavyweights have been included in the empire; first The Madeira Wine Company, in which the Symington family acquired the majority of shares in 1988, and a year later, the large Quinta do Vesúvio, which was bought from

Andrew James Symington, in the family known as "AJS", founder of the dynasty.

Dona Antónia Ferreira's descendants who sadly could not agree amongst themselves on how to run the company. Since James Symington's retirement in 1999, when he was 65 - that is a family rule - the active members are:

Peter Ronald Symington (born 1944), youngest son of John D. Symington, joined the company in 1964 having studied in Bordeaux. He has always been on the production side and today is recognised as one of the finest and most experienced tasters/blenders in Port business. He is responsible

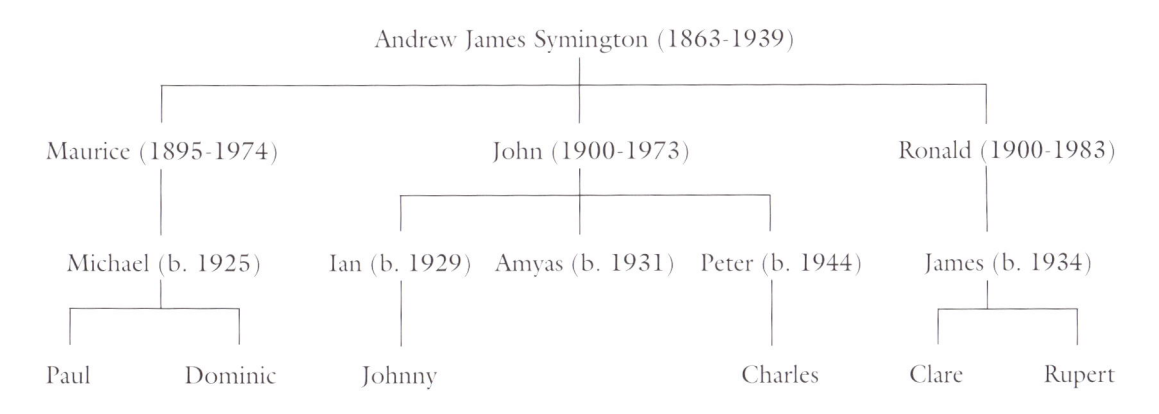

```
                    Andrew James Symington (1863-1939)
                                   |
        ┌──────────────────────────┼──────────────────────────┐
 Maurice (1895-1974)        John (1900-1973)           Ronald (1900-1983)
        |                          |                          |
        |              ┌───────────┼───────────┐              |
 Michael (b. 1925)  Ian (b. 1929) Amyas (b. 1931) Peter (b. 1944)  James (b. 1934)
        |              |                                          |
   ┌────┴────┐         |                   |                  ┌───┴───┐
  Paul   Dominic     Johnny            Charles              Clare   Rupert
```

for all the recent and spectacularly successful Vintage Ports produced by the family.

Charles Symington (born 1969), son of Peter, joined the company in 1995. He studied food sciences in England and oenology in Spain followed by extensive vineyard experience in Chile, Australia, South Africa, etc. He is now in charge of all the family vineyard properties in the Douro Valley and works with his father in the tasting room.

Paul Symington (born 1953), eldest son of Michael, joined the company in 1979. He has overall responsibility for sales and marketing as well as having specific markets under his direct control.

Dominic Symington (born 1956), youngest son of Michael, has been in the company since 1985, initially at the UK office. He is responsible for the family's sales in many European markets including Denmark and Nordic countries. He also regularly visits the USA specifically to support the Warre's brand.

Johnny Symington (born 1960), son of Ian. He joinde the firm in 1985. Like other members of the family he has many specific markets under his control but he also has the imPortant responsibility for the developement and control of the family's Vintage Ports.

Rupert Symington (born 1964), son of James. He joined the business in 1992. After obtaining a degree in mathematics at Oxford he was trained in financial management and took an MBA at Insead. He is in charge of the financial and legal affairs of the family business but also has responsibility for the US and Canadian markets.

Clare Jackson, née Symington (born 1962). Elder daughter of James. After five years in the UK wine trade including three years in Christie's wine department, she joined the family business in the UK where she deals in the older Vintage Ports no longer available in the family's cellars in OPorto.

Life goes on, and development continues. But hardly anybody will meet with the same revolution

Most of the Symington family gathered in Gaia in the mid 1990'ies. From left: Johnny, Ian, Michael, Peter, Amyas, James, Paul and Dominic.

as Michael Symington's generation. When he retired in 1988 one af the his last duties was to represent the family (and the Confraria) at the big Port Festival in Copenhagen. On that occasion he told me about the progress since his start in the company in 1947:

"Oh yes, at that time the company had 45 employees, 30 of which were coopers. Almost all letters were written by hand and we sold 1300 pipes of Port a year. Today we have more than 400 employees, of which only 6 are coopers. We sell 20.000 pipes of Port every year and the offices are crowded with typewriters. Yes, things have changed!"

And they have changed even more. Today the Symingtons sell 28.000 pipes of Port per year and it is due to them that the US market has become the biggest in the world for Vintage Port.

Taylor's
(Taylor, Fladgate & Yeatman)

Founded: 1692.
Owner: Limited company
Taster/Blender: David Bruce Fonseca Guimaraens
Quintas: Quinta de Vargellas and Quinta de Terra Feita

Say Port and the name of Taylor's lies on the tip of your tongue! This is how well Taylor's, Fladgate's and Yeatman's descendants have distinguished themselves with regard to brand as well as quality. Year after year, Taylor's manages to produce some of the best Port always obtaining the best prices and giving anybody relishing a fine glass of Port a hopeful expression on their face. And this in spite of the company's rather agitated life - if not in objectives then in name. Modern marketing people would have had many a sleepless night at the constant change of company names changing as the owners joined and left the company. The present name, Taylor, Fladgate & Yeatman (usually just called Taylor's) actually only dates from 1844. Until then, Taylor's were known under the following names, which are printed on all the old bottles and include all the partners' names:

1692:	Job Bearsley
1709:	Peter Bearsley
1723:	Bearsley & Brackley
1732:	Bearsley, Brackley & Bearsley
1736:	Peter Bearsley & Co.
1739:	Peter & Charles Bearsley
1742:	Peter, Bartholomew & Charles Bearsley
1744:	Bartholomew Bearsley & Co.
1747:	Peter & Francis Bearsley
1749:	Francis Bearsley
1758:	Bearsley & Co.
1766:	Bearsley & Webb
1769:	Bearsley, Webb & Sandford
1806:	Webb, Campbell & Grey
1808:	Webb, Campbell, Grey & Camo
1813:	Webb, Campbell, Grey & Co.
1816:	Campbell, Bowden & Taylor
1825:	Campbell, Taylor & Co.
1826:	Joseph Taylor & Co.
1837:	Taylor, Fladgate & Co.
1844:	Taylor, Fladgate & Yeatman

(Source: Taylor's archives)

As you can see, the first Taylor entered the company in 1816, whilst Job Bearsley, who founded the company in 1692 "or around that time", as Huyshe Bower diplomatically put it, when the company was making preparations for its 300-years anniversary in 1992. But traces are faint. We do know, however, that a former Job Bearsley, presumably from Yorkshire, England, worked in the northern part of Portugal in the 1670'ies, and that he certainly in 1692 was involved in shipments of Monção wine, but not only wine, for at that time trade was a multifarious business, a time when you fetched wool and dried cod from England and returned with corn, fruit and wine. And according to archives, Taylor's famous logo, 4XX, is a typical brand in the wool industry.

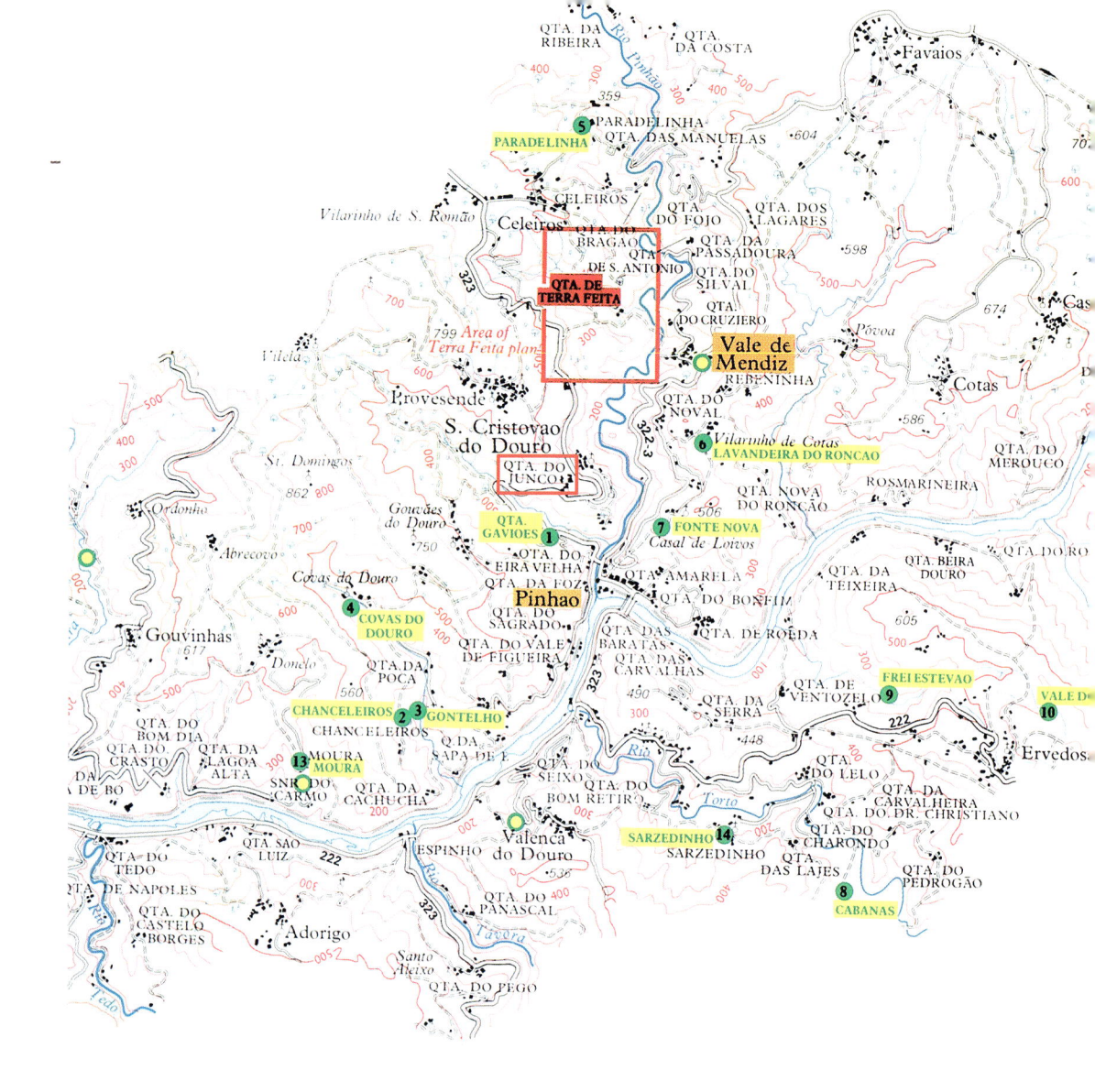

Job Bearsley did not reside permanently in Porto, but lived a bit north of the city in Viana do Castelo, and it was not till the beginning of the 18th Century that his son, Peter, moved to Porto and started to take an interest in wine from the Douro Valley. In 1727, he dared what no other wine exporter had dared before: he went East to see where the wine grew, and even though it must have been a jungle-like experience to arrive in Régua to find no lighting nor paving, he returned in 1744 with his brother, Bartholemew, and bought Casa dos Alambiques in Salgueiral, which as far as we know was the first British-owned property in the Douro Valley. And it does still belong to Taylor's.

Times were prosperous. Trade boomed, and Peter Bearsley was blessed with three, very active sons: Charles, Francis and William, who each had issue of 6 children, a total of 11 girls and 7 boys. Oddly enough, it was through Francis' two daughters, Margaret (wed Sandford) and Elizabeth (wed Grey) that the wine exports continued, as H.W. Sandford became partner in 1769 and

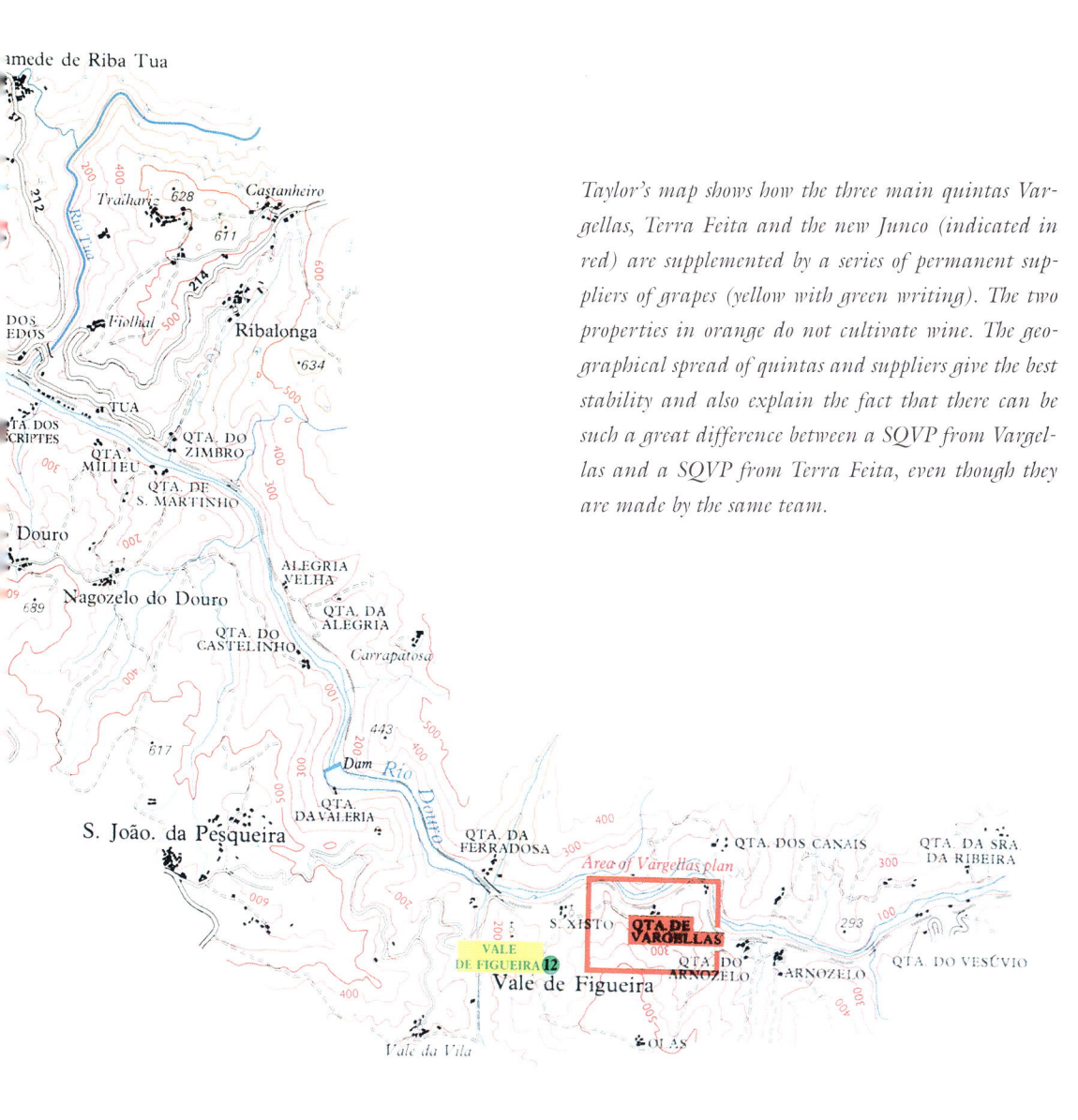

Taylor's map shows how the three main quintas Vargellas, Terra Feita and the new Junco (indicated in red) are supplemented by a series of permanent suppliers of grapes (yellow with green writing). The two properties in orange do not cultivate wine. The geographical spread of quintas and suppliers give the best stability and also explain the fact that there can be such a great difference between a SQVP from Vargellas and a SQVP from Terra Feita, even though they are made by the same team.

Elizabeth's son, Francis, became partner in 1806. Upon Peter Bearsley's death, however, the Bearsley name disappeared from the list of partners all together.

When the British exporters founded The Factory House in 1786 (see page 319) the company was consolidated as a shipper of Port and was no longer a trading company dealing in various merchandise, often on the basis of commission and without any other experience than a nose for business. But the good times were soon replaced by wartimes, and during part of the Napoleonic wars, which in England and Portugal are known as "The Peninsular War", Francis Grey had to flee to England when French troops conquered Porto. These were bad times for the British in Porto, and in 1808 American-born Joe Camo was taken in as a partner after Webb, Campbell and Grey had had to flee the country.

It was however a good fortune in these unfortunate times to find a man with Camo's qualifications, and it is undoubtedly due to "our Mr. Camo" that Taylor's could celebrate their illustrious 300-years anniversary in 1992. Joe Camo managed to keep the company close to neutral and cleverly ran the company through the French siege which cost so many British tradesmen, if not their lives, then at least their company. When the fierce French general Soult took over command in North Portugal in 1809, even Camo had to flee for his life, although he only fled to Lisbon, from where he could return only three months' later when Wellesley threw the French troops out of Porto. In a miraculous way, Camo had succeeded in hiding the company's best Port onboard a ship in the harbour, maybe in the hope that it would reach England safely. But when he returned, the ship was still in the harbour with the Port untouched.

When Francis Grey died in 1815 and Joe Camo a year later, Joseph Taylor became a partner in the company, and his significance to the reputation to and fame of the firm is best documented in the fact that his name is the only one of all the owners of the company that has survived. When he started in the company in 1816, he was one of the three nearly equal co-owners, but ten years later the company was renamed to Joseph Taylor & Co. which very precisely indicates his important role in the partnership.

The civil war in 1832-1834 between the King's sons, Miguel and Pedro, was a disaster for many Portuguese and a costly affair for many people in the British colony, but according to archives, Joseph Taylor's greatest sorrow in this war was that the family's well-grown magnolia was shattered by a bombshell, so that when the war was over, new and golden times could start anew. Joseph Taylor had great plans and when he met a young, friendly Englishman by the name of John Fladgate, he made him a partner in 1836.

However, Taylor never lived to see many of his great ideas to be realized, for he suddenly died a year later whithout leaving any heirs, so 29-years-old John Fladgate had to go out and find a new partner, which he found two years later in Morgan Yeatman from Dorchester, England, a wine dealer and a well-to-do person. With great respect for Taylor's efforts, the now-deceased Taylor's name was maintained as part of the company name that was now renamed *Taylor, Fladgate & Yeatman*.

Fladgate consecrated his life to Port and apparently also the life of his children. His son, Francis Pedro Gauntlett, became partner in 1867, and his four daughters were all married into the Port business. Marian married Albert Morgan (Morgan Bros.), Janet married Charles Wright (Croft & Co.), Florence married Pedro Golçalves Guimaraens (forefather to Bruce, Gordon, and David Guimaraens), and Catherine Mary married J.J. Forrester, later the famous Baron Forrester.

Fladgate was a great success and met great recognition to such an extent that he was appointed Baron with the right to wear a wig. This was a "kick upstairs" for the young wine merchant from London who lost the place name of his barony, Quinta da Roêda, when his daughter married, to Croft, but he managed to profile Taylor, Fladgate & Yeatman well through the prosperous years in the mid 19th Century. He survived both his partners, first Taylor and then Morgan Yeatman. Yeatman died in 1849 and was succeeded by his son, Morgan Jr., who at the time was only 24-yearss old and was therefore sent to London to learn the trade. When John Fladgate's son, Francis, died in 1888, and Morgan Yeatman Jr. a year later, a completely new management had to be formed again, but for once the new management lasted for many years. Harry Oswald and Frank Pym Stanley Yeatman entered the company at a very young age, but they were the ones who led the old Port house into a new era, although this did take place from London, first by taking over the old Quinta de Vargellas in 1893-99 (see page 194ff) and then by entering the new centu-

Quinta de Vargellas was purchased from Dona Antónios heirs in 1899. It lies in the valley, close to the river and is here seen from the very top of the vineyard. The white house with the swimming-pool is habitation, the buildings to the left is the vinification center. The white quinta on the opposite bank of the Douro River is Cockburn's Quinta dos Canais. (Photo: HO)

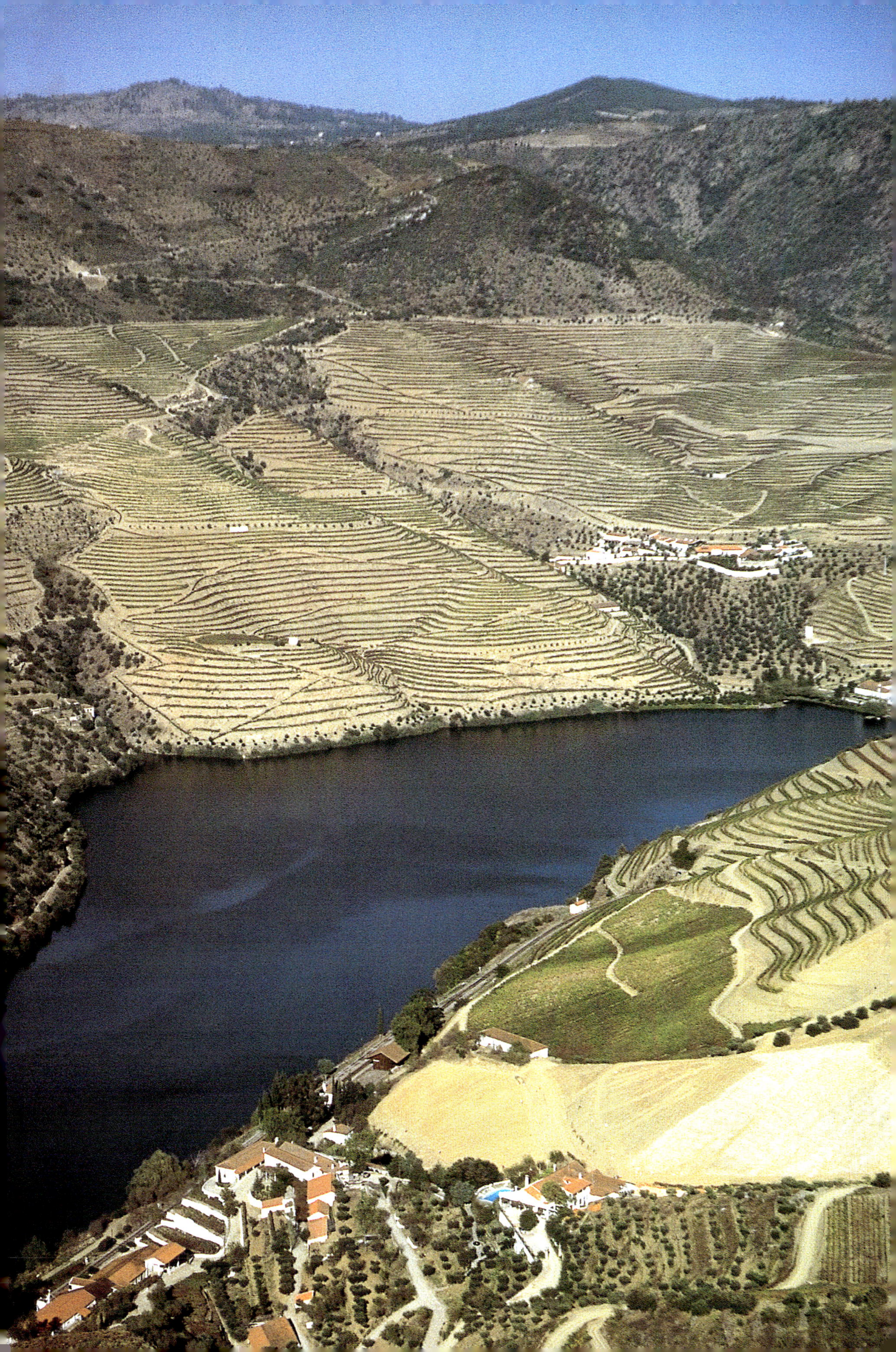

ry with Taylor, Fladgate & Yeatman as one of the front figures in the Port business. Frank "Smiler" Yeatman even became a legendary person by being the first British Port producer to produce 50 vintages. According to the archives, he was oddly enough also the first Yeatman to settle down in Porto; the others all remained in England.

Upon Frank "Smiler" Yeatman's death in 1950, his son, Richard "Dick" Stanley Yeatman, became the strong man at Taylor's with his cousin Stanley. He was educated at the University of Montpellier, France, and returned to the Douro full of new ideas, as all young people have. In 1927 and again in 1935 he ordered the planting of blocks of single grapes at Vargellas, which was way ahead of his time. Otherwise, he is mostly known for a series of colourful anecdotes. He was very old-fashioned, typical for the British colonials, and is especially known for a rather noisy episode at the railway station at Pinhão. He was on his way to Vargellas and as usual he threw his trunk out of the window from the small slow train, expecting a Portuguese porter to grab it. But for once there was nobody there to catch it - and the trunk contained a West Indy coffee set!

"Dick" died in 1966 and left the majority of his shares to his widow, Beryl. She later gave the shares to her nephew, Alistair Robertson, and told him to either make Taylor's successful or sell the shares.

Thank goodness he chose the first option, and luckily there were a couple of golden eggs to go with the shares: Bruce Guimaraens and Huyshe Bower, who had both joined as partners in 1961. Bruce Guimareans came from the Fladgate branch of the family and Huyshe Bower from the Yeatman branch of the family. Now, Alistair Robertson joined from the Yeatman branch of the family, but the last Taylor was gone forever.

Apart from the Casa dos Alambiques, which the Bearsley brothers bought in 1744, and which now boasts a significant vinification plant, Taylor's owns two quintas, the famous Quinta de Vargellas and the less known Quinta da Terra Feita, neighbour to Warre's Quinta da Cavadinha. As all other quintas in the neighbourhood, Terra Feita originally consisted of several properties which Taylor's had purchased on two different occasions: Terra Feita de Baixo in 1974 and Terra Feita da Cima in 1990. The nearly 45 ha of vines (Class A) yield grapes of the best quality. They are foot-crushed in lagares and used for the production of the best wines, including Taylor's Vintage Port. With 1982 as the first SQVP from this property.

The last part of Quinta de Vargellas was bought by Taylor's in 1899 from Dona Antónia's daughter, Maria. The property originally consisted of three parts: Vargelas da Cima, Vargelas de Meio and Vargelas Baixo, which was then spelt with one "l" like the village. On the statement of 1896 of Dona Antónia's property (see page 195), 2/3 was owned by Ferreira and out of production, first due to phylloxera, then due to mildew, but new plants from American roots were quickly planted, and Taylor's archives show that 80 pipes of Port were produced in 1911. Today, production has nearly tripled, and in 1998 a significant number of new plants were planted.

The quinta is a model property with a unique location, beautiful buildings, wonderful fields, and state-of-art vinification equipment. When Frank Yeatman ordered the new planting after the purchase in 1899, the 5 noble grape varieties were applied, but Vargellas has always been known as having a preference for Touriga Francesa which is however toned down in the newest plantings by also using Touriga Nacional. The grapes are foot-crushed in the traditonal lagares, and thanks to foresight, the planting has since the 1920'ies been carried out in blocks so that the grape varieties are separated from each other.

The grapes from Vargellas have been the backbone of Taylor's best wines since 1908 and the first vintage of grapes exclusively from the quinta - the first Single Quinta Vintage Port - was produced in 1910. Christie's of London has a record of selling a Quinta de Vargellas in 1912. Taylor's continued to do this, long before it became a popular thing to do, but mostly due to demands from certain customers. Since 1958, Taylor's have been making their Single Quinta Vintage Port from Vargellas in the good years. In the great years the wine is used as the backbone af Taylor's classic Vintage Port.

Since the purchase of the Port Wine part of Borges & Irmão in 1998, Taylor's have also possessed the famous Quinta do Junco a little south of Terra Feita.

It might be somewhat simplified to say that Taylor's unique and international success is only due to hard work, talent, skilled management and a non-compromised seeking for quality. But there does not seem to be any other explanation to the fact that the quinta, which Dona Antónia's daughter had sold because the grapes were of a poor quality, produces the world's finest Port year after year. There is only one other Port house who can measure up to Taylor's in the art of making Vintage Port - Fonseca, which is also owned by Taylor's!

RUBY

In the preface to Taylor's jubilee book "A Celebration of Port" from 1992, Michael Broadbent calls Taylor's Vintage Port "the Latour of Port" at least, he says, with regard to power, robustness and durability. He has tasted more bottles of Taylor's Vintage Port than I probably ever will, but still I dare say that if you can make comparisons of that sort, I believe that Taylor's Vintage reminds me more of a Mouton due to its characteristic taste of concentrated juice of black berries (especially blackberries!) whilst the severe, opulent Latour reminds me much more of Fonseca's Vintage Port. But these are just my humble remarks and we cannot do must more than compare and analyze – and enjoy! Let us start at the low end of the scale: "First Estate" is a solid Ruby type that is comparable to Fonseca's "Bin no. 27" and maybe it is too during production – it is made by the same team. In Late Bottled Vintage, Taylor's likes, oddly enough, a filtered, drinkable type. The philosophy seems to be that LBV should not be a replacement for Vintage Port, but an independent Ruby type with the characteristic of a smooth, friendly fruit, a self-confident power, immediately drinkable. The evidence is that Taylor's both made Vintage Port and LBV in 1994 with the remark on the back label of the latter that it was drinkable and did not need decanting. The price on the Danish market is 12-15% of what a newly declared Vintage Port costs.

But the Vintage Port has placed Taylor's on the unofficial Ruby throne. When Taylor's celebrated its 3rd centennial in 1992, a fashionable tasting of old vintages from this century was held, and I understand from Michael Broadbent that especially Vintage 1945 was the sensation of the tasting, a bit at the expense of the previous and later fantastic vintages 1912 and 1948 (also excellent), 1955, and the deep sleeper 1963.

Among my more humble tasting notes I have the following impressions from 1997-1999:

Vintage 1966: "Deep nose. The fruit just streams out of the glass with berries – and liquorice. Soft, wonderful juice with both depth and length. But especially the berries, black berries. Creamy, delicious interlude and then a late, short explosion. Still vivid, but also drinkable". (92/100)

Vintage 1970: "Super potent and extremely fruity. A concentrate of field crops with lots of blackberries and some black currant. Velvety, with a fabulous sweetness changing into ascetic dryness. Explodes in your mouth that fills up with stars and small flags. Long taste, long aftertaste, long durability". (98/100)

Vintage 1977: "Dark and sinister. Berries and pepper, chocolate and oriental spices. Deep-sleeping giant with one eye half open. Again the natural sweetness changes into straightforward dryness. Great potency, which requires patience". (98/100)

Vintage 1985: "Great berry nose. Dry matter in both nose and mouth. Exquisite fruit, liquorice, tobacco, black berries. Enormous explosion of berries in the mouth, but just about to leave a period of outgoing friendliness and go underground. Great potential, lots of dry matter, lots of potency". (96/100)

Vintage 1994: "Cinnamon nose changing into a berry nose. Intense fruit, great muscle. Long powerful taste with tannin and an impressive length. Juice and power. Incredibly potent. Long, convincing taste. Promising – and durable for many years to come". (95-98/100)

Taylor's SQVP from Quinta de Vargellas is famous for a reason – also for its reliability. Vintage 1978 was the first vintage I noticed, and it was a sympathetic introduction to an acquaintance which was relived in 1998-1999:

Quinta de Vargellas Vintage 1978: "Fruity, polished, juicy. If you know Taylor's Vintage, it is obvious that this is the little brother with the same genes. It is more friendly, slightly more drinkable, has a shorter skeleton and lacks the big muscles, but it is very decent and well-structured". (89/100)

Quinta de Vargellas Vintage 1984: "Concentrated with a dense, very nice fruit. Soft and glossy with a long, polished taste of berries. The very nice fruit makes it drinkable and decent now. Not a wine for keeping, but wine to enjoy". (89/100)

Quinta de Vargellas Vintage 1987: "Rather mild and very pure taste of berries, black currant and blackberry. Berry and fruit, sweetness and friendliness. Young and not yet developed". (91/100)

Quinta de Terra Feita 1987: "More potent than Vargellas, more uncivilized and more unpolished. Uncouth, violent, disharmonious. Give it time". (88/100)

Both SQVPs are orthodox types, only made from grapes from their quintas, but Taylor's Vintage may also contain purchased grapes, although they are usually made from grapes from the two quintas. It will be exciting to see what the recently purchased Quinta do Junco will supply.

The two SQVPs are more different from Taylor's Vintage Port than the LBV, and this follows the house philosophy. Taylor's want the two SQVPs to reflect the quinta's terroir, to be individual and to express each their (and the vintage's) personality. The hierarchy is therefore somewhat different at Taylor's than at Fonseca's (see page 210).

TAWNY

Co-owner Huyshe Bower stresses that whilst Taylor's and Fonseca are Ruby producers, who also make Tawny, Romaríz, who have some of the same owners, is a Tawny house who also make Ruby types.

And it would be wrong to say that Tawny is of no interest to Taylor's, but I believe that they would admit that they prefer Vintage Port to maturation in casks. On that basis Taylor's series of old Tawnies is irritatingly good:

10-years Tawny: "Mild, and soft, a bit hard in the fruit, but nice, honest and fruity". (90/100)

20-years Tawny: "Brown sugar. Nice style, very nice depth and just a touch of aggression. Again dominated by fruit, and again a hard straightforward fruit content. Robust style with more fruit than sweetness and richness". (92/100)

30-years Tawny: "Robust, very robust even with a characteristic fruity taste. Very solid of a 30-years Tawny with a dash of acetone and more fruit than richness". (88/100)

Over 40-years Tawny: "Mild and decent, soft and friendly, no real depth. Robust of an Over 40-years Tawny, and yet friendly and drinkable. Powerful"! (92/100)

Like Fonseca, Taylor's do not produce Colheitas. The more common Tawny types are characterised by solid fruit and are among the most Ruby-like Tawnies I know.

Vasconcellos

Visitors to Gaia will know the name Vasconcellos, for they have the most aggressive "tourist hunters" and even fetch their own visitors off the streets – whether they want to or not. A visit is no special treat, neither are the wines. But the visit is free and popular. The address: Rua Barão Forrester 73.

Viera de Souza

see Hutcheson.

Vallegre
(Vista Alegre)

Founded: 1973
Owner: Barros Family
Taster/Blender: Manuel F. de Pinho Tavares
Quintas: Quinta da Vista Alegre, Quinta de Vilarinho, Quinta de Valongo, and Quinta da Lameira

This agricultural society has nothing to do with the Barros-Almeida family but is a co-operative consisting of some of the Barros family's other properties, founded in 1973. The co-operative has four quintas: Quinta da Vista Alegre, Quinta de Vilarinho, Quinta de Valongo and Quinta da Lameira, of which quinta da Vista Alegre has the best wines, a series of old Tawnies and Vintage Port. The family produces nearly 600 pipes of Port Wine a year, all produced in Régua and its surroundings. In May 1998, the family decided to change the name of the producer from the long Sociedade Agrícola Barros to Vallegre.

Warre's
(Warre & Ca. S.A.)

Founded: 1670
Owner: Symington Family
Taster/Blender: Peter Ronald Symington
Quintas: Quinta da Cavadinha

Warre should actually not have been called Warre at all, for the first Warre by the first name of William, did not enter the company until 59 years after its establishment. It all began with the colourful account of two young Englishmen who by curiosity went far into the dark and dangerous Douro Valley (see page 20), and when 23-years-old William Warre from Somerset entered the scene in Porto in 1729, John Clark was the company owner. He became a partner of the company *Messrs. Clark, Thornton & Warre* and later became sole owner and founder of the Warre dynasty and thus of the oldest, still-existing British-owned Port house.

At the time, young Warre and his predecessors did not deal in Port but in a table wine added alcohol for the sake of keeping qualities - and maybe also for its taste. But whether or not the wine was anything special, history was in its favour, and that was the good fortune. In 1689, France declared war on England, and the English immediately stopped all import of French wine. When this short war was replaced by a more important war in 1702, the so-called Spanish War of Succession, and Portugal after some consideration entered and sided with the British against the French, Portugal thus became wine supplier to the Royal British crown. This was also confirmed in the previously mentioned Methuen treaty (see page 21f) in 1703, and notes prove that in 1708, 7 of 10 bottles of wine which were consumed at the British Court were from Portugal. So things were looking good for John Clark whom we meet for the first time in 1718 as owner of the company in which young William Warre is taken on as partner in 1729, and shortly after his name is added to the company name.

When William Warre married, it was a marriage of convenience with the British consul's sister. They had 7 children, of which the eldest son James succeeded his father. James was succeeded by his son William who lived to play a brilliant boyish prank: he glued a sleeping Portuguese employee's pigtail to his desk with sealing wax and disappeared. He also disappeared from the company and got another job where boyish pranks might have been more comme-il-faut. He became a general in the army and never missed a moment to promote the family's good Ports, so even Lord Wellington was convinced to order a hogshead of Warre's best Port. A document in Warre's archives proves this.

Quinta da Cavadinha which the Symingtons bought in 1980 is attached to Warre's. In 1988 the adega was completely renovated. (Photo. HO)

It is dates 15/5 1810 and sent from officer Warre to his father, the Port producer, and says: "Lord Wellington ... has applied to me to procure him one hogshead of very fine old Port. He does not care about the price and wishes me to get you to take care of it for him in London".

A couple of years after this famous order, the first bottle of Warre's Port was printed on a price list dated 18/11 1812 when 12 bottles are offered at the lavish price of 56 shillings. Wellington's sworn enemy, Napoleon, could have used a couple of cases. The same month, the Russian winter stopped his Russian campaign at Beresina which inspired Tjaikowski to his 1812 ouverture.

But Wellington won the war against Napoleon, and Warre's was successful too and grew in the course of the 19th century, at the same time as George Acheson Warre, a nephew of the general and building up Silva & Cosens, was able to build ambitious lodges in Vila Nova de Gaia where an enormous cask was erected which could hold 178,091 bottles. It is still the world's largest cask for Port. These were also the years when close bonds were tied to other British Port houses such as Quarles Harris, Gould Campbell as well as Silva and Cosens, whose own brand "Dow's" was about to be introduced.

When Warre celebrated its 3rd centennial in 1970, the last Warre had left the company (1955). In 1912 Warre's was taken over by the Symingtons who had been co-owners since 1905. When the Symingtons bought the Quinta da Cavadinha in 1980, it was allotted to Warre's, which had never had its own quinta before. According to the Symingtons, the purchase of Cavadinha had originally been planned so that the grapes from this quinta would eventually become the life blood of Warre's Vintage Ports together with the grapes from Quinta do Bom Retiro Pequeno, owned by the Serôdio family, and which until this time had formed the basis of Warre's Vintage Ports. Four generations of Symingtons have done business with five generations of Serôdios and today Bom Retiro

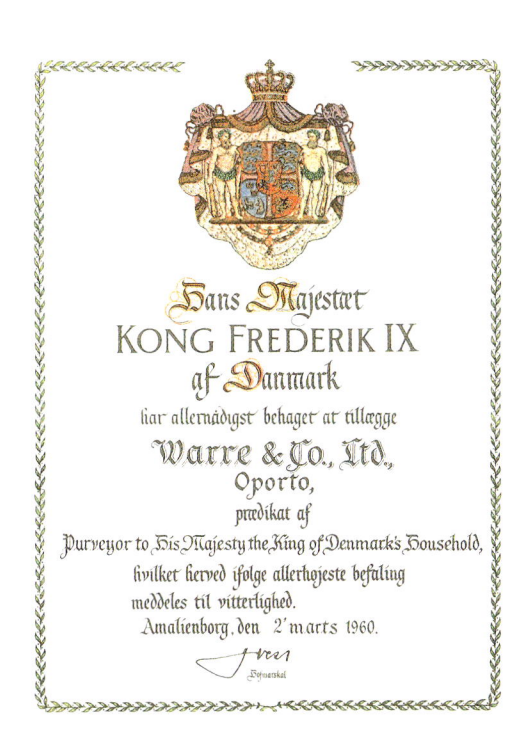

With Royal permission Warre's can write "Purveyor to HM the Queen of Denmark's Household" on the label.

Pequeno still forms an important part of Warre's Vintage Ports. Quinta da Cavadinha lies to the west of Rio Pinhão with its fields lying towards the southeast, joining Taylor's fields at Quinta da Terra Feita and looking towards Quinta do Noval on the other side of the river. So the location is quite exclusive. The annual production is of 178 pipes of Port which come from 30-40 year-old vines. The quinta's production is vinified on the spot in the small adega on the top of the hill, 400 metres above the sea. And the house might be a bit lopsided and crooked, but the technique most certainly is not. In 1988, the quinta's adega was rebuilt and converted to include a state-of-art vinification plant of stainless steel with small fermentation tanks, all designed and realized by Peter Symington. From the vintage year of 1978 and again in 1979, 1982, 1986, and 1987 a Single Quinta Vintage Port has been produced at Cavadinha bearing the Cavadinha name.

Warre has a special military relation to Denmark. For many years it has been common practice in the Queen's regiment that the Queen's guard leaving duty and the guard taking over the duty at the different castles salute each other with a glass of Warre's "Warrior", which supposedly got its warrior name after Wellington. Warre's is also the only Port company who can write "Purveyor to HM the Queen of Denmark's Household" on the label.

RUBY

The aforementioned warrior wine "Warre's Warrior" does not have a very fierce taste, but is a solid, fruity, rather sweet and nice Ruby. Warre's LBV is quite different, as it is not filtered before bottling, but matures in the bottles at Warre's for 6-8 years before it is sold on the market. LBV 1986 has just been released, bottled in 1990, and clearly marked "Bottle matured" and "Traditional – Unfiltered" on the label. Luckily it is worth both the effort and the patience, for it is among the most characteristic and best LBVs around.

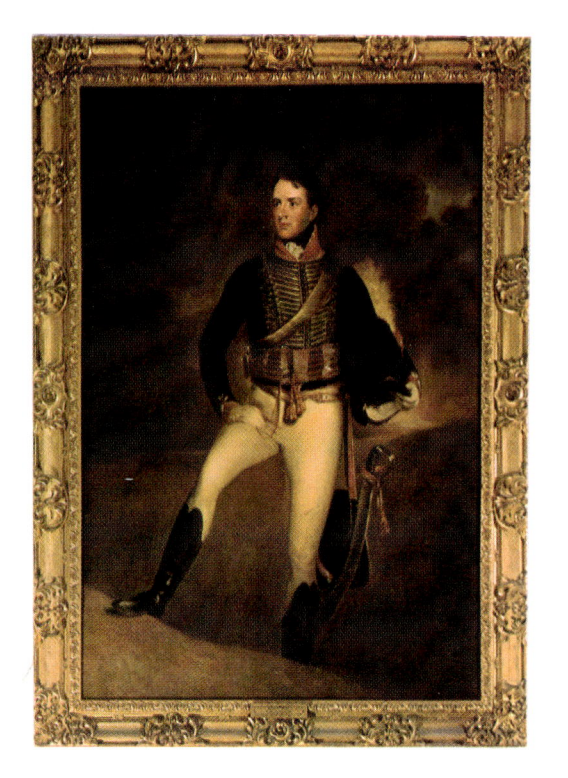

Warre's Vintage Port is also rightly among the best and most reliable wines, not so much due to the SQVP from Quinta da Cavadinha, which I tasted as Vintages 1982 and 1992 and was not especially impressed with, other than with their fruity friendliness. But Warre's Vintage Port, which I tasted as the following vintages in the course of 1998-1999, all at the Symingtons' in Gaia, most certainly is:

Vintage 1970: "Refined, well-balanced with a very nice fruit, which goes well with the fine sweetness. Light and fine elderberry taste. Graceful. I would drink it now". (90/100)

Vintage 1977: "Youthful fruity nose. Mild, soft taste full of character. Self-confident medium style – especially compared to the elegant Graham's and the potent Dow's". (90/100)

Vintage 1983: "Dry, fruity nose. Dense and nice taste with wholesome fruit. Easily drinkable and wonderful now. Lots of potency, long, fruity and delicious finish". (90/100)

Vintage 1985: "Almost black with an intense berry nose. Concentrated elderberry juice and very decent fruit. A lighter style than Graham's and without Dow's power but all in all very nice, even

William Warre - the warrior who sold Port to Wellington.

though it is a bit unpredictable and matures quickly". (91/100)

Vintage 1991: "Power, berries and sweetness. Seems rather potent for the vintage and is more complex than both Graham's and Dow's". (86/100)

Vintage 1994: "Intense berry nose. Slightly spicy taste with a fine sweetness and a nice amount of power behind the sweetness. The friendly sweetness covers up a significant amount of potency. Well-built. Promising, but still too young and too sweet". (89/100)

To put it simply, I believe that Warre's combines these Vintages with a bit of Dow's power and a bit of Graham's elegance, but without being a match for them at all. On the other hand, it is often more well-balanced and harmonic - 1991 is a good example of this. In the summer of 1999, I had the occasion of tasting Warre's Vintage 1960 which is considered as one of the gems of this Vintage. And most rightly so: "Dynamic, both in the nose and in the mouth, with a soft, slightly smoky, deep and wonderful taste. Clingy, long and delicious. A wonderful Vintage Port without any signs of age".

TAWNY ♥♥♥--

Quite a modest selection. The best known Tawny is probably the undefined "Nimrod Tawny" and the following:

10-years Tawny ("Sir William"): "Rather light, mild, slightly smoky, a bit more fruity and very friendly. Pure, nice and very useful medium style". (89/100)

Wiese & Krohn

Founded: 1865
Owner: Falcão Carneiro Family
Taster/Blender: Iolanda Falcão Carneiro & Rui Cunha
Quintas: Quinta do Retiro Novo by Pinhão was purchased in 1989

Dried cod can lead to many things - if you sell it in time. Theodor Wiese and Dankert Krohn would no doubt confirm this. They started their collaboration by fetching the salted fish from the clothes lines of Norway and selling it in Porto, but they soon found out that it was a smart idea to fill the empty ships with something to sell in Oslo and Bergen in Norway. They wisely chose Port and founded the company *Wiese & Krohn* in 1865 for this good purpose. In 1910, they became partners to Edmundo Falcão Carneiro who knew more about Port than about dried cod, and eventually he took over management completely. In 1937, he became sole owner. Today, his son Fernando and Fernando's children, Iolanda and José Falcão Carneiro, run the company - which does not include dried cod! But they have not forgotten their ancestors. I, myself, have enjoyed a meal of dried cod with the family at a lovely lunch in 1998.

In 1989, Wiese & Krohn purchased the Quinta do Retiro Novo by Pinhão. Originally it was called Quinta do Lapa after a previous owner, but it was renamed with the purchase. The family Carneiro's coat-of-arms was allowed to hang though, for the previous owner's wife's grandmother had been a Carneiro. When the Carneiro family took over the quinta, water had only been installed in a few places, and the field work was still being carried out by a local farmer and his mules. Even though this conception is somewhat romantic, modern times have invaded the quinta, and after the patamares were built in the 1990'ies, the approx. 15 ha of vines will soon provide the family with high-quality grapes. Until the quinta is extended, the family must buy its grapes from small farmers for the production of their best wines. Wiese and Krohn are very much a Tawny producer, and the family has for many years made Colheita from the best grapes instead of Vintage. In exceptional years they do, however, make a small quantity of Vintage, but they prefer to allow the pipes to mature even further. They must know quite a lot of small farmers because they make Tawnies of a superb quality. What Taylor's and Fonseca are to Vintage, Wiese & Krohn and Burmester are to Colheita.

RUBY

"We are not as good as the British producers in making sellable Vintage. We have another style", José Falcão Carneiro told me when he and his sister, Iolanda, in the autumn of 1998 introduced me to an impressive collection of Vintage Ports and new bottlings of old Tawnies, a total of 35!

The family prefers making Colheitas, even though they know from the foreign markets that the profits and big money is made in Vintage Port.

These are my impressions of the eight Vintage Ports which I had the occasion of tasting:

Vintage 1957: "Deep nose, drinkable but not overmature, quite durable, a bit of a short taste, but nice".

Vintage 1958: "Sweet and very friendly, nice, somewhat dull, pure and honest, also its style".

Vintage 1960: "Light, decent, nice with an emphasis on friendly fruit and sweetness".

Vintage 1961: "Massive sweetness, too sweet and too rich, too short and gone too fast".

Vintage 1963: "Serene, nice and decent, but a bit too dull. Richness and body, but lacks fruit and power. Develops nicely in the glass, but not exaggerated".

Vintage 1965: "Delicious - easily drinkable with more sweetness than fruit. Still nice, no power".

Vintage 1967: Serene, mature, nice. Nice version from a not so nice vintage, a tendency of sweetness".

The nice family, Falcão Carneiro is gathered around the table to enjoy a freshly baked gingerbread and a Colheita 1966. From the left: José, Fernando, and Iolanda Falcão Carneiro. (Photo: HO)

An impressive collection of Krohn's Colheitas was poured to this book's author in 1998. (Photo: HO)

Vintage 1970: "The first vintage with a fruity taste. Still a bit potent and friendly too, very nice and easily drinkable".

Light and friendly style, not aggressive, mild, as if Krohn's Vintage Ports were made with Tawny hands. And they are, actually.

TAWNY 🍷🍷🍷🍷🍷

Krohn sits, together with Burmester, on top of the Colheita mountain. Let us take a look at the concentrated tasting impressions from 1998. They speak for themselves. All bottles were first bottlings (full bottles):

Colheita 1989: "Young and powerful, potent, impressive dense and massive fruit". (94/100)

Colheita 1985: "Rich and delicious. Aggressive sweetness from sweets. Incredibly young". (92/100)

Colheita 1983: "Rather mild and light with a taste of syrup and nuts". (93/100)

Colheita 1982: "Light and elegant, discrete and supple – and quite delicious". (95/100)

Colheita 1978: "Refined, soft, clingy. Very nice balance. Delicious and harmonic". (96/100)

Colheita 1977: "Delicious, delicious, soft and affectionate. Incredibly well-proportioned. An angelic voice is heard". (98/100)

Colheita 1976: "Richness and good stuff. Does not have the 1977s firm character but a delicious nutty taste". (90/100)

Colheita 1968: "Smoke and dark honey. Intense sweetness. Rich, but not too rich, harmonic, affectionate and full of character with a characteristic power". (96/100)

Colheita 1967: "Clingy, oily structure with brown rock candy and syrup. Delicious and very friendly". (93/100)

Colheita 1966: " Rather dark. Intense taste with a delicious, concentrated sweetness, but also body and muscle. Incredibly great wine. Complex. Well-proportioned. No, not great: fantastic with a big explosion in the mouth and a long aftertaste". (100/100)

Colheita 1965: "Intense nose and taste. In spite of its age no flaws. Great and intense and with a character of its own, just a grape or two from 1966s perfect elegance". (99/100)

Colheita 1963: "Smoke and discrete sweetness. Richness, body, structure, wild gestures but all in all well-made. Utterly delicious with more rich sweetness than the 1966. Impressive". (99/100)

Colheita 1961: "Brown sugar and brown rock candy. Nice body, taunted by sweetness". (93/100)

Colheita 1960: "Powerful, not only with affectionate muscle but dominating, full of power and just as full of polished sweetness. Perfect balance. More sweetness but also more muscle than the 1966. Majestic". (100/100)

Colheita 1958: "Sweet, sweet as sweets, sweet as syrup. Wonderful, but not challenging. Very nice wine, but not in the league of the 1960". (90/100)

Colheita 1957: "Again an intense sweetness, but not much else. Rich and dense, but lacks character compared to the great vintage years". (89/100)

Reserva 1896: "I would have guessed 40-50 years old with a nose that makes you want to jump into the glass, as sweet and noble as an old unmarried lady of the noble rank. Stupendous aroma".

Reserva 1863: "Very dark, the colour of Coca Cola, with a noble deep nose and the taste of brown sugar with no richness at all. Dense and surprisingly vivid, smoky with a disciplined sweetness. The real great Colheitas are really enduring. I bow my head"

The family has a lot of experience in this area. They made their first Colheita in 1834 when it was still called "Reserva", and the word "Colheita" was not used before around 1930.

I cannot help noticing that in the autumn of 1999 Krohn's delicious Colheita 1977 cost 1/4 of what is the most expensive Vintage Ports 1997 are expected to cost. That's the world of Port for you. Wiese & Krohn also produce a mixed Colheita, "VVO" from old casks and naturally also a 10-years and a 20-years Tawny, all of which are excellent. It's all a question of skills – and a sweet tooth. And they do have a sweet tooth at Krohn's – but it is under control.

Nobody should doubt who owns Quinta do Retiro Novo. The family bought the quinta in 1989. (Photo: HO)

Chapter 8

PORT ASSOCIATIONS

Port Associations

Two domestic events influenced the Port industry dramatically in the 20th Century: first prime minister António Salazar's decision to split up the discorded wine business in 1932-1933 by establishing Casa do Douro, the Port Wine Institute, and Grémio dos Exportadores, and then the collapse of the system at the Carnation Revolution on 25 April 1974 when all of Salazar's corporative ideas were discarded which resulted in a new structure of the entire Port Wine industry as per September 1974.

AEVP

(Associacão das Empresas de Vinho do Porto) The AEVP is better known under its English name, Shippers' Association. It was founded on 4 May 1995 as a re-organization of the Associacão do Exportadores de Vinho do Porto (AEVP), which was founded on 10 January 1975, to replace Salazar's establishment of Grémio dos Exportadores de Vinho do Porto that was dissolved in 1974 following a re-organization of the wine sector.

The AEVP is a private non-profit association whose objective it is to strengthen the export situation on behalf of the producers. The main objective is, according the statutes, to "promote and defend the trade and industry of Port Wine, and to represent and protect the members' interests with regard to finances".

The AEVP represents the exporters towards the State and all official bodies. The AEVP contributes by protecting the name and quality of Port Wine. All the most important producers of Port Wine are members of the AEVP - except the Real Companhia Velha.

To become a member of AEVP and to be recognized as a Port shipper you must present proof:

- that you have a stock of 500 pipes of Port
- that you only sell 1/3 of your stock every calendar year

The objective of the latter stipulation ("Lei do Terço") is to ensure that every single bottle of Port, which is sold, has matured for a certain amount of time. This guarantees that no producer can sell more than 1/3 of the previous year's stock at any one time.

AVEPOD

AVEPOD is the association of winegrowers and bottlers of Port and Douro wines (table wines) in the Douro Valley. It was established as a counterweight to the concentration of these good men in Gaia, and its domicile is naturally in Régua.

Casa do Douro

Casa do Douro was established by prime minister Salazar by decree of 18 November 1932 under the name of Federação dos Viticultores da Região do Douro. After a few amendments the Casa do Douro obtained its final shape by decree of 30 April 1940. The objective of the establishment of Casa do Douro was, as was the establishment of the Grémio dos Exportadores de Vinho do Porto and the establishment of the Port Institute (IVP), to preserve peace in the Port industry by splitting up the involved parties' interests (see page 62). In other words, this trinity can be explained thus that Casa do Douro was now responsible for the quantities of Port produced, the IVP for its quality, and the Grémio for sales and exports.

Casa do Douro with domicile in Régua was designated to be the association of the winegrowers and the producers, and all the producers of Port Wine are still by definition under the supervision of the Casa do Douro which today counts approx. 24,000 winegrowers and farmers as well as 22 large-scale and small-scale Port houses. As one member has always counted as one vote in the Casa do Douro, this does still signify some controversy, and there have been violent disputes in and around the Casa do Douro for several years, especially with regard to the affair about the acquisition of shares in the Real Companhia Velha (See page 84f).

In the many years that António José Borges Mesquita Montes was the powerful president of Casa do Douro, there was no realistic possibility of a fruitful dialogue with the IVP or with the Shippers' Association. Montes was as hard as a rock, but it should be said to his defence that it was not his job to speak on behalf of Port Wine but to speak on behalf of the small winegrowers and inefficient co-operatives, and this he did very well indeed. Naturally, there is more focus on the 22 dissatisfied Port houses than on the 24,000 small farmers - and this book is a living proof thereof! However, one can only hope for a dialogue with Montes' successor, Manuel António Araújo dos Santos, who replaced Mesquita Montes in 1998. One of Casa do Douro's most important functions was to be the advocate of the small winegrowers and producers as well as for the independent co-operatives by, among other things, by purchasing their grapes and wine. In theory, this could be justified by the fact that the Casa do Douro then could supply the shippers who needed Port for the purpose of exports. But often the Casa do Douro purchased Port of such an inferior quality that even the most needy shippers would not buy it. The Casa do Douro is responsible for the classification of all lots within the demarcated area. By the amendment of the Act of 15 March 1991 the monopoly of the Casa do Douro was abolished with regard to the sale of aguardente to the producers - which until then had been a considerable extra income to Casa do Douro.

When the CIRDD was founded in 1995, Casa do Douro lost more influence, and it seems to be a side effect of Mesquita Montes' unlighted autocracy that the power of the Casa do Douro gradually decreased.

CIRDD

(The Interprofessional Commission for the demarcated area Do Douro) was established by decree of 19 April 1995 as a public body under the Ministry of Agriculture and Fishery and as an autonomous body for both Port Wine and table wine from the demarcated area. The objective of the CIRDD is to join the interests of the producers and the shippers as well as to defend the infrastructure of the region, to decide how much of the harvest of a particular year may be used for Port, as well as to monitor and control the production and sales of Port. Today, the CIRDD also estimates and recommends the prices of grapes. At the establishment of the CIRDD, the statutes of the Casa do

Douro were changed, and its influence reduced. The domicile of the CIRDD is in Régua. The issues related to Port Wine are handled by CIRDD's 12 members, of which 6 members handle production (appointed by Casa do Douro) - 6 members handle the trade (appointed by the sector).

Confrario do Vinho do Porto

The Confrario do Vinho do Porto is a brotherhood that was established in 1982, but it had been on the drawing table since 1964. At that time, it had not, however, been possible to establish a private association in Portugal, so the brotherhood had to wait for the fall of the dictatorship and the revolution in 1974 before their dream came true in November 1982.

The overall objective of the brotherhood was and still is to spread the knowledge and love of Port. The brotherhood is headed by a Chanceler, who is responsible for the daily management, and he is assisted by a Almoxarife (Secretary), a Copeiro-Mor (cellar master), a Almotacé (Treasurer), and a Fiel das Usanças (Master of Ceremony). When the Confraria was established in 1982, top management consisted of Fernando Nicolau de Almeida, Robin Reid, José António Ramos-Pinto Rosas, Michael Symington, and Manuel Pintão Poças. The other members of the brotherhood are called confrades. They are divided into three ranks: Cavaleiros, Infançãos and Cancelários. The two latter ranks are reserved statesmen and royalty.

In its 17-year existence, the Confraria has only had two Chancelers, first Fernando Nicolau de Almeida (left), who was one of the founders of the brotherhood, and present Chanceler António Filipe (right).

The brotherhood has Infante Dom Henrique (Henry the Seafarer) as patron and wears a copy of his hat. The brothers always meet in full dress, including the hat, for the enthronement of new members. This takes place upon recommendation of two members of the brotherhood. The new members participate in a solemn ceromony and must sign to the following:

"I swear to lend my support to the Confraria and to continue fighting for the Dignification of Port Wine."

All new members, around 700, are enthroned at the beautiful Stock Exchange (a Bolsa) in Porto and then join a fabulous galla dinner, which is served in the famous "Arabian hall". Due to practicalities, the brotherhood does permit the enthronement of new brothers under the Confraria's overseas voyages, for example in the U.S.A or in the Far East, but within the boundaries of Europe even royalties must travel to Porto to receive their diploma and the red and green band with the Port tasters' wine logo.

Today, the Port Wine's brotherhood has become part of the profile of Porto, and when heads of State and royal guests come to Porto they are usually invited to join the brotherhood. Danish Prince Henri is also a member, and the only royal confrade who not only is royalty but also a winegrower with his own castle.

The Confraria also works to serve Port Wine, and every single speach and ceremony is concluded by the Chanceler's solemn salute: "For Port Wine, for the Confraria, for the Confrades."

Confraria Vintage

When a minimum of 10 shippers have declared Vintage Port, the Confraria declares its own Confraria Vintage (the first one was the vintage year of 1982). The Confrades walk in procession through Porto. At Cais da Ribeira they go aboard an old Barco Rabelo and sail to the opposite bank of Douro to the Vila Nova de Gaia where they go to a Lodge and supervise that every Port house who has declared vintage contributes 25 litres of the Vintage Port to the Confraria's 600-litre pipe - a genuine mixed wine! Later the wine is bottled, and the bottles are laid in the Confraria's cellar for later use on special occasions.

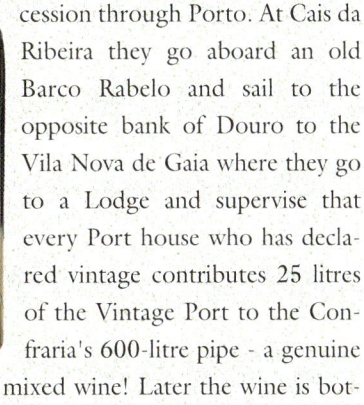

Tulipa Porto

In 1996, Port Wine had its own tulip, which year after year will blossom and remind the happy owners that a new flowering season has started for both the vines and the tulips. The tulip is (naturally) Dutch and has the Confraria as godmother. Its Latin name is Tulipa Porto.

At the important Port Wine Festival at Sølyst in Copenhagen in 1988, the Confraria was represented by many of its members to spread the interest of good Port. The Chanceler, Fernando Nicolau de Almeida, is surrounded by (from the left): Rogério Leandro da Silva, Robin Reid, Manuel Poças Pintão, José Ramos-Pinto Rosas, Dirk van der Niepoort, Mario Saraiva Pinto, Julio Valente, Fátima Burmester, Michael Symington, and Arnold Gilbert. Peter M. Cobb, David Sandeman, David Delaforce and Bruce Guimaraens also participated. (Photo: BJS)

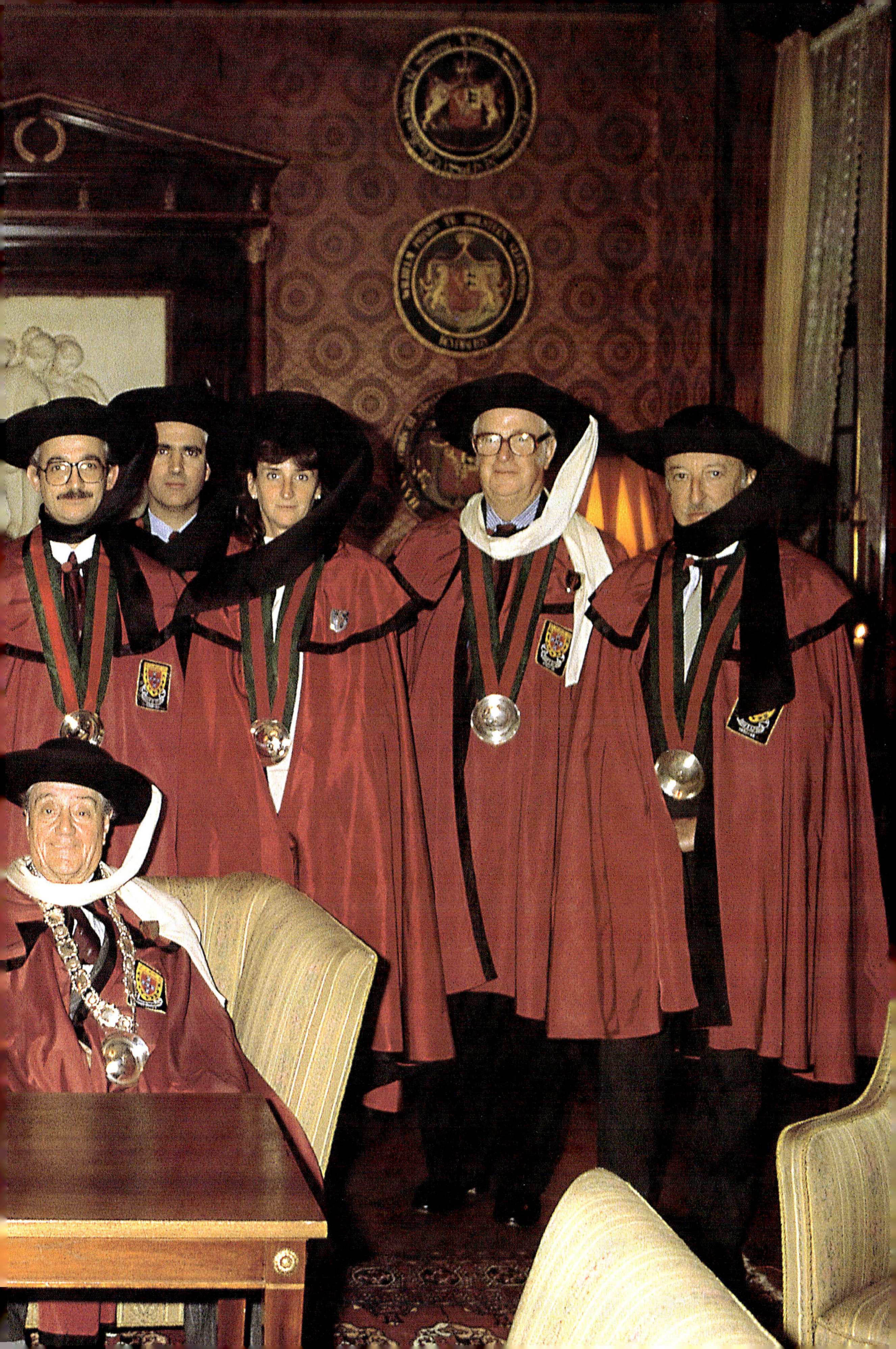

The annual boat race

In the 200 years from the time that the Douro became navigable and until the railway crossed the Spanish border in the 1880'ies, Port Wine was shipped from the Douro Valley to Vila Nova de Gaia in the long, slim flat-bottomed *barcos rabelos*. But then the railway took over, and later the damn made it impossible to sail on the Douro. In the 1950'ies more than 300 barcos rabelos were still in use, but in 1964 the last barco rabelo sailed on its long, slow journey to Vila de Gaia.

Therefore, this beautiful, once so indispensable boat, which may even descend from the Vikings, has since 1983 been celebrated in an annual boat-race on the Douro river by Porto and Gaia. The race, which takes place on the 24th June every year, on the day of São João, for he his the patron of Porto. The organizers of this event are the Confrario and the Port Institute.

This is really an important day. It starts with the rigging of the boats and ends with an impressive firework. But the race is naturally the most important event, and even though the important thing is to participate, it is fun to win - otherwise you will never hear the end of it!

The boats of the 15-20 participants start at the mouth of the Atlantic Sea (Foz do Douro), and at the starting signal from the accompanying boat they sail towards Porto with the Dom Luis I bridge as the finish line. A trip covering a couple of kilometers, but it is the wind not the crew who decides how fast to sail, and sometimes even in which direction to sail!

The winning team is duly celebrated with silver plated tastewines and after the race all the boat crews are invited to a sailer's lunch and a couple of "salute's" for São João and Port Wine.

The festive barcos rabelos sail approx. 2 kilometres from the mouth of the Douro to the Dom Luis I bridge. Only one thing is at stake: honour! (Photo: HO)

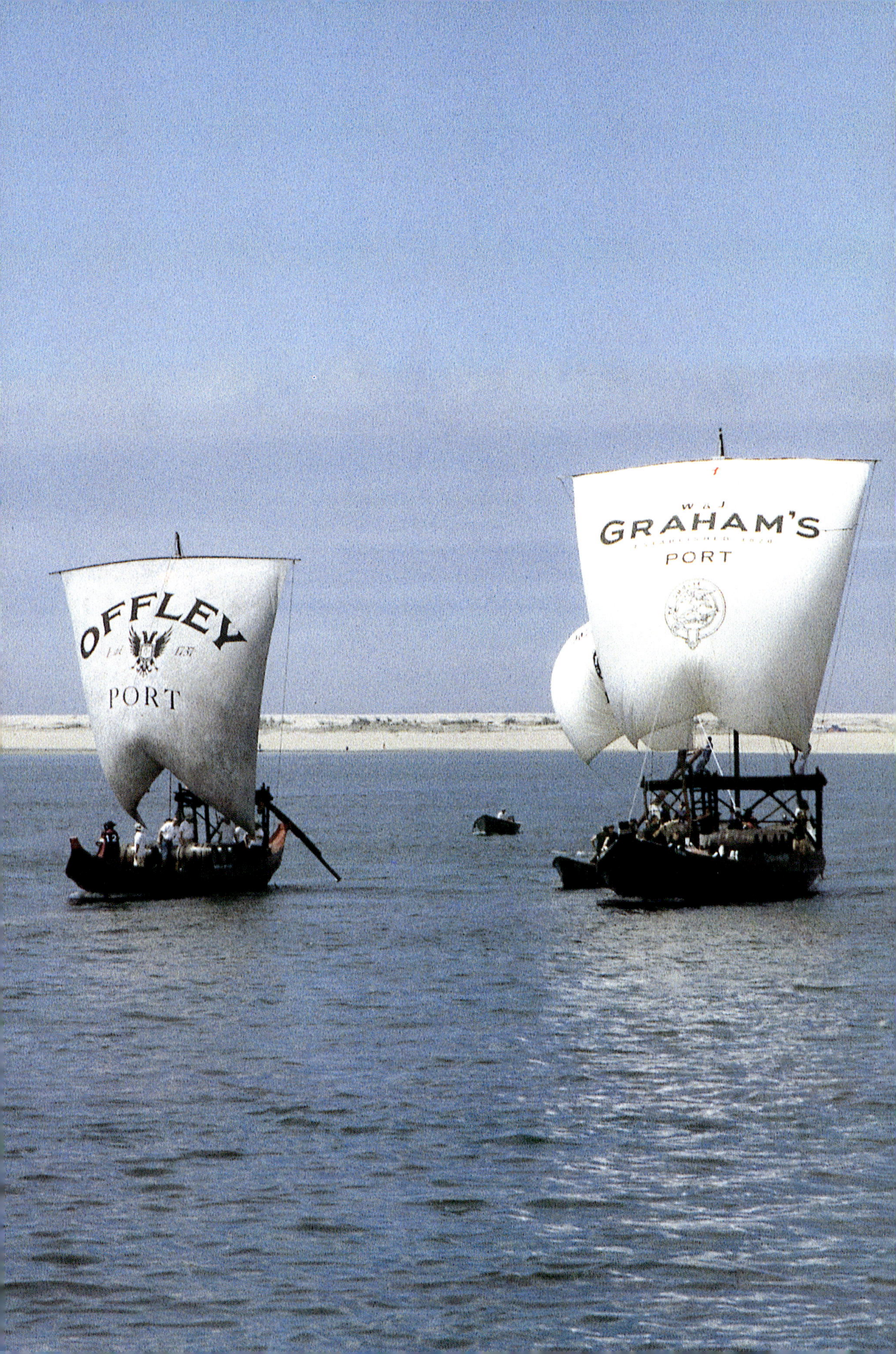
OFFLEY
PORT
GRAHAM'S
PORT

Even a Prince must follow the Confraria's strict rules and travel to Canossa, in this case Porto, to be admitted as a member. On the top photo, Danish Prince Henrik is recommended in 1996 at the castle of Fredensborg, Denmark, by Chanceler António Filipe, assisted by Almoxarife, Robin Reid, who invites the Prince to Porto to be admitted as a member of the Confraria at the usual ceremony taking place at the Portuguese Stock Exchange. (Photo: Klaus Moeller). In the summer of 1998, Prince Henrik arrives in manner to Porto to be formally admitted to the Confraria (bottom).

Factory House

Already in the beginning of the 17th Century, Portuguese tradesmen, under the supervision of the state, had established feitorias in foreign countries, especially in Africa. The word became the English word factory, and the idea spread to the British trade colonies abroad, first to India, since to Portugal, where such factories are known in Lisbon, Porto and Viano do Castelo around year 1700.

The purpose of these factories was to solve problems together, to support each other as much as possible with regard to competition and to meet at parties and to join in church activities together. The basis of the latter was a fixed duty on all merchandise which was exported to England. This duty was handled by the state and went to paying the priest, doctors and hospital personnel so that the British wine merchants of Porto could have both church services, vaccinations, and a hospital stay - all in English.

In the years 1786-90, the present Factory House was built in Rua Nova dos Inglezes (now Rua Infante D. Henrique), a pompous building, which has ever since been the meeting place of the British in the Port Wine business in Porto. But it is more than just that. It is an institution, which was duly celebrated at a British Ball on its 200-year Centennial in June 1990. The house is a genuine, irreplacable small piece of England in Portugal's next to largest city, a sad salute from Queen Victoria and the grand old times of the British Empire and at the same time a meeting place, lodge, church and consulate. At first, the house was not known as the Factory Housefor a long time, for when Napoleon invaded Portugal in 1810, the word Factory was forbidden, and the British trade colony had to change its name to the British Association. When the house was re-opened in 1811, it was naturally under its original name, and to celebrate the event and the expulsion of the French troops, the 11 members gathered for a luncheon on the 11th November 1811, at 11 a.m.

Everything was back to normal, except for the fact that the silverware and the archives had been stolen by the French. As a curio, which could only be English, the 11 members of the Factory House met again on the 11 November 1911 for a luncheon at 11 a.m. to taste 11 wines!

Outside of the Factory House, you can still see the long wooden benches, upon which the bearers could rest whilst their lords and masters were at a luncheon or at a meeting. On the first floor there are reading and writing rooms where guests are registered. You are only welcome here upon a formal, written invitation or accompanied by a member. There is also a library from 1817 with more than 15,000 books.

On the second floor, you will find the famous Supper Room (with room for up to 40 guests) as well as the Dessert Room. These rooms are identical for the practical reason that the dining gentlemen - women were not allowed in the more serious rooms of these premises - after a digested dinner would continue their discussions with a couple of decanters of Port in the Dessert Room, whilst the Supper Room was being tidied up. They sat at the same places as they had sat in the Supper Room. Elementary and pure elitism!

These rooms which hold so many memories and in which all British in the Port Wine business of some significance have dined, are open once a week, on Wednesdays, for lunch when members meet and discuss small and big issues, especially relating to Port Wine. They meet in the Drawing Room for a glass of white Port or Fino Sherry, a remnant from the good old days of Sherry, where many Port Wine producers also made Sherry (Sandeman, Croft, Osborne, etc.), and when everybody has arrived, the doors of the Dining Room are opened, and they proceed to having lunch with the relevant wines to accompany every course of the meal. While they are having their lunch, decanters are set on the table, first Tawny Port, called the "mouthwash", and then the clou of the day: decanters of Vintage Port which the clever noses now have to explore. The selected wines are from the House's private collection of Vintage Ports, to which all members contribute with 20 cases, every time a Vintage is declared. It only improves a member's image if he can guess the correct vintage year and/or the correct producer. I, myself, have been so fortunate as to have been invited to a lunch three times - a very special experience I will never forget!

Four Portuguese monarchs have visited the Factory House, but the culmination point is no doubt the visit of Queen Elizabeth II in 1957, and one could only imagine the diplomatic conflicts that would emerge, should she be denied access to the famous gentlemen's lunch! The major events of the year are the Christmas Ball and the annual dinner, which, as many other events, are organized by the Treasurer. Not a task to be envied, and members do take turns. Today, there are 12 members of the Factory House, all British, most of whom have roots to 18th and 19th Century Porto. The Factory House in Porto is the last of its

Rua do Inglezes, the street of the English, with groups of noble Englishmen in front of the Factory House, seen and painted by Baron Forrester in 1834.

kind. All other British institutes of this kind around the world have disappeared, have been demolished, closed down or taken over for other purposes.

Only the male directors of the British-owned Port Houses may participate in the meetings at the Factory House, all British of course, apart from a couple of statistically irritating exceptions, as for example Reginal Cobb (Cockburn's) who as a fate of destiny was born with a New Zealand citizenship, or, and even worse, as when the Cockburn's took on a Portuguese managing director, the present head of the Port Wine brotherhood, António Filipe! Otherwise, all is as it always has been, and nobody would dare touch the Wednesday Luncheon at the Factory House in Porto, or even the house itself, which naturally had a well-deserved book dedicated to it a long time ago: John Delaforce's "The Factory House at Oporto" from 1983, Christie's Wine Publications.

Instituto do Vinho do Porto (IVP)

The Port Wine Institute was established by decree of 10 April 1933 on the order of prime minister Salazar (see page 62). The main objective was to establish a supreme Port Wine body for all issues relating to quality and (to a certain degree) to the quantity of Port Wine produced.

This was a versatile task. According to the wording of the Act, the IVP was in charge of supervising the quality of the produced Port Wine, guaranteeing its origins and issuing a seal of guarantee, functioning as arbitrator or umpire in disputes with the farmers and the wine merchants, seeing to technical development and financial growth, and spreading the knowledge of Port via PR activities and information. After the first three years of a rather shaky start, the IVP was re-organized by decree of 22 August 1936. The provisions from 1936 are the same provisions in force today, apart from a new section on a tasting jury under the IVP, which was introduced by decree of 21 October 1959.

Today, the IVP is an independent body under the Ministry of Agriculture and Fishery. The president, who is the supreme authority, is elected politically, whilst the IVP managers are employed as an administrative body. Under the long conflict with the Casa do Douro concerning the sale of the shares of the Real Companhia Velha, the management structure proved to be unfavourable, as the board of directors were not legally competent in a period of around three years.

The then president Leopoldo Mourão was replaced by recognized researcher and professor at the University of Vila Real, Dr. Fernando Bianchi de Aguiar, in September 1991, and then things settled down in the IVP. Bianchi was replaced by Armando Pimentel in 1998, but he died only shortly afterwards, and it was not until April 1999 that Jorge Monteiro was appointed new president.

In 1993, the IVP finally got a branch in Régua after many years of planning, but it has no controlling function at all. All samples to the IVP still have to be forwarded to Porto, also from the producers exporting direct from the Douro Valley.

Every year on the 31st December the IVP makes a statement on the basis of every single producer's stock and purchases as to how much Port Wine may be sold in the following year, as every importer may only sell max. 1/3 of his stock.

As a more outgoing activity, the IVP runs two port wine bodegas (Solar de Vinho do Porto), one situated in Lisbon, the other in Porto (Please see page 375).

World's best wine control

The IVP's domicile is an old bank, which is situated 100 metres from Porto's stock exchange, and this is where all Port Wine is estimated and controlled. In principle, every lot of Port Wine which is to be sold/exported and which therefore requires a seal of guarantee, must be approved by the IVP through laboratory analyses and sensory (blind) tasting. Among its many functions, this is IVP's most important task.

Let us follow a sample on its way through the system at IVP:

1) The Port Wine producer's car drives into the yard, and he hands over samples of all his Port Wines to the reception desk. Here, every bottle is equipped with a black spring lever stopper and is wrapped in black plastic so that the bottle remains anonymous. Then the computer registers the bottle under the next order number with an indication of the producer's code number and wine type. A label with the order number is placed on the bottle and thus becomes the identification of the bottle at all times. Any decoding may only take place via the reception computer with regard to any information on the submitting producer.

2) The black bottles are now carried up to the first floor. The organizer of the tasting pours the content in numbered glasses and inserts all the necessary information in the tasting room's computers with regard to wine type. The tasters in the tasting room can only see this information on the computer monitors. They know nothing of the producer, and they see neither bottles nor names. The only information available on the computer monitor is the wine type (for example Vintage Port, 1999, or 10-years Tawny).

3) The six tasters (all from the IVP), consisting usually of 5 tasters and one co-ordinator - taste each their wines in small separate rooms. They usually seek information on the computer monitor and read what type of wine is in all the glasses and mark them accordingly as the computer automatically asks them for each wine's typicity, colour, clearness, aroma, taste, etc. The taster can adjust the light at desk making it white, red, green, or the

like, to exclude the colour during the tasting phase. The tasters do not speak to each other, they only consult the computer, to which they have access only upon entering a password. As the tasters answer the computer questions, the co-ordinator collects their comments and prepares the results on the monitor.

4) If the evaluations vary to such an extent that the wine should be rejected, the producer may resend it for a new approval at a later stage as many times as he wishes. But the stock of the wine in question will be blocked, until the producer accepts that the wine is rejected. If he does, he may only use the wine for mixing with other wines, unless it is diseased and must be discarded. The IVP has information about the size of the producer's stock as well as all relevant dates for the wine and can thus keep a constant eye on the wines.

5) If the producer is not satisfied with the IVP's decision, he may appeal this decision to the only Appellate Body which is the so-called "Council of the Wise", a council consisting of 5 skilled professionals (outside of the IVP). Their decision cannot be appealed.

6) As mentioned, all the Port Wines are thoroughly examined, in principle both in the lab and through an organoleptic test, and both tests must be passed for the Port Wine to obtain its seal of guarantee. Physically, it is impossible to check every single bottle, so what one does is take a representative number of each lot.

7) All approved Port Wines must be assigned a seal of guarantee, but can then proudly boast of having been through the world's most severe wine control.

The best Vintages of the century

The Port Institute's most ambitious project till this day was the presentation of the "Vintages of the Century" which was held on the premises of the old Stock Exchange in Porto on Saturday, 12 June 1999. 62 wine journalists from all over the world were invited to participate and to taste a total of 277 Vintage Ports from a total of 47 producers and ranging from the year 1900 til 1995. Sandeman alone was represented by 45 vintages.

Early in the morning, the employees at the Port Institute started to burn the necks of the oldest bottles. Then one of the oenologists or one of the directors was given the great responsibility of decanting the wines. When all the decanted wines stood handsomely in one line, the wine journalists just had to sit down in their designated seats and make their "orders" on the appropriate list. Young sommelieres and waiters then brough one glass after another on silver trays. This was my impression from this incredible tasting that was carried out to such perfection that they even serves the wines on silver trays!

All the gilted-edged vintage years were represented: 1900 (Ferreira, Sandeman), 1904 and 1908, 1912, 1917, 1920, 1924, 1927, the legendary 1931 (Cálem, Ramos-Pinto, Sandeman), the historic war vintage year of the war 1945, and post-war valuable 1955, 1960, 1963, 1966, and 1970, and naturally the "young generations" of 1982/3, 1985, 1991/92 and 1994/5.

It was hard work from the early morning with the decantation of the many precious drops. Here Cockburn's António Graça carefully decanting a Martínez Vintage 1987. (Photo: HO)

Four of the famous tasting's curios are ready to be poured to the excited wine journalists. (Photo: HO)

A. A. Ferreira, Succrs.
OPORTO
VINTAGE 1900
FERREIRA
PORTO
VINTAGE 1904
CALEM
1908
VINTAGE PORT
A. A. Ferreira, Succrs.
OPORTO
VINTAGE 1912

Port Wine clubs

Denmark is the land of wine clubs! This is confirmed with great enthusiasm by the Danish Port Wine drinkers. In 1998, a Port Wine club was founded in the town of Horsens, which means that there are now four active wine clubs in Denmark, apart from the many "private get-togethers" that indulge in Port Wine.

The club in Copenhagen on the island of Zealand was the first one. "Portvinsklubben af 1981" (The Port Wine club of 1981) is the oldest and the largest club with approx. 75 members with an everlasting waiting list. The club has tastings, arranges travels to the land of Port and establishes itself at any major Port Wine event in Denmark. The club also has its own wine cellar, and a pecial "hardcore" group of Swedish Port Wine drinkers cross the Baltic Sea faithfully every time a bottle of Port is set forth on the meeting table.

"Fynske Portvinsklub af 13. September 1989" (The Portwine club of Funen of 13 September 1989) was Denmark's next Port Wine club, situated on the island of Funen. It has just celebrated its 10th anniversary with a mini Port Wine festival in the capital of Odense, home town of H.C. Andersen. There is also a Port Wine club in Jutland, the Danish peninsula, and then the new club in the town of Horsens, also situated on the peninsula.

The Danish Port Wine clubs are also an oasis for the lovers of Port Wine from Sweden. The Port Wine club of 1981, situated in Copenhagen, has a special group of "hardcore" members from the southern part of Sweden who are seen here at the annual Port Wine festival at the old Danish Stock Exchange in Copenhagen. (Photo: BJS)

Chapter 9

VINTAGE YEARS

Vintage Years

Terroir, micro climate, rain and thunder, hail and frost, drought and heat waves as well as mildew, botrytis, oidium, and coulure - and at the end a winemaker: this is the codex of the vintage year. As the landscape of Port Wine is vast in number of kilometres, nature does play at least a minor role in the annual harvest for a producer of Port Wine than it does for a château in Bordeaux or a quinta in Vinho Verde where all the grapes grow within a limited area and are thus much more vulnerable. As Port Wine is a dessert wine where the subtleties of table wine can be corrected by adding alcohol, technically there would be nothing wrong in making a Vintage Port every year. The wines would not have the same stable quality every year, but then neither do the wines from Bordeaux' classified châteaux. However, there is no tradition of making Vintage Port that often - and upon that issue the producers agree with the market. So the versatile nature and the changing weather does play a role after all, and the good and not so good vintage years are confronted with one other. However, it is long proven that a bad worksman can make a bad Port Wine even in a good year, and that a true artist can make great wines in bad years, so there is no point in giving a vintage points or stars. It is far more important to know the name of the producer. Anyway, the potential of each vintage is indicated by the number of producers who have declared Vintage (the number in parenthesis following the number of the year!)

DRINKABLE: These are only guidelines and are not to be considered directives. Please note that especially in the fine vintage years there may be good Ports and not so good Ports. An unimpressive Vintage 1994 will probably be drinkable in year 2005, whilst one of the vintage classics may not be until 60 - 70 years later! In the following I have put a focus on the Vintages which are still drinkable.

1900

Civil war in South Africa and uprise in China. But in the Douro Valley life goes on as usual. The harvest is late this year - in certain places not before October, but the quality is high as are quantities. The wine is light both in taste and colour - and stays that way for almost a century. Sandeman's is the best I have tasted.
DRINKABLE: Now.

1904

This vintage year was met with some scepticism, for there was not enough brandy, which was then replaced by German spirits of wine! But the vintage became much better than its reputation. The weather was perfect with lots of sunshine and just enough rain in the middle of September. Unofficially, 25 shippers declared Vintage. Even the best wines are gone now - or almost.
DRINKABLE: Now.

1908

A successful year for the British Port houses with darker and more durable wines than the Vintages 1900 and 1904. Very good yields after a cool winter, a heatwave in spring and in the summer and extreme hot weather during harvest. The biggest problem this year was to control fermentation. All 26 shippers declared Vintage, and the best wines are still impressive.
DRINKABLE: Now.

1912

This is the year when everything was perfect and ran smoothly. Both the heat and the rain came as requested and the human efforts consisted in picking the grapes mid September and avoiding a quick fermentation. A bit of rain in September did more harm than good. This Vintage became a classic, the first one after Portugal had declared itself a Republic. 25 shippers declared Vintage.
DRINKABLE: Now - 2012.

1917

While the First World War was raging, the summer was long overdue, as was the sun. When it did appear, it stayed too long. Harvest in late October but it yielded a historical Vintage with small quantities. Due to the war and to the national crisis in general, only 15 shippers declared Vintage.
DRINKABLE: Now.

1920

The spring of this year was nice and cool and very humid, but the summer was stifling hot with drought in July-August, and the late harvest gave healthy, fine grapes. 23 shippers declared Vintage, even though the harvest yielded somewhat small quantities. Graham's is the best I have tasted.
DRINKABLE: Now.

1927

Both Lisbon and Porto both suffered during the revolution against the regime, but life went on. The summer was rather chilly, and a bit of rain in September delayed the harvest, but the grapes had enough sun in the beginning of October and were picked under ideal conditions. The first perfect vintage since 1912 and for some the vintage was a bit lighter thanVintage 1912. According to Bruce Guimaraens it is "one of the greatest Vintages ever declared!". A total of 30 shippers declared Vintage, the largest number ever. When the wine was bottled and sold in 1929, the depression had paralyzed the European economies. Most British wine merchants had to give up selling the expensive wines and used it for mixtures instead!
DRINKABLE: Now - 2010

1931

When the grapes were picked in September, the Bank of England abolished the possibility of cash in gold and devaluated the pound. Countries like Denmark and Portugal were forced to do the same. When the wine was bottled and sold in 1933, Hitler had gained power, and trouble swept through Europe. Also, the Port Wine market still offered the fine Vintage 1927, and it did not help this Vintage that the few shippers who declared it called it outstanding. The weather was as unreliable as were the predictions of selling wine. The summer was chilly, August and September rainy, but towards the end of September the sun returned, and the grapes were actually picked in sunny weather. Noval and Naconal, 1931, have become legendary as the most expensive Port Wines ever sold.
DRINKABLE: Now - 2010.

When the Port Institute (IVP) was established in 1933, this was the first time a body was responsible for the quality for Port Wine and who accurately noted the number of producers who declared Vintage Port. The source of the figures in parentheses is therefore IVP's.

1935 (15)

As 12 shippers had declared Vintage 1934, only 15 shippers chose to declare Vintage Port 1935, which was actually considered to be of a higher quality. The vintage years 1934/35 were the first examples of "double vintages" as were 1982/83 and 1991/92. This vintage was the last of the great vintages before the Second World War with spring frost and summer rain, but luckily with ideal conditions for harvesting in September. Sandeman is still very excellent.
DRINKABLE: Now - 2015.

1945 (8)

The war was over, but this did not change everyday life in the Douro Valley. Portugal had not participated in the war, and there was enough man power available when the grapes had to be picked. But during the summer up until harvest, the shippers had been frowning a lot, for once because the weather was nearly too good. The winter gave the smallest rainfall ever recorded. The flowering season started too soon. The summer was long, hot and very dry, and there was a lot of sun and heat all during the harvest season which started early September. Not all producers produced the same quality of wines, but in 1945 nobody could blame it on nature. Taylor's is said to be monumental, and other houses produced fantastic wines too, which will keep well into the next century. This Vintage is a big, classic Vintage with small quantities. Due to restrictions, a total of only 20,000 pipes was allowed, and the climate saw to it that not even this number was achieved.
DRINKABLE: Now - 2030.

1948 (3)

Bruce Guimaraens writes in his book "Vintage Port": "1948 was, like 1945, a true classic. These wines are enormous and will last and last". This vintage will be remembered as the vintage year when the weather was so hot with frequent temperatures of 45°C that the grapes became overripe and fermentation was hard to control. But when things went well, they went very well. The harvest yielded small quantitites, also due to the hot weather and drought, but it is a good Vintage Port.
DRINKABLE: Now - 2020.

1952 (4)

A cool month of May and hail in June and July reduced harvest yields even before the first grape had ripened. But then the weather turned out quite nicely with a lot of sun but without getting too hot. Fermentation was slow, as many grapes were simply not ripe enough. The vintage was small in quantity.
DRINKABLE: Now.

1954 (3)

A dry, cold winter was followed by a dry, cold spring. The flowering was late and the harvest was late. However, quality was better than feared and some good cool nights helped the patient producers. Concentrated wines for the few lucky/clever producers.
DRINKABLE: Now.

1955 (23)

This is the best vintage since 1945 both with regard to temperature and quality. Spring was nice and dry with a heatwave in April/May, the summer was long and warm, and August which is so important for the maturing grapes, was dry and very hot. The grapes would have benefited from a bit of rain, but the only rain they encountered was a small shower on 22 September so many chose to pick their grapes shortly after - but patience paid off. More rain came on 2 and 3 October followed by dry weather. Most of the grapes were perfect, concentrated, some maybe too hot and wild, but the best grapes yielded classical, durable wines which will keep for years to come.
DRINKABLE: Now - 2010.

1956 (none)

1957 (11)
First a dull spring, then a nearly just as dull summer. A small harvest of a dubious quality with a lot of unripe grapes. A vintage for the Tawny houses - and for Taylor's!
DRINKABLE: Now.

1958 (21)
The weather was very homogeneous in both winter and summer, mostly cool and wet, but autumn finally brought a bit of hot weather, and the harvest was carried out under perfect conditions. A bit too late for most producers for anything else than light wines. Some producers had problems in selling the excellent Vintage 1955, and did not declare.
DRINKABLE: Now.

1959 (1)
A rainy winter and a cold spring. July and August brought hot weather, but more rain in September resulted in rot. As the rain seemed never to stop, many started to harvest too soon and this resulted in a lot of unripe grapes. Sandeman declared.
DRINKABLE: Now.

1960 (41)
The spring this year was mild and sunny, and the summer very hot and dry. Many would have loved a spot of rain, but it never came, and this is why the picking season already started in early September, before the grapes would become overripe, so when the rain finally did come on 23 and 24 September, the picking season was nearly over. Many had problems with the heat during fermentation, but the the best wines are really excellent. They do not, however, have the same durability as vintage 1963, which has always overshadowed the vintage year of 1960. According to the Symington family, Dow's Vintage 1960 is the first Vintage Port to be sold on the market both as original bottling and on pipes.
DRINKABLE: NOW - 2010.

1961 (4)
This great Bordeaux year was not a good year for Port wine. A terrible thunder rolled over Portugal on 2 July, and the remaining grapes had a slow development and reluctantly. But both Taylor's and Fonseca declared Vintage.
DRINKABLE: Now.

1962 (6)
The winter rain which caused a major flood in Pinhão and surroundings on 3 January was followed by mild and dry weather until mid September. The flowering season came almost two weeks' later than usual, but the harvest season started early than usual due to the hot and dry summer. The short maturation time gave unripe grapes with a low sugar content, and even though the grapes were nice and free from rot and disease, they could only give light wines. But the harvest yielded large quantities.
DRINKABLE: Now.

1963 (44)
This Vintage was a classic even as a mere seedling. The spring of this year was actually rather cool and wet with only a bit of sun under the important phase of flowering, but then the hot weather started in July and August - some did not see a drop of rain from Whitsun till 10 September - and in September the weather was exceptionally good with an intense heat and nearly no rain. The grapes developed perfectly - and willingly - and then came the miracle: the many days of massive heat had not overripened the grapes, for the Douro Valley's cool nights saved them and also stopped early fermentation. Late maturation, the latest since 1946, but this did not matter. Neither did the fact that the harvest only started in October. Everything went well for the producers, even market prices were good. They agreed quite early that this vintage would keep well into the next century, and so would the best wines, but the next to best wines have matured quite rapidly in recent years.
DRINKABLE: Now - 2040

1964 (10)

After the fantastic Vintage year of 1963 only a few producers wanted another miracle. And luckily, the weather was not too good. Taylor's, Fonseca, and Noval were among the 10 producers to declare Vintage and produced nice, light wines.
DRINKABLE: Now.

1965 (10)

The shortage of rain after a dry winter gave the grapes a low concentration of fruit. The harvest was wet, but even though this might be uncomfortable for the pickers, it was quite an advantage for the grapes! They did, however, lack concentration and gave yet another vintage year of light wines.
DRINKABLE: Now.

1966 (29)

Just as 1960 surpassed 1963, it also surpassed 1966. But excellent wines were produced this year with Fonseca as unique producer. The wet winter was replaced by a very long, dry summer with low yields but a high quality. Temperatures in August reached a maximum of 45°C twice. The grapes were small and intense with a good balance. The harvest started around 21 September with a few rainfalls during the picking season, which only gave freshness and no problems. Fermentation was slow, the colour fine. The best wines of this vintage year have proven to be more durable than one could have expected for many years. "It will be surprising indeed, if 1966 does not prove to be an excellent Vintage for Ports", Michael Symington wrote in his diary at Quinta do Bomfim in October 1966. And he turned out to be right.
DRINKABLE: Now - 2020.

1967 (16)

This vintage year was a joke for most producers, but there were some nice, light wines to be found, somewhat lighter than the Vintages 1963 and 1966. Spring was cold, the flowering season late, slow and not at all satisfactory. The summer gave heat, but also thunder, and the picking had to be stopped several times. The best wines of this vintage year are nice and light.
DRINKABLE: Now.

1968 (3)

The winter had been quite mild with a few scattered rain showers. June was exceptionally hot, but then the weather turned capricious, and the harvest season lasted from late September and until mid October. The cool nights gave a good concentration, but the quality of the grapes varied a great deal. Only Taylor's, Fonseca, and Sandeman declared Vintage.
DRINKABLE: Now.

1969 (1)

Only Taylor's (Vargellas) declared Vintage Port.
DRINKABLE: Now.

1970 (41)

After a few, very small vintage years, finally a fantastic season. It started with a cold and wet winter, but this gave good water reserves, and the spring was mild and dry, the summer hot, so nobody could wish for better weather. A thunder storm on 26 - 28 August cleared the air, and a few rain showers on the first few days of September were luckily good for the crop too, so when the harvest season started on 21 September with temperatures of up to 35°C, the weather conditions were perfect for picking. From 26 September till 6 October the weather was ideal with hot days and cool nights. Fermentation was a quick, hot process, but with a promising colour. Everything was promising and ended perfectly - but still this vintage year has never been considered as fine as Vintage 1963. Its homogeneous, high quality has only been recognized in recent years. The best wines of this vintage year will keep for years to come. This is the last of the great Vintages which was bottled outside of Gaia.
DRINKABLE: Now - 2030.

1971 (None)

1972 (6)

This vintage was declared in the light of the devastating synthetic alcohol scandal (see page 70f), and this is the only reason why it was more neglected than it actually deserved to be. A cold and wet winter with three months' of intensive rain (December - February) was followed by a dry spring and an even drier hot summer. But then the weather became unstable. Small quantities of grapes, which everyone knew meant a small harvest. The sugar content was also lower than usual and some of the grapes had rot. The grapes had to be firmly trodden upon to get fermentation going, and a lot of hard work had to be put in to get the wines sold - even though the harvest had been quite small.
DRINKABLE: Now.

1973 (None)

1974 (11)

In June, 1/3 of the rain fall, which should have given water reserves in October-March, fell. Now there was enough water, just at the wrong time! August-October had no rain nor heat. The harvest began in early October and gave grapes which were healthy but lacked sugar concentration, so it would never be a great vintage year. It was, however, a vintage year for the Tawny producers - and for Taylor's and Fonseca.
DRINKABLE: Now.

1975 (34)

It was a hot year in 1975. Both nature and politics exploded - it was year 1 after the carnation coup, and nobody knew whether or not the entire port wine industry would be nationalized. Furthermore, the shippers needed a Vintage Port, so if for nothing else then for this reason nearly all declared vintage. The winter had been long and wet, but September, which started out with dreadful rainfalls, rapidly changed to hot, sunny weather and justified some of the enthusiasm, but not as much as the fact that there was a shortage of Vintage Port on the market. The market welcomed this Vintage Port nicely, even though prices went up because the Casa do Douro doubled the price of Aguardente. But unfortunately for 1975, it was declared at the same time that 1977 was born. The late harvest yielded wines which are not durable for much longer.
DRINKABLE: Now - 2005.

1976 (3)

The extremely dry winter was followed by an extremely hot summer, which in some places resulted in a drought so that streams and sources dried out. The soil was exhausted, several old vines died from lack of water, and the producers did not even have water to spare for tears. Finally the rain did come in late August and lasted till September so that the grapes were thrown into the lagar with rot and botrytis. Only 3 declared: Taylor's, Fonseca and Messias.
DRINKABLE: Now

1977 (33)

Just like 1963, this vintage year was a classic from its birth, but the enthusiasm was more forced, because the need of a great vintage was enormous. The weather was troublesome, so it was actually a paradox that all things ended well. It was the first real wet winter for several years. The spring was cold in the Douro, with scattered local frosty spells and hail storms, and the summer was rather chilly, so everything was delayed this year. But just as everybody was starting to dread the awful autumn rain, an Indian summer came with a heat wave, which lasted far into September, and it did not start to rain until 7 October, so long after the picking season had started (on 28 September), most of the grapes were big and healthy, and the remaining grapes were picked in late October and were dry and healthy. The producers feared the worst, but they

had no reason to. As Bruce Guimaraens once said: "The year 1977 taught us that the most important thing is not whether we get the right amount of rain and sun, because the weather has always been so unpredictable. Juicy, potent wines with long-lasting durability. Small harvest, high quality. And this was the year that Cockburn's did not declare
DRINKABLE: Now - 2060.

1978 (27)

The weather was unreliable. And so were the wines. Spring was unstable, summer was unstable, flowering was slow and not too good. But from July and until the picking season there was no rain of any significance. This gave low yields, and the warm month of September resulted in mature grapes and full wines which in many cases lack elegance. Quinta do Infantado produced the first estate-bottled SQVP.
DRINKABLE: Now - 2010.

1979 (13)

The winter was wet with endless and heavy rainfalls in October 78 - March 79, but spring was perfect with a perfect fructification, followed by a hot sumer. Everything looking promising, but the rain came on 16 September and resulted in a much larger harvest, but a much lower quality of grapes. The picking season started one week later, and the good weather returned with dry weather and sun. After this, everything went by the book, but the grapes never obtained the desired concentration. This vintage year would have been more appreciated, if it had not followed 1978 and 1977. Only a few Tawny houses declared Vintage.
DRINKABLE: Now - 2010.

1980 (31)

This vintage year followed a couple of shaky vintage years and followed three years after the very durable 1977, so it received mixed reviews. However, it has improved over time, and just as underestimated it was, just as drinkable it is now. The winter was one of the driest winters ever measured with no winter rain for the vines to absorb during the long summer. Spring was cool with rain and sleet, the flowering season was delayed, but the weather in July and August and until mid September was very good. But then the rain came on 19 and 20 September and was replaced by a heatwave when the picking season started on 29 September. In spite of all the problems, the grapes were healthy with a nice sugar content. The heat resulted in a short fermentation process, bu the grapes had a good colour and aroma so a lot of decent wines were produced. However with the inflation in Portugal, the opening prices were so high that the wines were difficult to sell, and on top of all that, Casa do Douro doubled the price of aguardente - just as they had done in 1975! Graham's is my personal favourite. A lot of the wines are drinkable now!
DRINKABLE: Now - 2010.

1981 (1)

Exceptionally hot year with an average temperatures in June-August of 24.7°C and high humidity. Only one producer declared Vintage: Quinta do Infantado.

1982 (39)

A dry winter was followed by a mild spring and a fairly hot summer. It rained a bit in May-June during the flowering season, but otherwise it was nice weather with average temperatures. The producers agreed quite early that the harvest would be a small one, but quite reasonable with regard to quality, and that the grapes would develop so that they would give delicious, sweet, but hardly pompous, wines. Robin Reed (Croft's) expected quite a lot from this vintage already in 1985, and contrary to many critics he also believed in 1990 that the vintage would be quite durable, for it may not have a substantial and truculent tannin, but it had a very nice structure and a good balance. At Quinta do Noval, Cristiano van Zeller compared 1982

with 1966 and 1970 at an early stage, because the harvest after the start of the picking season on 20 September had gone very well. Especially after the 1983's had been bottled, it was proclaimed that 1982 matured more rapidly than the 1983's. Maybe, maybe not. It seems to vary from producer to producer. This is one of the most versatile vintage years, I have ever experienced.
DRINKABLE: Now - 2030.

1983 (36)
From the first bottle there was good opportunity to make comparisons between 1982 and 1983. Once again, the winter was dry, very dry indeed, and cold with snow in Pinhão on 11 February for the first time in 20 years. And it was followed by a cool and rather humid spring, which did not seem promising. On the contrary, there was too much coulure. But then June and July looked promising, August was disappointing, however, but then again a very hot September and October meant that the grapes were harvested in perfect condition. Maturation was more than perfect, seen from a classical point of view, compared to 1982, for the development was slower than in 1983 due to the chilly weather, and there was nice hot weather before and during the picking season without the grapes scorching. The harvest started late, around 1 October. The Syminton's were enthusiastic for the rigid and good aroma, but Taylor's noted that the day temperatures in September were 5°C higher than usual so that the grapes ripened perfectly and the harvest was completed in ideal weather. This vintage was from its birth very promising with quantities of 20 - 25 % less than in 1982. All in all, it seems as if the 1983's are developing slower than the 1982's.
DRINKABLE: Now - 2040.

1984 (15)
After three winters in a row with a shortage of water, the rain finally came - and it kept on raining with lots of water in the last months of 1983 and the first months of 1984. Late in the spring, development was behind, and the weather was cool and dull. But late in the summer and in the beginning of autumn the sun came out resulting in hot weather and a heatwave, which continued till the last grapes had been harvested. A three-day period of water-spouts in the middle of the harvest season put back development once again and reduced concentration and sugar content, but the hot weather returned, and the harvest was completed under perfect weather conditions. But the exceptionally wet winter had put its mark on this Vintage which is very uneven quality-wise.
DRINKABLE: Now - 2020.

1985 (46)
"Not a vintage year, but good quinta Ports," William Warre wrote in "Decanter" in January 1986, a bit premature, for one year later 46 shippers had declared Vintage. The weather had been quite capricious. The winter of 1984-85 was rugged in the Douro Valley with a cold and wet climate and the largest rainfall since 1979. I remember that January was cold with rare temperatures below 0°C, for I had only brought summer clothes with me and caught a chill - like the grapes. Fructification was two weeks behind schedule. April was cold and wet, but the rain was good for the flowering in May. In the beginning of June, the hot weather came and stayed with a heatwave in July and August. The vines suffered, but now the huge rainfall in the winter was an advantage. Furthermore, a bit of thunder rain in the beginning of September came to an advantage for once, for it had not rained for three months (!), so the prospects were quite promising. Then the hot weather returned, and the picking season was carried out in sunny and dry weather - without any rot, quite early in the season, but the producers had not dared wait any longer, for the grapes looked as if they were drying out. Harvest began already in Mid September. Some feared that the grapes had become too Douro-baked, but most of the grapes were mature and concentrated. In the third week of October the

harvest ended and was great in both quality and quantity. "Never can the grapes have been gathered under better weather conditions than this 1985 vintage", Michael Symington wrote in his diary at Quinta do Bomfim. The opening prices were 30 - 40% higher than for 1983, especially due to the thirsty American market.
DRINKABLE: Now - 2050.

1986 (5)

This was a very dry summer, but from the second week of September a lot of rain fell. The grapes were small and dry but suddenly grew big and full. Later the weather improved but kept on changing, and some of the heat from the rainy weather in September resulted in rot and some concern. Some of the producers started picking already in late September (from the 22nd) in a bit of a panic and under difficult conditions, by fear of more rain. This resulted in grapes of a low sugar content, and the heat in the beginning of October proved that they should have waited. But it is always easy to be wise after the event. The producers who were patient harvested many fine grapes in Upper Douro.
DRINKABLE: Now - 2010.

1987 (30)

Again this year, a long and dry summer, with a heatwave and no rain in June, July and August after a long reasonably dry spring with a perfect flowering season in a very mild month of May. But this year the rain did not arrive until the third week of September. The biggest difference is that in 1986 the harvest season had not started yet when the rain arrived, but it had in 1987. Many bone-dry grapes were picked and stored in rainy and muddy weather. The rain resulted in many producers picking in a panic, but actually the good weather did return, again in favour of the patient ones who now had to deal with a very hot fermentation process. But all in all, in spite of the difficult conditions, there was good possibility of decent, although not first-class, wines. This was already obvious at an early stage. "A typical LBV vintage" was the unanimous agreement from all in Gaia, but 30 producers declared Vintage.
DRINKABLE: Now - 2025.

1988 (5)

An odd season with showers and local hail storms in April and May, a bad flowering season and 5-6 times more rain than usual for June. But then the weather changed. Dry but never really hot in July-August, but very hot in September, which helped the damage already done, except for the damage from the hail. I remember temperatures of above 40°C in September! "I have never experienced a worse summer in Portugal," Michael Symington wrote. And even before the last grapes had been picked, there were rumours that it would be one of the rare "minus years" in which the allowed quantities of Port Wine would not be even be obtained (140,000 pipes) and in which production would be 25 - 30% lower than usual. On the global market Port Wine set a new record in 1988 by around 9,000,000 cases!
DRINKABLE: Now - 2015.

1989 (19)

The winter was dry, the spring mild with a spot of rain, and the summer early and warm. Local problems of hail and coulure in June, a heatwave in July, and scattered showers in August, but some quintas that had perfect weather all the way through. The producers realized that yields would be limited, so some of them started their picking season already in the last week of August, and a major producer as Sandeman started as early as on 4 September which was unheard of. A bit more rain in the second week of September did good for the remaining grapes which obtained a better sugar balance, so several producers actually produced a better Port Wine from the grapes which were picked late than of the best grapes which were picked early!
DRINKABLE: Now - 2020.

1990 (10)

This season was odd, heterogeneous - "patchy", as Michael Symington called it in March 1991. The winter was exceptionally wet, so wet that 80% of this year's total rainfall fell in only a few weeks. It recreated the water balance in the soil after the drought in 1989. But it was from one extreme to the other, and a veritable heatwave in July and August damaged the grapes, locally called queima. The grapes were cooled off by thunder and rain, which saved some of them, but others were scorched. The harvest began in the first days of September, which was very early once again, and the grapes had matured unevenly. Surprisingly many grapes were not sweet enough and contained too much acid. Some said that this was due to duress. The grapes benefited from a bit of rain on 19 and 20 September and were a bonus for the producers who had waited. They harvested many big and well-balanced grapes, but when they were about to celebrate it, the Casa do Douro informed them that they had "unfortuntely" bought too little aguardente, so some of the producers could whistle for it and had to make tablewine from the grapes that could have produced an excellent Port.

DRINKABLE: 2000 - 2020.

1991 (41)

A certain impatience was spreading among the producers. It had now been six years since the last really good vintage year, and both producers and the market really needed a good vintage year. But things did not go as desired. The winter was cool and wet, which was necessary to build up a reserve. The spring was dry and hot, and the summer even hotter, which was OK. But on 11 and 12 September heavy rain fell in and around Pinhão and again in the weekend of 21 and 22 September. Miraculously all this rain was beneficial and did not cause any damage, for the soil had dried out in several places, and the rain thus ensured the acid balance in the grapes. The drought had reduced quantities by 25 - 30%, but the quality was quite excellent, and combined with a bit of patience, 41 shippers could declare Vintage (as in 1970) only surpassed by 1963. Dow's who had not declared for six years - the biggest vacuum since the Second World War - declared this year.

DRINKABLE: 2005 - 2030.

1992 (21)

After an exceptionally dry winter and a very dry spring, both grapes and producers were yearning for rain. When it did come in August, the grapes were in great need of "first aid", as Peter Cobb put it. The late summer was warmer drier than average, so again the grapes yearned for rain. And it did came. The picking season had merely started around 23-24 September when it became cloudy and the cool weather arrived. It rained cats and dogs for the next 3-4 weeks, but again in scattered areas. Some producers had to heat the must to get fermentation going, whilst others had very nice grapes and were very satisfied with the sugar content. This was a vintage year with a significant content of tannin and fruit and the vintage year that Taylor's and Fonseca declared after only having produced SQVP in 1991. And Cálem declared it for the 11th year in a row!

DRINKABLE: 2005 - 2030.

1993 (1)

All in all a hopeless year when everything went wrong and when only Quinta da Romaneira declared Vintage. It had been a long, hard and wet winter. It rained more or less from April till June, and by then prospects were dull. A bit of sun in July and August did not save much, and September was capricious, cool and humid. The harvest season started late, and the producers who dared wait a bit longer, were only rewarded by more rain. Even the happy pickers had difficulty in smiling. Yields were 50 - 60% lower compared to the year before.

DRINKABLE: 2005 - 2010.

1994 (46)

But the good times soon returned. The winter rain improved the water balance, but things did not go according to plan as it continued to rain in April and May. I visited the Douro Valley that spring, wearing my raincoat every day. The flowering season was irregular, and the grapes did not mature as they were supposed to. But then one of the rare, wonderfully perfect summers came, which is not too warm, but just warm enough, and not too wet, but with just enough rain. When I visited the Douro again in September, spirits were high, even though the producers knew that the harvest would not be big this year. The slow maturation process gave the grapes a good concentration, and the rainfall ensured the acid balance, so prospects were suddenly quite good. But once again patience proved to be a virtue. The producers who had learned their lesson in 1993 started their picking season quite early, which resulted in medium Port Wines, but the producers who were patient and waited till late September harvested grapes with a very good sugar content, and they also had dry weather in their picking season. American hysteria (see page 87) made prices soar.
DRINKABLE: 2010 - 2070.

1995 (42)

The mild spring suddenly changed around 20 April with a drastic fall in temperatures, in some places even with frost. Then a mild month of May with scattered showers arrived followed by a unreliable June with both rain, cold weather and hail, which caused great damage by late June. Even though the first days of July were cloudy, the sun returned and gave four weeks of warm weather - and drought. Especially Tinta Barroca were experiencing hard times, and again the harvest season would be uneven and unreliable. Some producers chose to start their picking season early to save the grapes, but also this vintage year gave the best wines to the producers who chose to wait and to the producers who had water in the soil from the spring rain.

When I visited Cálem's Quinta da Foz, the first lagar was full as early as on 26 August, and the sugar content was very good. Some producers estimate this vintage year as being as successful as Vintage 1994.
DRINKABLE: 2010 - 2060.

1996 (26)

Heavy rainfall in the winter period resulted in great damage but also hope for the dry soil to be soaked. It did not, however, and spring was dry with no rain until just before harvest. But then it rained a lot, many producers had full grapes but with an uneven quality. Most of the producers used their yields for LBV or SQVP, Noval made Nacional.
DRINKABLE: 2010 - 2050.

1997 (still uncertain)

February, March, and April had exceptionally hot and dry weather in the north of Portugal, which caused an early flowering, scorching and uneven maturation, but all depending on microclimate and geography. After this somewhat tough start, the rest of the season was more or less ideal. The hot weather continued until well into September, and the picking season started mid September under perfect conditions. The grapes were perfect too in many places, but there were not many of them. The total yield was approx. 20% lower than usual, but the quality was high as predicted. The best wines matured at a slower rate than the 1994's but were more fruity. The vintage year had in Johnny Graham's words "a steel girder", i.e. a good tannin structure matching the fruitiness. It will develop slowly but steadily. The Vintage was declared by many producers in 1999.

1998 (still uncertain)

Changing and capricious weather with a harvest giving small yields. The slight hopes were washed away with the rain that fell in the first days of the harvest. This Vintage will be declared more out of necessity than out of desire.

Chapter 10

THE PLEASURES OF PORT

The pleasures of Port

Maturation

People have always said that there is a fine balance between being a Port Wine drinker and a Port Wine drunk. The typical image of a Port Wine drinker is an elderly sober gentleman with podagra and a dominant blue nose spending most of his time in his rocking chair staring at his bottles which have been lying for years in a dark cellar.

Well, those times are long gone, for the young generation has done justice to Port Wine, and most dark cellars are history.

Actually, Port Wine does not belong in cellars at all, as most Port Wines do not improve from maturing in cellars - on the contrary:

Only Vintage Port and unfiltered Late Bottled Vintage Port improve from maturation. All other Port Wines are by definition drinkable as soon as they are bottled.

What should you store?

White Port: Not suitable for maturation. (With the exception of a few houses, who mature their white Port Wine in casks, that can be kept for several years and develop as Sherries do).

Port without quality: Not suitable for maturation.

Crusted Port: Not suitable for maturation.

10-years, 20-years, 30-years, and over 40-years Tawnies: Not suitable for maturation.

Colheitas: Not suitable for maturation.

Filtered LBV: Not suitable for maturation.

Unfiltered LBV: Suitable for maturation in bottles, but a LBV should not be more than 15-20 years old.

Vintage Port: Suitable for maturation / requires maturation, depending on vintage year and producer. Impossible to set any time limit. Some SQVP's should not be more than 10 years - but great Vintage Ports in good vintage years can keep for 100 years.

THE PLEASURES OF PORT

Storage

- No Port improves from standing in a vertical position compared to lying down.
- Vintage Ports and unfiltered LBV's should always be laid down
- Just as some wines, Port should be kept in a cool and dark place
- The temperature should always be kept as constant as possible

Temperatures:
Changing temperatures result in the wine maturing quicker and more unevenly than stable temperatures which are either too low or too high in relation to the ideal temperature.

Dépôt:
Regardless of the temperature, all Port will deposit dregs during maturation, which in Port language is called dépôt. The more irregular the temperature, the more dépôt is deposited.

Preparation

A bottle of Port, which is expected to deposit dregs, should be placed in a vertical position for a day or so before opening it. This way, the dépôt slowly falls to the bottom - where it belongs - and the wine is easier to decant.

The older the Port, the longer it takes for the dregs to deposit on the bottom of the bottle. My own routine is as follows:

15-20-year-old Vintage Port in a vertical position for min. 1 day.
20-40-year-old Vintage Port in a vertical position for min. 2 days
40-80-year-old Vintage Port in a vertical position for min. 3 days

The cork wagon is taking a break just outside of Pinhão. Portugal is the world's largest producer of cork, of which a good part goes to the wine industry. A cork is still the best way to close a bottle, which must mature for many years, but even the best cork has its limits. Under ideal conditions, a cork in a Vintage Port can last for 20-25 years at the most.

Up with the cork

When the bottle has been in a vertical position for as long as it takes the dregs to deposit, it is uncorked. During this process, the bottle should be shaken the least possible and kept in as vertical a position as possible - otherwise the dregs will mix with the wine again.

The cork:
Even the best cork in a Vintage Port cannot be expected to stay resilient and compact for more than 20-25 years - even under the best conditions of maturation. After that many years, the bottom of the cork will have broadened, whilst the top will have shrunk so much that the cork cannot be pulled out with a traditional cork screw without breaking and resulting in pieces of cork in the Port.

The cork of this Vintage Port 1970 has been in the bottle for 29 years, and the top of the cork is dry and cylindrical and the bottom of the cork is wet and fan-shaped. Even the special Port Wine cork screw with its long screw thread cannot do the trick. The cork cannot be pulled out in one piece, but must be removed with Port Wine pincers.

There is no tradition of re-corking Vintage Port, not even with the producers in Gaia. There are, however, special Port Wine cork screws with a long screw thread and a pointed top which may often save an old cork, but if you are unlucky and uncork the bottle ending up with a cork in two pieces you will have to filter the content. Therefore:

A Vintage Port which is more than 25 years old should be opened with a pair of pincers.

1. The grip of the pincers is heated over an open fire (fireplace or grill).

2. When it is hot enough, squeeze the pincers around the bottleneck below the cork!

The Port Wine pincers have been in the grill or the fireplace for 10-15 minutes and are burning hot. The pincers are squeezed around the bottleneck below the cork but above the surface of the wine. They are squeezed tightly around the bottleneck for 30-60 seconds, depending on the temperature of the pincers and of the quality of the bottle.

3. When the bottle is heated, the bottleneck is sprinkled or swabbed with cold water which then gives a slight crack.

4. Now, you can lift off the top part of the bottle containing the cork and pour direct from the "decapitated" bottle.

If the Port Wine pincers are hot enough, and cold water is quickly applied on the bottleneck, there is a neat cut and no risk of glass fragments. The bottle is now ready for decanting.

Nothing happens when you remove the pincers, but when you quickly sprinkle or dab cold water on the bottleneck, it breaks off and the top part (containing the cork) can be removed. The bottle on the photo was not of a high quality so the cut was not completely horizontal - but there were no fragments of glass in the Port Wine!

Decanting Port

All Port with dépôt should be decanted, i.e. the wine is poured into a decanter and the dépôt remains in the bottle.

Which Ports should be decanted?

The age of the Port Wine is of no significance - only when the bottling was carried out.

A Colheita 1920, bottled in 1998, will not have to be decanted in year 2000, for it has not yet deposited dregs in the only two years it has been bottled.

A Vintage Port 1990, which is enjoyed in the year 2000, has matured in its bottle for approx. 8 years and will have to be decanted.

The 29 year old Vintage Port is decanted very carefully through a fine-meshed strainer on the top of the decanter. It will keep back any deposit. Please notice that the Port is decanted by a lady's hand. In Denmark it is absolutely legal for women to drink Port - and even to decant it!

A Port which is drunk more than 5 years after it has been bottled, should be decanted.

However, there is no tradition for decanting old Tawnies/Colheitas - but they should never lie so long that they deposit dregs.

Decanting by hand:
The Port Wine is gently poured from the bottle to a (clean) decanter, preferably in one continuous jet, as the purpose is to separate the wine from the dregs - and not to oxidize the wine.

Sieve or tea bag:
A small-meshed sieve or a tea bag is an excellent aid for decanting wine. But remember to choose tea bags, and especially filtering bags used in making coffee, which have a neutral smell.

If you do not use a sieve nor a tea bag, you should stop pouring before the dépôt reaches the top of the bottleneck. The rest of the Port is then poured through the sieve or the tea bag into a glass - or perhaps into the decanter - if you dare!

The dépôt from a good Vintage Port can be used for gravies.

Decanting by machine:
Even in the Port Wine business there are different opinions about how an old Vintage Port should be treated. Most prefer to hold the bottle in a vertical position and carefully pour, lifting the bottle towards a horizontal position. Others put the bottle in a decanting machine which has an oblique position and fasten the bottle in a horizontal position so that the wine runs out. Then it does not matter if your hand shakes, but there is a greater risk of the dépôt following.

Candles:
In old books about Port you can read that it is important to hold a lit candle under the bottle when you decant (to avoid the dregs). This was relevant in the time of the light bottles. Today, the first bottling of Port Wines is carried out in dark-coloured bottles, so the candlelight has no function anymore.

Resting time:
When a Vintage Port is decanted it should rest in the decanter - uncovered or corked. How long it has to do so depends on the age and sturdiness of the wine. According to Bruce Guimaraens who has produced some of the sturdiest Vintage Ports for Taylor's and Fonseca, a Vintage Port, which is served after dinner, should be decanted at 10 a.m. in the morning and then left to rest in the decanter uncorked. He also prefers to cork the decanter a couple of hours before the wine is served.

Decanter

A decanter is a stoppered bottle, usually of glass, but you can easily decanter into any other bottle or jug and then pour the decanted Port back into its original (rinsed) bottle.
You can find decanters in all kinds of shapes and sizes, especially beautiful, artistically made crystal decanters. The Port Wine Brotherhood has its own decanter with a broad bottom to made it stand solidly on the table (see page 343). This could be a relic from past times when a quite a lot of Port was consumed aboard the British ships.

Temperature

Most people enjoy a glass of Port with a cellar temperature or room temperature. It is merely a matter of preference. A Port should rather be too cold than too warm. Some producers even store their 10-year Tawnies in the fridge.

Glasses

All glass series include a Port Wine glass. None of the ones I know are suitable for Port Wine. They are simply too small. In most cases, the white wine glass of the series is must more suitable.

A Port Wine, especially a good Port Wine, deserves a glass, in which it can expand - much of the pleasure of drinking Port Wine is through inhaling its aroma. This is why I do not like the so-called "tulip glasses". There is simply no room for your nose so that you can take in the aroma of the Port Wine - at least not without your nose getting stuck in the glass!

The glass should rather be too big than too small. If the Port Wine is carefully decanted, there is no reason to used coloured glass either.

Many professional Port Wine drinkers have their personal Port Wine glass - so do I - and for them there are no other rules other than Port Wine tastes better from your own glass.

Never believe Port Wine writers when they declare on behalf of a glassblower that a particular glass (often very expensive) is the only genuine Port Wine glass.

I would rather drink a good Port out of a bad glass than a bad Port out of a good glass!

A Port Wine glass should not be too small and not too narrow at the top. On the photo you can see four glasses of Vintage 1970 poured out of the bottle that was opened and decanted on page 343. To the left a simple and cheap everyday glass. No. 2 from the left is an antique glass with a large practical surface. The third glass is a crystal glass from the series "Prelude", but it is the white wine glass, for glass designers have no sense of Port Wine. Finally to the right, my own private Port Wine glass, a hand-cut crystal glass, which I bought from a second-hand shop in Italy!

PASS THE PORT!!!

The elderly gentleman on the drawing is apparently in good company, but his table companion to his left has probably asked him the question: "Have you ever heard of the Archbishop of Canterbury?" If he hasn't the answer will be: "Well, he came to a bad end. He forgot to pass the Port"! Always pass it to your left, i.e. clockwise, and always with your right hand. Maybe because the right hand is then busy and cannot be up to any monkey business, but most probably because Port in the sailor's language means "on the port side", i.e. the left side.

A third important rule is that you only pour yourself a glass of Port. You take the decanter, which your table companion to the right has passed to you, you pour yourself a glass of Port, and place the decanter in front of your table companion to the left using your right hand. Never pour a glass of Port - even to a lady! If she has ventured into this man's world, she has to follow the rules and pour herself a glass of Port. Some say that they have met well-educated ladies who could not quench their thirst because they could not get themselves to pour their own glass of Port.

Some practical decanters have a round bottom signifying so that they cannot stand on the table. This forces everyone to keep on passing the Port. This solution is, however, quite an expensive one. The informative drawing is from an old ad for Taylor's Port.

Keeping Qualities

The older the Port, the quicker it should be enjoyed. This, at least, is the rule-of-thumb.

How long can Port Wine keep?

Old Vintage:
An old Vintage Port (more than 25 - 30 years) should not be kept longer than until one day after opening. It can keep for several days, but it loses its subtleties and intensity every minute.

Young Vintage:
The younger a Vintage Port / an unfiltered LBV, the longer it can keep in a decanter (corked). But no decanted Port should be kept for more than 3-4 days.

Young Tawny:
A 10-years Tawny and all younger Tawnies usually improve from oxidization. Therefore an 10-years Tawny is often better, or more harmonic, the day after opening the bottle. Young Tawnies can easily be kept in the bottle (corked) for up to one week, but they do not improve. A 10-years Tawny already begins to lose some of its intensity after 3-4 days.

Old Tawny:
A Colheita and an older Tawny of a certain age (20-years, 30-years, and over 40-years) should be enjoyed in max. 2-3 days. Already the day after opening they lose some of their intensity, and especially for old Colheitas, we are not talking about days, but hours.

Food and Port

In consideration of how Port, from a historical point of view, has developed from being a table wine to a dessert wine, it is incredible how traditionally Port is used when it is placed on the table. Even if you ask the producers of Port Wine what they serve with their wine, they all answer: "Tawny with cake, Vintage with cheese". Some of the British producers even go further and say: "Tawny with nut cake, Vintage with Stilton!"

But some of the British producers have also surprised me and served simple menus, as for example fresh strawberries in a chilled LBV at Cockburn's and a Quiche Lorraine with a cold 20-year Tawny at Sandeman's.

But thank heaven: Port Wine is much more versatile than tradition gives it credit for, and especially the young generation of chefs dare challenge the adopted rules of how to serve Port Wine.

Sometimes they may go to extremes and serve a very young Vintage Port to red meat, but this is more to provoke than due to their imagination. And it actually tastes quite good.

However, an endless imagination was found and tradition overruled when we asked a new generation of 10 talented Danish chefs to taste and choose a Port and tell what the taste inspired them to prepare and serve:

Dry White Port

Kurt Kjær Jensen, "Fru Larsen", Langaa:

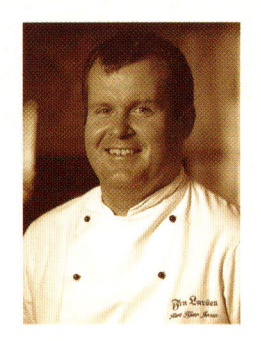

"It says dry aperitif on the label of this Churchill's White Port that has matured in casks for 10 years. This Port Wine has a beautiful golden colour and light nutty taste and should be enjoyed before dinner. But the nutty taste inspired us to prepare a dish made of raw materials which complements the nutty taste".

Lobster with pickled green tomatoes and Rucola salad with walnut oil

(4 persons)

2 lobsters of 400 g each
Lemon juice (1/2 lemon), 2 bay leaves
Sprinkle with dill

Lobster stock:
Shells from the lobsters
2 cloves garlic, 1/2 onion
Olive oil
7 white pepper corns
1 sprig of thyme
1 teaspoon tomato purée
A pinch of paprika
1 litre of water or fish stock

Lobster bisque:
Lobster stock
2 finely chopped shallots
1 dl white wine
1/2 dl Churchill's White Port
50 g cold butter

Sauté:
50 g olives
2-3 bunches Rucola
1 shallot
1/2 dl walnut oil
8 pickled green tomatoes

Place the lobsters in boiling water, add the lemon juice and the bay leaves, and boil the lobsters for 5 minutes over high heat. Put them in cold water. Remove the meat from the shells and set the shells aside.

Lobster stock: Sauté the garlic in olive oil, add onion, white pepper corns and thyme without letting the ingredients take colour.
Add the lobster shells, tomato purée and paprika. Brown thoroughly, add water or fish stock and reduce for 1/2 hour uncovered. Sieve the stock.

Lobster bisque: Sauté the shallots in olive oil, pour in the white wine and white Port Wine, reduce to half. Add the lobster stock and reduce to 1/3. Monté with butter.

Sauté: Chop the shallots and sauté in walnut oil until glazed. Add the Rucola salad and sauté with the olives and pickled tomatoes cut into boats.

Arrange the sauté on soup plates and put pieces of lobster on top. Place the lobster bisque around the edge of the plate. Sprinkle with dill.

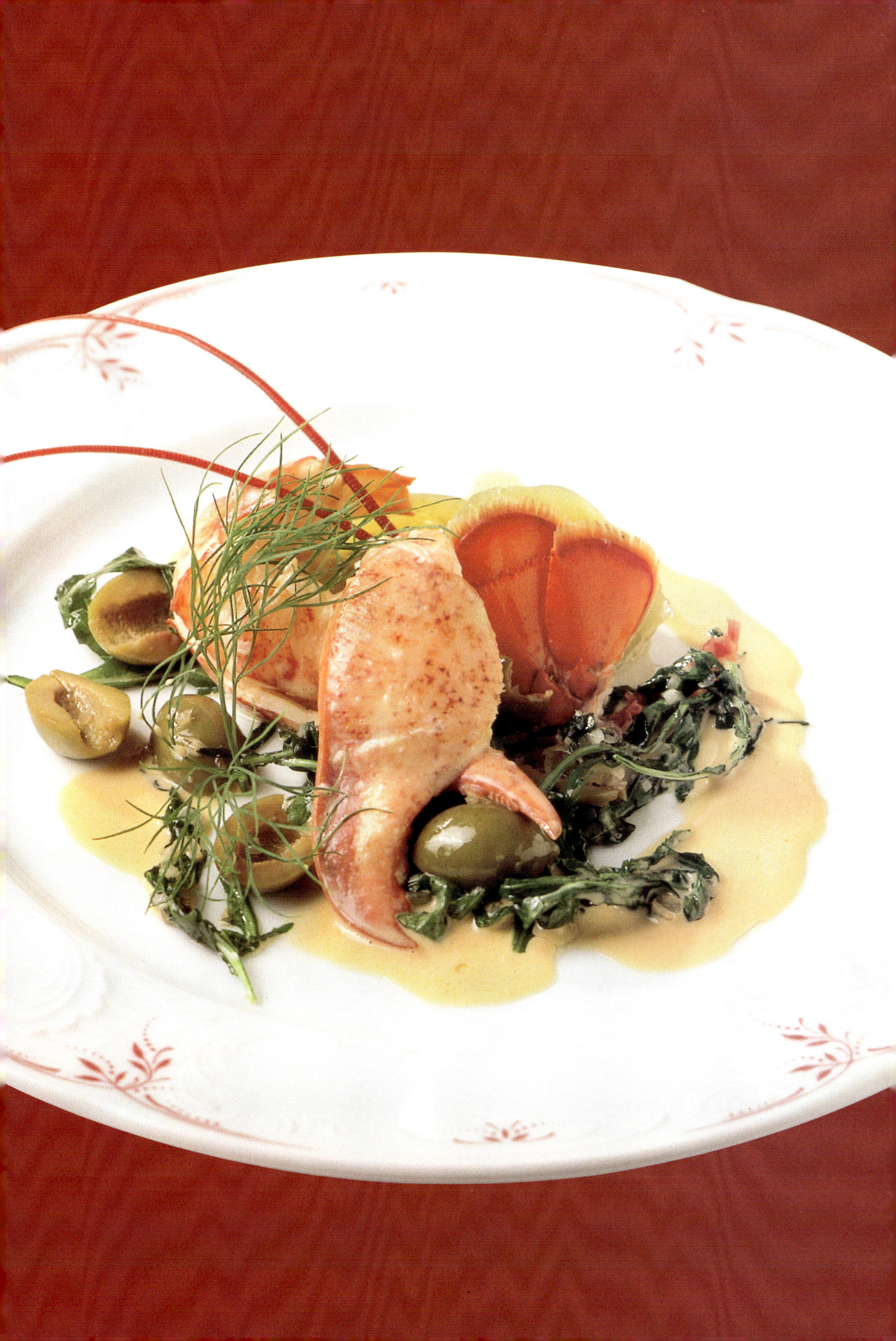

10-years Tawny

Allan Schultz, "Kirk", Copenhagen

"This composition with the southern Spanish blue cheese, Valdeon, made from cow's milk and wrapped and cured in vine leaves, suits this chilled Tawny Port incredibly well. This is a dish, in which Port Wine is an ingredient, but which is also enhanced when it is served slightly chilled to the dish instead of the usual glass of white wine".

Tortellini with Valdeon crème in a Port-tomato fondue

4 persons)

Pasta dough:
6 eggs
1 kg durum wheat flour
2 tablespoons olive oil
1 teaspoon salt
1 egg yolk for sealing

Valdeon crème:
250 g Valdeon blue cheese
2 egg yolks
Salt and pepper

Port-tomato fondue:
20 large, peeled, butterflied shrimps
250 g red cherry tomatoes
250 g yellow cherry tomatoes
1 finely chopped shallot
1 finely chopped garlic
5 tablespoons olive oil
1 dl Tawny Port
Salt and pepper

Pasta dough: Knead all the ingredients together until the dough is flexible and elastic. Let it rest in a plastic bag in the fridge for a couple of hours.

Valdeon crème: Beat the eggs and the cheese to a smooth mix, season with salt and pepper, and fill the creamy substance into a pastry bag.

Run the pasta dough through the pasta machine several times, until it cannot get any thinner. Use something round, e.g. a glass, with a diameter of approx. 8 cm to cut out the dough and make 25 round pasta shapes (the recipe is for min. 20 tortellini). Pipe a little of Valdeon crème onto each pasta shape. Brush the edge of the pasta with the egg yolk, and close the pasta so that it has the shape of a half-moon. Lay the tortellini one by one onto a baking tray, well-sprinkled with flour, cover the baking tray with film, and put it in the fridge.

Port-tomato fondue: Heat 4 tablespoons of olive oil in a sauté pan over high heat. Add the whole, rinsed cherry tomatoes and the shallot and sauté carefully until the ingredients are warmed through. Add Port Wine, salt and pepper and bring to boil. The sauce is ready.

Put 1 teaspoon of salt in a large pot of boiling water and add the 20 tortellini. Let them boil 'al dente' for 5-6 minutes. Take out the tortellini one by one and let them drain. Serve in soup plates with the hot Port-tomato fondue.

Sauté the shrimps in a very hot frying pan with 1 tablespoon of olive oil, garlic, salt and pepper and garnish the tortellini.

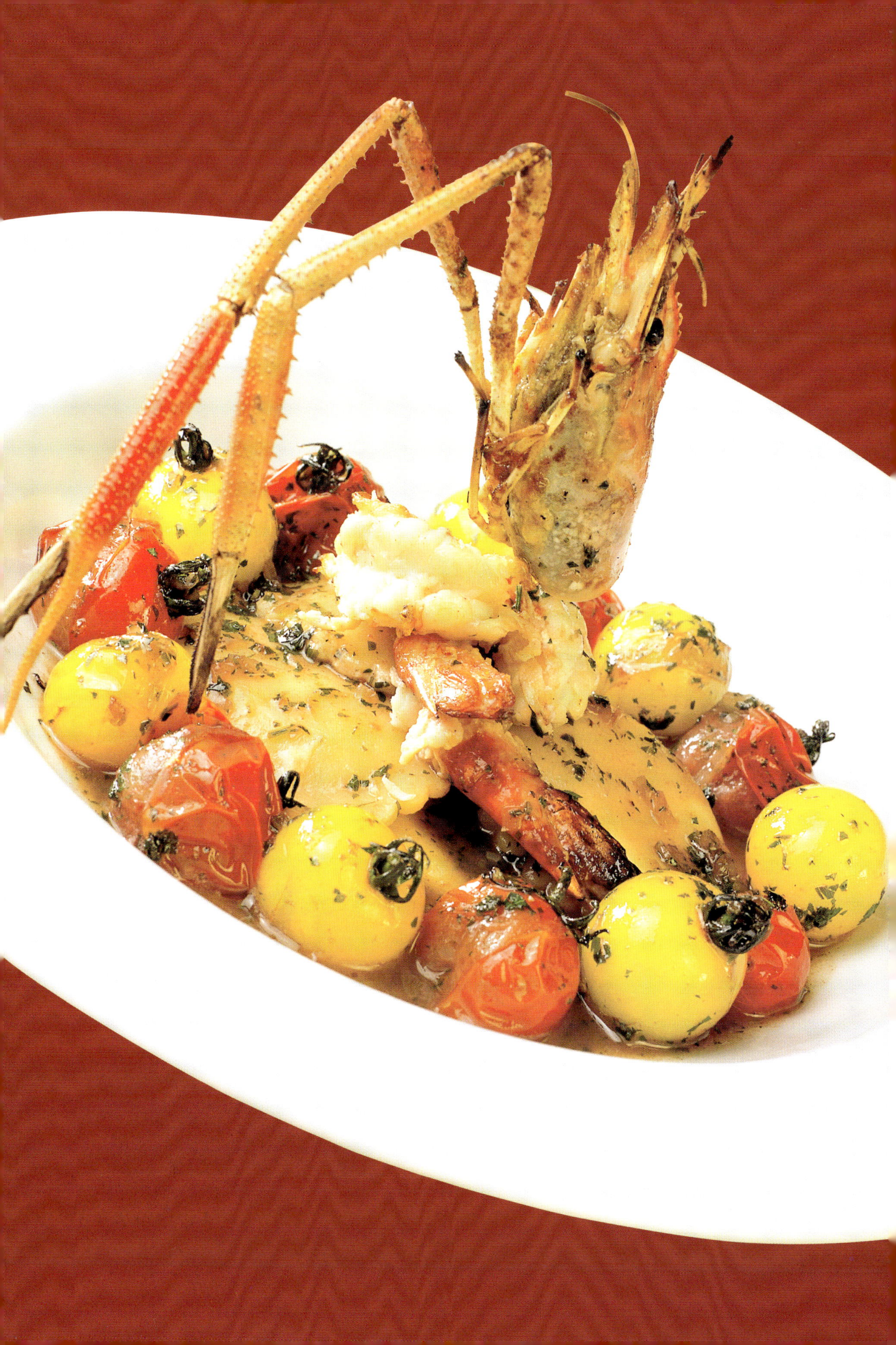

20-years Tawny

Vivi Schou, "Babette", Vordingborg:

"At Babette's we usually aim to create a complexity between the food and the wine. But in this case we have aimed for total harmony so that the solids are united with the liquids: currants, fruit acid, sweetness - and full body".

Sweetbreads in a cream sauce with port wine currants, walnuts, Mutzo apples and celery

((4 persons)

500 g sweetbreads
2 onions
2 leaks
4-5 cloves of garlic
1-2 sprigs of thyme
4-5 sprigs of parsley
10 black pepper corns
1/2 litre of veal stock
50 g currants
3 dl of 20-year Tawny
2 1/2 dl double cream
Salt and pepper

Garnish:
1-2 Mutzo apples
200 g celeriac
100 g fresh walnuts
1-2 sprigs of coriander

Rinse the sweetbreads. Put them in a pot, add just enough cold water to cover them, and give them a quick boil. Pour out the water and remove the large membranes.

Clean and cut the herbs into cubes, sauté them. Put the sweetbreads on top of the herbs, pour in the veal stock, cover and let the sweetbreads braise for approx. 20 minutes over a low heat.

Sauce: Add the currants and 2 dl of Port Wine in a sauce pan and boil until almost all of the Port Wine is reduced. Lift the sweetbreads off of the braised herbs, sieve the stock over the sauce pan, bring to a boil, and season with salt and pepper.

Cut the sweetbreads into cubes of 1 1/2 cm x 1 1/2 cm. Roast them on a non-stick pan, add 1 dl of Port Wine and boil to reduce. Add the double cream, reduce until a creamy taste and consistency is obtained. Season with salt and pepper.

Garnish: Peel and cut the apples and celeriac into small cubes of 1/2 x 1/2 cm. Blanch the walnuts in hot water. Roast first celeriac, then the apples and walnuts in the same pan, and finish by sprinkling with fresh coriander.

Place the sweetbreads together with the creamy sauce, on plates decorated with currants and Port Wine glace and the garnish.

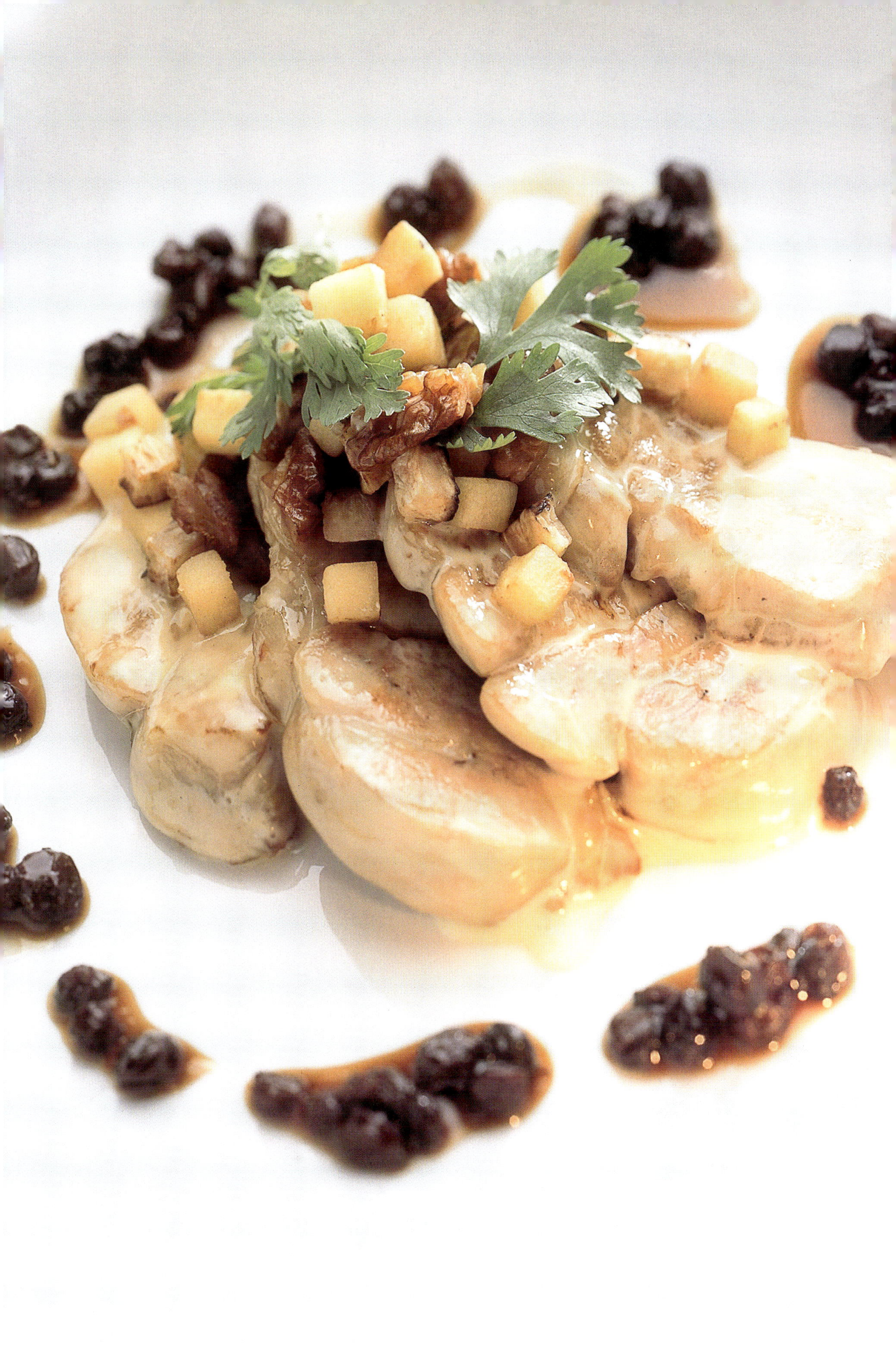

Young Colheita

Lars Kyllesbech, "Nouvelle", Copenhagen

"This young Colheita from Burmester contains a lot of conflicting taste sensations, but it has a good bouquet starting off with pepper and going towards dark, mature fruit, plums, liquorice, leather and tobacco. It fills your mouth to the brim with its fruity taste, and it contains quite a bit of tannin. This is a Port Wine, which urges up for a challenge - and that is what it will get"!

Duck pâté with pepper and Agen prunes

(6-10 persons)

1 kg of duck legs
Thyme
1/2 dl olive oil
Pickled, green pepper corns
200 g Agen prunes
4-5 dl Port Wine
Bay leaves
1 liquorice root
4 eggs
1 litre of cream
Granary bread or similar
Redcurrant jelly

Start preparations at least 3 days ahead of the planned meal:

Cut off the meat from the legs of duck into large chunks, but do not remove the skin. Marinate the meat in half of the Port Wine, add the thyme, a small handful of pickled pepper corns, the liquorice root and the bay leaves. Leave to marinate for at least 24 hours. Put the prunes in the remaining Port Wine.

Take the meat and the prunes out of their marinades, dry off the meat and keep the two ingredients separate.
Brown the meat in very hot olive oil and put aside to cool.
Chop the prunes.

Blend the cooled meat until smooth. Add salt and pepper and the eggs, one by one, followed by the cream and the Port Wine marinade until the mix has a smooth consistency.

Fill a buttered terrine form with the mix (preferably a terrine of chinaware), cover with a lid and place in a Bain Marie, in the oven at 160°C for 50-60 minutes. Let the pâté cool for 5-6 hours. Can keep for several days if refrigerated.
Serve the duck pâté with redcurrant jelly and a good loaf of granary bread.

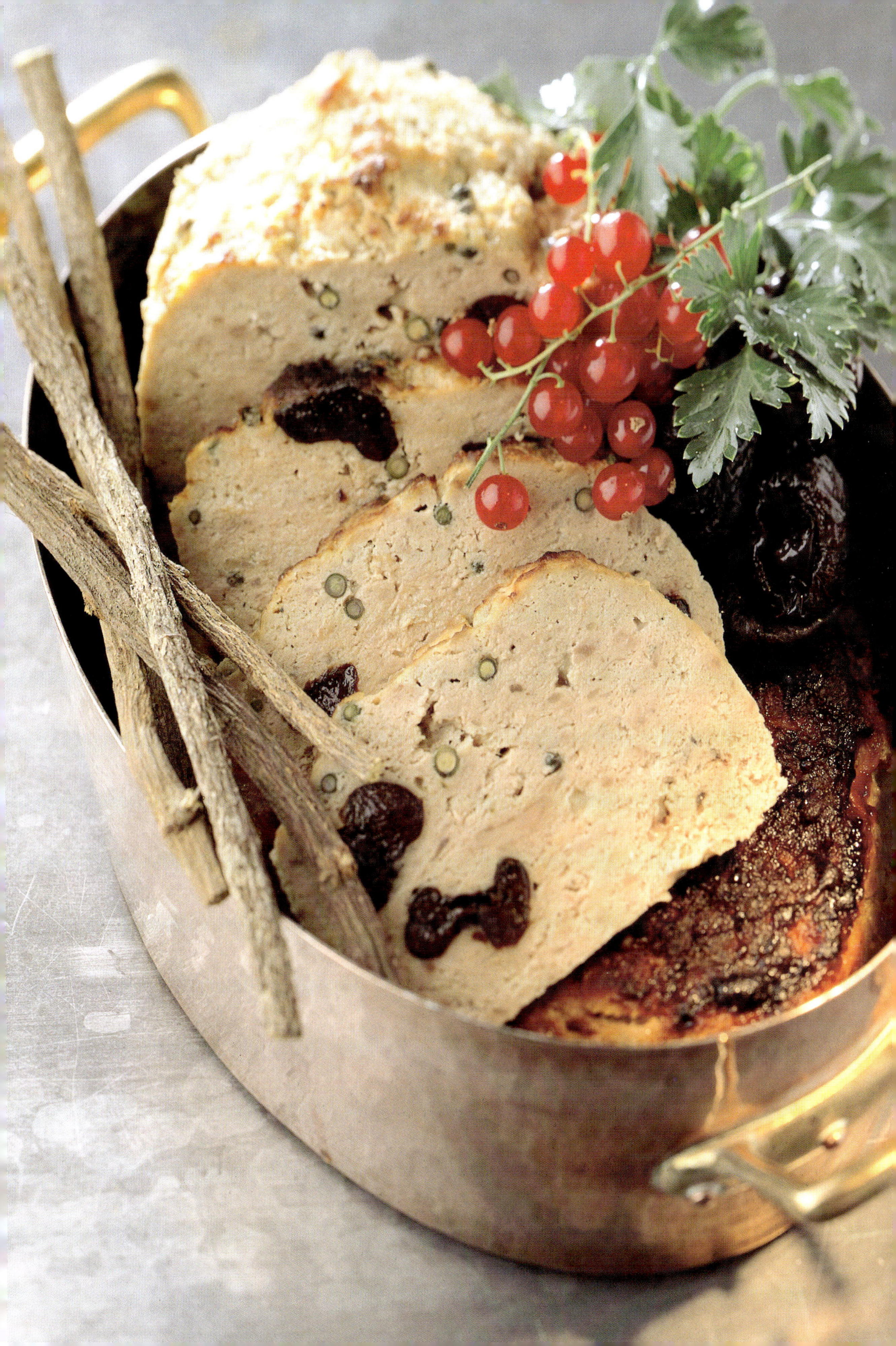

Old Colheita

Frank Lantz, "Krogs Fiskerestaurant", Copenhagen

"Romariz 1963 is a Colheita, which with its intense taste of ripe and concentrated grapes goes well in harmony with the spices and nuts of this dish. Even though this is an old Port Wine, it has no signs of weakness, and it tolerates the challenge".

Roasted pike perch on pear Carpaccio, Panis and Port Wine Bordelaise with Sultanas, walnuts and olives

(5 persons)

1 pike perch of 3-4 kg
Olive oil, extra virgin
Fresh, hard pears
Salt
Freshly ground pepper
Grapeseed oil

Port Wine Bordelaise:
3 dl brown veal stock
3 dl chicken broth boiled with herbs
4 cl Port Wine vinegar (preferably homemade)
100 g fresh walnuts
60 g pitted Nice olives
50 g Sultanas
1 glass of white Port
1 glass of Romariz, 1963, Colheita
Lemon juice

Panis:
4 dl cold water
1 dl apple juice
125 g chick pea flour
1 tablespoon Harissa (hot mixed spices)
1/4 dl olive oil

Marinate the Sultanas in the Romariz Port for one week.

Scale the fish, cut the pike perch into fillets and remove the bones.

Port Wine Bordelaise: Bring the Port Wine vinegar to boil, add white Port, stock and broth. Reduce the sauce to half. Dry-roast the walnuts in a sauté pan, add the olives and the Sultanas in the Port Wine marinade, bring to the boil and add the reduced sauce. Boil until a nice consistency and taste, and finish with a little lemon juice.

Panis: Mix the water, apple juice, chick pea flour, harissa, salt and pepper, and press the mixture through a sieve into a pot. Add the olive oil, and boil while whisking the mixture until it begins to stick to the pot. Roll out the dough on a baking tray greased with olive oil (you may to use greaseproof paper). Set aside the mixture for at least 4 hours. Cut the dough into sticks/panisses and bake them golden in hot oil on a pan just before serving. Sprinkle with salt.

Roast the pike perch, skin side down, in oil until the skin is crispy.

Cut the pears into thin slices and place them on a dinner plate so that they cover the whole plate. Put stripes of the Bordelaise sauce on top of the pears and stripes of olive oil in between. Arrange 3 pieces of panis in the form of a triangle with the pike perch on top. Season with salt and pepper.

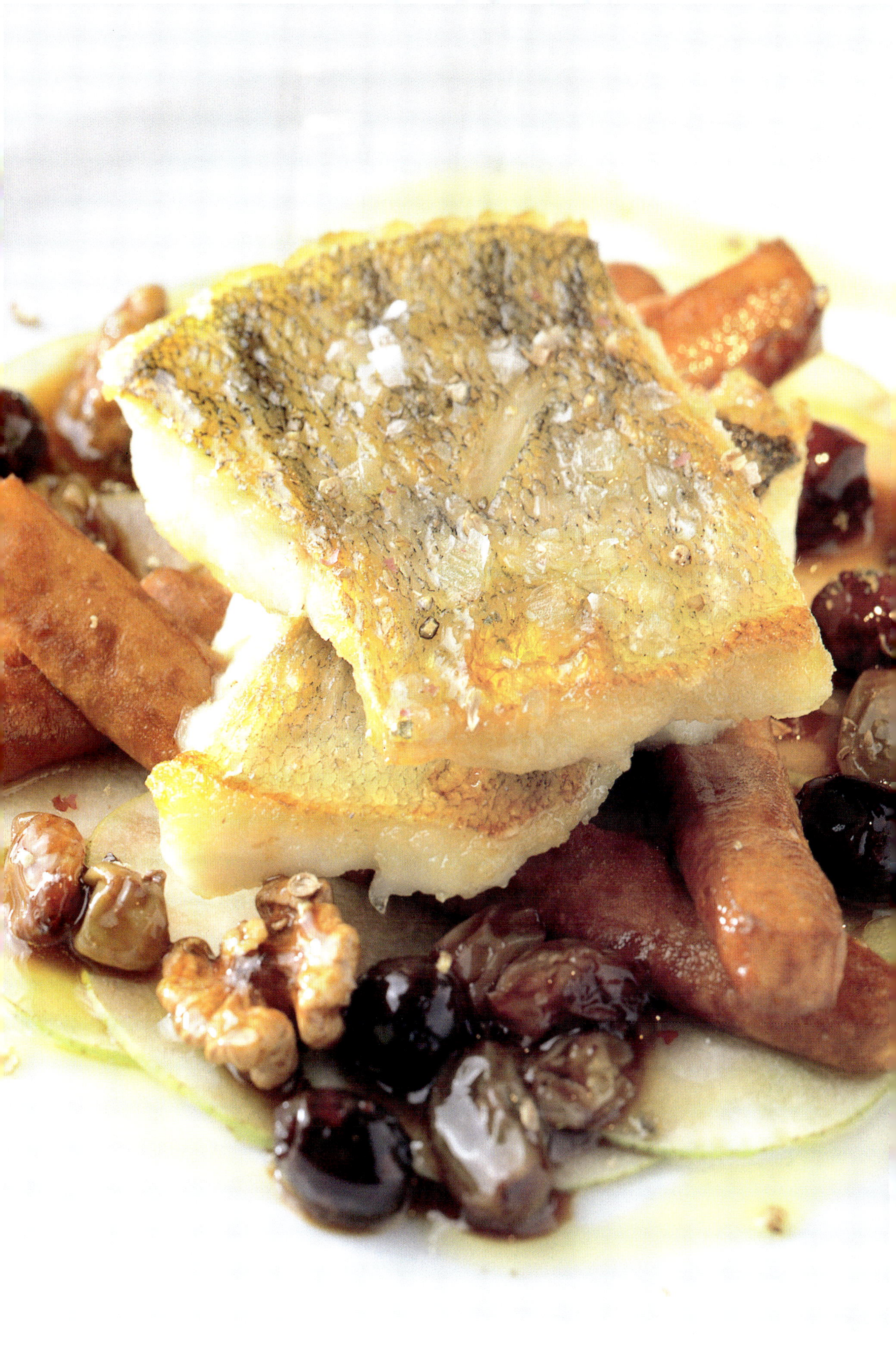

Vintage Character

René Knudsen, "René", Aarhus:

"A Vintage Character such as Fonseca's Bin No. 27 is rich and full-bodied and goes well with this first course because it keeps its rich taste, even after the dish is prepared".

Pigeon in a Port Wine Pot-au-feu

(4 persons)

1/2 litre of light chicken stock
4 young pigeons of 300-400 g
Butter

Sauce:
2 finely chopped shallots
3-4 dl Port, Fonseca Bin No. 27
2 tablespoons olive oil
1 tablespoon chopped, slightly smoked morels
2 blanched, finely chopped, large peaches
Salt and pepper

Garnish:
2 turnips
2 carrots
4 spring onions

Brown the rinsed and cleaned pigeons in butter and add the chicken stock. Braise the pigeons for approx. 20 minutes in the pot covered with a lid.

Sauce: Heat 1 tablespoon of olive oil in a saucepan and sauté the shallots until just softened but not browned. Add the Port and reduce by half. Add the pigeon gravy and boil down to a good, light sauce. Season with the Port Wine. Add salt, pepper and morels to taste. Add the pieces of peach.

Garnish: Cut the vegetables as you please, steam them 'al dente', and tuck them between the pigeons on plates. Pour the sauce over the pigeons.

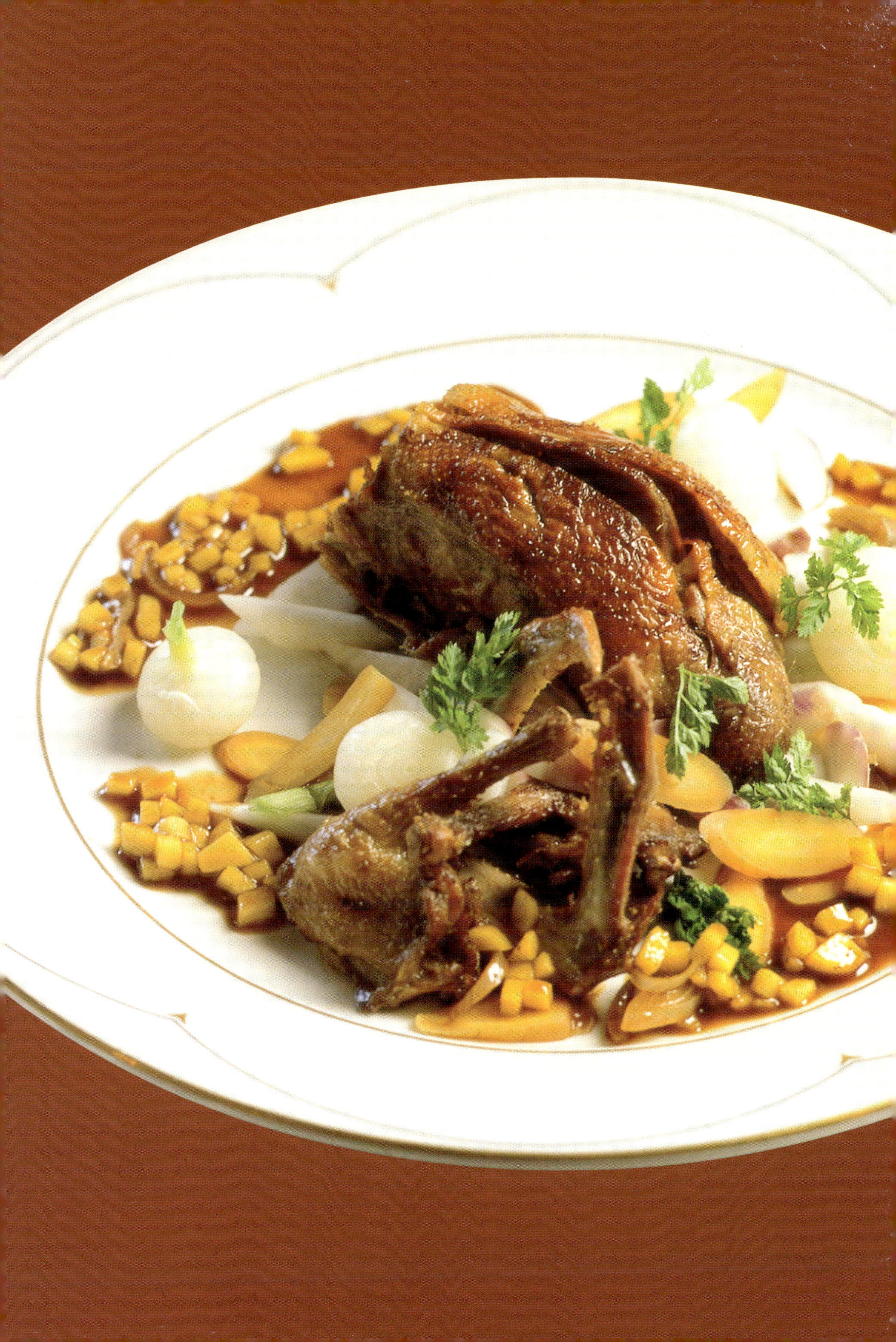

Late Bottled Vintage Port

Henrik Rosdahl, "Penny Lane", Aalborg:

"This Graham's Late Bottled Vintage, 1992, is still young and contains quite a lot of acid, that is why basil and salad are a good combination. Behind the fresh taste you can taste the sweetness which upon maturation will make this Port Wine sensational. To enhance the sweetness I have chosen to roast the celeriac in butter and a sweet stock. Taste the Port Wine before preparing the food and then taste it again with the finished dish".

Crottin de Chavignol on basil toast with rucola salad and Port Wine glace

(4 persons)

4 fresh Crottin de Chavignol of 60 g each
4 pieces of toast
1/2 celeriac
1 bunch of rucola
Fresh basil leaves
4 dl Port Wine
2 dl veal stock
75 g butter
3 tablespoons olive oil
Salt

Blend the olive oil and basil into a green pesto sauce.

Cut 8 round shapes from the 4 pieces of toast and put them to soak in the pesto sauce until they are green.

Bake the bread pieces crispy in the oven at 180°C.

Cut the celeriac into thin, round slices and roast them in a little butter until tender.

Put a slice of celeriac on a slice of the toast, a slice of goat's cheese on top, then a slice of the celeriac again, and then another piece of toast. Finish with another slice of goat's cheese on top. Bake the 'burgers' in the oven at 180°C for 6-8 minutes.

Boil the Port Wine and the veal stock until the mixture has a good consistency and is glazed. Pour a little olive oil on the rucola salad and season with salt. Whisk the reduced, cooled Port Wine stock.

Arrange the 'burgers' in the middle of the plate, garnish with the salad, and draw a circle with the Port Wine glace around it.

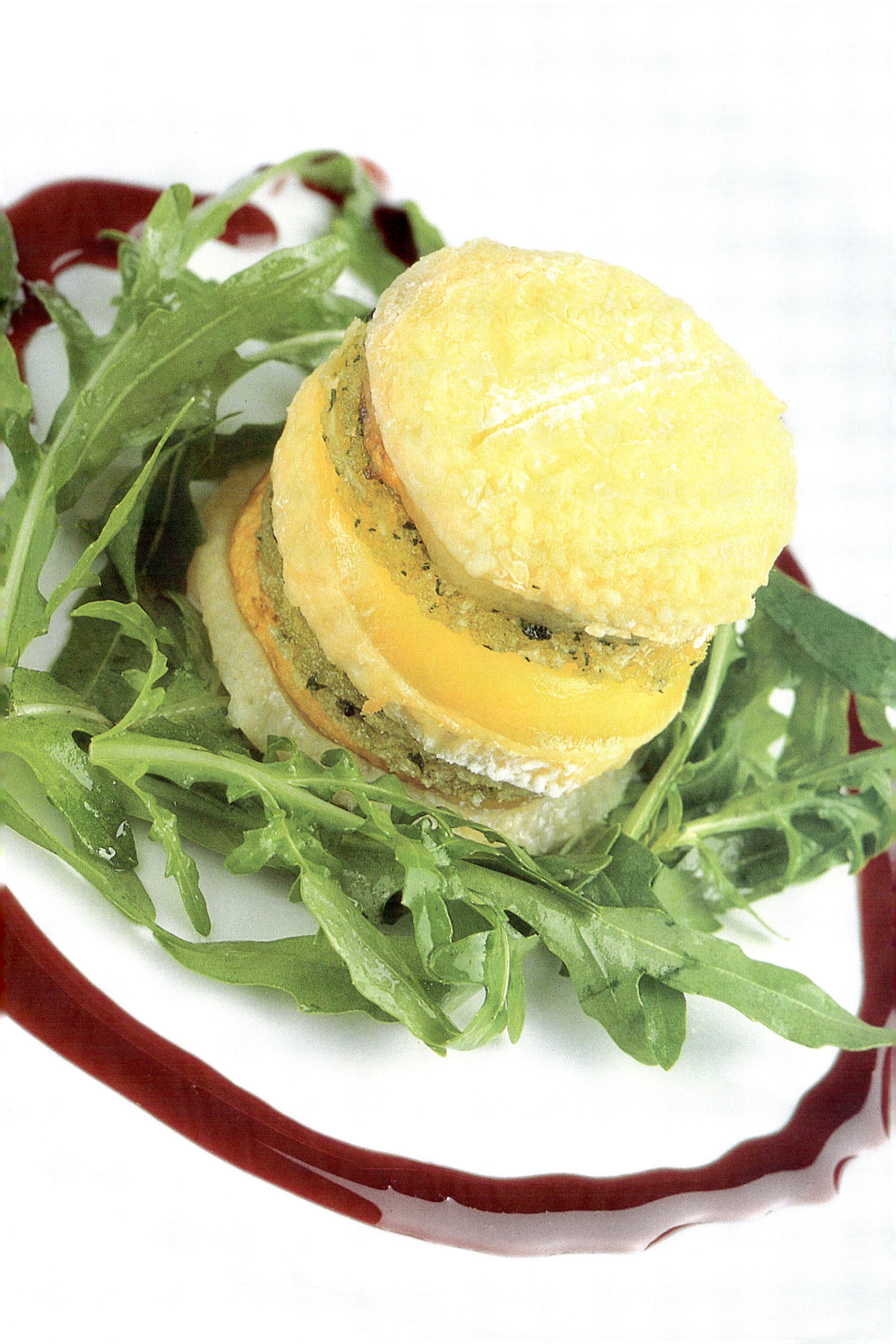

Young Single Quinta Vintage Port

Palle Enevoldsen, "Le Canard", Aarhus:

"Quinta da Ervamoira, 1994, is a great full-bodied Port Wine. It has a crimson colour and is bursting of youth. You can smell red berries and prunes, and it tastes of delicious, full bodied fruit and has just a dash of sweetness, which is supported by the tannin. There is a good interplay with the Manjari chocolate, which has a fruity taste, the berries as well as with the preserved fruit, especially the prunes, which suppress the tannin and produce a brilliant harmony with the rich fruit".

Chocolate truffle with compote of stewed fruit in Port Wine

(10 persons)

Chocolate cake:
100 g Caraibe Valrhôna chocolate
100 g butter
35 g plain flour
3 eggs
100 g sugar

Truffle mixture:
4 dl cream
150 g Manjari Valrhôna

Compote of preserved fruit*:
200 g apricots ★
200 g Agen prunes ★
200 g pears ★
4 dl Ramos Pinto

Chocolade border:
100 g Caraque Valrhôna
10 pcs. plastic film of 3 cm x 8 cm

★All the fruit in the compote must be preserved via osmosis, i.e. added sugar and drained.

Chocolate cake: Melt the chocolate and the butter in a Bain Marie at approx. 55°C and cool down to 40°C.

Whisk the eggs and sugar to a light consistency, sieve in the flour, and mix all of the remaining ingredients carefully.

Pour the chocolate mix into a baking tin of 30 x 30 cm lined with grease-proof paper so that the chocolate cake is easily removed.

Bake the cake for 30 minutes at 130°C and let it rest for 12 hours.

Truffle mix: Cut the chocolate into small pieces and pour boiling cream on top. Stir until melted, set aside to cool, and then chill in the fridge for min. 12 hours.

Compote: Cut the apricots, prunes, and pears into cubes, pour the Port Wine on top and cook over a slow heat for 10 minutes. Set aside to cool.

Cut out, e.g. with a cup, 10 circles from the large chocolate cake. Whisk the truffle mix until it has the same consistency as whipped cream. Fill it in the pastry bag and pipe the small chocolate circles with it.

Chocolate border: Melt the Caraque chocolate in a Bain Marie at 55°C, brush the pieces of plastic film and wrap them around the chocolate truffles. Put them in the fridge for 3-4 hours and then pull off the plastic pieces.

Arrange the chocolate truffles on dessert plates along with the compote of preserved fruits.

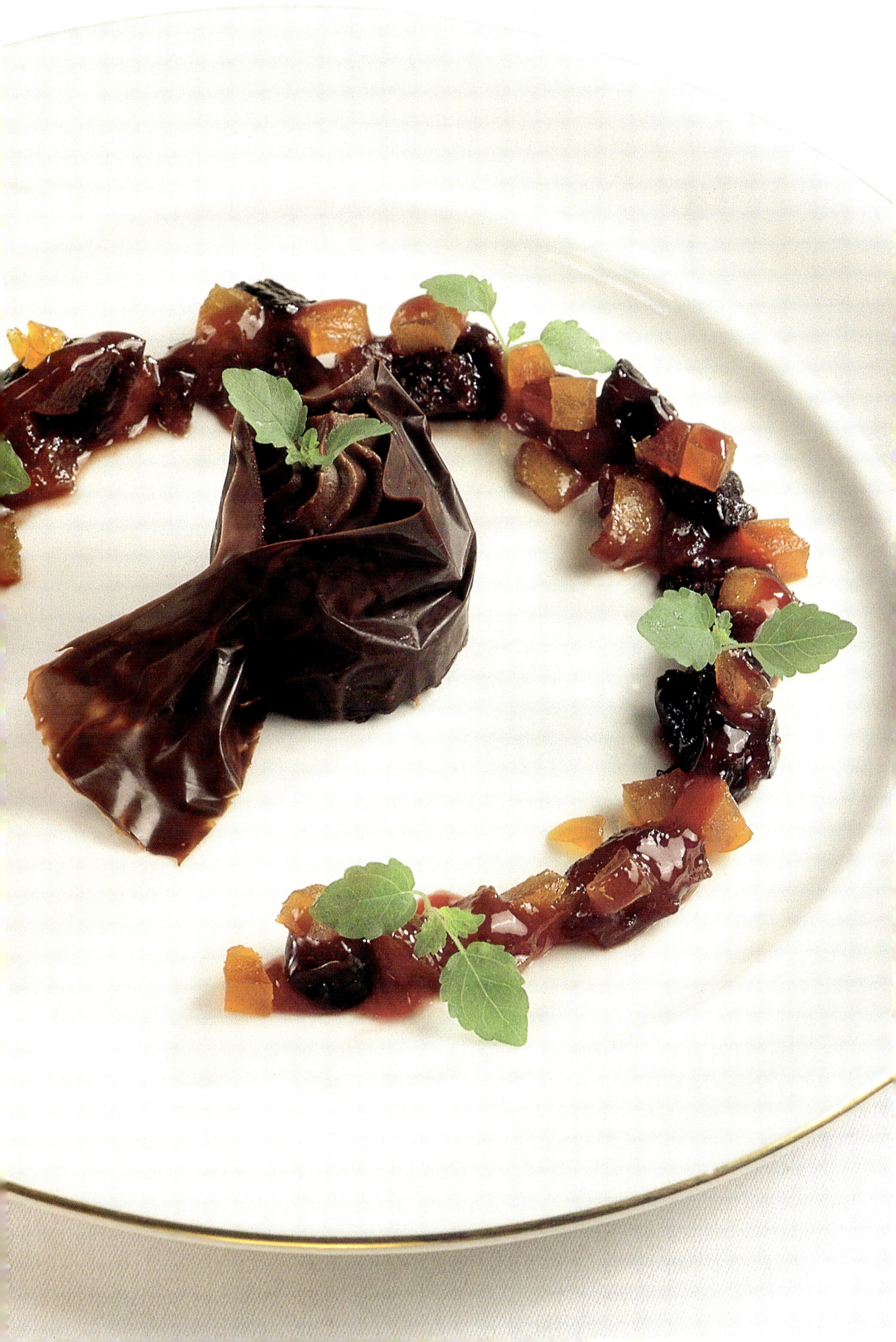

Young Vintage Port

Claus Christensen, "Gammel Mønt 41", Copenhagen:

"It is pure infanticide! But a young and virile Vintage Port contains both intensity, sweetness and fruit that goes well with pheasant. Pheasant and Port is a perfect marriage with cheese as the bridesmaid"!

Baked breast of pheasant with Port Wine, grapes and nuts

(2 persons)

1 pheasant (cock bird)
Salt and pepper
Butter
2 dl Vintage Port
1 dl Muscat grapes
1 dl fresh hazelnuts
1 dl forest mushrooms + truffles - according to your budget
100 g goat cheese
1 thin slice Jabugo ham
1 dl pheasant stock
1/4 dl Eau de Vie de Prunes
1 sprig rosemary
Puff pastry
1 egg yolk

Season the inside and the outside of a whole pheasant with salt and pepper, brown it on its back in clarified butter in a hot oven at 200-220°C for 3-4 minutes. Take out the bird, turn it on its breast, and the juice goes back into the breast.

When the pheasant is at room temperature, cut off the breasts and marinate them for one hour in 1 dl of this wonderful Port Wine.

Put small, green Muscat grapes, fresh hazelnuts, forest mushrooms, and truffles if available, in a small ovenproof dish or a copper cocotte.
Turn the breasts and place a bar of fat, soft Corsican goat's cheese or another good goat's cheese between the breasts and the small side fillets. Place the breasts close together with the cutting edge towards each other and wrap them in a very thin slice of Jabugo or another excellent Spanish air-dried ham - just a dab, as you would put on perfume!
Put the breasts in between the mixture of grapes, mushrooms and nuts.

Reduce the Port Wine marinade plus 1 dl of extra Port Wine and 1 dl of a good pheasant stock, pour it over the breasts and correct with a little Eau de Vie de Prunes. Add knobs of butter and rosemary. Cover with puff pastry (do not make holes in it with a fork!). Brush with egg yolk and put the dish at the bottom of an oven at 180-200°C for 25-30 minutes.

Put a towel over the head of each of your guests, and let them lean over the dish when the puff pastry lid is cut open so that they can smell the aroma.
Serve with a cellar chilled Vintage Port 1994.

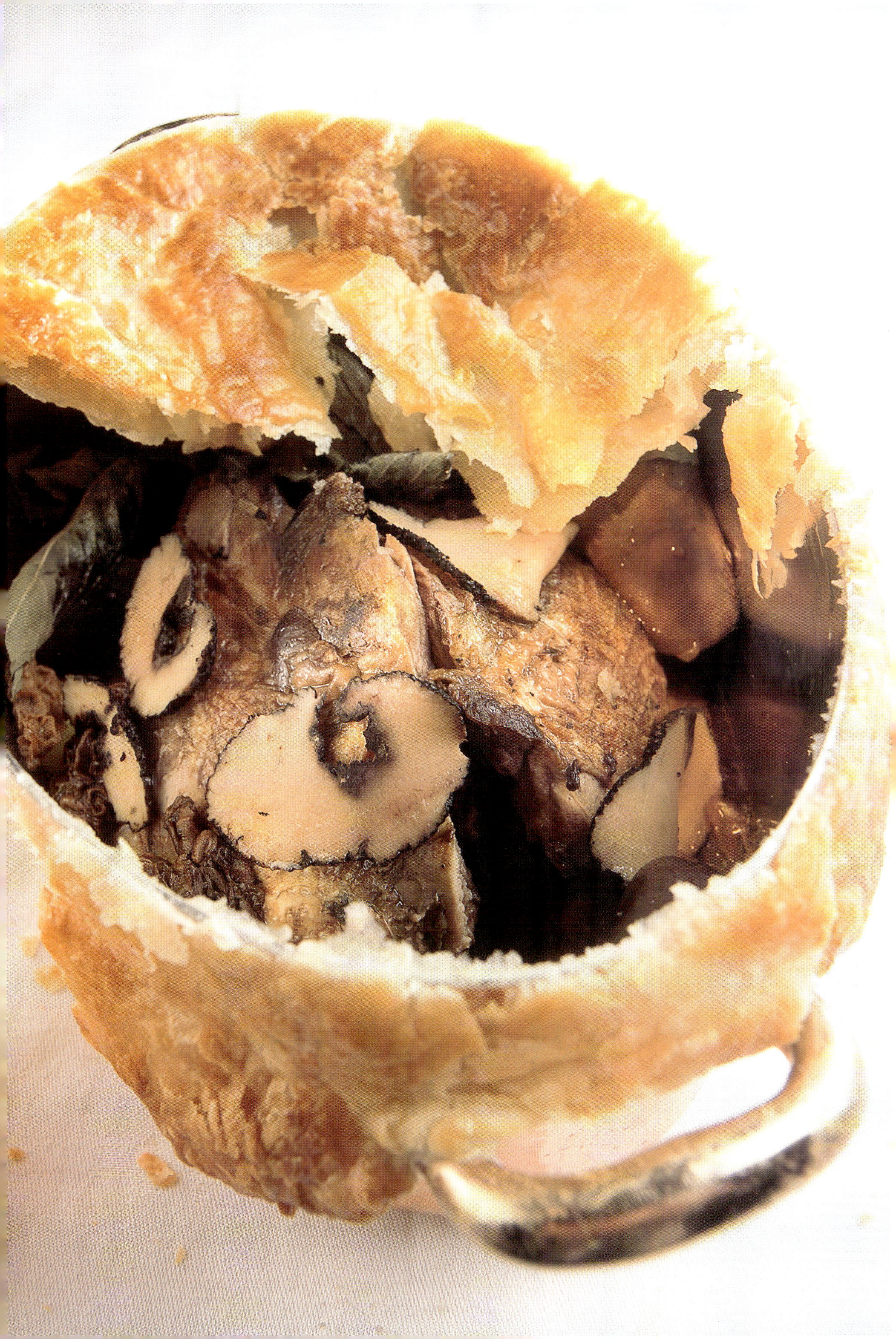

Matured Vintage Port

Francis Cardenau, "Kommandanten", Copenhagen:

"Rozès Vintage Port, 1985, is a rather heavy Port Wine with a high alcohol content and strong sweetness and richness. It is served chilled to suppress the alcohol and richness. The fatty/sweet foie gras and the mousse challenge the Port's consistency and sweetness. It is enhanced by glazed artichokes and the reduced Port - rather like a caramel consistency. The puff pastry is rich and the salt suppresses the sweetness of the wine. The artichokes and their acid taste of freshness give complete harmony."

Roasted foie gras de canard en croûte with reduced Port Wine with figs

(4 persons)

1 foie gras of duck of 500 g
100 g pig's caul
Thyme, Olive oil
100 g puff pastry made with butter
Salt and pepper

Mousse:
50 g pigeon heart and liver
50 g meat of chicken breast
20 g ventrêche (air-dried pig's breast)
2 chopped shallots
1 tablespoon duck fat
1/2 teaspoon Cognac
1/2 egg white
1/2 dl whipped cream

Port with figs:
4 dried figs
3 dl Rozès Vintage 1985

Glazed artichoke and artichoke salad:
8 small artichoke hearts
1 large artichoke heart
Vinaigrette (Sherry vinaigre, olive oil, salt and pepper)
1 dl poultry broth
2 chopped shallots, Butter

.Port with figs: Boil the figs in Port Wine and let them marinate for 48 hours.

Cut the foie gras into 4 equal thick slices. Use the rest for mousse.

Mousse: Blend the chicken breast and the rest of the foie gras with egg white, whipped cream, salt and pepper to a soufflé mousse. Let the two chopped shallots simmer for 10 minutes in the duck fat without browning. Brown the giblets and the ventrêche in a frying pan, set aside to cool. Chop and season with salt and pepper, thyme, Cognac and shallots. Then add the soufflé mousse and mix gently.

Brown the four pieces of foie gras on one side, set aside to cool and spread the mousse on the browned side. Wrap each piece in a pig's caul and roast them for a second in a frying pan.

Artichokes: Brown the small hearts in olive oil. Add chopped shallots, thyme, poultry broth, and braise the artichokes until tender. Glaze with a knob of butter. Cut the large artichoke heart into Julienne and marinade with the vinaigrette.

Take the figs out of the Port Wine marinade and reduce with a touch of salt to a thick caramel syrup. Cut the figs in small cubes and put them in the glaze just before arranging the dish and serving on hot plates.

Puff pastry tuiles: Cut the puff pastry in thin slices and sprinkle with coarse sea salt. Bake until golden at 220°C.

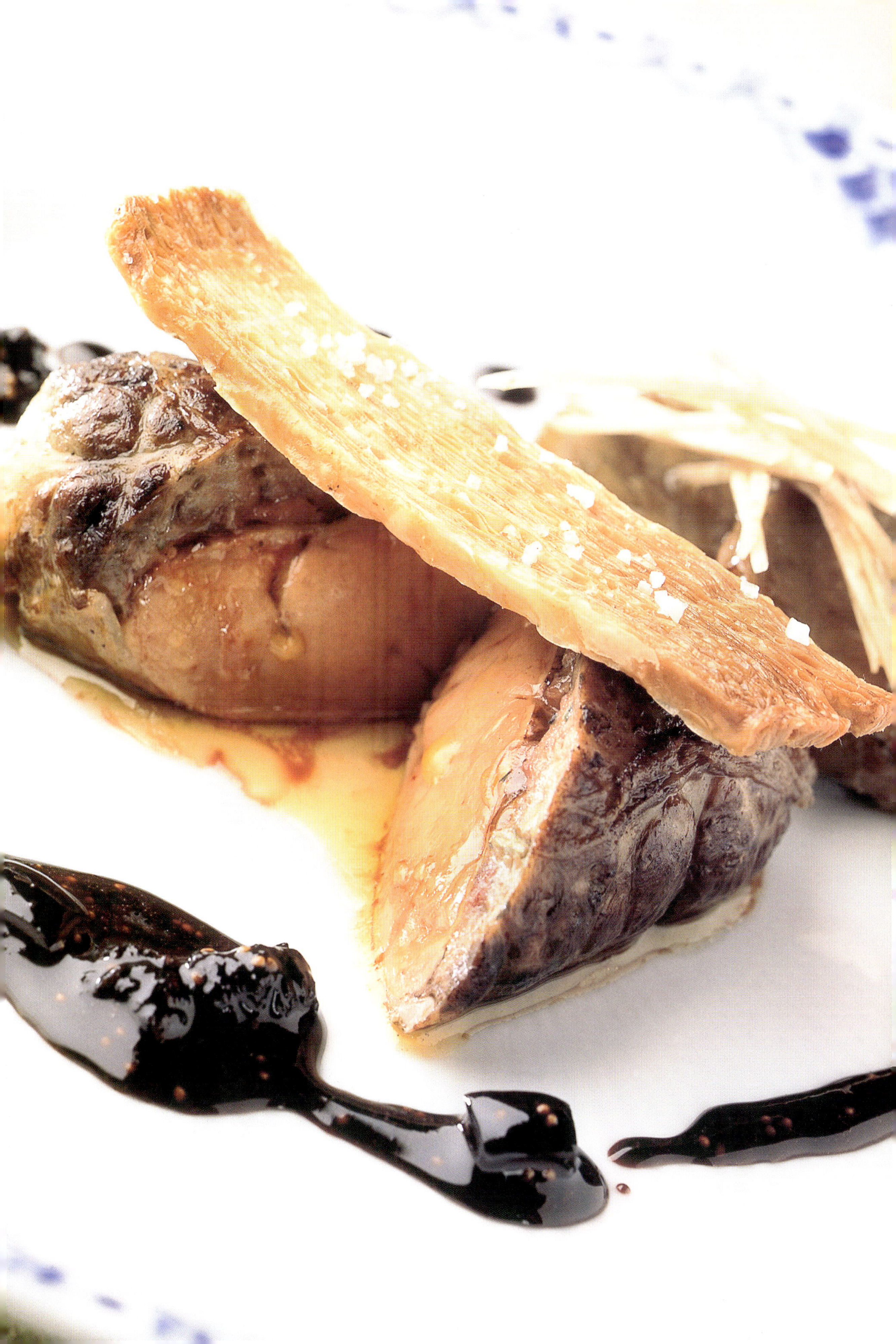

From decanter to bottle

The first bottles of glass had both function and shape as decanters. But as it became more common to bottleage Port and therefore also to pile the bottles, they had to be more cylindrical. From about 1770 bottles have had the shape we still use. The bottles on this page come from Sandeman's unique collection.

1715

1738

1755

1764

Chapter 11

TOURIST IN THE COUNTRY OF PORT

Porto

Hotels:

The hotels in Porto are scattered in a very practical way so that the nice and cosy - and cheapest hotels - are in the city centre and the big international box-shaped hotels lie along the east-to-westbound Avenida da Boavista leading from the city centre to the Atlantic Sea.

Naturally, there is a big difference in price and comfort between a humble hotel or a boarding house (pensão) in the middle of Porto and the Sheraton or Le Meridien Parc Atlantic, both on the Avenida da Boavista.

Especially the hotels in the de luxe category are looking forward to the year 2001 when Porto has been appointed the Cultural City of Europe.

Eating out:

Don't expect to travel to Portugal for the cuisine. You won't find it in Porto either. The city has excellent primary produce, but bad chefs and a tradition of uniting the most drab recipes from the Portuguese farms (cooking for hours on end) and Queen Victoria's prettified British roastbeef dishes. Even fish, which should be the city's pride, is often fried, cooked or grilled beyond recognition, and vegetables can usually be enjoyed without the use of teeth or cutlery.

The best restaurants are:

Portucale,
Rua da Alegria 598

The restaurant is situated in a high-rise building in the outskirts of the city centre and is according to Michelin's Porto's best restaurant. Well I don't agree. I find it just as drab as the building.

Portofino,
Rua do Padrão 103

In the quarter called Foz in a byroad off the posh coastal road of Avenida do Brasil. Old-fashioned style, service and furniture, but one of the best restaurants in town. The fish is marvellous here.

Bull & Bear,
Avenida da Boavista 3431

Porto's new in-spot (opened in 1997) is situated in a high-rise building on Avenida da Boavista. One of the few places where you sense the chef's ambitions and skills and where the dishes are served before they are boiled to a mash or overdone. The price level is rather high for Portugal but not according to Scandinavian, British or American standards. Try their *Carpaccio do Polvo prensado* (cuttle fish in a delicious aspic) or *Franguinho recheado com Figados de Pato* (a small chicken stuffed with mushrooms and duck liver) or the local special dish *Carré de Borrego com Ervas e Port* (lamb chops in a rich, spicy Port sauce).

Bol a d'Água,
Loja 28,
Rua Formosa

One of my private oases. A very humble place with 3-4 tables on the balcony of the market hall in Rua Formosa in the middle of Porto. You can sit here in the midday sun (open from 7 a.m. to 5 p.m.) and enjoy 2 medium-sized grilled soles and a bowl of fresh fruit salad for 5 £/7 $.

Garrafão
Rua António Nobre 53
Leça da Palmeira

If you want to try fresh fish or good shellfish you have to go to the suburbs, especially to Matosinhos or to Leça da Palmeira. If you are lucky, you get to choose your fish, drink a glass or two of wine whilst they prepare the fish - and then you can enjoy the fresh catch from the great Atlantic Sea. Sole (linguado) is a special dish here and the shellfish come in all sizes (mariscos).

Mercearia
Cais da Ribeira

The small restaurants along the many-coloured wharf of Cais da Ribeira was for many years more variegated than any good. But something is happening. Some of them have been renovated very nicely and you eat very well here. At "Mercearia" has a first floor overlooking the Douro river and the Port houses in Gaia. They also have a tourist menu (3 course menu + wine/water and coffee: 14 £/20 $), but the special dish is Linguado grelhado (grilled sole) at 12 £/17 $.

Gaia's wharf

The restaurants in Gaia have also improved. Unfortunately, the Port houses' small outdoors restaurants at the water's edge have closed down temporarily because the municipal government of Gaia decided to ask for an exorbitant rate. This was a wonderful spot overlooking Porto and looking at the colourful barcos rabelos for free to a glass of draught beer (fino) at 1 £/1 $, a wonderful plate of freshly cut ham (presunto) at 6 £/8 $ and a large glass of 10-years Tawny at 2,5 £/3,5 $ from Cálem's "Adega e Presuntaria". But this string of pearls has unfortunately closed down until the spring of 2000.

The restaurants lie side by side along the Cais da Ribeira. In recent years, quality has improved. (Photo: HO)

Ramos-Pinto's João Nicolau de Almeida is co-owner of the Wine Bar/Restaurant "DiVino" where you eat good food and drink good wine. (Photo: HO)

I have good news for the wine people who want to dine and drink well. A new place has opened, and you would never find it, if you did not know where to look. It is called Wine Bar/Restaurant and is situated in a byroad to Avenida da Boavista. Here you can sit at the bar and buy wine by the glass: Portuguese wines and foreign wines of the best quality, and then you can sit down at your table and dine and drink well. The wine is in good hands. Ramos-Pinto's clever winemaker, João Nicolau de Almeida is the co-owner:

Wine Bar/Restaurant
DiVino
R.S. Joao de Brito 383

The curious reader has a right to know where to go in Porto's city centre when he or she is sick and tired of eating the two dishes that even the Portuguese chefs cannot spoil: chicken (frango) and omelette. Well, eat Chinese! Just like any other place in Portugal you will find Chinese from the colony of Macão trying their hand as chefs or restaurant keepers, and two of the best restaurants in Porto are actually Chinese:

The best according to Michelin is in my opinion the second best:

King Long,
Largo Dr. Tito Fontes 115

The second best according to Michelin is in my opinion the best:

Chinés
Avenida Vimara Peres 38

Here they serve the famous Peking duck (Pato de Peking) in an excellent and almost authentic version. But they serve good food in both restaurants with good helpings at a reasonable price.

Visiting the Port houses:

Naturally you cannot visit Porto without visiting the Port Wine houses in Gaia. Even though some of them look like small tourist hotels from the outside and will accept unannounced visitors, they are all places of work producing and selling Port.

An increasing number of Port Wine houses have a tour of the premises and a tasting for free or for a very modest sum, and they do allow unannounced visits. Sandeman's and Cálem's are the first port houses you see when you cross the Dom Luis I bridge, and they also have the best facilities for groups or unannounced visits.

Naturally, you will always be treated kindly and professionally, but if you have not booked your visit, but if you want a more personal approach, or if you want to visit one of the Port Wine houses who do no accept unannounced visitors, then you must make arrangements before leaving for Portugal. Ask your local wine merchant. This will give you a great experience and will make your visit to Gaia something special.

From the centre of Porto you cross the Douro by the Dom Luis I bridge and before you reach the other side you have to make your first big decision: Whom to visit. The Port Institute has prepared this index map showing where the port wine houses are situated in Gaia. See next page.

PORTO
Cidade Património da Humanidade
World Heritage

The numbers on the map refer to the following Port producers:

- ✓ 1. Cálem
- ✓ 2. Ferreira
- ✓ 3. Ramos-Pinto
- ✓ 4. Barros
- ✓ 5. Kopke
-   6. Da Silva
-   7. Churchill Graham
- ✓ 8. Cockburn's
-   9. Croft
- 10. Delaforce
- ✓ 11. Fonseca
- 12. Offley Forrester
- 13. Gran Cruz
- 14. Hunt Constantino
- 15. Carvalho Macedo
- 16. Andrésen
- 17. Burmester
- 18. Poças
- ✓ 19. Martínez
- 20. Niepoort
- ✓ 21. Osborne
- 22. Quarles Harris
- ✓ 23. Noval
- 24. Romariz
- ✓ 25. Rozès
- ✓ 26. Sandeman
- 27. Dow's
- 28. Smith Woodhouse
- 29. Messias
- ✓ 30. Borges
- ✓ 31. Taylor's
- ✓ 32. Graham's
- 33. Warre's
- 34. Wiese & Krohn
- 35. IVP-kontor

The Port houses who according to the IVP receive unannounced visits and organise a conducted tour - and maybe a small tasting - are marked with a ✓.
Source: IVP

Port Wine bars:

As in Lisbon, Porto also has a Port Wine bar equipped and run by the Port Institute (IVP). Here they have a wine list with several hundred Ports from which you may choose a glass or bottle of Port at a reasonable price. It is very tempting to buy by the glass, but I recommend to buy un-opened bottles. I have had so many bad experiences with half-emptied bottles that have been open for too long so that the Port Wine had become dull and indifferent. And who needs that!

Solar do Vinho do Porto,
Rua de S. Pedro de Alcántara 45,
Lisboa

Solar do Vinho do Porto,
Rua de Entre-Quintas 220,
Porto

No phone number is necessary. You just enter like you enter any other shop.

Transportation:

It is both cheap and easy to take the bus or tram in Porto. It is also cheap to take a cab according to Scandinavian standards. Porto and Gaia are two different towns, and in Porto the taxis run by taxi-meter and in Gaia by kilometre, so they are a bit more expensive.

Douro Valley

Hotels:

Only 3-4 years ago it was just as difficult to find a hotel on the North Pole as it was in the Douro Valley. But even here things are changing. The village of Pinhão has actually got a new de luxe hotel, furnished and owned by Taylor's who was just as annoyed as the visitors because there were no possibility of spending the night:

The Vintage House Hotel,
Lugar da Ponte
5085 Pinhão.
Tlf: 054 73 02 30.
Fax: 054 73 02 38.

The hotel opened in April 1998. It is situated on a large 18th century quinta. In 1999, it offered 43 rooms (approx. 50-100 £ or 70-150 $ per room) all with a view of the river. The restaurant seats 90 persons.

Staying the night:

Small private farmers have signs on the road offering bed and breakfast at a very reasonable price and this popular, often primitvive "agroturismo" is becoming more and more popular. Some quintas also have overnight stays. Ask the ICEP.

In 1998, Casa do Visconde de Chanceleiros, which is a small country house, was made into hotel flats, all modern, and offering meals:

Casa do Visconde de Chanceleiros,
5085 Pinhão.
Tlf: 054 730 190
Fax: 054 730 199

A German couple have rebuilt an old patrician villa, neighbour to Offley's Quinta da Boa Vista a bit west of Pinhão. Free sporting facilities and the possibility of making your own food. A room, including breakfast, costs 60 £/80 $ Lunch costs 10 £/14 $ and dinner 14 £/20 $.

The wine route:

A collaboration between the Port Wine Institute, Casa do Douro, and the local tourist organisations was celebrated on 21 September 1996 when Portugal's first wine route "Rota do Vinho do Porto" was opened with the objective of bringing tourists to the Douro Valley.

After the usual doubts and scepticism have settled down, the wine route is becoming more and more popular. The first 54 places to visit of interest to tourists were pinpointed on the map, and in 1998 another 11 places of interest were added.

The marks represent overnight stays, visits to Port houses, landmarks and sights to see and other objects of interest.

On the inauguration tour to the Douro Valley in September 1996, the organisers stressed the importance of promoting both small farmers, co-operatives, quintas and Port Wine producers. After a somewhat slow start, some of the large quintas have caught on to the idea and offer conducted tours and meals and overnight stays.

These quintas include: Quinta da Casa Amarela, Quinta da Foz (Cálem), Quinta das Quartas (Poças), Quinta de la Rosa, Quinta de Santa Maria (Cockburn's), Quinta do Castelinho, Quinta do Côtto, Quinta do Crasto, Quinta do Panascal (Fonseca), Quinta do Portal, Quinta do Seixo (Ferreira) and Quinta de São Luiz (Barros).

An increasing number of quintas are joining and have more and more to offer. Quinta do Noval has postponed a project, including refurbishing a small hotel by the Casa do Abrau with a restaurant, but the famous quinta is very interested in attracting tourists to the Douro Valley.

ICEP has maps and brochures and information about interesting topics. The idea is that the visitors on the wine route may be inspired on their tour and improvise their itinerary so they do not have to arrange visits and book overnight stays – however this would still probably be a good idea.

I have not visited all the quintas and production places accepting visitors, but of the ones I do know, I can recommend the following:

Taylor's "The Vintage House Hotel" is a real de luxe hotel in a large, old quinta in Pinhão on the bank of River Douro and with Croft's Quinta da Roéda as opposite neighbour. (Photo: HO)

Quinta do Panascal,
Valença do Douro,
5120 Tabuaço.
Tlf: 054 72 321
Open: Monday-Friday 10 a.m. - 5.30 p.m.

The pedagogical "Audio Tour" provides you with your own tape recorder and headset and a map. This way you can follow the work in the field and the production of wine. There is a choice of 5 languages. The tour is concluded by a small tasting.

Quinta das Quartas
Lugar das Quartas-Fontelas
5050 Peso da Régua.
Tlf: 054 336645

ICEP

ICEP is an abbreviation of Investimentos, Comércio e Turismo de Portugal, i.e. Portugal's trade and tourist organisation with offices in many countries. One of ICEPs objectives is to bring tourists to Portugal. They will provide you with brochures, maps, prices and inform of any practicalities.
Ask your local ICEP or:

ICEP
Gammel Torv 4
1457 Copenhagen
Phone: + 45 33 13 43 62
Fax: + 45 33 93 88 85

Quinta de la Rosa
5085 Pinhão.
Tlf: 054 72254

Overnight stay, conducted tour, shop where you can buy the quinta's products.

Casa de Santa Clara
Vale de Mendiz
5070 Alijó.
Tlf: 054 72333

Exhibition of old vinification equipment which is fully operational so that you can follow the traditional production of wine.

Quinta do Côtto
Citadelhe
5040 Mesão Frio.
Tlf: 054 899269

The most westwards quinta on the wine route and one of the few resembling a château. A rebuilding with a small hotel/restaurant is planned.

Quinta de São Luiz
Adorigo
5120 Tabuaço.
Tlf: 02 3752320

The "Omnibus Quinta" (see page 26f) where you can see a modern winery and vineyards with very nice patamares.

The miracle at Côa

I have already told you that Ramos-Pinto's Quinta da Ervamoira in the beginning of the 1990'ies was on the verge of being expropriated and flooded but was fortunately estimated as being "extraordinarily worth preserving" by UNESCO (see page 270f). Today the quinta and Vale do Côa is among the Douro Valley's landmarks, but it is still not a tourist attraction because it is far from the public highway.

In 1992, archaeologists found traces of manmade writings on the rocks, the so-called petroglyphs (signs which are carved in the stone). In the course of 1993 and 1994, more petroglyphs were found, and a major excavation looking for prehistoric existence began in the summer of 1995. Here traces of a village, which was approx. 22,000 years old, was found by Salto do Boi, and in November 1995 the Portuguese government, supported by UNESCO, declared the whole area of Côa worth preserving and declared it an "Archaeological National Park".

Also foreign archaeologists have emphasised the Côa Valley's unique historic landscape, which partly is the first place in the world where manmade traces from so many different epochs and eras have been found, and which partly have the largest number of outdoors paleolithic drawings yet known.

Preliminary analyses show that the drawings (or engravings) are made over a time span of approx. 20,000 years (from approx. 30,000 to approx. 10,000 B.C.). The drawings include drawings of horses, prehistoric cattle types and wild goats. But there are also drawings of iron-age men, horsemen and weaponry.

The drawings are from the very long geological epoch called the Paleolithic period which covered nearly 2,5 million years from the time of the first tools till the late Glacial Age around 10,000 years ago. All drawings are outdoors drawings unlike the famous cave drawings in Altamira and Niaux (12-15,000 years B.C.)

The new "Parque Arqueológico Vale de Côa" is only open to visitors by appointment. Contact:

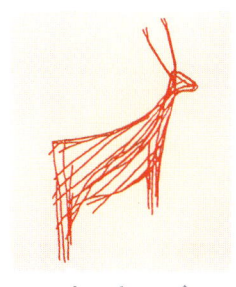

Vale do Côa

The buoyant Bordeaux-red goat has become the trade mark of the new findings

Parque Arqueológico Vale do Côa,
Avenida Gago Coutinho 19,
5150 Vila Nova de Foz Côa.
Phone: 079 764317
Fax: 079 764317

The meeting place for guided tours (compulsory guide) is at Castelo Melhor. Phone: 079 73344.

On Quinta da Ervamoira Ramos-Pinto has made a small museum with some of the findings that were dug up just before the expropriation. The address is:

Chãs
5150 Vila Nova de Foz Côa.

Please contact:
Phone: 02 370 7000
Fax: 02 379 3121

This engraving shows a horse lifting his head and looking back. Across the horse's tail there are some engravings of a new extinct race of oxen. The engraving is from approx. 18,000 B.C. (Rock 3, Penascosa).

INDEX

Italicized letters refer to illustrations

AEVP 310
Afonso Henriques, Port. king 16
Afonso II, Port. King 16
Afonso III, Port. King 17
ageing 340ff
Agrellos, António 258,265
Aguiar, Fernando Bianchi de 99,321
Alfons VI, King of Castilla-León 16
Allen, Warner 41,139
Almeida, Fernando Nicolau de 66,*66*,67,82,118, 196ff,312,*312*
Almeida, João Nicolau de 78,97ff,104,106ff,*136*, 269ff,*270,372*,379
Almeida, Manoel de 156
Alves, Martins 166ff
Anacleto, Joaquim 254
Andersen,H.C. 10
Andrade, Luis de Beleza 28
Andrésen, João Henrique 153
ao alto, see: vinha ao alto
autovinifikation 126f
AVEPOD 310
AXA Millésimes 258ff

Barca Velha 66f
barcos rabelos *63,133,*
Barros, João de 18
Barros, Manoel de 156
Barros, Manuel Ângelo 99,*119*
Barros-Almeida,Family 75,128,156f,191f,202, 221,222ff,253
Baverstock, David 256
Bearsley, Bartholomew 25
Bearsley, Family 293ff
Bearsley, Peter 25
Beatrix of Castile,Queen 17

benefício 82f,111ff,
Beresford, William, Eng. general 46
Bergqvist, Family 253
Borges, Jorge Serodio 240
Bourgogne, Peter 141
Bower, Huyshe 88,145,*150*,293
Bradford, Sarah 139
Branco, Family 266
British Association 24,319
British Factory 20
Broadbent, Michael 299
Browne, Manuel de Clamouse 160f
Burmester, Family 159ff
Burmester, Heinz "Henry" 24
Burnett, John *136*,143,179ff,*182*
Byron, Lord, Eng. poet 172

Cálem, Alfredo Holzer 254
Cálem, Family 166ff
Camo, Joe 193f
Campbell, Family 213
Campos, Maria Emilia *171*,
Carlos I, Port. King 57
Cardenau, Francis 366,*366*
Carnation Revolution 70ff
Carvalho e Melo, José de: see Marquês de Pombal
Carvalho, Manuel 172,227
Carvalho, Paulo de 28
Casa do Douro 62,70,72,74,76,82ff,102,112ff, 128,130,149,274,310f,333,337
Castro, Fidel, Cub. politician 81f,313
Catarina de Bragança, Eng. Queen 18,21
Cazes, Jean-Michel 260,265
cestos 121
Champalimuad, Miguel 142f,230ff,*232*
Charles II, Eng. King 18,20
Château Lafite 41
Château Margaux 141
Christensen, Claus 364,*364*

Christie's auctions 40f,139,252
Churchill, Caroline 170
Churchill, Winston, 207
Cid, Alonso 222
CIRDD 86,112,128,311
Clark, John 302f
climate 103ff
Clos de Tart 16
Clos de Vougeot 16
Cobb, Family 173ff
Cobb, Peter M. 84,140,147,*173*,173ff,
Cobb, Reginald 173ff,207,321
Cockburn, Ernest 150
Cockburn, Family 172ff
Cockburn, Robert 49
Colbert, Jean Baptiste 20
Comissão de Viticultura... 57
Companhia Geral da Agricultura..., see: Real Companhia Velha
Company, the, see Real Companhia Velha
Confraria do Vinho do Porto, see: Port Wine Brotherhood
Conselho Consultivo 112
Correia, Pedro 253
Corte Real, Miguel 172,175,227
Cosens, William 187ff
Costa, Jaime 159,164
Costa, José Manuel Soares de 252
Croft, Family 179ff
Croft, John 41,139
Cromwell, Oliver 18
crushing 123ff
crushing by foot 123f
crushing by robot 124f,262
Cunhal, Alvaro, Port. politician 72

da Costa, Gomes, Port. general 59
Dagge, Arthur 179f
decanting 343f,*343*
Decius Junius Brutus 14
Delaforce, David 185
Delaforce, Family 184ff

Delaforce, John 321
Delaforce, Nicholas 179
desavinho 104
Dinis I, Port. King 17
Disney, Walt 59
Dona Antónia Adelaide Ferreira
19,52,54,127,192ff,*199*,207,266ff,296
Douro Valley, tourist in... 376ff
Dow, John Ramsay 187ff
Dunlop, Hugh, Eng. captain 172

Eanes, Ramalho, Port. general 72
Elizabeth II, Eng. Queen 65,82,313,320
Enevoldsen, Palle 362,*362*
Entreposta de Gaia 59,59,70,79

Factory House 24,49,160,319f,320
Falcão Carneiro, Family 305ff
Falcão Carneiro, Fernando *306*
Falcão Carneiro, Iolanda 305ff,*306*
Falcão Carneiro, José *306*
Federação dos Viticultores..., see: Casa do Douro
Feist, Family 191
Feitoria 30f,37,101,319
Ferdinand VII, Sp. King 46
Ferdinand of Sachsen-Koburg 47
fermentation 122f
Fernandes, Joaquim 98ff,*99*,
Fernandes, Ruy 106
Fernando I, Port. King 17
Ferreira, António Bernardo 46
Ferreira, Family 192ff
Ferreira, Luís 46
Ferreira, Nanuel Maria de Magalhães 282
Feuerheerd, Family 202
ficha cadastral 116
Filipe, António 174,*312,318*,320
Fladgate, Family 193ff
Fladgate, John 180,204,296f
flood 58
Flores, Carlos 153,*153*

Fonseca, Álvaro Moreira da 106,116
Forrester, baron Joseph James 15,50,*51*,54,127
Franco, João, Port. politician 57,102
Franz Joseph, Aust. Emp 162
Frei João de Mansilha 28,34
Frei, Eduardo, Chil. politician 82,313
fungus disease 110

Gaia freeport, see: Entreposta
Galvão, Henrique, Port. captain 68
Gassiot, Family 226ff
geios 94
Gilbert, Arnold *31*,159ff,165
Gilbert, Karl 162ff
Gilbey, Family 179f
glasses 345
Gonçalves, Manoel Pedro 203
Gonçalves, Vasco, Port. politician 72
Gould, Family 213
Graça, António 177,*324*
Graça, António Américo da Rocha 118,*119*,198
Graham, Colin 142
Graham, Family 170ff
Graham, John 49,214ff
Graham, John(ny) L 170f,338
Graham, William 49,214f
grape varieties 105ff
Greig, William, eng. captain 172
Grey, Francis 295f
Guimaraens, Bruce (Duncan) 88f,92,100,107,109, 119, 123,133,*137*,203ff,*205*,277,329f
Guimaraens, David Bruce Fonseca *137*,203ff,*209*, 277,293ff
Guimaraens, Family 203ff
Guimaraens, (John) Gordon 87,133,174,178,204,227f,*229*
Guimaraens, Magdalena Gorrell 203f
Guimaraens, Manuel Pedro 49

Harveys of Bristol 62,174
Heath, Nick *150*

Henderson, A 139
Henry af Burgundy 16
Henrik, prince of Denmark *318*
Henry the Seafarer 18,82
Hitler, Adolf 59,329
Hotel, The Vintage House 376,*377*

ICEP 378
Instituto do Vinho do Porto: see Port Wine Institut

Jacob II, Eng. King 21
Jensen, Kurt Kjaer 348,*348*
João I, Port. King 17f
João VI, Port. King 46f
Johnson, Samuel 40
José I, Port. King 34,274
Juan Carlos, Sp. King 82,313
Junta Nacional do Vinho 62

Karberg, Flemming 189
Katarina II, Russ. emperor 36
Kebe, Eduard 238
Kendall, Basil 180
Knudsen, René 358,*358*
Kopke, Cristiano Nicolau 18,222ff
Kopke, Family 222ff
Krohn, Dankert 305f
Kyllesbech, Lars 354,*354*

lagares 121f,*122*,129
Lameiras, Rui 277,*277*
Lantz, Frank 356,*356*
Leão, José Estrela 10,
Lei do Terço 76,310
Link, Heinrich Friedrich, Germ. botanist 126f
Louzada, Manuel 279
Ludvig XIV, Fr. King 21,184
Ludvig XVI, Fr. King 41
Luis, Port. crown prince 57

Luso-Magyar agreement 75

Machado, Port. politician 60
Macmillan, Harold, Eng. politician 69
Magalhães, Nuno 103
Manso, José 100
Mao Tse Tsung, Chin. politician 71f
Maria I, Port. Queen 34ff,46
Maria II, Port. Queen 47,50
maromba 110
Martínez, Family 226ff
Marx, Karl, Germ. philosopher 72
Máximo, Joaquim 46
Menem, Carlos, Arg. politician 82,313
Methuen, Lord 21f,52,302
Miguel, Port. King 47,49
mildew 56,110
Miquelino, Ana 254
Monteiro, Jorge 321
Montes, Mesquita *83*,84ff,311
Morris, Dominique 256
Mourão, Leopoldo 86
Mussolini, Benito, Ital. politician 59

Napoleon I, Fr. emperor 42,44,46,48,172,303,319
Nash, John 24
Nelson, Lord Horatio 42,*43*,
Newman, Family 220,227
Niepoort, Family 238ff
Niepoort, Dirk van der 238ff,*239*,240
Niepoort, Rolf van der 238ff,*239*
Nobel, Alfred 92
Noble, Charles 49
Nogueira, "Zeze" 238,240
novidade *140*
Nugent, F.J. 174

oidium 56,110
Olazabal, Francisco "Vito" 106,192ff,*193*,*200*,243
Olazabal, Maria Luisa 195,200
Olazabal, Ramon de 195
Oliveira, António 156,191,202,221
Oliveira Marques, A.H. de 46
Oporto 370ff
Oporto, restaurants 370ff
Oporto Customs House 57

Pancorbo, Bartholomeu 28f
Parker, Robert M 87
Parnell, Colin 142
"Pass the Port" 346
patamares 96ff
Pedro I, Braz. emperor 47,49
Pedro III, Port. King 34
Peel, Robert, Eng. politician 48
Pereira, Gaspar Martins 126f,195
Philip, Eng. prince 82,313
phylloxera 56,94f
picking 121
Pimenta,Fátima Burmester *162*,*163*
Pimentel, Armando 321
Pintão, Jorge Manuel Soeiro e Silva 245
Pitt, William, Eng. politician 282
Pombal, Marquês de 25,28f,34f,37,40,50,100,274
Poças, Family 245ff
Poças, Manuel Pintão 82,84,86,245ff,*249*,312
Port Wine Brotherhood 81f,86,312ff,*314f*,

PORT PRODUCERS
(according to main name)

Andrésen 153f
Barão de Vilar 155
Barros 26,59,*61*,*90*,100,125
Borges & Irmão 61,158,336
Burmester 24,31,65,141,159ff
Cálem 19,50,58,124,166ff,254,279, 329, 336ff,371

Carvalho Macedo 170
Churchill Graham 75,150,170ff
Cockburn 19,48f,63,65,*71*,75,88,125f,128,
130,140,147,172ff,330,334,347
Croft 22,75,104,128,133,143
da Silva (Noval) 141,233ff,258ff
da Silva C 183
Delaforce 50,75,184ff
Dow 39,146,290,331,337
Feist 191f
Ferreira 19,26,46,49,64,75,94,98f,106,110,
118,125,127,192ff
Feuerheerd 141,202,253
Fonseca 26,48f,87f,123,203ff,330,333,336f
Gould Campbell 39,213
Graham 48f,75,142,147,214ff,329f,334
Gran Cruz 220
Hunt, Constantino 220
Hutcheson 221
Kopke 141,222ff,266
Martínez 39,75,130,226ff
Messias 230
Morgan Brothers 233
Nacional 233ff,264,329,332,338
Niepoort 50,238ff
Noval 24,67,75,83,87f,90,233ff,244,258ff,
329,338
Offley-Forrester 75,94,106,243
Osborne 244
Quarles Harris 22,251
Poças 59,62,245ff
Porto Cruz 75
Prod. Associados 250
Ramos-Pinto 59,*61*,75,79,143,146,254,269ff, 329
Robertson 75,276,284
Romaríz 50,277f,300
Rozès 50,75,279f
Sandeman 26,39ff,49,59,*61*,65,75,96,100,126f,
133,243,276,281ff,328ff,336,347
Smith Woodhouse 39,75,146,288f
Taylor 22,25,67,87f,90,100,107,123,125,141,
145,*150*,158,167,180,195,204,277,279,293ff,
330,333,335ff,346

Vallegre 301
Vasconcellos 301
Warre 20,22,41,139,146,*147*,290,302ff
Wiese & Krohn 50,305ff

Port houses, visit to 374f
Port Wine Clubs 326f
Port Wine Institut 30,62,72,81,136ff,310f,312ff,
321ff

PORT TYPES

Colheita 136,149,340,*354*,356
Crusted Port 136,150,340
Full Port 150
Late Bottled Vintage 67,89,144ff,340ff,360
Single Quinta Vintage Port 67,89,141ff,*362*
Tawny with age 136,148,340ff,350,*352*
Vintage Character 89,150,*358*
Vintage Port 89,*131*,132ff,138ff,340ff,*364*,*366*
White Port 150,340,*348*

post phylloxera 94
pre phylloxera 94f
pruning 110

QUINTAS
(according to main name)

Abelheira 266
Aciprestes 275
Água Alta 170
Alambiques 25
Aranhas 155
Atayde 172ff,*176*
Boa Vista 62,94,106,243,376
Bomfim 20,75,77,128,187ff,330
Bom Retiro 79,97,143,269ff
Bom Retiro Pequeno 303
Bons Ares 269ff

Cachão 230
Caêdo 192ff
Canais 172ff
Carril 238
Carvalhas *73*,274
Carvoeira 156
Casa Amarela 251
Casa Nova 158
Casal de Celeirós 266
Castelinho 166,254f,*254*
Cavadinha 302ff,*302*
Chouse 172ff
Confradeiro 266
Côrte 184ff,*184*,186
Côtto 79,142f,230ff,378
Crasto 256,*256*
Cruzeiro 208
Dona Matilde 156f
Eira Velha 18,220,226ff,*227*
Enxodreiro 156
Ervamoira 97,269ff,379
Figueiras 194ff,268
Fojo 170
Foz 54,*55*,124,166ff,338
Granja 52
Gricha 170f
Infantado 79,142f,257f,334
Junco 87,158,*158*,300,
Lagas 142
Leda 125,192ff
Liceiras 252
Madalena 288f
Malvedos 125,*125*,142,175,214ff,219,
Manuela 170
Muros 266
Nogueiras 52,195
Montes 56
Nápoles 238
Nossa Senhora do Carmo 31, 159ff,*160*,
Noval 19,62,79f,*125*,141,145,155,233ff,
258ff,*259*,261,334
Panascal 26,119,203ff,*206*,378
Passadouro 238

Portal 266
Porto *26*,192ff,196
Quartas 245ff,*247*,378
Retiro Novo 305,*308*
Roêda 104,128,179ff,
Romaneira 79,87,252
Romarigo
Roncão Pequeno 170
Roriz 141,260,262,266
Rosa 141,202,253,253,378
Sagrado 166,168
Santa Barbara 245,248
Santa Clara 378
Santa Maria 172ff
Santo António 208
São Domingos 254
São Luiz *26*,99,*100*,125,128,156f,*157*,191f,
221ff,*223*,378
Senhora da Ribeira 87,187ff
Seixo 98,*98*,99,118,119,192ff,*197*
Soalheira 158
Terre Feita *141*,293ff
Tua 19,64,172ff,175
Urtiga 269ff
Val Coelho 172ff
Val de Figueira 254,*254*
Vale de Cavalos 245
Vale do Meão 66,196
Vale Dona Maria 290
Vargel(l)as 52,*100*,107,125,141,*141*,145,194ff,
293ff,297,
Vau *26*,96,281ff,*285*
Ventozelo 87,88,
Vesúvio 52,75,127,129,194ff,266ff,*267*
Zimbro 188

Ramos-Pinto, Family 269ff
Reader, Jim 172,227
Real Companhia Velha
28ff,34,36ff,45f,49,52f,56,79,84f,100,274ff
Reid, Robin 82,180,*181*,312,*318*,334
Reis, Batalha 56

Regueiro, Laura 251
Remarque, Erich Maria 63
remontage 128f
Reynolds, Raymond 253
Rhee, Frank, Eng. captain 173
Roberston, Alistair 298ff
Robertson, George 179
Robertson, James Nisbet 276
Roquette, Family 256
Romaríz, Manoel da Rocha 277
Rosas, Jorge 146,270ff,270,
Rosas, José Ramos-Pinto 78,82,97f,106f,270ff,312
Rosdahl, Henrik 360,*360*
Roseira, Family 257f
Roseira, João 143,257f
Rota do Vinho do Porto 26,86f,376ff
Rouzaud, Jean-Claude 272
Rozès, Ostende 279
Rutherford, Jack 67,145

Saintsbury, George 189,289
Salazar, António Oliveira de, Port.politician 60,64,68,82,310,321
Saldanha, Duque de, Port. politician 194
Sandeman, David Patrick *286*
Sandeman, Family 281ff
Sandeman, George Thomas David 281ff,*282*
Sandeman, George 41f,52f,140,207,281ff,*286*
Sandeman, Patrick 65
Sankey, George 174
Santos, Manuel António Araújo dos 311
Saraiva, Family 254
Saraiva, Manuel António C. 166f,254
Santos, António 153
schist 92ff
Schou, Vivi 352,*352*
Schubert, Max 66
Schultz, Allan 350,*350*
Seely, Christian 90,233ff,*234*,259ff,*263*,
Shippers' Association 310
Silva e Sousa, Albino Jorge 277f,*277*
Silva, Bruno Evaristo Ferreira da 187f

Silva, Carlos 276,281
Silva, José Teles Dias da 244f
Silva, Rogério Leandro da 166ff,*167,279f*
Silva Reis, Family 274ff
Silva Reis, Manuel da 71,73,84,274ff
Silva Reis, Pedro
Smithes, Family 172ff
Smithes, John Henry 63f,125,207
Soares Franco, José Maria d'Orey 192ff,243
Soares, José Sosa 156,202,221
Soares, Mário, Port. politician 72f,82,313
SOGRAPE 94,192ff,243
Soltau, Hermann Lukas 160
Spinola, António, Port. general 71
Steinmetz, Hans 162f
storing 341
Swift, Jonathan 42
Symington, Andrew James 187ff,214ff,290ff,*291*
Symington, Charles 125,217,292
Symington, Family 64,75,87,100,128,142,146,187ff,197,213ff,266ff,288f,290ff,
302ff,331f,335
Symington, Ian D.F. 146,*291*
Symington, James 70,77,88,125,142,188,215ff,290ff
Symington, Michael 77,82,84,87,115,143,187,*187*,290ff,312,332f,335ff
Symington, Paul 146,292
Symington, Peter Ronald 125,213f,217,251,266ff,288,292,302,

Talleyrand, Fr. politician 46
Tavares, Manuel F. de Pinho 301
Taylor, Family 293ff
Teage, Family 173ff
Teage, John 173ff,226
Tiberius Gracchus, Roman politician 14
Tjaikovski, Peter, Russ. composer 303
Tomba Geral das Duas Costas 30
Torres, Francisco José da Silva 54,194
Tovar, Francisco Barata de 244

Treaty of Lord Methuwn, see: Methuen

Vale de Côa 379f
van Zeller, Cristiano 83,86,256,334
van Zeller, Family 67,80,145,155,233ff,244,258ff,266
van Zeller, Fernando 155,260
van Zeller, Frederico 163
Vasconcelos Porto, Luis 67,145,155,258f
Victoria I, Eng. Queen 48
Vilhelm III of Orange, Eng. King 21,22
Vinagre, António Borges 252
vinha ao alto 97ff
vinha tradicional 94
Vintages 328ff
Virgiano, J.M. 49,193

Warre, Family 187ff,302ff
Warre, William 44,302ff,*304*
Watson, Hugh 179
Wellesley, Arthur, see: Wellington
Wellington, Duke of 44f,48,302f
Wiese, Thedor 305
World Bank 81
Wright, J.R. 133

Yeatman, "Dick" Stanley 67,298
Yeatman, Family 293ff
Yeatman, Frank "Smiler" 207,296ff